Spring Enterprise Recipes

A Problem-Solution Approach

**Gary Mak and
Josh Long**

Apress®

Spring Enterprise Recipes: A Problem-Solution Approach

Copyright © 2009 by Gary Mak and Josh Long

ISBN-13 (pbk): 978-1-4302-2497-6

ISBN-13 (electronic): 978-1-4302-2498-3

Trademarked names may appear in this book. Rather than use a trademark symbol with every occurrence of a trademarked name, we use the names only in an editorial fashion and to the benefit of the trademark owner, with no intention of infringement of the trademark.

Java™ and all Java-based marks are trademarks or registered trademarks of Sun Microsystems, Inc., in the US and other countries. Apress, Inc., is not affiliated with Sun Microsystems, Inc., and this book was written without endorsement from Sun Microsystems, Inc.

President and Publisher: Paul Manning
Lead Editor: Steve Anglin
Technical Reviewer: Manuel Jordan
Editorial Board: Clay Andres, Steve Anglin, Mark Beckner, Ewan Buckingham, Tony Campbell, Gary Cornell, Jonathan Gennick, Michelle Lowman, Matthew Moodie, Jeffrey Pepper, Frank Pohlmann, Ben Renow-Clarke, Dominic Shakeshaft, Matt Wade, Tom Welsh
Coordinating Editor: Jim Markham
Copy Editor: Nancy Sixsmith
Compositor: folio 2
Indexer: Potomac Indexers
Artist: April Milne
Cover Designer: Anna Ishchenko

Distributed to the book trade worldwide by Springer-Verlag New York, Inc., 233 Spring Street, 6th Floor, New York, NY 10013. Phone 1-800-SPRINGER, fax 201-348-4505, e-mail orders-ny@springer-sbm.com, or visit http://www.springeronline.com.

For information on translations, please contact Apress directly at 2855 Telegraph Avenue, Suite 600, Berkeley, CA 94705. Phone 510-549-5930, fax 510-549-5939, e-mail info@apress.com, or visit http://www.apress.com.

Apress and friends of ED books may be purchased in bulk for academic, corporate, or promotional use. eBook versions and licenses are also available for most titles. For more information, reference our Special Bulk Sales–eBook Licensing web page at http://www.apress.com/info/bulksales.

The source code for this book is available to readers at http://www.apress.com. You will need to answer questions pertaining to this book in order to successfully download the code.

To my wife, Ivy, and our baby

Gary Mak

To my wife, Richelle

Josh Long

Contents at a Glance

Contents

About the Authors

Gary Mak, founder and chief consultant of Meta-Archit Software Technology Limited, has been a technical architect and application developer on the enterprise Java platform for over seven years. He is the author of the Apress books *Spring Recipes: A Problem-Solution Approach* and *Pro SpringSource dm Server*. In his career, Gary has developed a number of Java-based software projects, most of which are application frameworks, system infrastructures, and software tools. He enjoys designing and implementing the complex parts of software projects. Gary has a master's degree in computer science and his research interests include object-oriented technology, aspect-oriented technology, design patterns, software reuse, and domain-driven development.

Gary specializes in building enterprise applications on technologies such as Spring, Hibernate, JPA, JSF, Portlet, AJAX, and OSGi. He has been using the Spring framework in his projects for five years, since Spring version 1.0. Gary has been an instructor of courses on enterprise Java, Spring, Hibernate, Web Services, and agile development. He has written a series of Spring and Hibernate tutorials as course materials, parts of which are open to the public, and they're gaining popularity in the Java community. In his spare time, he enjoys playing tennis and watching tennis competitions.

Josh Long is an enterprise architect, developer, consultant, speaker and author. When he's not hacking on code, he can be found at the local Java user group or at the local coffee shop. Josh likes building solutions that push the boundaries of the technologies that enable them. His interests include high availability/scalability, business process management, grid processing, mobile computing, and so-called "smart" systems.

Josh is a Sun-certified Java programmer with many years of professional experience. He has been using the Spring framework since it debuted and has followed with excitement as Spring has enabled one complex solution after another. Josh lives in sunny Southern California with his wife. He maintains a blog where he can be reached at http://www.joshlong.com.

About the Technical Reviewer

Manuel Jordan Elera is a freelance Java developer. He designed and developed personal systems for his customers, using powerful frameworks based in Java, such as Spring, Hibernate, and others. Manuel is now an autodidact developer and enjoys learning new frameworks to get better results in his projects.

Manuel got a degree in Systems Engineering with public congratulations and he was a professor at Universidad Católica de Santa María in Perú. In his rare free time he likes reading the Bible and composing music with his guitar. Manuel is a senior member in the Spring community forums and is known as dr_pompeii.

Acknowledgments

First of all, I'd like to thank all the people who read the first edition of *Spring Recipes*. The popularity of Spring Recipes is the reason this book could be written.

I'd also like to thank Steve Anglin and Josh Long. Steve Anglin supported me in updating *Spring Recipes* and found Josh Long, a very hard-working and humble person with deep knowledge of Spring, to work with me on this book. Josh Long updated many topics of *Spring Recipes* for Spring 3.0 and added new topics in Spring enterprise development. He often finished his jobs much better and more quickly than I expected.

Gary Mak

It may sound like a cliché, but I can't even begin to name all the people who helped get this book out the door. I'd like to thank my family, especially my wife Richelle, without whose unremitting support I wouldn't have dared take the unsure leaps that I've taken. She is my garbage collection routine, my safety net. I couldn't, and wouldn't, have done it without her. Additionally, my father Clark, my mother Kathy, and my stepfather Gordon have proved to be invaluable sources of inspiration and support. Thank you. I'd also like to thank my close friend and professional colleague Mario Gray. At first it was annoying having someone be that good a friend to me *and* be that smart... scratch that, it's still annoying! I've benefited profoundly from our friendship, both as a technologist and a person. Thank you for pushing (and pulling) me, kicking and screaming.

As engineers, we build on abstractions, reusing where possible. We say that we are "standing on the shoulders of giants." This book is an update of Gary Mak's incredible *Spring Recipes* book. He is a figurative giant, and I can't thank him enough for working with me, mentoring me, and giving me the high bar I've constantly strived to meet. I'm not sure that I ever will!

I'd like to thank Steve Anglin, who saw fit after months and many proposals to let me write this book with Gary Mak. Without his enthusiasm for the concept and his support for (and confidence in) us, both at inception and throughout the process, this book wouldn't have worked.

This book passed through many inboxes. It is a much better book for their work, and if any error somehow still remains, they are our own. The editors at Apress are amazing. I worked as hard as I could to not need the editors. I went into the process thinking their involvement would be a formality. "Humbled" doesn't even begin to describe how I felt when the editors finished. They are rock stars. I truly hope everybody gets a chance to work at least once with people as professional and capable as they are.

Tom Welsh provided substantive guidance on the literary quality of this book. James Markham helped guide the work, providing a clear roadmap and lighting the way for the next steps in the process. Manuel Jordan, our technical reviewer, provided innumerable suggestions and expansions, resulting in a dramatic improvement of both the book and the clarity with which some topics are discussed. I'd also like to thank Nancy Sixsmith, who worked hard to beat some very tight deadlines to refine the copy and give it some missing polish.

Finally, I'd like to acknowledge and thank Mike Ray for giving me a new perspective on some of the technologies discussed in this book.

Josh Long

Introduction

The Spring framework is growing. While Java EE has largely been a prescription of architecture (the Java Pet Store and the Sun blueprints, for example), the Spring framework has always been about choice. Java EE focused on a best-practices-oriented solution, largely to the detriment of alternative solutions. When the Spring framework debuted, few would have agreed that Java EE represented the best-in-breed architectures of the day. Each release sees the introduction of a myriad of new features designed to both simplify and enable solutions.

With Spring 2.0 and later, the Spring platform started targeting multiple platforms. The framework provided services on top of existing platforms, as always, but was decoupled from the underlying platform wherever possible. Java EE is still a major reference point, but not the only target. OSGi (a promising technology for modular architectures) has been a big part of the SpringSource strategy. Additionally, with the introduction of annotation-centric frameworks and XML schemas, SpringSource could build frameworks that effectively modeled the domain of the problem itself, in effect creating DSLs. In short order, frameworks built on top of the Spring framework emerged supporting application integration, batch processing, Flex integration, OSGi, and much more.

When it came time to update the seminal *Spring Recipes*, we decided to split the book into two, with focuses on both enterprise programming and web programming. This book is for the enterprise programmer, noble and gray-haired. For every pretty widget deployed on some application UI, there is business logic driving it, and this book discusses solutions for building the heart of any application. This book walks the reader from the basics (databases, remoting, messaging, and transactions) to the more nuanced (EAI using Spring Integration, BPM, batch processing, and distributed computing). A sizable portion of this book focuses not on simplifying APIs on top of the Java EE platform, but enabling API (for which, quite simply, there is no good solution in Java EE).

The topics in this book are introduced by complete and real-world code examples that you can follow step by step. Instead of abstract descriptions on complex concepts, you will find live examples in this book. When you start a new project, you can consider copying the code and configuration files from this book and then modifying them for your needs. This can save you a great deal of work when creating a project from scratch.

Who This Book Is For

This book is for Java developers who want to simplify their architecture and solve problems outside the scope of the Java EE platform. If you are already a developer using Spring in your projects, the more advanced chapters present a discussion of newer technologies that you might not have known about. You can also use this book as a reference and you'll find the code examples very useful.

This book assumes that you have some familiarity with Spring, although there is a breakneck speed introduction and refresher. It also assumes that you have a feel for the basic services offered by the Spring framework and want to expand your toolkit to include some of the new frameworks coming from

SpringSource. This book also assumes a focus on service-oriented architectures. If you're looking for a discussion of Spring and web frameworks, this book might not be for you.

How This Book Is Structured

This book covers Spring 3.0 from the basic to the advanced and introduces several common Spring projects that will bring significant value to your application development. It is divided into 12 chapters, with each chapter progressively more advanced than its predecessor.

Chapter 1: "Introduction to Spring." This chapter introduces the core features of the Spring framework as well as the underlying principle of Inversion of Control (IoC). Additionally, this chapter provides an introduction to the life cycle of beans deployed in the Spring application context and an introduction to Spring's support for AOP.

Chapter 2: "What's New in Spring 3.0?" This chapter provides a breakneck introduction to the refinements and additions to the Spring framework in version 3.0. Read this chapter if you're quite sure you understand the thrust of Chapter 1 but aren't familiar with version 3.0 of the Spring framework.

Chapter 3: "Data Access." This chapter shows how Spring can simplify JDBC's uses through its JDBC support. It also serves as an introduction to Spring's data access module.

Chapter 4: "Transaction Management in Spring." This chapter discusses Spring's different transaction management approaches and explains transaction attributes in detail.

Chapter 5: "EJB, Spring Remoting and Web Services." This chapter covers Spring's support for various remoting technologies, including RMI, Hessian, Burlap, HTTP Invoker, and Web Services. It also introduces developing contract-first Web Services using Spring Web Services.

Chapter 6: "Spring in the Enterprise." Sometimes the devil is in the details. This chapter discusses Spring's broad support for various application concerns, such as monitoring via JMX, e-mail via JavaMail, and scheduling using Quartz.

Chapter 7: "Messaging." This chapter introduces JMS, the basic principles of message-oriented architectures, and Spring's support for JMS. This chapter will set the stage for Chapter 8, in which we discuss more-advanced message-oriented solutions.

Chapter 8: "Spring Integration." No application is an island. Modern applications exist to serve multiple masters and often need to interoperate with other applications. Sharing services and data is hard. This chapter discusses Spring Integration, a Spring framework that enables high-level integration solutions.

Chapter 9: "Spring Batch." Many applications deal with long-running tasks such as file processing or database updates. If you're coming from an environment such as CICS on mainframes, you'll find the tools available in Java EE a bit lacking. Spring Batch is a Spring framework that is oriented around long-running batch processes. This chapter discusses batch processing and Spring Integration.

Chapter 10: "Distributed Spring." The era of the monolithic client/server architecture is gone, and although three-tier architectures have their place, there is something to be said for grid-oriented architectures. This chapter discusses Terracotta to help cluster your dataset, and GridGain to implement an effective grid-processing framework.

Chapter 11: "jBPM and Spring." Business process management (BPM) is a technology often mired in buzzwords. However, a lightweight application of BPM can provide significant value to a business and can enable service reuse. This chapter introduces BPM and then discusses how to integrate Spring with jBPM 4.

Chapter 12: "OSGi and Spring." Applications are more and more pieced together, à la carte, assembled from the best-of-breed pieces. There's less and less need for a proper Java EE container. Indeed, applications can profit both in computer throughput and elegance by building modular solutions, using only what's required. This chapter introduces OSGi and then describes the Spring technologies built on and for this powerful platform.

Each chapter of this book discusses a Spring topic with multiple problem-solution recipes. You can look up a solution for a particular problem and see how the solution works in the "How It Works" section. Each chapter demonstrates a topic with complete examples. The example within a chapter is coherent, but examples are independent between chapters.

Conventions

Sometimes when we want you to pay particular attention to a part within a code example, we will make the font bold. Please note that bold doesn't reflect a code change from the last version. In cases when a code line is too long to fit the page's width, we will break it with a code continuation character (➡). Please note that when you try out the code, you have to concatenate the line by yourself without any spaces.

Prerequisites

Because the Java programming language is platform independent, you are free to choose any supported operating system. However, some of the examples in this book use platform-specific paths. Translate them as necessary to your operating system's format before trying out the examples. To make the most of this book, you should install JDK version 1.5 or higher. You should also have a Java IDE installed to make development easier. For this book, the sample code is Maven-based. If you're running Eclipse and you install the M2Eclipse plug-in, you can open the sample code in Eclipse, and the classpath and all dependencies will be filled in by the Maven metadata.

Alternatively, IntelliJ IDEA features fantastic support for Maven. The company behind IntelliJ IDEA has just released the IntelliJ Community Edition as this book was going to press. This is a good open source IDE that can open Maven projects with no hassle and should prove quite capable. Finally, newer releases of Netbeans feature fantastic support for opening Maven projects. If you're building from the command line, you will need Maven 2.1 or better. For some of these examples, you will have an easier time running the samples using the Eclipse IDE because some of the SpringSource tooling supporting many of these technologies is built on Eclipse.

Downloading the Code

The source code for this book is available from the Apress web site (http://www.apress.com) in the Source Code/Download section. The source code is organized by chapters, each of which includes one or more independent examples.

Contacting the Authors

We always welcome your questions and feedback regarding the contents of this book. You can reach Gary Mak at springrecipes@metaarchit.com and visit his web site at http://www.metaarchit.com. You can reach Josh Long at josh@joshlong.com and visit his site at http://www.joshlong.com.

CHAPTER 1

■■■

Introduction to Spring

In this chapter, you will be given a crash course refresher on Spring, the core container, as well as some of the globally available facilities provided by the container, such as *aspect-oriented programming (AOP)*. You will also become acquainted with the Spring XML configuration format as well as the annotation-driven support. The core framework has changed in many ways, and coverage of the additional configuration options is available in Chapter 2.

One of the most notable shifts in the core framework was the change from AOP support in the 1.x release of Spring to the AOP support starting from version 2.0. The Spring framework overhauled its AOP support, integrating with AspectJ_a separate project whose functionality can mostly be leveraged entirely from the familiar Spring *Inversion of Control (IoC)* environment. Typically, you will deal very little with AOP directly in the course of your Spring framework programming. You will interface with it indirectly in some of the more core support (such as with transactions), but only as a client of the functionality.

This chapter will give you the knowledge you need to deal with the concepts introduced in the rest of the book."

1-1. Instantiating the Spring IoC Container

Problem

You have to instantiate the Spring IoC container for it to create bean instances by reading their configurations. Then you can get the bean instances from the IoC container to use.

Solution

Spring provides two types of IoC container implementation. The basic one is called *bean factory*. The more advanced one is called *application context*, which is a compatible extension to the bean factory. Note that the bean configuration files for these two types of IoC containers are identical.

The application context provides more advanced features than the bean factory while keeping the basic features compatible. So I strongly recommend using the application context for every application unless the resources of this application are restricted, such as when running in an applet or a mobile device.

The interfaces for the bean factory and the application context are BeanFactory and ApplicationContext, respectively. The interface ApplicationContext is a subinterface of BeanFactory for maintaining compatibility.

1

How It Works

Instantiating an Application Context

ApplicationContext is an interface only. You have to instantiate an implementation of it. The ClassPathXmlApplicationContext implementation builds an application context by loading an XML configuration file from the classpath. You can also specify multiple configuration files for it.

```
ApplicationContext context = new ClassPathXmlApplicationContext("beans.xml");
```

Besides ClassPathXmlApplicationContext, there are several other ApplicationContext implementations provided by Spring. FileSystemXmlApplicationContext is used to load XML configuration files from the file system, while XmlWebApplicationContext and XmlPortletApplicationContext can be used in web and portal applications only.

Getting Beans from the IoC Container

To get a declared bean from a bean factory or an application context, you just make a call to the getBean() method and pass in the unique bean name. The return type of the getBean() method is java.lang.Object, so you have to cast it to its actual type before using it.

```
SequenceGenerator generator =
    (SequenceGenerator) context.getBean("sequenceGenerator");
```

Up to this step, you are free to use the bean just like any object you created using a constructor. The complete source code for running the sequence generator application is given in the following Main class:

```
package com.apress.springenterpriserecipes.sequence;

import org.springframework.context.ApplicationContext;
import org.springframework.context.support.ClassPathXmlApplicationContext;

public class Main {

    public static void main(String[] args) {
        ApplicationContext context =
            new ClassPathXmlApplicationContext("beans.xml");

        SequenceGenerator generator =
            (SequenceGenerator) context.getBean("sequenceGenerator");
```

```
        System.out.println(generator.getSequence());
        System.out.println(generator.getSequence());
    }
}
```

If everything is fine, you should see the following sequence numbers output, along with some logging messages that you might not be interested in:

```
30100000A
30100001A
```

1-2. Configuring Beans in the Spring IoC Container

Problem

Spring offers a powerful IoC container to manage the beans that make up an application. To utilize the container services, you have to configure your beans to run in the Spring IoC container.

Solution

You can configure your beans in the Spring IoC container through XML files, properties files, annotations, or even APIs.

Spring allows you to configure your beans in one or more bean configuration files. For a simple application, you can simply centralize your beans in a single configuration file. But for a large application with a lot of beans, you should separate them in multiple configuration files according to their functionalities. One useful division is by the architectural layer that a given context services.

How It Works

Suppose that you are going to develop an application for generating sequence numbers. In this application, there may be many series of sequence numbers to generate for different purposes. Each one of them will have its own prefix, suffix, and initial value. So, you have to create and maintain multiple generator instances in your application.

Creating the Bean Class

In accordance with the requirements, you create the SequenceGenerator class that has three properties_prefix, suffix, and initial_that can be injected via setter methods or a constructor. The private field counter is for storing the current numeric value of this generator. Each time you call the getSequence() method on a generator instance, you will get the last sequence number with the prefix and suffix joined. You declare this method as synchronized to make it thread-safe.

3

```
package com.apress.springenterpriserecipes.sequence;

public class SequenceGenerator {

    private String prefix;
    private String suffix;
    private int initial;
    private int counter;

    public SequenceGenerator() {}

    public SequenceGenerator(String prefix, String suffix, int initial) {
        this.prefix = prefix;
        this.suffix = suffix;
        this.initial = initial;
    }

    public void setPrefix(String prefix) {
        this.prefix = prefix;
    }

    public void setSuffix(String suffix) {
        this.suffix = suffix;
    }

    public void setInitial(int initial) {
        this.initial = initial;
    }

    public synchronized String getSequence() {
        StringBuffer buffer = new StringBuffer();
        buffer.append(prefix);
        buffer.append(initial + counter++);
        buffer.append(suffix);
        return buffer.toString();
    }
}
```

As you see, this SequenceGenerator class can be configured by getters/setters or by the constructor. When configuring them with the container, this is called constructor injection and setter injection.

Creating the Bean Configuration File

To declare beans in the Spring IoC container via XML, you first have to create an XML bean configuration file with an appropriate name, such as beans.xml. You can put this file in the root of the classpath for easier testing within an IDE.

The Spring configuration XML allows you to use custom tags from different schemas (tx, jndi, jee, and so on) to make the bean configuration simpler and clearer. Here's an example of the simplest XML configuration possible.

```
<beans xmlns="http://www.springframework.org/schema/beans"
    xmlns:xsi="http://www.w3.org/2001/XMLSchema-instance"
    xsi:schemaLocation="http://www.springframework.org/schema/beans
        http://www.springframework.org/schema/beans/spring-beans-3.0.xsd">
    ...
</beans>
```

Declaring Beans in the Bean Configuration File

Each bean should provide a unique name or id and a fully qualified class name for the Spring IoC container to instantiate it. For each bean property of simple type (e.g., String and other primitive types), you can specify a <value> element for it. Spring will attempt to convert your value into the declaring type of this property. To configure a property via setter injection, you use the <property> element and specify the property name in its name attribute. A <property> requires that the bean contain a corresponding setter method.

```
<bean name="sequenceGenerator"
    class="com.apress.springenterpriserecipes.sequence.SequenceGenerator">
    <property name="prefix">
        <value>30</value>
    </property>
    <property name="suffix">
        <value>A</value>
    </property>
    <property name="initial">
        <value>100000</value>
    </property>
</bean>
```

You can also configure bean properties via constructor injection by declaring them in the <constructor-arg> elements. There's not a name attribute in <constructor-arg> because constructor arguments are position-based.

```
<bean name="sequenceGenerator"
    class="com.apress.springenterpriserecipes.sequence.SequenceGenerator">
    <constructor-arg>
        <value>30</value>
    </constructor-arg>
    <constructor-arg>
        <value>A</value>
    </constructor-arg>
    <constructor-arg>
        <value>100000</value>
    </constructor-arg>
</bean>
```

In the Spring IoC container, each bean's name should be unique, although duplicate names are allowed for overriding bean declaration if more than one context is loaded. A bean's name can be defined by the name attribute of the <bean> element. Actually, there's a preferred way of identifying a bean: through the standard XML id attribute, whose purpose is to identify an element within an XML document. In this way, if your text editor is XML-aware, it can help to validate each bean's uniqueness at design time.

```
<bean id="sequenceGenerator"
    class="com.apress.springenterpriserecipes.sequence.SequenceGenerator">
    ...
</bean>
```

However, XML has restrictions on the characters that can appear in the XML id attribute, but usually you won't use those special characters in a bean name. Moreover, Spring allows you to specify multiple names, separated by commas, for a bean in the name attribute. But you can't do so in the id attribute because commas are not allowed there.

In fact, neither the bean name nor the bean ID is required for a bean. A bean that has no name defined is called an *anonymous bean*. You will usually create beans like this that serve only to interact with the Spring container itself; that you are sure you will only inject by type later on; or that you will nest, inline, in the declaration of an outer bean.

Defining Bean Properties by Shortcut

Spring supports a shortcut for specifying the value of a simple type property. You can present a value attribute in the <property> element instead of enclosing a <value> element inside.

```
<bean id="sequenceGenerator"
    class="com.apress.springenterpriserecipes.sequence.SequenceGenerator">
    <property name="prefix" value="30" />
    <property name="suffix" value="A" />
    <property name="initial" value="100000" />
</bean>
```

This shortcut also works for constructor arguments.

```
<bean name="sequenceGenerator"
    class="com.apress.springenterpriserecipes.sequence.SequenceGenerator">
    <constructor-arg value="30" />
    <constructor-arg value="A" />
    <constructor-arg value="100000" />
</bean>
```

Spring 2.0 provides another convenient shortcut for you to define properties. It's by using the p schema to define bean properties as attributes of the <bean> element. This can shorten the lines of XML configuration.

```
<beans xmlns="http://www.springframework.org/schema/beans"
    xmlns:xsi="http://www.w3.org/2001/XMLSchema-instance"
    xmlns:p="http://www.springframework.org/schema/p"
    xsi:schemaLocation="http://www.springframework.org/schema/beans
        http://www.springframework.org/schema/beans/spring-beans-3.0.xsd">
```

```xml
<bean id="sequenceGenerator"
    class="com.apress.springenterpriserecipes.sequence.SequenceGenerator"
    p:prefix="30" p:suffix="A" p:initial="100000" />
</beans>
```

Configuring Collections for Your Beans

List, Set, and Map are the core interfaces representing three main types of collections. For each collection type, Java provides several implementations with different functions and characteristics from which you can choose. In Spring, these types of collections can be easily configured with a group of built-in XML tags, such as <list>, <set>, and <map>.

Suppose you are going to allow more than one suffix for your sequence generator. The suffixes will be appended to the sequence numbers with hyphens as the separators. You may consider accepting suffixes of arbitrary data types and converting them into strings when appending to the sequence numbers.

Lists, Arrays, and Sets

First, let's use a java.util.List collection to contain your suffixes. A *list* is an ordered and indexed collection whose elements can be accessed either by index or with a for-each loop.

```java
package com.apress.springenterpriserecipes.sequence;
...
public class SequenceGenerator {
    ...
    private List<Object> suffixes;

    public void setSuffixes(List<Object> suffixes) {
        this.suffixes = suffixes;
    }

    public void setPrefixGenerator(PrefixGenerator prefixGenerator) {
            this.prefixGenerator = prefixGenerator;
    }

    public synchronized String getSequence() {
        StringBuffer buffer = new StringBuffer();
        ...
        for (Object suffix : suffixes) {
            buffer.append("-");
            buffer.append(suffix);
        }
        return buffer.toString();
    }
}
```

7

To define a property of the interface java.util.List in the bean configuration, you specify a <list> tag that contains the elements. The elements allowed inside the <list> tag can be a simple constant value specified by <value>, a bean reference by <ref>, an inner bean definition by <bean>, or a null element by <null>. You can even embed other collections in a collection.

```
<bean id="sequenceGenerator"
    class="com.apress.springenterpriserecipes.sequence.SequenceGenerator">
    <property name="prefixGenerator" ref="datePrefixGenerator" />
    <property name="initial" value="100000" />
    <property name="suffixes">
        <list>
            <value>A</value>
            <bean class="java.net.URL">
                <constructor-arg value="http" />
                <constructor-arg value="www.apress.com" />
                <constructor-arg value="/" />
            </bean>
            <null />
        </list>
    </property>
</bean>
```

Conceptually, an *array* is very similar to a list in that it's also an ordered and indexed collection that can be accessed by index. The main difference is that the length of an array is fixed and cannot be extended dynamically. In the Java Collections framework, an array and a list can be converted to each other through the Arrays.asList() and List.toArray() methods. For your sequence generator, you can use an Object[] array to contain the suffixes and access them either by index or with a for-each loop.

```
package com.apress.springenterpriserecipes.sequence;
...
public class SequenceGenerator {
    ...
    private Object[] suffixes;

    public void setSuffixes(Object[] suffixes) {
        this.suffixes = suffixes;
    }
    ...
}
```

The definition of an array in the bean configuration file is identical to a list denoted by the <list> tag.

Another common collection type is a *set*. Both the java.util.List interface and the java.util.Set interface extend the same interface: java.util.Collection. A set differs from a list in that it is neither ordered nor indexed, and it can store unique objects only. That means no duplicate element can be contained in a set. When the same element is added to a set for the second time, it will replace the old one. The equality of elements is determined by the equals() method.

```
package com.apress.springenterpriserecipes.sequence;
...
public class SequenceGenerator {
    ...
    private Set<Object> suffixes;
```

```
    public void setSuffixes(Set<Object> suffixes) {
        this.suffixes = suffixes;
    }
    ...
}
```

To define a property of java.util.Set type, use the <set> tag to define the elements in the same way as a list.

```
<bean id="sequenceGenerator"
    class="com.apress.springenterpriserecipes.sequence.SequenceGenerator">
    ...
    <property name="suffixes">
        <set>
            <value>A</value>
            <bean class="java.net.URL">
                <constructor-arg value="http" />
                <constructor-arg value="www.apress.com" />
                <constructor-arg value="/" />
            </bean>
            <null />
        </set>
    </property>
</bean>
```

Although there's not an order concept in the original set semantics, Spring preserves the order of your elements by using java.util.LinkedHashSet, an implementation of the java.util.Set interface that does preserve element order.

Maps and Properties

A *map* is a table that stores its entries in key/value pairs. You can get a particular value from a map by its key, and also iterate the map entries with a for-each loop. Both the keys and values of a map can be of arbitrary type. Equality between keys is also determined by the equals() method. For example, you can modify your sequence generator to accept a java.util.Map collection that contains suffixes with keys.

```
package com.apress.springenterpriserecipes.sequence;
...
public class SequenceGenerator {
    ...
    private Map<Object, Object> suffixes;

    public void setSuffixes(Map<Object, Object> suffixes) {
        this.suffixes = suffixes;
    }

    public synchronized String getSequence() {
        StringBuffer buffer = new StringBuffer();
        ...
        for (Map.Entry entry : suffixes.entrySet()) {
            buffer.append("-");
            buffer.append(entry.getKey());
```

```
            buffer.append("@");
            buffer.append(entry.getValue());
        }
        return buffer.toString();
    }
}
```

In Spring, a map is defined by the <map> tag, with multiple <entry> tags as children. Each entry contains a key and a value. The key must be defined inside the <key> tag. There is no restriction on the type of the key and value, so you are free to specify a <value>, <ref>, <bean>, <idref>, or <null> element for them. Spring will also preserve the order of the map entries by using java.util.LinkedHashMap.

```
<bean id="sequenceGenerator"
    class="com.apress.springenterpriserecipes.sequence.SequenceGenerator">
    ...
    <property name="suffixes">
        <map>
            <entry>
                <key>
                    <value>type</value>
                </key>
                <value>A</value>
            </entry>
            <entry>
                <key>
                    <value>url</value>
                </key>
                <bean class="java.net.URL">
                    <constructor-arg value="http" />
                    <constructor-arg value="www.apress.com" />
                    <constructor-arg value="/" />
                </bean>
            </entry>
        </map>
    </property>
</bean>
```

There are shortcuts to defining map keys and values as attributes of the <entry> tag. If they are simple constant values, you can define them by key and value. If they are bean references, you can define them by key-ref and value-ref.

```
<bean id="sequenceGenerator"
    class="com.apress.springenterpriserecipes.sequence.SequenceGenerator">
    ...
    <property name="suffixes">
        <map>
            <entry key="type" value="A" />
            <entry key="url">
                <bean class="java.net.URL">
                    <constructor-arg value="http" />
                    <constructor-arg value="www.apress.com" />
                    <constructor-arg value="/" />
                </bean>
```

```
            </entry>
        </map>
    </property>
</bean>
```

In all the collection classes seen thus far, you used values to set the properties. Sometimes the desired goal is to configure a null value using a Map instance. Spring's XML configuration schema includes explicit support for this. Here is a map with null values for the value of an entry:

```
<property name="nulledMapValue">
        <map>
<entry>
        <key> <value>null</value> </key>
</entry>
        </map>
    </property>
```

A java.util.Properties collection is very similar to a map. It also implements the java.util.Map interface and stores entries in key/value pairs. The only difference is that the keys and values of a Properties collection are always strings.

```
package com.apress.springenterpriserecipes.sequence;
...
public class SequenceGenerator {
    ...
    private Properties suffixes;

    public void setSuffixes(Properties suffixes) {
        this.suffixes = suffixes;
    }
    ...
}
```

To define a java.util.Properties collection in Spring, use the <props> tag with multiple <prop> tags as children. Each <prop> tag must have a key attribute defined and the corresponding value enclosed.

```
<bean id="sequenceGenerator"
    class="com.apress.springenterpriserecipes.sequence.SequenceGenerator">
    ...
    <property name="suffixes">
        <props>
            <prop key="type">A</prop>
            <prop key="url">http://www.apress.com/</prop>
            <prop key="null">null</prop>
        </props>
    </property>
</bean>
```

If you define your beans with inheritance, a child bean's collection can be merged with that of its parent by setting the merge attribute to true. For a <list> collection, the child elements will be added.

1-3. Auto-Wiring Beans with XML Configuration

Problem

When a bean requires access to another bean, you can wire it by specifying the reference explicitly. However, if your container can wire your beans automatically, it can save you the trouble of configuring the wirings manually.

Solution

The Spring IoC container can help you to wire your beans automatically. You only have to specify the auto-wiring mode in the autowire attribute of <bean>. Table 1-1 lists the auto-wiring modes supported by Spring.

Table 1-1. Auto-Wiring Modes Supported by Spring

Mode	Description
no*	No auto-wiring will be performed. You must wire the dependencies explicitly.
byName	For each bean property, wire a bean with the same name as the property.
byType	For each bean property, wire a bean whose type is compatible with that of the property. If more than one bean is found, an UnsatisfiedDependencyException will be thrown.
constructor	For each argument of each constructor, first find a bean whose type is compatible with the argument's. Then pick the constructor with the most matching arguments. In case of any ambiguity, an UnsatisfiedDependencyException will be thrown.
autodetect	If a default constructor with no argument is found, the dependencies will be auto-wired by type. Otherwise, they will be auto-wired by constructor.

* The default mode is no, but this can be changed by setting the default-autowire attribute of the <beans> root element. This default mode will be overridden by a bean's own mode if specified.

Although the auto-wiring feature is very powerful, the cost is that it will reduce the readability of your bean configurations. Because auto-wiring is performed by Spring at runtime, you cannot derive how your beans are wired from the bean configuration file. In practice, I recommend applying auto-wiring only in applications whose component dependencies are not complicated.

How It Works

Auto-Wiring by Type

You can set the `autowire` attribute of the `sequenceGenerator` bean to `byType` and leave the `prefixGenerator` property unset. Then Spring will attempt to wire a bean whose type is compatible with `PrefixGenerator`. In this case, the `datePrefixGenerator` bean will be wired automatically.

```
<beans ...>
    <bean id="sequenceGenerator"
        class="com.apress.springenterpriserecipes.sequence.SequenceGenerator"
        autowire="byType">
        <property name="initial" value="100000" />
        <property name="suffix" value="A" />
    </bean>

    <bean id="datePrefixGenerator"
        class="com.apress.springenterpriserecipes.sequence.DatePrefixGenerator">
        <property name="pattern" value="yyyyMMdd" />
    </bean>
</beans>
```

The main problem of auto-wiring by type is that sometimes there will be more than one bean in the IoC container compatible with the target type. In this case, Spring will not be able to decide which bean is most suitable for the property, and hence cannot perform auto-wiring. For example, if you have another prefix generator generating the current year as the prefix, auto-wiring by type will be broken immediately.

```
<beans ...>
    <bean id="sequenceGenerator"
        class="com.apress.springenterpriserecipes.sequence.SequenceGenerator"
        autowire="byType">
        <property name="initial" value="100000" />
        <property name="suffix" value="A" />
    </bean>

    <bean id="datePrefixGenerator"
        class="com.apress.springenterpriserecipes.sequence.DatePrefixGenerator">
        <property name="pattern" value="yyyyMMdd" />
    </bean>

    <bean id="yearPrefixGenerator"
        class="com.apress.springenterpriserecipes.sequence.DatePrefixGenerator">
        <property name="pattern" value="yyyy" />
    </bean>
</beans>
```

Spring will throw an UnsatisfiedDependencyException if more than one bean is found for auto-wiring.

```
Exception in thread "main"
org.springframework.beans.factory.UnsatisfiedDependencyException: Error creating
bean with name 'sequenceGenerator' defined in class path resource [beans.xml]:
Unsatisfied dependency expressed through bean property 'prefixGenerator': No unique
bean of type [com.apress.springenterpriserecipes.sequence.PrefixGenerator]
is defined:
expected single matching bean but found 2: [datePrefixGenerator,
yearPrefixGenerator]
```

Auto-Wiring by Name

Another mode of auto-wiring is byName, which can sometimes resolve the problems of auto-wiring by type. It works very similarly to byType, but in this case, Spring will attempt to wire a bean whose class name is the same as the property name, rather than with the compatible type. As the bean name is unique within a container, auto-wiring by name will not cause ambiguity.

```
<beans ...>
    <bean id="sequenceGenerator"
        class="com.apress.springenterpriserecipes.sequence.SequenceGenerator"
        autowire="byName">
        <property name="initial" value="100000" />
        <property name="suffix" value="A" />
    </bean>

    <bean id="prefixGenerator"
        class="com.apress.springenterpriserecipes.sequence.DatePrefixGenerator">
        <property name="pattern" value="yyyyMMdd" />
    </bean>
</beans>
```

However, auto-wiring by name will not work in all cases. Sometimes it's not possible for you to make the name of the target bean the same as your property. In practice, you often need to specify ambiguous dependencies explicitly, while keeping others auto-wired. That means you employ a mixture of explicit wiring and auto-wiring.

Auto-Wiring by Constructor

The auto-wiring mode constructor works like byType, but it's rather more complicated. For a bean with a single constructor, Spring will attempt to wire a bean with a compatible type for each constructor argument. But for a bean with multiple constructors, the process is more complicated. Spring will first attempt to find a bean with a compatible type for each argument of each constructor. Then it will pick the constructor with the most matching arguments.

Suppose that SequenceGenerator has one default constructor and one constructor with an argument PrefixGenerator.

```
package com.apress.springenterpriserecipes.sequence;

public class SequenceGenerator {

    public SequenceGenerator() {}

    public SequenceGenerator(PrefixGenerator prefixGenerator) {
        this.prefixGenerator = prefixGenerator;
    }
    ...
}
```

In this case, the second constructor will be matched and picked because Spring can find a bean whose type is compatible with PrefixGenerator.

```
<beans ...>
    <bean id="sequenceGenerator"
        class="com.apress.springenterpriserecipes.sequence.SequenceGenerator"
        autowire="constructor">
        <property name="initial" value="100000" />
        <property name="suffix" value="A" />
    </bean>

    <bean id="datePrefixGenerator"
        class="com.apress.springenterpriserecipes.sequence.DatePrefixGenerator">
        <property name="pattern" value="yyyyMMdd" />
    </bean>
</beans>
```

However, multiple constructors in a class may cause ambiguity in constructor argument matching. The situation may be further complicated if you ask Spring to determine a constructor for you. So, if you use this auto-wiring mode, take great care to avoid ambiguity.

Auto-Wiring by Auto-Detection

The auto-wiring mode autodetect asks Spring to decide the auto-wiring mode between byType and constructor. If at least a default constructor with no argument is found for that bean, byType will be chosen. Otherwise, constructor will be chosen. Because the SequenceGenerator class has a default constructor defined, byType will be chosen. That means the prefix generator will be injected via the setter method.

```
<beans ...>
    <bean id="sequenceGenerator"
        class="com.apress.springenterpriserecipes.sequence.SequenceGenerator"
        autowire="autodetect">
        <property name="initial" value="100000" />
        <property name="suffix" value="A" />
    </bean>
```

```
    <bean id="datePrefixGenerator"
        class="com.apress.springenterpriserecipes.sequence.DatePrefixGenerator">
        <property name="pattern" value="yyyyMMdd" />
    </bean>
</beans>
```

Auto-Wiring and Dependency Checking

As you have seen, if Spring finds more than one candidate bean for auto-wiring, it will throw an UnsatisfiedDependencyException. On the other hand, if the auto-wiring mode is set to byName or byType, and Spring cannot find a matching bean to wire, it will leave the property unset, which may cause a NullPointerException or a value that has not been initialized. However, if you want to be notified when auto-wiring cannot wire your beans, you should set the dependency-check attribute to objects or all.

In that case, an UnsatisfiedDependencyException will be thrown whenever auto-wiring doesn't work. objects tells Spring to raise an error when a collaborating bean can't be found in the same bean factory. all tells the container to raise an error when any simple property types (a String or a primitive) expressed as dependencies on a bean haven't been set, in addition to the functionality of objects.

```
<bean id="sequenceGenerator"
    class="com.apress.springenterpriserecipes.sequence.SequenceGenerator"
    autowire="byName" dependency-check="objects">
    <property name="initial" value="100000" />
    <property name="suffix" value="A" />
</bean>
```

1-4. Auto-Wiring Beans with @Autowired and @Resource

Problem

Auto-wiring by setting the autowire attribute in the bean configuration file will wire all properties of a bean. It's not flexible enough to wire particular properties only. Moreover, you can auto-wire beans only either by type or by name. If neither strategy satisfies your requirements, you must wire your beans explicitly.

Solution

Spring 2.5 made extensive enhancements to the auto-wiring feature. You can auto-wire a particular property by annotating a setter method, a constructor, a field, or even an arbitrary method with the @Autowired annotation or the @Resource annotation defined in JSR-250: Common Annotations for the Java Platform. That means you have one more option besides setting the autowire attribute to satisfy your requirements. However, this annotation-based option requires you to be using Java 1.5 or higher.

How It Works

To ask Spring to auto-wire the bean properties with @Autowired or @Resource, you have to register an AutowiredAnnotationBeanPostProcessor instance in the IoC container. If you are using a bean factory, you have to register this bean post processor through the API. Otherwise, you can just declare an instance of it in your application context.

```
<bean class="org.springframework.beans.factory.annotation.↩
    AutowiredAnnotationBeanPostProcessor" />
```

Or you can simply include the <context:annotation-config> element in your bean configuration file, and an AutowiredAnnotationBeanPostProcessor instance will automatically get registered.

```
<beans xmlns="http://www.springframework.org/schema/beans"
    xmlns:xsi="http://www.w3.org/2001/XMLSchema-instance"
    xmlns:context="http://www.springframework.org/schema/context"
    xsi:schemaLocation="http://www.springframework.org/schema/beans
        http://www.springframework.org/schema/beans/spring-beans-3.0.xsd
        http://www.springframework.org/schema/context
        http://www.springframework.org/schema/context/spring-context-3.0.xsd">

    <context:annotation-config />
    ...
</beans>
```

Auto-Wiring a Single Bean of Compatible Type

The @Autowired annotation can be applied to a particular property for Spring to auto-wire it. As an example, you can annotate the setter method of the prefixGenerator property with @Autowired. Then Spring will attempt to wire a bean whose type is compatible with PrefixGenerator.

```
package com.apress.springenterpriserecipes.sequence;

import org.springframework.beans.factory.annotation.Autowired;

public class SequenceGenerator {
    ...
    @Autowired
    public void setPrefixGenerator(PrefixGenerator prefixGenerator) {
        this.prefixGenerator = prefixGenerator;
    }
}
```

If you have a bean whose type is compatible with PrefixGenerator defined in the IoC container, it will be set to the prefixGenerator property automatically.

```xml
<beans ...>
    ...
    <bean id="sequenceGenerator"
        class="com.apress.springenterpriserecipes.sequence.SequenceGenerator">
        <property name="initial" value="100000" />
        <property name="suffix" value="A" />
    </bean>

    <bean id="datePrefixGenerator"
        class="com.apress.springenterpriserecipes.sequence.DatePrefixGenerator">
        <property name="pattern" value="yyyyMMdd" />
    </bean>
</beans>
```

By default, all the properties with @Autowired are required. When Spring can't find a matching bean to wire, it will throw an exception. If you want a certain property to be optional, set the required attribute of @Autowired to false. Then when Spring can't find a matching bean, it will leave this property unset.

```java
package com.apress.springenterpriserecipes.sequence;

import org.springframework.beans.factory.annotation.Autowired;

public class SequenceGenerator {
    ...
    @Autowired(required = false)
    public void setPrefixGenerator(PrefixGenerator prefixGenerator) {
        this.prefixGenerator = prefixGenerator;
    }
}
```

In addition to the setter method, the @Autowired annotation can also be applied to a constructor. Then Spring will attempt to find a bean with the compatible type for each of the constructor arguments.

```java
package com.apress.springenterpriserecipes.sequence;

import org.springframework.beans.factory.annotation.Autowired;

public class SequenceGenerator {
    ...
    @Autowired
    public SequenceGenerator(PrefixGenerator prefixGenerator) {
        this.prefixGenerator = prefixGenerator;
    }
}
```

The @Autowired annotation can also be applied to a field, even if it is not declared as public. In this way, you can omit the need of declaring a setter method or a constructor for this field. Spring will inject the matched bean into this field via reflection. However, annotating a non-public field with @Autowired will reduce code testability because the code will be difficult to unit test (there's no way black-box testing can manipulate that state, such as with mock objects).

```
package com.apress.springenterpriserecipes.sequence;

import org.springframework.beans.factory.annotation.Autowired;

public class SequenceGenerator {

    @Autowired
    private PrefixGenerator prefixGenerator;
    ...
}
```

You may even apply the @Autowired annotation to a method with an arbitrary name and an arbitrary number of arguments. Then Spring will attempt to wire a bean with the compatible type for each of the method arguments.

```
package com.apress.springenterpriserecipes.sequence;

import org.springframework.beans.factory.annotation.Autowired;

public class SequenceGenerator {

    ...
    @Autowired
    public void inject(PrefixGenerator prefixGenerator) {
        this.prefixGenerator = prefixGenerator;
    }
}
```

Auto-Wiring All Beans of Compatible Type

The @Autowired annotation can also be applied to a property of array type to have Spring auto-wire all the matching beans. For example, you can annotate a PrefixGenerator[] property with @Autowired. Then Spring will auto-wire all the beans whose type is compatible with PrefixGenerator at one time.

```
package com.apress.springenterpriserecipes.sequence;

import org.springframework.beans.factory.annotation.Autowired;

public class SequenceGenerator {

    @Autowired
    private PrefixGenerator[] prefixGenerators;
    ...
}
```

If you have multiple beans whose type is compatible with the PrefixGenerator defined in the IoC container, they will be added to the prefixGenerators array automatically.

```
<beans ...>
    ...
    <bean id="datePrefixGenerator"
        class="com.apress.springenterpriserecipes.sequence.DatePrefixGenerator">
        <property name="pattern" value="yyyyMMdd" />
    </bean>

    <bean id="yearPrefixGenerator"
        class="com.apress.springenterpriserecipes.sequence.DatePrefixGenerator">
        <property name="pattern" value="yyyy" />
    </bean>
</beans>
```

In a similar way, you can apply the @Autowired annotation to a type-safe collection. Spring can read the type information of this collection and auto-wire all the beans whose type is compatible.

```
package com.apress.springenterpriserecipes.sequence;

import org.springframework.beans.factory.annotation.Autowired;

public class SequenceGenerator {

    @Autowired
    private List<PrefixGenerator> prefixGenerators;
    ...
}
```

If Spring notices that the @Autowired annotation is applied to a type-safe java.util.Map with strings as the keys, it will add all the beans of the compatible type, with the bean names as the keys, to this map.

```
package com.apress.springenterpriserecipes.sequence;

import org.springframework.beans.factory.annotation.Autowired;

public class SequenceGenerator {

    @Autowired
    private Map<String, PrefixGenerator> prefixGenerators;
    ...
}
```

Auto-Wiring by Type with Qualifiers

By default, auto-wiring by type will not work when there is more than one bean with the compatible type in the IoC container. However, Spring allows you to specify a candidate bean by providing its name in the @Qualifier annotation.

```
package com.apress.springenterpriserecipes.sequence;

import org.springframework.beans.factory.annotation.Autowired;
import org.springframework.beans.factory.annotation.Qualifier;

public class SequenceGenerator {

    @Autowired
    @Qualifier("datePrefixGenerator")
    private PrefixGenerator prefixGenerator;
    ...
}
```

Then Spring will attempt to find a bean with that name in the IoC container and wire it into the property.

```
<bean id="datePrefixGenerator"
class="com.apress.springenterpriserecipes.sequence.DatePrefixGenerator">
    <property name="pattern" value="yyyyMMdd" />
</bean>
```

The @Qualifier annotation can also be applied to a method argument for auto-wiring.

```
package com.apress.springenterpriserecipes.sequence;

import org.springframework.beans.factory.annotation.Autowired;
import org.springframework.beans.factory.annotation.Qualifier;

public class SequenceGenerator {
    ...
    @Autowired
    public void inject(
            @Qualifier("datePrefixGenerator") PrefixGenerator prefixGenerator) {
        this.prefixGenerator = prefixGenerator;
    }
}
```

You can create a custom qualifier annotation type for the auto-wiring purpose. This annotation type must be annotated with @Qualifier itself. This is useful if you want a specific type of bean and configuration injected wherever an annotation decorates a field or setter method.

```
package com.apress.springenterpriserecipes.sequence;
import java.lang.annotation.Target;
import java.lang.annotation.Retention;
import java.lang.annotation.ElementType;
import java.lang.annotation.RetentionPolicy;import
org.springframework.beans.factory.annotation.Qualifier;
```

```
@Retention(RetentionPolicy.RUNTIME)
@Target({ElementType.FIELD, ElementType.PARAMETER })
@Qualifier
public @interface Generator {

    String value();
}
```

Then you can apply this annotation to an @Autowired bean property. It will ask Spring to auto-wire the bean with this qualifier annotation and the specified value.

```
package com.apress.springenterpriserecipes.sequence;

import org.springframework.beans.factory.annotation.Autowired;

public class SequenceGenerator {

    @Autowired
    @Generator("prefix")
    private PrefixGenerator prefixGenerator;
    ...
}
```

You have to provide this qualifier to the target bean that you want to be auto-wired into the preceding property. The qualifier is added by the <qualifier> element with the type attribute. The qualifier value is specified in the value attribute. The value attribute is mapped to the String value() attribute of the annotation.

```
<bean id="datePrefixGenerator"
    class="com.apress.springenterpriserecipes.sequence.DatePrefixGenerator">
    <qualifier type="Generator" value="prefix" />
    <property name="pattern" value="yyyyMMdd" />
</bean>
```

Auto-Wiring by Name

If you want to auto-wire bean properties by name, you can annotate a setter method, a constructor, or a field with the JSR-250 @Resource annotation. By default, Spring will attempt to find a bean with the same name as this property. But you can specify the bean name explicitly in its name attribute.

■Note   To use the JSR-250 annotations, you have to include common-annotations.jar (located in the lib/j2ee directory of the Spring installation) in your classpath. However, if your application is running on Java SE 6 or Java EE 5, you needn't include this JAR file.

```
package com.apress.springenterpriserecipes.sequence;

import javax.annotation.Resource;

public class SequenceGenerator {

    @Resource(name = "datePrefixGenerator")
    private PrefixGenerator prefixGenerator;
    ...
}
```

1-5. Scanning Components from the Classpath

Problem

In order for the Spring IoC container to manage your components, you declare them one by one in the bean configuration file. However, it can save you a lot of work if Spring can automatically detect your components without manual configuration.

Solution

Spring provides a powerful feature called *component scanning*. It can automatically scan, detect, and instantiate your components with particular stereotype annotations from the classpath. The basic annotation denoting a Spring-managed component is @Component. Other more particular stereotypes include @Repository, @Service, and @Controller. They denote components in the persistence, service, and presentation layers, respectively.

How It Works

Suppose you are asked to develop your sequence generator application using database sequences, and store the prefix and suffix of each sequence in a table. First, you create the domain class Sequence containing the id, prefix, and suffix properties.

```
package com.apress.springenterpriserecipes.sequence;

public class Sequence {

    private String id;
    private String prefix;
    private String suffix;

    // Constructors, Getters, and Setters
    ...
}
```

Then you create an interface for the Data Access Object (DAO), which is responsible for accessing data from the database. The getSequence() method loads a Sequence object from the table by its ID, while the getNextValue() method retrieves the next value of a particular database sequence.

```
package com.apress.springenterpriserecipes.sequence;

public interface SequenceDao {

    public Sequence getSequence(String sequenceId);
    public int getNextValue(String sequenceId);
}
```

In a production application, you should implement this DAO interface using a data access technology such as JDBC or object/relational mapping. But for testing purposes, let's use maps to store the sequence instances and values.

```
package com.apress.springenterpriserecipes.sequence;
...
public class SequenceDaoImpl implements SequenceDao {

    private Map<String, Sequence> sequences;
    private Map<String, Integer> values;

    public SequenceDaoImpl() {
        sequences = new HashMap<String, Sequence>();
        sequences.put("IT", new Sequence("IT", "30", "A"));
        values = new HashMap<String, Integer>();
        values.put("IT", 100000);
    }

    public Sequence getSequence(String sequenceId) {
        return sequences.get(sequenceId);
    }

    public synchronized int getNextValue(String sequenceId) {
        int value = values.get(sequenceId);
        values.put(sequenceId, value + 1);
        return value;
    }
}
```

You also need a service object, acting as a façade, to provide the sequence generation service. Internally, this service object will interact with the DAO to handle the sequence generation requests. So it requires a reference to the DAO.

```
package com.apress.springenterpriserecipes.sequence;

public class SequenceService {

    private SequenceDao sequenceDao;
```

```
    public void setSequenceDao(SequenceDao sequenceDao) {
        this.sequenceDao = sequenceDao;
    }

    public String generate(String sequenceId) {
        Sequence sequence = sequenceDao.getSequence(sequenceId);
        int value = sequenceDao.getNextValue(sequenceId);
        return sequence.getPrefix() + value + sequence.getSuffix();
    }
}
```

Finally, you have to configure these components in the bean configuration file to make the sequence generator application work. You can auto-wire your components to reduce the amount of configurations.

```
<beans ...>
    <bean id="sequenceService"
        class="com.apress.springenterpriserecipes.sequence.SequenceService"
        autowire="byType" />

    <bean id="sequenceDao"
        class="com.apress.springenterpriserecipes.sequence.SequenceDaoImpl" />
</beans>
```

Then you can test the preceding components with the following Main class:

```
package com.apress.springenterpriserecipes.sequence;

import org.springframework.context.ApplicationContext;
import org.springframework.context.support.ClassPathXmlApplicationContext;

public class Main {

    public static void main(String[] args) {
        ApplicationContext context =
            new ClassPathXmlApplicationContext("beans.xml");

        SequenceService sequenceService =
            (SequenceService) context.getBean("sequenceService");

        System.out.println(sequenceService.generate("IT"));
        System.out.println(sequenceService.generate("IT"));
    }
}
```

Scanning Components Automatically

The component scanning feature provided by Spring since version 2.5 can automatically scan, detect, and instantiate your components from the classpath. By default, Spring can detect all components with a stereotype annotation. The basic annotation type that denotes a Spring-managed component is @Component. You can apply it to your SequenceDaoImpl class.

```
package com.apress.springenterpriserecipes.sequence;

import org.springframework.stereotype.Component;

@Component
public class SequenceDaoImpl implements SequenceDao {
    ...
}
```

Also, you apply this stereotype annotation to the SequenceService class for Spring to detect it. In addition, you apply the @Autowired annotation to the DAO field for Spring to auto-wire it by type. Note that because you're using the annotation on a field, you don't need a setter method here.

```
package com.apress.springenterpriserecipes.sequence;

import org.springframework.beans.factory.annotation.Autowired;
import org.springframework.stereotype.Component;

@Component
public class SequenceService {

    @Autowired
    private SequenceDao sequenceDao;
    ...
}
```

With the stereotype annotations applied to your component classes, you can ask Spring to scan them by declaring a single XML element: <context:component-scan>. In this element, you need to specify the package for scanning your components. Then the specified package and all its subpackages will be scanned. You can use commas to separate multiple packages for scanning.

The previous stereotype is enough to be able to use the bean. Spring will give the bean a name created by lowercasing the first character of the class and using the rest of the camelcased name for the bean name. Thus, the following works (assuming that you've instantiated an application context containing the <context:component-scan> element).

```
SequenceService sequenceService =
            (SequenceService) context.getBean("sequenceService");
```

Note that this element will also register an AutowiredAnnotationBeanPostProcessor instance that can auto-wire properties with the @Autowired annotation.

```
<beans xmlns="http://www.springframework.org/schema/beans"
    xmlns:xsi="http://www.w3.org/2001/XMLSchema-instance"
    xmlns:context="http://www.springframework.org/schema/context"
    xsi:schemaLocation="http://www.springframework.org/schema/beans
        http://www.springframework.org/schema/beans/spring-beans-3.0.xsd
        http://www.springframework.org/schema/context
        http://www.springframework.org/schema/context/spring-context-3.0.xsd">

    <context:component-scan base-package=➥
"com.apress.springenterpriserecipes.sequence" />
</beans>
```

The @Component annotation is the basic stereotype for denoting components of general purposes. Actually, there are other specific stereotypes denoting components in different layers. First, the @Repository stereotype denotes a DAO component in the persistence layer.

```
package com.apress.springenterpriserecipes.sequence;

import org.springframework.stereotype.Repository;

@Repository
public class SequenceDaoImpl implements SequenceDao {
    ...
}
```

Then the @Service stereotype denotes a service component in the service layer.

```
package com.apress.springenterpriserecipes.sequence;

import org.springframework.beans.factory.annotation.Autowired;
import org.springframework.stereotype.Service;

@Service
public class SequenceService {

    @Autowired
    private SequenceDao sequenceDao;
    ...
}
```

There's another component stereotype, @Controller, which denotes a controller component in the presentation layer.

Filtering Components to Scan

By default, Spring will detect all classes annotated with @Component, @Repository, @Service, @Controller, or your custom annotation type that is itself annotated with @Component. You can customize the scan by applying one or more include/exclude filters.

Spring supports four types of filter expressions. The annotation and assignable types are for you to specify an annotation type and a class/interface for filtering. The regex and aspectj types allow you to specify a regular expression and an AspectJ pointcut expression for matching the classes. You can also disable the default filters with the use-default-filters attribute.

For example, the following component scan includes all classes whose name contains the word Dao or Service, and excludes the classes with the @Controller annotation:

```
<beans ...>
    <context:component-scan base-package=➥
"com.apress.springenterpriserecipes.sequence">
        <context:include-filter type="regex"
            expression="com\.apress\.springenterpriserecipes\.sequence\..*Dao.*" />
        <context:include-filter type="regex"
            expression="com\.apress\.springenterpriserecipes\.sequence\..➥
*Service.*" />
```

```
    <context:exclude-filter type="annotation"
            expression="org.springframework.stereotype.Controller" />
    </context:component-scan>
</beans>
```

Because you have applied `include` filters to detect all classes whose name contains the word Dao or Service, the SequenceDaoImpl and SequenceService components can be auto-detected even without a stereotype annotation.

Naming Detected Components

By default, Spring will name the detected components by lowercasing the first character of the non-qualified class name. For example, the SequenceService class will be named as sequenceService. You can define the name for a component explicitly by specifying it in the stereotype annotation's value.

```
package com.apress.springenterpriserecipes.sequence;
...
import org.springframework.stereotype.Service;

@Service("sequenceService")
public class SequenceService {
    ...
}

package com.apress.springenterpriserecipes.sequence;

import org.springframework.stereotype.Repository;

@Repository("sequenceDao")
public class SequenceDaoImpl implements SequenceDao {
    ...
}
```

You can develop your own naming strategy by implementing the BeanNameGenerator interface and specifying it in the name-generator attribute of the <context:component-scan> element.

1-6. Setting Bean Scopes

Problem

When you declare a bean in the configuration file, you are actually defining a template for bean creation, not an actual bean instance. When a bean is requested by the getBean() method or a reference from other beans, Spring will decide which bean instance should be returned according to the bean scope. Sometimes you have to set an appropriate scope for a bean other than the default scope.

Solution

In Spring 2.0 and later, a bean's scope is set in the scope attribute of the <bean> element. By default, Spring creates exactly one instance for each bean declared in the IoC container, and this instance will be shared in the scope of the entire IoC container. This unique bean instance will be returned for all subsequent getBean() calls and bean references. This scope is called singleton, which is the default scope of all beans. Table 1-2 lists all valid bean scopes in Spring.

Table 1-2. *Valid Bean Scopes in Spring*

Scope	Description
singleton	Creates a single bean instance per Spring IoC container
prototype	Creates a new bean instance each time when requested
request	Creates a single bean instance per HTTP request; valid only in the context of a web application
session	Creates a single bean instance per HTTP session; valid only in the context of a web application
globalSession	Creates a single bean instance per global HTTP session; valid only in the context of a portal application

How It Works

To demonstrate the concept of bean scope, consider a shopping cart example in your shop application. First, you create the ShoppingCart class as follows:

```
package com.apress.springenterpriserecipes.shop;
...
public class ShoppingCart {

    private List<Product> items = new ArrayList<Product>();

    public void addItem(Product item) {
        items.add(item);
    }

    public List<Product> getItems() {
        return items;
    }
}
```

Then you declare some product beans and a shopping cart bean in the IoC container as usual:

```
<beans ...>
    <bean id="aaa" class="com.apress.springenterpriserecipes.shop.Battery">
        <property name="name" value="AAA" />
        <property name="price" value="2.5" />
    </bean>

    <bean id="cdrw" class="com.apress.springenterpriserecipes.shop.Disc">
        <property name="name" value="CD-RW" />
        <property name="price" value="1.5" />
    </bean>

    <bean id="dvdrw" class="com.apress.springenterpriserecipes.shop.Disc">
        <property name="name" value="DVD-RW" />
        <property name="price" value="3.0" />
    </bean>

    <bean id="shoppingCart" class="com.apress.springenterpriserecipes.shop.➥
ShoppingCart" />
</beans>
```

In the following Main class, you can test your shopping cart by adding some products to it. Suppose that there are two customers navigating in your shop at the same time. The first one gets a shopping cart by the getBean() method and adds two products to it. Then the second customer also gets a shopping cart by the getBean() method and adds another product to it.

```
package com.apress.springenterpriserecipes.shop;

import org.springframework.context.ApplicationContext;
import org.springframework.context.support.ClassPathXmlApplicationContext;

public class Main {

    public static void main(String[] args) {
        ApplicationContext context =
            new ClassPathXmlApplicationContext("beans.xml");

        Product aaa = (Product) context.getBean("aaa");
        Product cdrw = (Product) context.getBean("cdrw");
        Product dvdrw = (Product) context.getBean("dvdrw");

        ShoppingCart cart1 = (ShoppingCart) context.getBean("shoppingCart");
        cart1.addItem(aaa);
        cart1.addItem(cdrw);
        System.out.println("Shopping cart 1 contains " + cart1.getItems());

        ShoppingCart cart2 = (ShoppingCart) context.getBean("shoppingCart");
        cart2.addItem(dvdrw);
        System.out.println("Shopping cart 2 contains " + cart2.getItems());
    }
}
```

As a result of the preceding bean declaration, you can see that the two customers get the same shopping cart instance.

```
Shopping cart 1 contains [AAA 2.5, CD-RW 1.5]
Shopping cart 2 contains [AAA 2.5, CD-RW 1.5, DVD-RW 3.0]
```

This is because Spring's default bean scope is singleton, which means Spring creates exactly one shopping cart instance per IoC container.

```
<bean id="shoppingCart"
    class="com.apress.springenterpriserecipes.shop.ShoppingCart"
    scope="singleton" />
```

In your shop application, you expect each customer to get a different shopping cart instance when the getBean() method is called. To ensure this behavior, you should change the scope of the shoppingCart bean to prototype. Then Spring will create a new bean instance for each getBean() method call and reference from the other bean.

```
<bean id="shoppingCart"
    class="com.apress.springenterpriserecipes.shop.ShoppingCart"
    scope="prototype" />
```

Now if you run the Main class again, you can see that the two customers get a different shopping cart instance.

```
Shopping cart 1 contains [AAA 2.5, CD-RW 1.5]
Shopping cart 2 contains [DVD-RW 3.0]
```

1-7. Customizing Bean Initialization and Destruction

Problem

Many real-world components have to perform certain types of initialization tasks before they are ready to be used. Such tasks include opening a file, opening a network/database connection, allocating memory, and so on. Also, they have to perform the corresponding destruction tasks at the end of their life cycle. So, you have a need to customize bean initialization and destruction in the Spring IoC container.

Solution

In addition to bean registration, the Spring IoC container is also responsible for managing the life cycle of your beans, and it allows you to perform custom tasks at particular points of their life cycle. Your tasks should be encapsulated in callback methods for the Spring IoC container to call at a suitable time.

The following list shows the steps through which the Spring IoC container manages the life cycle of a bean (this list will be expanded as more features of the IoC container are introduced):

1. Create the bean instance either by a constructor or by a factory method (a static method or a method on a bean instance).

2. Set the values and bean references to the bean properties.

3. Call the initialization callback methods.

4. The bean is ready to be used.

5. When the container is shut down, call the destruction callback methods.

There are three ways that Spring can recognize your initialization and destruction callback methods. First, your bean can implement the `InitializingBean` and `DisposableBean` life cycle interfaces and implement the `afterPropertiesSet()` and `destroy()` methods for initialization and destruction. Second, you can set the `init-method` and `destroy-method` attributes in the bean declaration and specify the callback method names. In Spring, you can also annotate the initialization and destruction callback methods with the life cycle annotations `@PostConstruct` and `@PreDestroy`, which are defined in JSR-250: Common Annotations for the Java Platform. Then you can register a `CommonAnnotationBeanPostProcessor` instance in the IoC container to call these callback methods.

How It Works

To understand how the Spring IoC container manages the life cycle of your beans, let's consider an example involving the checkout function. The following `Cashier` class can be used to check out the products in a shopping cart. It records the time and the amount of each checkout in a text file.

```
package com.apress.springenterpriserecipes.shop;
...
public class Cashier {

    private String name;
    private String path;
    private BufferedWriter writer;

    public void setName(String name) {
        this.name = name;
    }

    public void setPath(String path) {
        this.path = path;
    }

    public void openFile() throws IOException {
        File logFile = new File(path, name + ".txt");
        writer = new BufferedWriter(new OutputStreamWriter(
                new FileOutputStream(logFile, true)));
    }
```

```
    public void checkout(ShoppingCart cart) throws IOException {
        double total = 0;
        for (Product product : cart.getItems()) {
            total += product.getPrice();
        }
        writer.write(new Date() + "\t" + total + "\r\n");
        writer.flush();
    }

    public void closeFile() throws IOException {
        writer.close();
    }
}
```

In the Cashier class, the openFile() method opens the text file with the cashier name as the file name in the specified system path. Each time you call the checkout() method, a checkout record will be appended to the text file. Finally, the closeFile() method closes the file to release its system resources.

Then you declare a cashier bean with the name cashier1 in the IoC container. This cashier's checkout records will be recorded in the file c:/cashier/cashier1.txt. You should create this directory in advance or specify another existing directory. (On a Unix derivative, you might put it in your home directory: ~/cashier.)

```
<beans ...>
    ...
    <bean id="cashier1" class="com.apress.springenterpriserecipes.shop.Cashier">
        <property name="name" value="cashier1" />
        <property name="path" value="c:/cashier" />
    </bean>
</beans>
```

However, in the Main class, if you try to check out a shopping cart with this cashier, it will result in a NullPointerException. The reason for this exception is that no one has called the openFile() method for initialization beforehand.

```
package com.apress.springenterpriserecipes.shop;

import org.springframework.context.ApplicationContext;
import org.springframework.context.support.FileSystemXmlApplicationContext;

public class Main {

    public static void main(String[] args) throws Exception {
      // checkout() throws an Exception
        ApplicationContext context =
            new FileSystemXmlApplicationContext("beans.xml");
        ...
        Cashier cashier1 = (Cashier) context.getBean("cashier1");
        cashier1.checkout(cart1);
    }
}
```

Where should you make a call to the openFile() method for initialization? In Java, the initialization tasks should be performed in the constructor. But would it work here if you call the openFile() method in the default constructor of the Cashier class? No, because the openFile() method requires both the name and path properties to be set before it can determine which file to open.

```
package com.apress.springenterpriserecipes.shop;
...
public class Cashier {
    ...
    public void openFile() throws IOException {
        File logFile = new File(path, name + ".txt");
        writer = new BufferedWriter(new OutputStreamWriter(
                new FileOutputStream(logFile, true)));
    }
}
```

When the default constructor is invoked, these properties have not been set yet. So you may add a constructor that accepts the two properties as arguments, and call the openFile() method at the end of this constructor. However, sometimes you might not be allowed to do so, or you might prefer to inject your properties via setter injection. Actually, the best time to call the openFile() method is after all properties have been set by the Spring IoC container.

Implementing the InitializingBean and DisposableBean Interfaces
Spring allows your bean to perform initialization and destruction tasks in the callback methods afterPropertiesSet() and destroy() by implementing the InitializingBean and DisposableBean interfaces. During bean construction, Spring will notice that your bean implements these interfaces and call the callback methods at a suitable time.

```
package com.apress.springenterpriserecipes.shop;
...
import org.springframework.beans.factory.DisposableBean;
import org.springframework.beans.factory.InitializingBean;

public class Cashier implements InitializingBean, DisposableBean {
    ...
    public void afterPropertiesSet() throws Exception {
        openFile();
    }

    public void destroy() throws Exception {
        closeFile();
    }
}
```

Now if you run your Main class again, you will see that a checkout record is appended to the text file c:/cashier/cashier1.txt. However, implementing such proprietary interfaces will make your beans Spring-specific and thus unable to be reused outside the Spring IoC container.

Setting the init-method and destroy-method Attributes
A better approach of specifying the initialization and destruction callback methods is by setting the init-method and destroy-method attributes in your bean declaration.

```
<bean id="cashier1" class="com.apress.springenterpriserecipes.shop.Cashier"
    init-method="openFile" destroy-method="closeFile">
    <property name="name" value="cashier1" />
    <property name="path" value="c:/cashier" />
</bean>
```

With these two attributes set in the bean declaration, your Cashier class no longer needs to implement the InitializingBean and DisposableBean interfaces. You can also delete the afterPropertiesSet() and destroy() methods as well.

Annotating the @PostConstruct and @PreDestroy Annotations

You can annotate the initialization and destruction callback methods with the JSR-250 life cycle annotations @PostConstruct and @PreDestroy.

■Note   To use the JSR-250 annotations, you have to include common-annotations.jar (located in the lib/j2ee directory of the Spring installation) in your classpath. However, if your application is running on Java SE 6 or Java EE 5, you needn't include this JAR file.

```
package com.apress.springenterpriserecipes.shop;
...
import javax.annotation.PostConstruct;
import javax.annotation.PreDestroy;

public class Cashier {
    ...
    @PostConstruct
    public void openFile() throws IOException {
        File logFile = new File(path, name + ".txt");
        writer = new BufferedWriter(new OutputStreamWriter(
                new FileOutputStream(logFile, true)));
    }

    @PreDestroy
    public void closeFile() throws IOException {
        writer.close();
    }
}
```

Then you register a CommonAnnotationBeanPostProcessor instance in the IoC container to call the initialization and destruction callback methods with the life cycle annotations. In this way, you no longer need to specify the init-method and destroy-method attributes for your bean.

```
<beans ...>
    ...
    <bean class="org.springframework.context.annotation.➥
        CommonAnnotationBeanPostProcessor" />
```

```
<bean id="cashier1" class="com.apress.springenterpriserecipes.shop.Cashier">
    <property name="name" value="cashier1" />
    <property name="path" value="c:/cashier" />
</bean>
</beans>
```

Or you can simply include the `<context:annotation-config>` element in your bean configuration file and a `CommonAnnotationBeanPostProcessor` instance will automatically get registered. But before this tag can work, you must add the `context` schema definition to your `<beans>` root element.

```
<beans xmlns="http://www.springframework.org/schema/beans"
    xmlns:xsi="http://www.w3.org/2001/XMLSchema-instance"
    xmlns:context="http://www.springframework.org/schema/context"
    xsi:schemaLocation="http://www.springframework.org/schema/beans
        http://www.springframework.org/schema/beans/spring-beans-3.0.xsd
        http://www.springframework.org/schema/context
        http://www.springframework.org/schema/context/spring-context-3.0.xsd">

    <context:annotation-config />
    ...
</beans>
```

1-8. Resolving Text Messages

Problem

For an application to support internationalization (I18N for short because there are 18 characters between the first character, *i*, and the last character, *n*), it requires the capability of resolving text messages for different locales.

Solution

Spring's application context can resolve text messages for a target locale by their keys. Typically, the messages for one locale should be stored in one separate properties file. This properties file is called a *resource bundle*.

`MessageSource` is an interface that defines several methods for resolving messages. The `ApplicationContext` interface extends this interface so that all application contexts can resolve text messages. An application context delegates the message resolution to a bean with the exact name `messageSource`. `ResourceBundleMessageSource` is the most common `MessageSource` implementation that resolves messages from resource bundles for different locales.

How It Works

As an example, you can create the following resource bundle, `messages_en_US.properties`, for the English language in the United States. Resource bundles will be loaded from the root of the classpath.

```
alert.checkout=A shopping cart has been checked out.
```

To resolve messages from resource bundles, you use `ResourceBundleMessageSource` as your `MessageSource` implementation. This bean's name must be set to `messageSource` for the

application context to detect it. You have to specify the base name of the resource bundles for
ResourceBundleMessageSource.

```
<beans ...>
    ...
    <bean id="messageSource"
        class="org.springframework.context.support.ResourceBundleMessageSource">
        <property name="basename">
            <value>messages</value>
        </property>
    </bean>
</beans>
```

For this MessageSource definition, if you look up a text message for the United States locale, whose
preferred language is English, the resource bundle messages_en_US.properties, which matches both the
language and country, will be considered first. If there's no such resource bundle, or the message can't
be found, the one messages_en.properties that matches the language only will be considered. If this
resource bundle still can't be found, the default messages.properties for all locales will be finally chosen.
For more information on resource bundle loading, you can refer to the javadoc of the
java.util.ResourceBundle class.

Now you can ask the application context to resolve a message by the getMessage() method. The first
argument is the key corresponding to the message, and the third is the target locale.

```
package com.apress.springenterpriserecipes.shop;

import org.springframework.context.ApplicationContext;
import org.springframework.context.support.FileSystemXmlApplicationContext;
...

public class Main {

    public static void main(String[] args) throws Exception {
        ApplicationContext context =
            new FileSystemXmlApplicationContext("beans.xml");
        ...
        String alert = context.getMessage("alert.checkout", null, Locale.US);
        System.out.println(alert);
    }
}
```

The second argument of the getMessage() method is an array of message parameters. In the text
message, you can define multiple parameters by index:

```
alert.checkout=A shopping cart costing {0} dollars has been checked out at {1}.
```

You have to pass in an object array to fill in the message parameters. The elements in this array will
be converted into strings before filling in the parameters.

```
package com.apress.springenterpriserecipes.shop;
...
public class Main {

    public static void main(String[] args) throws Exception {
        ...
```

```
        String alert = context.getMessage("alert.checkout",
                new Object[] { 4, new Date() }, Locale.US);
        System.out.println(alert);
    }
}
```

In the Main class, you can resolve text messages because you can access the application context directly. But for a bean to resolve text messages, it has to implement either the ApplicationContextAware interface or the MessageSourceAware interface. Now you can delete the message resolution from the Main class.

```
package com.apress.springenterpriserecipes.shop;
...
import org.springframework.context.MessageSource;
import org.springframework.context.MessageSourceAware;

public class Cashier implements MessageSourceAware {
    ...
    private MessageSource messageSource;

    public void setMessageSource(MessageSource messageSource) {
        this.messageSource = messageSource;
    }

    public void checkout(ShoppingCart cart) throws IOException {
        ...
        String alert = messageSource.getMessage("alert.checkout",
                new Object[] { total, new Date() }, Locale.US);
        System.out.println(alert);
    }
}
```

1-9. Loading External Resources

Problem

Sometimes your application may need to read external resources (e.g., text files, XML files, properties file, or image files) from different locations (e.g., a file system, classpath, or URL). Usually, you have to deal with different APIs for loading resources from different locations.

Solution

Spring's resource loader provides a unified getResource() method for you to retrieve an external resource by a resource path. You can specify different prefixes for this path to load resources from different locations. To load a resource from a file system, you use the file prefix. To load a resource from the classpath, you use the classpath prefix. You may also specify a URL in this resource path.

Resource is a general interface in Spring for representing an external resource. Spring provides several implementations for the Resource interface. The resource loader's getResource() method will decide which Resource implementation to instantiate according to the resource path.

How It Works

Suppose you want to display a banner at the startup of your shop application. The banner is made up of the following characters and stored in a text file called banner.txt. This file can be put in the current path of your application.

```
************************
*   Welcome to My Shop!   *
************************
```

Next you have to write the BannerLoader class to load the banner and output it to the console. Because it requires access to a resource loader for loading the resource, it has to implement either the ApplicationContextAware interface or the ResourceLoaderAware interface.

```java
package com.apress.springenterpriserecipes.shop;
...
import org.springframework.context.ResourceLoaderAware;
import org.springframework.core.io.Resource;
import org.springframework.core.io.ResourceLoader;

public class BannerLoader implements ResourceLoaderAware {

    private ResourceLoader resourceLoader;

    public void setResourceLoader(ResourceLoader resourceLoader) {
        this.resourceLoader = resourceLoader;
    }

    public void showBanner() throws IOException {
        Resource banner = resourceLoader.getResource("file:banner.txt");
        InputStream in = banner.getInputStream();

        BufferedReader reader = new BufferedReader(new InputStreamReader(in));
        while (true) {
            String line = reader.readLine();
            if (line == null)
                break;
            System.out.println(line);
        }
        reader.close();
    }
}
```

By calling the getResource() method from the application context, you can retrieve an external resource specified by a resource path. Because your banner file is located in the file system, the resource path should start with the file prefix. You can call the getInputStream() method to retrieve the input stream for this resource. Then you read the file contents line by line with BufferedReader and output them to the console.

Finally, you declare a BannerLoader instance in the bean configuration file to display the banner. Because you want to show the banner at startup, you specify the showBanner() method as the initialization method.

```
<bean id="bannerLoader"
    class="com.apress.springenterpriserecipes.shop.BannerLoader"
    init-method="showBanner" />
```

Resource Prefixes

The previous resource path specifies a resource in the relative path of the file system. You can specify an absolute path as well.

```
file:c:/shop/banner.txt
```

When your resource is located in the classpath, you have to use the classpath prefix. If there's no path information presented, it will be loaded from the root of the classpath.

```
classpath:banner.txt
```

If the resource is located in a particular package, you can specify the absolute path from the classpath root.

```
classpath:com/apress/springenterpriserecipes/shop/banner.txt
```

Besides a file system path or the classpath, a resource can also be loaded by specifying a URL.

```
http://springenterpriserecipes.apress.com/shop/banner.txt
```

If there's no prefix presented in the resource path, the resource will be loaded from a location according to the application context. For FileSystemXmlApplicationContext, the resource will be loaded from the file system. For ClassPathXmlApplicationContext, it will be loaded from the classpath.

Injecting Resources

In addition to calling the getResource() method to load a resource explicitly, you can inject it by using a setter method:

```
package com.apress.springenterpriserecipes.shop;
...
import org.springframework.core.io.Resource;

public class BannerLoader {

    private Resource banner;

    public void setBanner(Resource banner) {
        this.banner = banner;
    }
```

```
public void showBanner() throws IOException {
    InputStream in = banner.getInputStream();
    ...
}
}
```

In the bean configuration, you can simply specify the resource path for this `Resource` property. Spring will use the preregistered property editor `ResourceEditor` to convert it into a `Resource` object before injecting it into your bean.

```
<bean id="bannerLoader"
    class="com.apress.springenterpriserecipes.shop.BannerLoader"
    init-method="showBanner">
    <property name="banner">
        <value>classpath:com/apress/springenterpriserecipes/shop/banner.txt</value>
    </property>
</bean>
```

1-10. Enabling AspectJ Annotation Support in Spring

Problem

Spring version 2.0 and later support the use of POJO aspects written with AspectJ annotations in its AOP framework. But first you have to enable AspectJ annotation support in the Spring IoC container.

Solution

To enable AspectJ annotation support in the Spring IoC container, you only have to define an empty XML element `<aop:aspectj-autoproxy>` in your bean configuration file. Then Spring will automatically create proxies for any of your beans that are matched by your AspectJ aspects.

How It Works

Let's consider a calculator interface, whose interface is as follows:

```
package com.apress.springenterpriserecipes.calculator;

public interface ArithmeticCalculator {

    public double add(double a, double b);
    public double sub(double a, double b);
    public double mul(double a, double b);
    public double div(double a, double b);
}

package com.apress.springenterpriserecipes.calculator;

public interface UnitCalculator {
```

```
    public double kilogramToPound(double kilogram);
    public double kilometerToMile(double kilometer);
}
```

Then you provide an implementation for each interface with println statements to let you know when the methods are executed.

```
package com.apress.springenterpriserecipes.calculator;

public class ArithmeticCalculatorImpl implements ArithmeticCalculator {

    public double add(double a, double b) {
        double result = a + b;
        System.out.println(a + " + " + b + " = " + result);
        return result;
    }

    public double sub(double a, double b) {
        double result = a - b;
        System.out.println(a + " - " + b + " = " + result);
        return result;
    }

    public double mul(double a, double b) {
        double result = a * b;
        System.out.println(a + " * " + b + " = " + result);
        return result;
    }

    public double div(double a, double b) {
        if (b == 0) {
            throw new IllegalArgumentException("Division by zero");
        }
        double result = a / b;
        System.out.println(a + " / " + b + " = " + result);
        return result;
    }
}

package com.apress.springenterpriserecipes.calculator;

public class UnitCalculatorImpl implements UnitCalculator {

    public double kilogramToPound(double kilogram) {
        double pound = kilogram * 2.2;
        System.out.println(kilogram + " kilogram = " + pound + " pound");
        return pound;
    }
```

```
    public double kilometerToMile(double kilometer) {
        double mile = kilometer * 0.62;
        System.out.println(kilometer + " kilometer = " + mile + " mile");
        return mile;
    }
}
```

To enable AspectJ annotation support for this application, you just define an empty XML element, <aop:aspectj-autoproxy>, in your bean configuration file. Moreover, you must add the aop schema definition to your <beans> root element. When the Spring IoC container notices the <aop:aspectj-autoproxy> element in your bean configuration file, it will automatically create proxies for your beans that are matched by your AspectJ aspects.

```
<beans xmlns="http://www.springframework.org/schema/beans"
    xmlns:xsi="http://www.w3.org/2001/XMLSchema-instance"
    xmlns:aop="http://www.springframework.org/schema/aop"
    xsi:schemaLocation="http://www.springframework.org/schema/beans
        http://www.springframework.org/schema/beans/spring-beans-3.0.xsd
        http://www.springframework.org/schema/aop
        http://www.springframework.org/schema/aop/spring-aop-3.0.xsd">

    <aop:aspectj-autoproxy />

    <bean id="arithmeticCalculator"
        class="com.apress.springenterpriserecipes.➥
calculator.ArithmeticCalculatorImpl" />

    <bean id="unitCalculator"
        class="com.apress.springenterpriserecipes.calculator.UnitCalculatorImpl" />
</beans>
```

1-11. Declaring Aspects with AspectJ Annotations

Problem
Since merging with AspectWerkz in AspectJ version 5, AspectJ supports aspects written as POJOs annotated with a set of AspectJ annotations. Aspects of this kind are also supported by the Spring AOP framework, although they must be registered in the Spring IoC container to take effect.

Solution
You register AspectJ aspects in Spring simply by declaring them as bean instances in the IoC container. With AspectJ enabled in the Spring IoC container, it will create proxies for your beans that are matched by your AspectJ aspects.

Written with AspectJ annotations, an aspect is simply a Java class with the @Aspect annotation. An advice is a simple Java method with one of the advice annotations. AspectJ supports five types of advice annotations: @Before, @After, @AfterReturning, @AfterThrowing, and @Around.

How It Works

Before Advices

To create a *before* advice to handle crosscutting concerns before particular program execution points, you use the @Before annotation and include the pointcut expression as the annotation value.

```
package com.apress.springenterpriserecipes.calculator;

import org.apache.commons.logging.Log;
import org.apache.commons.logging.LogFactory;
import org.aspectj.lang.annotation.Aspect;
import org.aspectj.lang.annotation.Before;

@Aspect
public class CalculatorLoggingAspect {

    private Log log = LogFactory.getLog(this.getClass());

    @Before("execution(* ArithmeticCalculator.add(..))")
    public void logBefore() {
        log.info("The method add() begins");
    }
}
```

This pointcut expression matches the add() method execution of the ArithmeticCalculator interface. The preceding wildcard in this expression matches any modifier (public, protected, and private) and any return type. The two dots in the argument list match any number of arguments.

To register this aspect, you just declare a bean instance of it in the IoC container. The aspect bean may even be anonymous if there's no reference from other beans.

```
<beans ...>
    ...
    <bean class="com.apress.springenterpriserecipes.calculator.➥
CalculatorLoggingAspect" />
</beans>
```

You can test your aspect with the following Main class:

```
package com.apress.springenterpriserecipes.calculator;

import org.springframework.context.ApplicationContext;
import org.springframework.context.support.ClassPathXmlApplicationContext;

public class Main {

    public static void main(String[] args) {
        ApplicationContext context =
            new ClassPathXmlApplicationContext("beans.xml");
```

```
    ArithmeticCalculator arithmeticCalculator =
        (ArithmeticCalculator) context.getBean("arithmeticCalculator");
    arithmeticCalculator.add(1, 2);
    arithmeticCalculator.sub(4, 3);
    arithmeticCalculator.mul(2, 3);
    arithmeticCalculator.div(4, 2);

    UnitCalculator unitCalculator =
        (UnitCalculator) context.getBean("unitCalculator");
    unitCalculator.kilogramToPound(10);
    unitCalculator.kilometerToMile(5);
    }
}
```

The execution points matched by a pointcut are called *join points*. In this term, a pointcut is an expression to match a set of join points, while an advice is the action to take at a particular join point.

For your advice to access the detail of the current join point, you can declare an argument of type JoinPoint in your advice method. Then you can get access to join point details such as the method name and argument values. Now you can expand your pointcut to match all methods by changing the class name and method name to wildcards.

```
package com.apress.springenterpriserecipes.calculator;
...
import java.util.Arrays;

import org.aspectj.lang.JoinPoint;
import org.aspectj.lang.annotation.Aspect;
import org.aspectj.lang.annotation.Before;

@Aspect
public class CalculatorLoggingAspect {
    ...
    @Before("execution(* *.*(..))")
    public void logBefore(JoinPoint joinPoint) {
        log.info("The method " + joinPoint.getSignature().getName()
                + "() begins with " + Arrays.toString(joinPoint.getArgs()));
    }
}
```

After Advices

An *after* advice is executed after a join point finishes, whenever it returns a result or throws an exception abnormally. The following after advice logs the calculator method ending. An aspect may include one or more advices.

```
package com.apress.springenterpriserecipes.calculator;
...
import org.aspectj.lang.JoinPoint;
import org.aspectj.lang.annotation.After;
import org.aspectj.lang.annotation.Aspect;
```

```
@Aspect
public class CalculatorLoggingAspect {
    ...
    @After("execution(* *.*(..))")
    public void logAfter(JoinPoint joinPoint) {
        log.info("The method " + joinPoint.getSignature().getName()
                + "() ends");
    }
}
```

After Returning Advices

An after advice is executed regardless of whether a join point returns normally. If you want to perform logging only when a join point returns, you should replace the after advice with an *after returning* advice.

```
package com.apress.springenterpriserecipes.calculator;
...
import org.aspectj.lang.JoinPoint;
import org.aspectj.lang.annotation.AfterReturning;
import org.aspectj.lang.annotation.Aspect;

@Aspect
public class CalculatorLoggingAspect {
    ...
    @AfterReturning("execution(* *.*(..))")
    public void logAfterReturning(JoinPoint joinPoint) {
        log.info("The method " + joinPoint.getSignature().getName()
                + "() ends");
    }
}
```

In an after returning advice, you can get access to the return value of a join point by adding a returning attribute to the @AfterReturning annotation. The value of this attribute should be the argument name of this advice method for the return value to pass in. Then you have to add an argument to the advice method signature with this name. At runtime, Spring AOP will pass in the return value through this argument. Also note that the original pointcut expression needs to be presented in the pointcut attribute instead.

```
package com.apress.springenterpriserecipes.calculator;
...
import org.aspectj.lang.JoinPoint;
import org.aspectj.lang.annotation.AfterReturning;
import org.aspectj.lang.annotation.Aspect;

@Aspect
public class CalculatorLoggingAspect {
    ...
    @AfterReturning(
        pointcut = "execution(* *.*(..))",
        returning = "result")
```

```
    public void logAfterReturning(JoinPoint joinPoint, Object result) {
        log.info("The method " + joinPoint.getSignature().getName()
                + "() ends with " + result);
    }
}
```

After Throwing Advices

An *after throwing* advice is executed only when an exception is thrown by a join point.

```
package com.apress.springenterpriserecipes.calculator;
...
import org.aspectj.lang.JoinPoint;
import org.aspectj.lang.annotation.AfterThrowing;
import org.aspectj.lang.annotation.Aspect;

@Aspect
public class CalculatorLoggingAspect {
    ...
    @AfterThrowing("execution(* *.*(..))")
    public void logAfterThrowing(JoinPoint joinPoint) {
        log.error("An exception has been thrown in "
                + joinPoint.getSignature().getName() + "()");
    }
}
```

Similarly, the exception thrown by the join point can be accessed by adding a throwing attribute
to the @AfterThrowing annotation. The type Throwable is the superclass of all errors and exceptions in
the Java language. So the following advice will catch any of the errors and exceptions thrown by the
join points:

```
package com.apress.springenterpriserecipes.calculator;
...
import org.aspectj.lang.JoinPoint;
import org.aspectj.lang.annotation.AfterThrowing;
import org.aspectj.lang.annotation.Aspect;

@Aspect
public class CalculatorLoggingAspect {
    ...
    @AfterThrowing(
        pointcut = "execution(* *.*(..))",
        throwing = "e")
    public void logAfterThrowing(JoinPoint joinPoint, Throwable e) {
        log.error("An exception " + e + " has been thrown in "
                + joinPoint.getSignature().getName() + "()");
    }
}
```

However, if you are interested in one particular type of exception only, you can declare it as the
argument type of the exception. Then your advice will be executed only when exceptions of compatible
type (i.e., this type and its subtypes) are thrown.

```
package com.apress.springenterpriserecipes.calculator;
...
import java.util.Arrays;

import org.aspectj.lang.JoinPoint;
import org.aspectj.lang.annotation.AfterThrowing;
import org.aspectj.lang.annotation.Aspect;

@Aspect
public class CalculatorLoggingAspect {
    ...
    @AfterThrowing(
        pointcut = "execution(* *.*(..))",
        throwing = "e")
    public void logAfterThrowing(JoinPoint joinPoint,
            IllegalArgumentException e) {
        log.error("Illegal argument " + Arrays.toString(joinPoint.getArgs())
                + " in " + joinPoint.getSignature().getName() + "()");
    }
}
```

Around Advices

The last type of advice is an *around* advice. It is the most powerful of all the advice types. It gains full control of a join point, so you can combine all the actions of the preceding advices into one single advice. You can even control when, and whether, to proceed with the original join point execution.

The following around advice is the combination of the before, after returning, and after throwing advices you created before. Note that for an around advice, the argument type of the join point must be ProceedingJoinPoint. It's a subinterface of JoinPoint that allows you to control when to proceed with the original join point.

```
package com.apress.springenterpriserecipes.calculator;
...
import java.util.Arrays;

import org.aspectj.lang.ProceedingJoinPoint;
import org.aspectj.lang.annotation.Around;
import org.aspectj.lang.annotation.Aspect;

@Aspect
public class CalculatorLoggingAspect {
    ...
    @Around("execution(* *.*(..))")
    public Object logAround(ProceedingJoinPoint joinPoint) throws Throwable {
        log.info("The method " + joinPoint.getSignature().getName()
                + "() begins with " + Arrays.toString(joinPoint.getArgs()));
        try {
            Object result = joinPoint.proceed();
            log.info("The method " + joinPoint.getSignature().getName()
                    + "() ends with " + result);
            return result;
        } catch (IllegalArgumentException e) {
            log.error("Illegal argument "
```

```
                    + Arrays.toString(joinPoint.getArgs()) + " in "
                    + joinPoint.getSignature().getName() + "()");
            throw e;
        }
    }
}
```

The around advice type is very powerful and flexible in that you can even alter the original argument values and change the final return value. You must use this type of advice with great care because the call to proceed with the original join point may easily be forgotten.

■Tip   A common rule for choosing an advice type is to use the least powerful one that can satisfy your requirements.

1-12. Reusing Pointcut Definitions

Problem
When writing AspectJ aspects, you can directly embed a pointcut expression in an advice annotation. However, the same pointcut expression may be repeated in multiple advices.

Solution
Like many other AOP implementations, AspectJ also allows you to define a pointcut independently to be reused in multiple advices.

How It Works
In an AspectJ aspect, a pointcut can be declared as a simple method with the @Pointcut annotation. The method body of a pointcut is usually empty because it is unreasonable to mix a pointcut definition with application logic. The access modifier of a pointcut method controls the visibility of this pointcut as well. Other advices can refer to this pointcut by the method name.

```
package com.apress.springenterpriserecipes.calculator;
...
import org.aspectj.lang.annotation.Pointcut;

@Aspect
public class CalculatorLoggingAspect {
    ...
    @Pointcut("execution(* *.*(..))")
    private void loggingOperation() {}

    @Before("loggingOperation()")
    public void logBefore(JoinPoint joinPoint) {
        ...
    }
```

```java
    @AfterReturning(
        pointcut = "loggingOperation()",
        returning = "result")
    public void logAfterReturning(JoinPoint joinPoint, Object result) {
        ...
    }

    @AfterThrowing(
        pointcut = "loggingOperation()",
        throwing = "e")
    public void logAfterThrowing(JoinPoint joinPoint, IllegalArgumentException e) {
        ...
    }

    @Around("loggingOperation()")
    public Object logAround(ProceedingJoinPoint joinPoint) throws Throwable {
        ...
    }
}
```

Usually, if your pointcuts are shared between multiple aspects, it is better to centralize them in a common class. In this case, they must be declared as public.

```java
package com.apress.springenterpriserecipes.calculator;

import org.aspectj.lang.annotation.Aspect;
import org.aspectj.lang.annotation.Pointcut;

@Aspect
public class CalculatorPointcuts {

    @Pointcut("execution(* *.*(..))")
    public void loggingOperation() {}
}
```

When you refer to this pointcut, you have to include the class name as well. If the class is not located in the same package as the aspect, you have to also include the package name.

```java
package com.apress.springenterpriserecipes.calculator;
...
@Aspect
public class CalculatorLoggingAspect {
    ...
    @Before("CalculatorPointcuts.loggingOperation()")
    public void logBefore(JoinPoint joinPoint) {
        ...
    }
```

```
@AfterReturning(
    pointcut = "CalculatorPointcuts.loggingOperation()",
    returning = "result")
public void logAfterReturning(JoinPoint joinPoint, Object result) {
    ...
}

@AfterThrowing(
    pointcut = "CalculatorPointcuts.loggingOperation()",
    throwing = "e")
public void logAfterThrowing(JoinPoint joinPoint, IllegalArgumentException e) {
    ...
}

@Around("CalculatorPointcuts.loggingOperation()")
public Object logAround(ProceedingJoinPoint joinPoint) throws Throwable {
    ...
}
}
```

1-13. Writing AspectJ Pointcut Expressions

Problem

Crosscutting concerns may happen at different program execution points, which are called *join points*. Because of the variety of join points, you need a powerful expression language that can help in matching them.

Solution

The AspectJ pointcut language is a powerful expression language that can match many kinds of join points. However, Spring AOP only supports method execution join points for beans declared in its IoC container. For this reason, only those pointcut expressions supported by Spring AOP will be introduced here. For a full description of the AspectJ pointcut language, please refer to the AspectJ programming guide available on AspectJ's web site (http://www.eclipse.org/aspectj/).

Spring AOP makes use of the AspectJ pointcut language for its pointcut definition. Actually, Spring AOP interprets the pointcut expressions at runtime by using AspectJ's functionality.

When writing AspectJ pointcut expressions for Spring AOP, you must keep in mind that Spring AOP only supports method execution join points for the beans in its IoC container. If you use a pointcut expression out of this scope, an IllegalArgumentException will be thrown.

How It Works

Method Signature Patterns

The most typical pointcut expressions are used to match a number of methods by their signatures. For example, the following pointcut expression matches all of the methods declared in the ArithmeticCalculator interface. The preceding wildcard matches methods with any modifier (public, protected, and private) and any return type. The two dots in the argument list match any number of arguments.

```
execution(* com.apress.springenterpriserecipes.calculator.➡
ArithmeticCalculator.*(..))
```

You can omit the package name if the target class or interface is located in the same package as this aspect.

```
execution(* ArithmeticCalculator.*(..))
```

The following pointcut expression matches all the public methods declared in the ArithmeticCalculator interface:

```
execution(public * ArithmeticCalculator.*(..))
```

You can also restrict the method return type. For example, the following pointcut matches the methods that return a double number:

```
execution(public double ArithmeticCalculator.*(..))
```

The argument list of the methods can also be restricted. For example, the following pointcut matches the methods whose first argument is of primitive double type. The two dots then match any number of followed arguments.

```
execution(public double ArithmeticCalculator.*(double, ..))
```

Or, you can specify all the argument types in the method signature for the pointcut to match.

```
execution(public double ArithmeticCalculator.*(double, double))
```

Although the AspectJ pointcut language is powerful in matching various join points, sometimes you might not be able to find any common characteristics (e.g., modifiers, return types, method name patterns, or arguments) for the methods you want to match. In such cases, you can consider providing a custom annotation for them. For instance, you can define the following annotation type (this annotation can be applied to both method level and type level):

```
package com.apress.springenterpriserecipes.calculator;

import java.lang.annotation.Documented;
import java.lang.annotation.ElementType;
import java.lang.annotation.Retention;
import java.lang.annotation.RetentionPolicy;
import java.lang.annotation.Target;

@Target( { ElementType.METHOD, ElementType.TYPE })
@Retention(RetentionPolicy.RUNTIME)
@Documented
public @interface LoggingRequired {
}
```

Then you can annotate all methods that require logging with this annotation. Note that the annotations must be added to the implementation class but not the interface because they will not be inherited.

```
package com.apress.springenterpriserecipes.calculator;

public class ArithmeticCalculatorImpl implements ArithmeticCalculator {

    @LoggingRequired
    public double add(double a, double b) {
        ...
    }

    @LoggingRequired
    public double sub(double a, double b) {
        ...
    }

    @LoggingRequired
    public double mul(double a, double b) {
        ...
    }

    @LoggingRequired
    public double div(double a, double b) {
        ...
    }
}
```

Now you can write a pointcut expression to match all methods with this @LoggingRequired annotation.

```
@annotation(com.apress.springenterpriserecipes.calculator.LoggingRequired)
```

Type Signature Patterns

Another kind of pointcut expressions matches all join points within certain types. When applied to Spring AOP, the scope of these pointcuts will be narrowed to matching all method executions within the types. For example, the following pointcut matches all the method execution join points within the com.apress.springenterpriserecipes.calculator package:

```
within(com.apress.springenterpriserecipes.calculator.*)
```

To match the join points within a package and its subpackage, you have to add one more dot before the wildcard.

```
within(com.apress.springenterpriserecipes.calculator..*)
```

The following pointcut expression matches the method execution join points within a particular class:

```
within(com.apress.springenterpriserecipes.calculator.ArithmeticCalculatorImpl)
```

Again, if the target class is located in the same package as this aspect, the package name can be omitted.

```
within(ArithmeticCalculatorImpl)
```

You can match the method execution join points within all classes that implement the ArithmeticCalculator interface by adding a plus symbol.

```
within(ArithmeticCalculator+)
```

Your custom annotation @LoggingRequired can be applied to the class level instead of the method level.

```
package com.apress.springenterpriserecipes.calculator;

@LoggingRequired
public class ArithmeticCalculatorImpl implements ArithmeticCalculator {
    ...
}
```

Then you can match the join points within the classes that have been annotated with @LoggingRequired.

```
@within(com.apress.springenterpriserecipes.calculator.LoggingRequired)
```

Bean Name Patterns

Spring supports a new pointcut type that is used to match bean names. For example, the following pointcut expression matches beans whose name ends with Calculator:

```
bean(*Calculator)
```

■Caution This pointcut type is supported only in XML-based Spring AOP configurations, not in AspectJ annotations.

Combining Pointcut Expressions

In AspectJ, pointcut expressions can be combined with the operators && (and), || (or), and ! (not). For example, the following pointcut matches the join points within classes that implement either the ArithmeticCalculator or UnitCalculator interface:

```
within(ArithmeticCalculator+) || within(UnitCalculator+)
```

The operands of these operators can be any pointcut expressions or references to other pointcuts.

```
package com.apress.springenterpriserecipes.calculator;

import org.aspectj.lang.annotation.Aspect;
import org.aspectj.lang.annotation.Pointcut;

@Aspect
public class CalculatorPointcuts {

    @Pointcut("within(ArithmeticCalculator+)")
    public void arithmeticOperation() {}
```

```
@Pointcut("within(UnitCalculator+)")
public void unitOperation() {}

@Pointcut("arithmeticOperation() || unitOperation()")
public void loggingOperation() {}
}
```

Declaring Pointcut Parameters

One way to access join point information is by reflection (i.e., via an argument of type org.aspectj.lang.JoinPoint in the advice method). Besides, you can access join point information in a declarative way by using some kinds of special pointcut expressions. For example, the expressions target() and args() capture the target object and argument values of the current join point and expose them as pointcut parameters. These parameters will be passed to your advice method via arguments of the same name.

```
package com.apress.springenterpriserecipes.calculator;
...
import org.aspectj.lang.annotation.Aspect;
import org.aspectj.lang.annotation.Before;

@Aspect
public class CalculatorLoggingAspect {
    ...
    @Before("execution(* *.*(..)) && target(target) && args(a,b)")
    public void logParameter(Object target, double a, double b) {
        log.info("Target class : " + target.getClass().getName());
        log.info("Arguments : " + a + ", " + b);
    }
}
```

When declaring an independent pointcut that exposes parameters, you have to include them in the argument list of the pointcut method as well.

```
package com.apress.springenterpriserecipes.calculator;

import org.aspectj.lang.annotation.Aspect;
import org.aspectj.lang.annotation.Pointcut;

@Aspect
public class CalculatorPointcuts {
    ...
    @Pointcut("execution(* *.*(..)) && target(target) && args(a,b)")
    public void parameterPointcut(Object target, double a, double b) {}
}
```

Any advice that refers to this parameterized pointcut can access the pointcut parameters via method arguments of the same name.

```
package com.apress.springenterpriserecipes.calculator;
...
import org.aspectj.lang.annotation.Aspect;
import org.aspectj.lang.annotation.Before;
```

```
@Aspect
public class CalculatorLoggingAspect {
    ...
    @Before("CalculatorPointcuts.parameterPointcut(target, a, b)")
    public void logParameter(Object target, double a, double b) {
        log.info("Target class : " + target.getClass().getName());
        log.info("Arguments : " + a + ", " + b);
    }
}
```

1-14. Introducing Behaviors to Your Beans

Problem

Sometimes you may have a group of classes that share a common behavior. In OOP, they must extend the same base class or implement the same interface. This issue is actually a crosscutting concern that can be modularized with AOP.

In addition, the single inheritance mechanism of Java allows a class to extend only one base class at most. So you cannot inherit behaviors from multiple implementation classes at the same time.

Solution

Introduction is a special type of advice in AOP. It allows your objects to implement an interface dynamically by providing an implementation class for that interface. It seems as if your objects had extended the implementation class at runtime.

Moreover, you are able to introduce multiple interfaces with multiple implementation classes to your objects at the same time. This can achieve the same effect as multiple inheritance.

How It Works

Suppose you have two interfaces, MaxCalculator and MinCalculator, to define the max() and min() operations.

```
package com.apress.springenterpriserecipes.calculator;

public interface MaxCalculator {

    public double max(double a, double b);
}
```

```
package com.apress.springenterpriserecipes.calculator;

public interface MinCalculator {

    public double min(double a, double b);
}
```

Then you have an implementation for each interface with println statements to let you know when the methods are executed.

```
package com.apress.springenterpriserecipes.calculator;

public class MaxCalculatorImpl implements MaxCalculator {

    public double max(double a, double b) {
        double result = (a >= b) ? a : b;
        System.out.println("max(" + a + ", " + b + ") = " + result);
        return result;
    }
}
```

```
package com.apress.springenterpriserecipes.calculator;

public class MinCalculatorImpl implements MinCalculator {

    public double min(double a, double b) {
        double result = (a <= b) ? a : b;
        System.out.println("min(" + a + ", " + b + ") = " + result);
        return result;
    }
}
```

Now suppose you also want ArithmeticCalculatorImpl to perform the max() and min() calculation. As the Java language supports single inheritance only, it is not possible for the ArithmeticCalculatorImpl class to extend both the MaxCalculatorImpl and MinCalculatorImpl classes at the same time. The only possible way is to extend either class (e.g., MaxCalculatorImpl) and implement another interface (e.g., MinCalculator), either by copying the implementation code or delegating the handling to the actual implementation class. In either case, you have to repeat the method declarations.

With introduction, you can make ArithmeticCalculatorImpl dynamically implement both the MaxCalculator and MinCalculator interfaces by using the implementation classes MaxCalculatorImpl and MinCalculatorImpl. It has the same effect as multiple inheritance from MaxCalculatorImpl and MinCalculatorImpl. The brilliant idea behind introduction is that you needn't modify the ArithmeticCalculatorImpl class to introduce new methods. That means you can introduce methods to your existing classes even without source code available.

■Tip   You may wonder how an introduction can do that in Spring AOP. The answer is a *dynamic proxy*. As you may recall, you can specify a group of interfaces for a dynamic proxy to implement. Introduction works by adding an interface (e.g., MaxCalculator) to the dynamic proxy. When the methods declared in this interface are called on the proxy object, the proxy will delegate the calls to the back-end implementation class (e.g., MaxCalculatorImpl).

Introductions, like advices, must be declared within an aspect. You may create a new aspect or reuse an existing aspect for this purpose. In this aspect, you can declare an introduction by annotating an arbitrary field with the @DeclareParents annotation.

```
package com.apress.springenterpriserecipes.calculator;

import org.aspectj.lang.annotation.Aspect;
import org.aspectj.lang.annotation.DeclareParents;

@Aspect
public class CalculatorIntroduction {

    @DeclareParents(
        value = "com.apress.springenterpriserecipes.calculator.➥
ArithmeticCalculatorImpl",
        defaultImpl = MaxCalculatorImpl.class)
    public MaxCalculator maxCalculator;

    @DeclareParents(
        value = "com.apress.springenterpriserecipes.calculator.➥
ArithmeticCalculatorImpl",
        defaultImpl = MinCalculatorImpl.class)
    public MinCalculator minCalculator;
}
```

The value attribute of the @DeclareParents annotation type indicates which classes are the targets
for this introduction. The interface to introduce is determined by the type of the annotated field. Finally,
the implementation class used for this new interface is specified in the defaultImpl attribute.

Through these two introductions, you can dynamically introduce a couple of interfaces to the
ArithmeticCalculatorImpl class. Actually, you can specify an AspectJ type-matching expression in
the value attribute of the @DeclareParents annotation to introduce an interface to multiple classes. For
the last step, don't forget to declare an instance of this aspect in the application context.

```
<beans ...>
    ...
    <bean class="com.apress.springenterpriserecipes.calculator.➥
CalculatorIntroduction" />
</beans>
```

Because you have introduced both the MaxCalculator and MinCalculator interfaces to your
arithmetic calculator, you can cast it to the corresponding interface to perform the max() and min()
calculations.

```
package com.apress.springenterpriserecipes.calculator;

public class Main {

    public static void main(String[] args) {
        ...
        ArithmeticCalculator arithmeticCalculator =
            (ArithmeticCalculator) context.getBean("arithmeticCalculator");
        ...
        MaxCalculator maxCalculator = (MaxCalculator) arithmeticCalculator;
        maxCalculator.max(1, 2);
```

```
        MinCalculator minCalculator = (MinCalculator) arithmeticCalculator;
        minCalculator.min(1, 2);
    }
}
```

1-15. Introducing States to Your Beans

Problem

Sometimes you might want to add new states to a group of existing objects to keep track of their usage, such as the calling count, the last modified date, and so on. It should not be a problem if all the objects have the same base class. However, it's difficult for you to add such states to different classes if they are not in the same class hierarchy.

Solution

You can introduce a new interface to your objects with an implementation class that holds the state field. Then you can write another advice to change the state according to a particular condition.

How It Works

Suppose you want to keep track of the calling count of each calculator object. Because there is no field for storing the counter value in the original calculator classes, you need to introduce one with Spring AOP. First, let's create an interface for the operations of a counter.

```
package com.apress.springenterpriserecipes.calculator;

public interface Counter {

    public void increase();
    public int getCount();
}
```

Then just write a simple implementation class for this interface. This class has a count field for storing the counter value.

```
package com.apress.springenterpriserecipes.calculator;

public class CounterImpl implements Counter {

    private int count;

    public void increase() {
        count++;
    }

    public int getCount() {
        return count;
    }
}
```

To introduce the Counter interface to all your calculator objects with CounterImpl as the implementation, you can write the following introduction with a type-matching expression that matches all the calculator implementations:

```
package com.apress.springenterpriserecipes.calculator;
...
import org.aspectj.lang.annotation.Aspect;
import org.aspectj.lang.annotation.DeclareParents;

@Aspect
public class CalculatorIntroduction {
    ...
    @DeclareParents(
        value = "com.apress.springenterpriserecipes.calculator.*CalculatorImpl",
        defaultImpl = CounterImpl.class)
    public Counter counter;
}
```

This introduction introduces CounterImpl to each of your calculator objects. However, it's still not enough to keep track of the calling count. You have to increase the counter value each time a calculator method is called. You can write an after advice for this purpose. Note that you must get the *this* object but not the *target* object because only the proxy object implements the Counter interface.

```
package com.apress.springenterpriserecipes.calculator;
...
import org.aspectj.lang.annotation.After;
import org.aspectj.lang.annotation.Aspect;

@Aspect
public class CalculatorIntroduction {
    ...
    @After("execution(* com.apress.springenterpriserecipes.➥
calculator.*Calculator.*(..))"
            + " && this(counter)")
    public void increaseCount(Counter counter) {
        counter.increase();
    }
}
```

In the Main class, you can output the counter value for each of the calculator objects by casting them into the Counter type.

```
package com.apress.springenterpriserecipes.calculator;

public class Main {

    public static void main(String[] args) {
        ...
        ArithmeticCalculator arithmeticCalculator =
            (ArithmeticCalculator) context.getBean("arithmeticCalculator");
        ...

        UnitCalculator unitCalculator =
```

```
        (UnitCalculator) context.getBean("unitCalculator");
    ...

    Counter arithmeticCounter = (Counter) arithmeticCalculator;
    System.out.println(arithmeticCounter.getCount());

    Counter unitCounter = (Counter) unitCalculator;
    System.out.println(unitCounter.getCount());
    }
}
```

Summary

This chapter discussed the core Spring framework and the dependency injection container's features. You learned about some of the sophisticated practical options that the Spring framework offers for configuring applications, large or small. The chapter showed you how to receive various callbacks from the container and how to depend on the ApplicationContext interface explicitly to use some of its more advanced features such as resource bundles. Finally, you learned how to configure your beans with annotations to lessen the XML required for configuration and all about Spring's powerful AOP support (and how to use it to interact with the container).

In the next chapter, you will explore the many exciting new features of Spring framework 3.0.

CHAPTER 2

■ ■ ■

What's New in Spring 3.0?

Spring 3.0 is upon us. It marks an evolution of a framework that revitalized the state of enterprise Java forever. Since its debut, Spring has had decidedly ambitious goals, not the least of which was to simplify enterprise Java development. It attempted this before Ruby on Rails, Django, and Scala came out of the woodwork. The framework has in many ways shaped the evolution of Java and contributed to a change of mindset in the Java community at large.

When the first version debuted, it featured simple, common-sense libraries that tied together otherwise boilerplate idioms and reduced them to their simplest elements, as reusable libraries. It built these abstractions on top of a solid, Plain Old Java Object (POJO)–oriented dependency injection container. Spring 1.0 expressed the configuration format in a simple XML schema that mapped, one to one, to objects and properties. With Spring 1.0, you could create objects that would be wired in a hierarchy that looks exactly as it would if you showed the objects in Java. It was possible to get a little bit of indirection through the use of a BeanFactory, but otherwise the result was plain and easily understood. The BeanFactory hid the construction of the object that was created. One small BeanFactory could create a very complex object graph if it needed to.

This approach made the functionality in the libraries even more charming because there was very little to imagine. What you saw was what you got. The POJO-oriented approach meant that applications could be unit tested because it was easy to use interfaces. This was a feat worthy of praise because it flew in the face of the Java EE "best practices" being shopped at that point. It proffered that applications were essentially different variations of the same kind of stuff: plain objects in a container. It didn't presume to be better than everything else, but instead it took a conciliatory approach, integrating with anything and everything being used in any quantity by anybody: Struts, Hibernate, JDO, Java EE, JSP, servlets, Java Database Connectivity (JDBC), Enterprise JavaBeans (EJB), Java Message Service (JMS), and much more.

As the framework grew, it did more and more to relieve the complexity from building solutions in Java EE and popularized many patterns that would eventually be codified in the standards, including dependency injection. With the hard things made simple, the framework took the next step and worked to make possible the impossible. Solutions that were otherwise estranged or enjoyed only a niche place in the market suddenly surfaced in an easy-to-use manner. One example is AOP, which was considered largely a relic of academia.

Spring 2.0 brought XML schemas, which meant even more indirection. It became a little harder to understand what was going on in certain places, but it also brought an extra level of abstraction to the framework. This was an overall gain. It meant that many different idioms could be packaged and reused in a schema, sparing the user the tedium of reimplementation each time. It did for some of Spring's more hairy idioms what Spring had done for raw Java EE code years earlier. Spring 2.0 also saw dramatic changes in the Spring landscape. A much improved AOP solution was introduced, built on AspectJ. It introduced numerous new libraries for things that simply hadn't been introduced before. Dynamic languages (Groovy, Bean Shell, JRuby) gained broad support in the container, too.

Spring 2.5 saw the introduction of core support for annotations. It also brought the "schema-fication" of more technologies. The release broadened the presence of Spring, making it easier to leverage it. It set the foundations for Spring 3.0.

Other projects, such as the Spring model-view-controller (MVC), have evolved concurrently throughout the development of the core Spring framework, growing in tandem with—and sometimes influencing—the core Spring framework. The last few years have seen the introduction of more than five new major frameworks: Spring Integration; Spring Batch; the Spring/Flex integration; Spring Faces for JSF; and even a radically different version of Spring MVC, which many refer to as @MVC because of the annotation-centric approach that the framework espouses. These frameworks are often single-focused and extremely adept, built using the idioms you've come to take for granted in the core Spring framework such as IoC, schema, annotation and, of course, a POJO-friendly engine.

Indeed, the introduction of drastically new technologies has occurred in the supplementary frameworks, leaving the core stable. Spring 3.0 is, in many ways, an evolution of the ideas introduced in previous releases, a unifying release. The core Spring framework has remained pretty stable and backward compatible for the last few releases. Spring 3.0 represents a chance to clean house; to consolidate or deprecate as necessary. Spring 3.0 is also a chance to clean up and update some technologies debuted in earlier releases.

This release also brings the framework forward in keeping with the latest in technology. Sun has end-of-life'd Java 1.4, which is as fitting a reason as any for the Spring framework to drop official support for Java 1.4 and update the core framework for Java 1.5. Initial support for Java EE 6 is included, and functionality that evolved from other Spring frameworks in some cases has been folded into the core (for example, the Spring object-to-XML support and the new expression language[EL]).

Succinctly: Spring 3.0 represents a major leap forward.

Upgrades to the SpringSource Portfolio

Although there are many new projects coming out of SpringSource, some of them are simply out of the scope for this book. (Thank goodness! We'd need two volumes!) It's important to know what's out there, however.

One of the big-ticket items coming in Spring 3.0 is the support for Representational State Transfer (REST) in Spring MVC. REST will be supported fully, with annotations that are available on controller methods to specify which verb to respond to for which resource. This support will also see the introduction of a `RestTemplate`, in the same style of `JmsTemplate` or `HibernateTemplate`, which will facilitate accessing remote services.

What Is REST?

Representational State Transfer (REST) is an architectural style created by Roy Fielding (a principal author of HTTP 1.0 and 1.1). REST prescribes the most useful features of the Internet, wherein resources are accessed by unique URLs whose state may be modified with different types of requests: you would POST to add data to a resource, GET to read it, and so on.

As it applies to Spring, REST and RESTlets are part of a larger trend in the enterprise space (including a Java EE specification called JAX-RS, JSR-311) of enabling services whose endpoints are exposed on a URL as an HTTP endpoint. Because the platform is a well-known standard, REST services tend to be very open and very flexible.

For example, imagine needing to fetch the details on an object in a database for a customer record. In a traditional service layer, you might use EJB or SOAP, each very complex, and inflexible formats requiring sophisticated clients. With REST, it might be as easy as performing a GET on a URL (http://myservices.com/services/customers/24234, for example). Need security? Change it to HTTPS, and employ authentication. Need the customer record in XML, JSON, and HTML? You might change the suffix or send a parameter indicating the payload type. Creation of a new record could be as simple as a parameterized HTTP PUT against a URL. Deletion of existing records is as simple as an HTTP DELETE request against a URL. Needless to say, the model is flexible, and works with existing technology.

REST doesn't just *work with* HTTP; its main benefit is that it *is* HTTP. HTTP requests are inherently stateless, meaning they're proxy-friendly, cluster-friendly, and cache-friendly. It is standard HTTP, so requests travel through firewalls. Indeed, such endpoints work well with Ajax applications because the payload is a standard format (typically XML, JSON, HTML, or anything else you can imagine wanting to emit).

Spring Roo, a very exciting technology announced at SpringOne Europe in 2009, is a sophisticated round-tripping code generator that makes it quicker and easier than you've ever imagined to create and evolve Spring applications. This framework makes use of code generation and round-tripping to support dynamically building a request-response–oriented Spring MVC application with a working Maven build system, JUnit tests, JPA entities, and more. If you're thinking this all sounds like Ruby on Rails, you wouldn't be the only one. Naturally, Roo was designed to leverage Spring's capabilities and to provide tight integration with IDEs. Roo provides a shell that you can use to dynamically navigate the runtime model of your application. Spring Roo enables the creation of a meta model—a model of your application—that it uses to generate HTML views, services, entities, controllers, unit tests, Data Access Objects (DAOs) that you can extend, custom finder methods that you can add if you like, and more. Currently the "interface" to this model is the aforementioned shell, which is built on top of Maven, although there's no reason it couldn't also be surfaced through Ant or Buildr. The shell takes simple commands and generates the scaffolding needed to satisfy the requests. Because it's built on top of Maven, projects generated with Spring Roo open and work out of the box with all leading IDEs including Eclipse, Netbeans, and IntelliJ IDEA.

Spring is a powerful tool in Java, but it brings a lot to the table for other platforms, too. Spring.NET is a well known example. Spring Python released 1.0 recently. Spring Python provides a dependency injection container, an AOP container and a unified set of APIs—surfaced as the familiar template objects you're familiar with in the classic Spring. Spring Python offers an XML configuration, but it sometimes almost seems like overkill given how expressive and succinct Python itself is. So it's no surprise that Spring Python came out of the gate with Python Config, based on decorators (decorators are like Java annotations or .NET attributes but with more innate flexibility), à la Spring Java Config (which is discussed later in this chapter). Besides a very robust AOP facility and a Dependency Injection (DI) container, Spring Python provides support for database access, transactions, remoting, and security, among others. Spring Python ships with a console ("coily") and a plug-in system so that you can install functionality independent of the main release.

SpringSource bought G2One, the parent company behind the Groovy and Grails technologies in November, 2008. The purchase could herald many changes, not the least of which is tighter integration between Spring and Groovy. Already, SpringSource has announced a conference focused on both Spring and Groovy technologies called SpringOne 2GX.

In 2008, SpringSource announced a collaboration with Adobe to evolve the integration between the Spring framework and Adobe's open sourced middleware and Flash Action Message Format (AMF) server (formerly LiveCycle Data Services ES) BlazeDS. This integration includes the capability to export services, in typical Spring remoting and messaging fashion, as AMF-invokable services. AMF is the binary format that the Flash Virtual Machine reads and writes for RPC. While the Flash Virtual Machine also supports JSON, XML, and HTTP, AMF is remarkably quick, owing mainly to how well-compressed it is. Message queue functionality and Comet-style applications with server-side push and publish/subscribe architecture support are also offered.

Independently, a Spring Extension called Spring ActionScript—a rework of a framework formerly known as the Prana framework—is in incubation and being developed. The framework provides auto wiring, an IoC container based on Spring, a reflection API, utilities, and integrations with popular MVC frameworks Cairngorm and PureMVC.

The exciting list of new technologies is ever growing. For some bleeding-edge functionality that's definitely worth watching, visit the Spring Extensions page at `http://www.springsource.org/extensions` for more.

2-1. Getting Started with the Latest and Greatest Spring Framework

Problem

You've read enough and want to start using the Spring framework 3.0 right now!

Solution

You can download Spring framework 3.0 or use Maven/Ivy to obtain the relevant `.jar` files. To download the distribution manually, visit `http://www.springsource.com/download`. You'll see the latest milestones available for your consumption. If you're feeling adventurous, you can ride Spring's HEAD.

If you do use Maven/Ivy, however, there are a few things to be aware of because the framework's source layout has changed.

How It Works

They broke the build! The various packages of similar functionality have been broken out and moved into their own separate projects, with their own proper source and test directories. This enables easier development for the maintainers. Internally, the code is now standardized on the same Ivy-based build system: Spring Build.

The source code itself has moved, too! It used to be on SourceForge.net, but now you can get it from the SpringSource Subversion repository at `https://src.springsource.org/svn/spring-framework`. The migration of the source code won't affect you if you're not hacking on the code yourself.

If you're trying to build against it using Maven/Ivy, you need to be aware of a few things. First, because of the enhanced modularity of the projects, there are more potential jars to download. You can stipulate every one of them using Maven, or you can simply refer to the wrapper dependency, whose sole function is to transitively import them all. The wrapper dependency has a dependency on all the other dependencies, which means that they'll come with when you use a tool such as Maven or Ivy to fetch your dependencies. It functionally replaces the old `spring.jar` that was shipped, which contained the entire framework in one large `.jar` file. Naturally, you'll end up with quite a few more `.jar` files with this approach, but the effect is the same: the entire Spring framework is on your classpath come build or development time.

At the time of this writing, the release is not considered final because Spring 3.0 is still being developed and is still releasing 3.0 milestones. So the final .jar files are not on the central Maven repositories. You need to download them from the SpringSource Enterprise Repository, which is a special repository that SpringSource has established to provide access to Spring dependencies. One of the main advantages of this repository is that it provides OSGi-friendly jars. If you're using Maven, the configuration for the repositories looks like the following:

```
<repositories>
        <repository>
            <id>SpringSource Enterprise Bundle Repository - ➥
External Bundle Milestones</id>
                <url>http://repository.springsource.com/maven/bundles/milestone</url>
        </repository>
        <repository>
            <id>SpringSource Enterprise Bundle Repository - ➥
SpringSource Bundle Releases</id>
                <url>http://repository.springsource.com/maven/bundles/release</url>
        </repository>
        <repository>
            <id>SpringSource Enterprise Bundle Repository - ➥
External Bundle Releases</id>
                <url>http://repository.springsource.com/maven/bundles/external</url>
        </repository>
        <repository>
            <id>SpringSource Enterprise Bundle Repository - Library Milestones</id>
            <url>http://repository.springsource.com/maven/libraries/milestone</url>
        </repository>
</repositories>
```

Finally, to add the wrapper dependency to get most of the functionality you're likely to need, simply add the following to your Maven POM (pom.xml, the Maven "project object model") inside the dependencies element.

```
<dependency>
        <groupId>org.springframework</groupId>
        <artifactId>org.springframework.spring-library</artifactId>
        <type>libd</type>
        <version>3.0.0</version>
    </dependency>...
```

2-2. Using Java 5 Syntax in Spring

Problem

Spring has always worked in Java 5, of course. Indeed, it even provided extra functionality that worked only in Java 5, but it never exploited Java 5's features at the core of the framework. Some use cases practically beg to be reworked for Java 5.You should be aware of some of these things going forward because even though existing code shouldn't be broken, a lot of these new features are enticing and can save you a lot of conceptual complexity (not to mention keystrokes!)

Solution

Spring 3.0 requires Java 5 from the bottom up. Support has been added throughout, from the smaller convenience methods to methods that will likely be used a lot and whose use of the new features translates into *a lot* of saved typing. You will work through the major changes here.

How It Works

There are many changes related to Java 5 that are, in some cases, very relevant for the average user of Spring 3.0; some are decidedly less so. Some of the changes are mentioned here, and you'll be referred to a more advanced treatment of the topic in other chapters.

BeanFactory and FactoryBean

The most immediate visible use of generics in Spring 3.0 is apparent when dealing with BeanFactory. BeanFactory is the super interface for ApplicationContext, which you'll use in almost every application of Spring, at some level or another. Two methods—getBean() from the BeanFactory interface and getBeansOfType() from the ListableBeanFactory interface—are now generic-friendly. You can replace a lot of code with these new methods. The resultant code might be slightly more verbose, but it removes a lot of ambiguity from the original incantations. After all, incorrect usage could yield a compiler error!

Here you see two calls using the new methods. In the first invocation of getBean(), you specify the bean's name as the first parameter and the type of the bean as the second, which enables you to avoid a cast. The second example, getBeansOfType(), demonstrates that the returned Map (whose keys are the bean names and values the instances of the beans whose interface is castable to Cat) is parameterized to a type, which makes iteration more predictable and easier.

```
import java.util.Map;

import org.springframework.context.support.ClassPathXmlApplicationContext;

public class GenericFriendlyLookupExample {
    public static void main(String[] args) {
        ClassPathXmlApplicationContext context =
            new ClassPathXmlApplicationContext(args[0]);
        context.start();
        // without generics
        Cat catWithoutGenerics = (Cat) context.getBean("fluffy");
        // with generics
        Cat catWithGenerics = context.getBean("fluffy", Cat.class);
        // without generics
        Map catsWithoutGenerics = context.getBeansOfType(Cat.class);
        // with generics
        Map<String, Cat> catsWithGenerics =
            context.getBeansOfType( Cat.class);
        for(String key : catsWithGenerics.keySet()) {
            Cat cat = catsWithGenerics.get( key );
            // no need to cast!
        }
    }
}
```

FactoryBean is an `interface` implemented by beans to provide it with a chance to customize the creation of another type of object, above and beyond what the container knows how to do. FactoryBean is also generic-friendly. This is rarely something you'll deal with unless you write a custom FactoryBean or decide to inject another FactoryBean and manipulate it manually. The new interface looks like this:

```
public interface FactoryBean<T> {
        T getObject() throws Exception;
        Class<? extends T> getObjectType();
        boolean isSingleton();
}
```

ApplicationContext Events

ApplicationContext events let you bring another level of decoupling to your application, going one step farther than dependency injection. Beans declared in the application context can publish and subscribe to events published by other beans. You might use this as a sort of publish/subscribe infrastructure inside the virtual machine. It's a quick way to broadcast an event that other beans can subscribe to if they want to. If a bean implements the ApplicationListener interface, it receives every ApplicationEvent that is published. However, this quickly becomes burdensome after a few different components start publishing an ApplicationEvent, if only because of the requirement to filter incoming events with instanceof checks.

Now you can stipulate what type of ApplicationEvent your bean will receive by using a type parameter. To broadcast an event, your event must still subclass ApplicationEvent. In the following example, the ApplicationContext is used to publish a subclass of ApplicationEvent called CopiesExhaustedApplicationEvent, which is published only when the library has exhausted the available copies of a given book:

```
public class LibraryServiceImpl
  implements LibraryService, ApplicationContextAware, InitializingBean {

  private List<Book> books;
  private ApplicationContext context;
  // …
  public boolean checkOutBook(Book book) {
    if (this.books.contains(book)) {
      if (book.getTotalCopiesAvailable() > 0) {
        book.setTotalCopiesAvailable(
            book.getTotalCopiesAvailable() - 1);
        return true;
      } else {
        ApplicationEvent evt = new CopiesExhaustedApplicationEvent(
                this, book);
        context.publishEvent(evt);
        return false;
      }
    }
    return false;
  }
```

Any beans interested in subscribing to this event would normally need only to implement ApplicationListener:

```
public interface ApplicationListener<E extends ApplicationEvent>
extends EventListener {
    void onApplicationEvent(E event);
}
```

The revised Java 5 support allows you to parameterize the type of the interface in Spring 3.0. BookInventoryManagerServiceImpl, whose job it is to respond to inventory outages, would look like this:

```
import org.springframework.context.ApplicationListener;
import com.apress.springenterpriserecipes.spring3.events. ➥
CopiesExhaustedApplicationEvent;
public class BookInventoryManagerServiceImpl implements
        BookInventoryManagerService,
        ApplicationListener<CopiesExhaustedApplicationEvent> {

    public void onApplicationEvent(CopiesExhaustedApplicationEvent event) {
        System.out.printf("Received a CopiesExhausted"+
                          "ApplicationEvent for book %s\n",
                          event.getBook().getTitle());
        this.purchaseMoreCopiesOfABook(event.getBook());
    }
}
```

2-3. Achieving Concurrency with TaskExecutors

Problem
Options for building threaded, concurrent programs are myriad, but there's no standard approach. What's more, building such programs tends to involve creating lots of utility classes to support common use cases.

Solution
Use Spring's TaskExecutor abstraction. This abstraction provides numerous implementations for many environments, including basic Java SE Executor implementations, Java EE WorkManager implementations, and custom implementations. In Spring 3.0, all the implementations are unified and can be cast to Java SE's Executor interface, too.

How It Works
Threading is a difficult issue, and several difficult use cases remain unapproachable without a sizable amount of effort; others are at least very tedious to implement using standard threading in the Java SE environment. Concurrency is an important aspect of architectures when implementing server-side components and enjoys no standardization in the Java EE space. In fact, it's quite the contrary: some parts of the Java EE specs forbid the explicit creation and manipulation of threads!

Java SE

In the Java SE landscape, a myriad of options have been introduced over the years. First, there's the standard java.lang.Thread support present since day 1 and Java Development Kit (JDK) 1.0. Java 1.3 saw the introduction of java.util.TimerTask to support doing some sort of work periodically. Java 5 debuted the java.util.concurrent package as well as a reworked hierarchy for building thread pools, oriented around the java.util.concurrent.Executor.

The application programming interface (API) for Executor is simple:

```
package java.util.concurrent;
public interface Executor {
    void execute(Runnable command);
}
```

ExecutorService, a subinterface, provides more functionality for managing threads and providing support for raising events to the threads, such as shutdown(). There are several implementations that have shipped with the JDK since Java SE 5.0. Many of them are available via static factory methods on the java.util.concurrent.Executors class, in much the same way that utility methods for manipulating java.util.Collection instances are offered on the java.util.Collections class. What follows are examples. ExecutorService also provides a submit() method, which returns a Future<T>. An instance of Future<T> can be used to track the progress of a thread that's executing—usually asynchronously. You can call isDone() or isCancelled() to determine whether the job is finished or cancelled, respectively. If you submit an object of type Runnable, whose primary method (run) supports no return type, the get() on Future<T> method will return either null or a value that you specify as a parameter on submission of the job, like so:

```
Runnable task = new Runnable(){
  public void run(){
    Thread.sleep( 1000 * 60 ) ;
    System.out.println("Done sleeping for a minute, returning! " );
  }
};
ExecutorService executorService  = Executors.newCachedThreadPool() ;
if(executorService.submit(task, Boolean.TRUE).get().equals( Boolean.TRUE ))
    System.out.println( "Job has finished!");
```

With that in hand, you can explore some the characteristics of the various implementations. For example, you'll use the following Runnable instance:

```
package com.apress.springenterpriserecipes.spring3.executors;

import java.util.Date;
import org.apache.commons.lang.exception.ExceptionUtils;

public class DemonstrationRunnable implements Runnable {
  public void run() {
        try {
            Thread.sleep(1000);
        } catch (InterruptedException e) {
            System.out.println(
                ExceptionUtils.getFullStackTrace(e));
        }
```

```
        System.out.println(Thread.currentThread().getName());
        System.out.printf("Hello at %s \n", new Date());
    }
}
```

The class is designed only to mark the passage of time. You'll use the same instance when you explore Java SE Executors and Spring's TaskExecutor support:

```
import java.util.Date;
import java.util.concurrent.ExecutorService;
import java.util.concurrent.Executors;
import java.util.concurrent.ScheduledExecutorService;
import java.util.concurrent.TimeUnit;

public class ExecutorsDemo {

    public static void main(String[] args) throws Throwable {
        Runnable task = new DemonstrationRunnable();

        // will create a pool of threads and attempt to
        // reuse previously created ones if possible
        ExecutorService cachedThreadPoolExecutorService = Executors
            .newCachedThreadPool();
        if (cachedThreadPoolExecutorService.submit(task).get() == null)
            System.out.printf("The cachedThreadPoolExecutorService "
                    + "has succeeded at %s \n", new Date());

        // limits how many new threads are created, queueing the rest
        ExecutorService fixedThreadPool = Executors.newFixedThreadPool(100);
        if (fixedThreadPool.submit(task).get() == null)
            System.out.printf("The fixedThreadPool has " +
                    "succeeded at %s \n",
                    new Date());

        // doesn't use more than one thread at a time
        ExecutorService singleThreadExecutorService = Executors
            .newSingleThreadExecutor();
        if (singleThreadExecutorService.submit(task).get() == null)
            System.out.printf("The singleThreadExecutorService "
                    + "has succeeded at %s \n", new Date());

        // support sending a job with a known result
        ExecutorService es = Executors.newCachedThreadPool();
        if (es.submit(task, Boolean.TRUE).get().equals(Boolean.TRUE))
            System.out.println("Job has finished!");

        // mimic TimerTask
        ScheduledExecutorService scheduledThreadExecutorService = Executors
            .newScheduledThreadPool(10);
        if (scheduledThreadExecutorService.schedule(
                task, 30, TimeUnit.SECONDS).get() == null)
            System.out.printf("The scheduledThreadExecutorService "
                    + "has succeeded at %s \n", new Date());
```

```
    // this doesn't stop until it encounters
    // an exception or its cancel()ed
    scheduledThreadExecutorService.scheduleAtFixedRate(task, 0, 5,
        TimeUnit.SECONDS);

    }
}
```

If you use the version of the submit() method on the ExecutorService that accepts a Callable<T>, then submit() return whatever was returned from the Callable main method call().The interface for Callable is as follows:

```
package java.util.concurrent;

public interface Callable<V> {
    V call() throws Exception;
}
```

Java EE
In the Java EE landscape, different approaches for solving these sorts of problems have been created, often missing the point. Java EE has offered no threading issue help for a long time.

There are other solutions for these sorts of problems. Quartz (a job scheduling framework) filled the gap by providing a solution that provided scheduling and concurrency. JCA 1.5 (or the J2EE Connector Architecture; the JCA acronym is most used when referring to this technology, even though it was supposed to be the acronym for the Java Cryptography Architecture) is a specification that supports concurrency in that it provides a primitive type of gateway for integration functionality. Components can be notified about incoming messages and respond concurrently. JCA 1.5 provides primitive, limited Enterprise Service Bus–similar to integration features, without nearly as much of the finesse of something like SpringSource's Spring Integration framework. That said, if you had to tie a legacy application written in C to a Java EE application server and let it optionally participate in container services, and wanted to do it in a *reasonably* portable way before 2006, it worked well.

The requirement for concurrency wasn't lost on application server vendors, though. In 2003, IBM and BEA jointly created the Timer and WorkManager API. The API eventually became JSR-237, which was subsequently withdrawn and merged with JSR-236 with the focus being on how to implement concurrency in a managed (usually Java EE) environment. JSR-236 is still not final. The Service Data Object (SDO) specification JSR-235 also had a similar solution in the works, although it is not final. Both SDO and the WorkManager API were targeted for Java EE 1.4, although they've both progressed independently since. The Timer and WorkManager API, also known as the CommonJ WorkManager API, enjoys support on both WebLogic (9.0 or later) and WebSphere (6.0 or later), although they're not necessarily portable. Finally, open source implementations of the CommonJ API have sprung up in recent years.

Confused yet?

The issue is that there's no portable, standard, simple way of controlling threads and providing concurrency for components in a managed environment (or a nonmanaged environment!). Even if the discussion is framed in terms of Java SE–specific solutions, you have an overwhelming plethora of choices to make.

Spring's Solution
In Spring 2.0, a unifying solution was introduced in the org.springframework.core.task.TaskExecutor interface. The TaskExecutor abstraction served all requirements pretty well. Because Spring supported Java 1.4, TaskExecutor didn't implement the java.util.concurrent.Executor interface, introduced

in Java 1.5, although its interface was compatible. And any class implementing TaskExecutor could also implement the Executor interface because it defines the exact same method signature. This interface exists even in Spring 3.0 for backward compatibility with JDK 1.4 in Spring 2.x. This meant that people stuck on older JDKs could build applications with this sophisticated functionality without JDK 5. In Spring 3.0, with Java 5 the baseline, the TaskExecutor interface now extends Executor, which means that all the support provided by Spring now works with the core JDK support, too.

The TaskExecutor interface is used quite a bit internally in the Spring framework. For example, the Quartz integration (which has threading, of course) and the message-driven POJO container support make use of TaskExecutor:

```
// the Spring abstraction
package org.springframework.core.task;

import java.util.concurrent.Executor;

public interface TaskExecutor extends Executor {
  void execute(Runnable task);
}
```

In some places, the various solutions mirror the functionality provided by the core JDK options. In others, they're quite unique and provide integrations with other frameworks such as with a CommonJ WorkManager. These integrations usually take the form of a class that can exist in the target framework but that you can manipulate just like any other TaskExecutor abstraction. Although there is support for adapting an existing Java SE Executor or ExecutorService as a TaskExecutor, this isn't so important in Spring 3.0 because the base class for TaskExecutor is Executor, anyway. In this way, the TaskExecutor in Spring bridges the gap between various solutions on Java EE and Java SE.

Let's see some of the simple support for the TaskExecutor first, using the same Runnable defined previously. The client for the code is a simple Spring bean, into which you've injected various instances of TaskExecutor with the sole aim of submitting the Runnable:

```
package com.apress.springenterpriserecipes.spring3.executors;


import org.springframework.beans.factory.annotation.Autowired;
import org.springframework.context.support.ClassPathXmlApplicationContext;
import org.springframework.core.task.SimpleAsyncTaskExecutor;
import org.springframework.core.task.SyncTaskExecutor;
import org.springframework.core.task.support.TaskExecutorAdapter;
import org.springframework.scheduling.concurrent.ThreadPoolTaskExecutor;
import org.springframework.scheduling.timer.TimerTaskExecutor;

public class SpringExecutorsDemo {
        public static void main(String[] args) {
            ClassPathXmlApplicationContext ctx =
              new ClassPathXmlApplicationContext("context2.xml");
            SpringExecutorsDemo demo = ctx.getBean(
                "springExecutorsDemo", SpringExecutorsDemo.class);
            demo.submitJobs();
        }

        @Autowired
        private SimpleAsyncTaskExecutor asyncTaskExecutor;
```

```
        @Autowired
        private SyncTaskExecutor syncTaskExecutor;

        @Autowired
        private TaskExecutorAdapter taskExecutorAdapter;

        /*  No need, since the scheduling is already configured,
in the application context
           @Resource(name = "timerTaskExecutorWithScheduledTimerTasks")
        private TimerTaskExecutor timerTaskExecutorWithScheduledTimerTasks;
        */

        @Resource(name = "timerTaskExecutorWithoutScheduledTimerTasks")
        private TimerTaskExecutor timerTaskExecutorWithoutScheduledTimerTasks;

        @Autowired
        private ThreadPoolTaskExecutor threadPoolTaskExecutor;

        @Autowired
        private DemonstrationRunnable task;

        public void submitJobs() {
                syncTaskExecutor.execute(task);
                taskExecutorAdapter.submit(task);
                asyncTaskExecutor.submit(task);

                timerTaskExecutorWithoutScheduledTimerTasks.submit(task);

                /* will do 100 at a time,
                        then queue the rest, ie,
                        should take round 5 seconds total
                   */
                for (int i = 0; i < 500; i++)
                   threadPoolTaskExecutor.submit(task);
        }
}
```

The application context demonstrates the creation of these various TaskExecutor implementations. Most are so simple that you could create them manually. Only in one case (the timerTaskExecutor) do you delegate to a factory bean:

```xml
<?xml version="1.0" encoding="UTF-8"?>
<beans
 xmlns="http://www.springframework.org/schema/beans"
 xmlns:p="http://www.springframework.org/schema/p"
 xmlns:xsi="http://www.w3.org/2001/XMLSchema-instance"
 xmlns:util="http://www.springframework.org/schema/util"
 xmlns:context="http://www.springframework.org/schema/context"
 xsi:schemaLocation="
  http://www.springframework.org/schema/context
  http://www.springframework.org/schema/context/spring-context-3.0.xsd
  http://www.springframework.org/schema/beans
```

```
        http://www.springframework.org/schema/beans/spring-beans-3.0.xsd
        http://www.springframework.org/schema/util
        http://www.springframework.org/schema/util/spring-util-3.0.xsd">

<context:annotation-config />

<!-- sample Runnable -->
<bean
  id="task"
    class="com.apress.springenterpriserecipes.spring3. ➡
    executors.DemonstrationRunnable" />

<!-- TaskExecutors -->
<bean
  class="org.springframework.core.task.support.TaskExecutorAdapter">
  <constructor-arg>
   <bean
    class="java.util.concurrent.Executors"
    factory-method="newCachedThreadPool" />
  </constructor-arg>
</bean>

<bean
  class="org.springframework.core.task.SimpleAsyncTaskExecutor"
  p:daemon="false" />

<bean
  class="org.springframework.core.task.SyncTaskExecutor" />

<bean
  id="timerTaskExecutorWithScheduledTimerTasks"
  class="org.springframework.scheduling.timer.TimerTaskExecutor">
  <property
   name="timer">
   <bean
    class="org.springframework.scheduling.timer.TimerFactoryBean">
    <property
     name="scheduledTimerTasks">
     <list>
      <bean
       class="org.springframework.scheduling.timer.ScheduledTimerTask"
       p:delay="10"
       p:fixedRate="true"
       p:period="10000"
       p:runnable-ref="task" />
     </list>
    </property>
   </bean>
  </property>

</bean>
```

```xml
<bean
  id="timerTaskExecutorWithoutScheduledTimerTasks"
  class="org.springframework.scheduling.timer.TimerTaskExecutor"
  p:delay="10000" />

<bean
  class="org.springframework.scheduling.concurrent.ThreadPoolTaskExecutor"
  p:corePoolSize="50"
  p:daemon="false"
  p:waitForTasksToCompleteOnShutdown="true"
  p:maxPoolSize="100"
  p:allowCoreThreadTimeOut="true" />

<!-- client bean -->
<bean
  id="springExecutorsDemo"
  class="com.apress.springenterpriserecipes.spring3. ➡
  executors.SpringExecutorsDemo" />
</beans>
```

The previous code shows different implementations of the TaskExecutor interface. The first bean, the TaskExecutorAdapter instance, is a simple wrapper around a java.util.concurrence.Executor instance so that you can deal with in terms of the Spring TaskExecutor interface. This is only slightly useful because you could conceptually deal in terms of the Executor interface now because Spring 3.0 updates the TaskExecutor interface to extend Executor. You use Spring here to configure an instance of an Executor and pass it in as the constructor argument.

SimpleAsyncTaskExecutor provides a new Thread for each job submitted. It does no thread pooling or reuse. Each job submitted runs asynchronously in a thread.

SyncTaskExecutor is the simplest of the implementations of TaskExecutor. Submission of a job is synchronous and tantamount to launching a Thread, running it, and then join()ing it immediately. It's effectively the same as manually invoking the run() method in the calling thread, skipping threading all together.

TimerTaskExecutor uses a java.util.Timer instance and manages jobs (java.util.concurrent.Callable<T> or java.lang.Runnable instances) for you by running them on the Timer. You can specify a delay when creating the TimerTaskExecutor, after which all submitted jobs will start running. Internally, the TimerTaskExecutor converts Callable<T> instances or Runnable instances that are submitted into TimerTasks, which it then schedules on the Timer. If you schedule multiple jobs, they will be run serialized on the same thread with the same Timer. If you don't specify a Timer explicitly, a default one will be created. If you want to explicitly register TimerTasks on the Timer, use the org.springframework.scheduling.timer.TimerFactoryBean's scheduledTimerTasks property. The TimerTaskExecutor doesn't surface methods for more advanced scheduling like the Timer class does. If you want to schedule at fixed intervals, at a certain Date (point in time) or for a certain period, you need to manipulate the TimerTask itself. You can do this with the org.springframework.scheduling.timer.ScheduledTimerTask class, which provides a readily configured TimerTask that the TimerFactoryBean will schedule appropriately.

To submit jobs just as you have with other TaskExecutors, after a delay simply configure a TimerFactoryBean and then submit as usual:

```xml
<bean id ="timerTaskExecutorWithoutScheduledTimerTasks"
class="org.springframework.scheduling.timer.TimerTaskExecutor" p:delay="10000" />
```

More complex scheduling, such as fixed interval execution, requires that you set the TimerTask explicitly. Here, it does little good to actually submit jobs manually. For more advanced functionality, you'll want to use something like Quartz, which can support cron expressions.

```
<bean
  id="timerTaskExecutorWithScheduledTimerTasks"
  class="org.springframework.scheduling.timer.TimerTaskExecutor">
  <property
   name="timer">
   <bean
    class="org.springframework.scheduling.timer.TimerFactoryBean">
    <property
     name="scheduledTimerTasks">
     <list>
      <bean
       class="org.springframework.scheduling.timer.ScheduledTimerTask"
       p:delay="10"
       p:ixedRate="true"
       p:period="10000"
       p:runnable-ref="task" />
     </list>
    </property>
   </bean>
  </property>
</bean>
```

The last example is ThreadPoolTaskExecutor, which is a full on thread pool implementation building on java.util.concurrent.ThreadPoolExecutor.

If you want to build applications using the CommonJ WorkManager/TimerManager support available in IBM WebSphere 6.0 and BEA WebLogic 9.0, you can use org.springframework.scheduling.commonj.WorkManagerTaskExecutor. This class delegates to a reference to the CommonJ Work Manager available inside of WebSphere or WebLogic. Usually, you'll provide it with a JNDI reference to the appropriate resource. This works well enough (such as with Geronimo), but extra effort is required with JBoss or GlassFish. Spring provides classes that delegate to the JCA support provided on those servers: for GlassFish, use org.springframework.jca.work.glassfish.GlassFishWorkManagerTaskExecutor; for JBoss, use org.springframework.jca.work.jboss.JBossWorkManagerTaskExecutor.

The TaskExecutor support provides a powerful way to access scheduling services on your application server via a unified interface. If you're looking for more robust (albeit much heavier) support that can be deployed on any server (even Tomcat and Jetty!), you might consider Spring's Quartz support.

2-4. Using the Spring Expression Language

Problem

You want to dynamically evaluate some condition or property and use it as the value configured in the IoC container. Or perhaps you need to defer evaluation of something—not at design time but at runtime, as might be the case in a custom scope. Or if nothing else, perhaps you just need a way to add a strong expression language to your own application.

Solution

Use Spring 3.0's Spring Expression Language (SpEL), which provides functionality similar to the Unified EL from JSF and JSP, or Object Graph Navigation Language (OGNL). SpEL provides easy-to-use infrastructure that can be leveraged outside of the Spring container. Within the container, it can be used to make configuration much easier in a lot of cases.

How It Works

Today, there are many different types of expression languages in the enterprise space. If you use WebWork/Struts 2 or Tapestry 4, you've no doubt used the OGNL. If you've used JSP or JSF in recent years, you've used one or both of the expression languages that are available in those environments. If you've used JBoss Seam, you've used the expression language made available there, which is a superset of the standard expression language shipped with JSF (Unified EL).

The expression language draws its heritage from many places. Certainly, the expression language is a superset of what's available via the Unified EL. Spring.NET has had a similar expression language for awhile, and the feedback has been very favorable. The need to be able to evaluate certain expressions at arbitrary points in a life cycle, such as during a scoped beans initialization, contributed to some of the qualities of this expression language.

Some of these expression languages are very powerful, bordering on being scripting languages in their own right. The SpEL is no different. It's available almost everywhere you can imagine needing it—from annotations to XML configuration. The SpringSource Tool Suite also provides robust support for the expression language in the way of auto-completion and lookup.

Features of the Language Syntax

The expression language supports a long list of features. Table 2-1 briefly runs through the various constructs and demonstrates their usage.

Table 2-1. Expression Language Features

Type	Use	Example
Literal expression	The simplest thing you can do in the expression language; essentially the same as if you were writing Java code. The language supports String literals as well as all sorts of numbers.	`2342` `'Hello Spring Enterprise Recipes'`
Boolean and relational operator	The expression language provides the ability to evaluate conditionals using standard idioms from Java.	`T(java.lang.Math).random() > .5`
Standard expression	You can iterate and return the properties on beans in the same way you might with Unified EL, separating each dereferenced property with a period and using JavaBean-style naming conventions. In the example to the right, the expression would be equivalent to getCat().getMate().getName().	`cat.mate.name`
Class expression	T() tells the expression language to act on the type of the class, not an instance. In the examples on the right, the first would yield the Class instance for java.lang.Math-equivalent to calling java.lang.Math.class. The second example calls a static method on a given type. Thus, T(java.lang.Math).random() is equivalent to calling java.lang.Math.random().	`T(java.lang.Math)` `T(java.lang.Math).random()`

Accessing arrays, lists, maps	You can index lists, arrays, and maps using brackets and the key—which for arrays or lists is the index number, and for maps is an object. In the examples, you see a java.util.List with 4 chars being indexed at index 1, which returns 'b'. The second example demonstrates accessing a map by the index 'OR', yielding the value associated with that key.	`T(java.util.Arrays).asList(`
		`'a','b','c','d')[1]`
		
		`T(SpelExamplesDemo).MapOfStatesAndCa`
		`pitals['OR']`

Type	Use	Example
Method invocation	Methods may be invoked in instances just as you would in Java. This is a marked improvement over the basic JSF or JSP expression languages.	`'Hello, World'.toLowerCase()`
Relational operators	You can compare or equate values, and the returned value will be a Boolean.	`23 == person.age` `'fala' < 'fido'`

Calling constructor	You can create objects and invoke their constructors. Here you create simple String and Cat objects.	`new String('Hello Spring Enterprise`
		`Recipes, again!')`
		`new Cat('Felix')`

Ternary operator	Ternary expressions work as you'd expect, yielding the value in the true case.	`T(java.lang.Math).random() > .5 ?` `'She loves me' : 'She loves me not'`
Variable	The SpEL lets you set and evaluate variables. The variables can be installed by the context of the expression parser, and there are some implicit variables, such as #this, which always refer to the root object of the context.	`#this.firstName` `#customer.email`
Collection projection	A very powerful feature inside of SpEL is the capability to perform very sophisticated manipulations of maps and collections. Here, you create a projection for the list cats. In this example, the returned value is a collection of as many elements being iterated that has the value for the name property on each cat in the collection. In this case, cats is a collection of Cat objects. The returned value is a collection of String objects.	`cats.![name]`

Continued

Type	Use	Example
Collection selection	Selection lets you dynamically filter objects from a collection or map by evaluating a predicate on each item in the collection and keeping only those elements for which the predicate is true. In this case, you evaluate the `java.util.Map.Entry.value` property for each `Entry` in the `Map` and if the value (in this case a `String`), lowercased, starts with *s*, then it is kept. Everything else is discarded.	`mapOfStatesAndCapitals.?[value.toLowerCase().startsWith('s')]`
Templated expression	You can use the expression language to evaluate expressions inside of string expressions. The result is returned. In this case, the result is dynamically created by evaluating the ternary expression and including `'good'` or `'bad'` based on the result.	`Your fortune is ${T(java.lang.Math).random()> .5 ? 'good' : 'bad'}`

Uses of the Language in Your Configurations

The expression language is available via XML or annotations. The expressions are evaluated at creation time for the bean, not at the initialization of the context. This has the effect that beans created in a custom scope are not configured until the bean is in the appropriate scope. You can use them in the same way via XML or annotations.

The first example is the injection of a named expression language variable, `systemProperties`, which is just a special variable for the `java.util.Properties` instance that's available from `System.getProperties()`. The next example shows the injection of a system property itself directly into a `String` variable:

```
@Value("#{ systemProperties }")
private Properties systemProperties;

@Value("#{ systemProperties['user.region'] }")
private String userRegion;
```

You can also inject the result of computations or method invocations. Here you're injecting the value of a computation directly into a variable:

```
@Value("#{ T(java.lang.Math).random() * 100.0 }")
private double randomNumber;
```

The next examples assume that another bean is configured in the context with the name `emailUtilities`. The bean in turn has JavaBean-style properties that are injected into the following fields:

```
@Value("#{ emailUtilities.email }")
private String email;
```

```
@Value("#{ emailUtilities.password }")
private String password;

@Value("#{ emailUtilities.host}")
private String host;
```

You can also use the expression language to inject references to other named beans in the same context:

```
@Value("#{ emailUtilities }")
private EmailUtilities emailUtilities ;
```

In this case, because there's only one bean in the context with the interface EmailUtilities, you could also do this:

```
@Autowired
private EmailUtilities emailUtilities ;
```

Although there are other mechanisms for discriminating against beans of the same interface, the expression language becomes very handy here because it lets you simply discriminate by bean id.

You can use the expression language in your XML configurations in exactly the same way as with the annotation support. Even the prefix #{ and the suffix } are the same.

```
<bean  class="com.apress.springenterpriserecipes.spring3.➥
spel.EmailNotificationEngine"
 p:randomNumber="#{  T(java.lang.Math).random() * 100.0 }"
...
/>
```

Using the Spring Expression Language Parser

The SpEL is used primarily inside the XML configuration and annotation support provided with the Spring framework, but you're free to use the expression language. The centerpiece of the functionality is provided by the expression parser, org.springframework.expression.spel.antlr.SpelAntlrExpressionParser, which you can instantiate directly:

```
ExpressionParser parser = new SpelAntlrExpressionParser();
```

Conceivably, you could build an implementation that complies with the ExpressionParser interface and builds your own integration using this API. This interface is central for evaluating expressions written using the SpEL. The simplest evaluation might look like this:

```
Expression exp = parser.parseExpression("'ceci n''est pas une String'" );
String val = exp.getValue(String.class);
```

Here, you evaluate the String literal (notice that you're escaping the single quote with another single quote, not with a backslash) and return the result. The call to getValue() is generic, based on the type of the parameter, so you don't need to cast.

A common scenario is evaluation of expressions against an object. The properties and methods of the object no longer require an instance or class, and can be manipulated independently. The SpEL parser refers to it as the *root object*. Let's take an object named SocialNetworkingSiteContext, for example, which in turn has other attributes you want to traverse to iterate over the members of the site:

```
SocialNetworkingSiteContext socialNetworkingSiteContext =
new SocialNetworkingSiteContext();
// ... ensure it's properly initialized ...
Expression firstNameExpression = parser.parseExpression("loggedInUser.firstName");
StandardEvaluationContext ctx = new StandardEvaluationContext();
ctx.setRootObject(socialNetworkingSiteContext);
String valueOfLoggedInUserFirstName = exp.getValue(ctx, String.class );
```

Because you set the socialNetworkingSiteContext as the root, you could enumerate any child property without qualifying the reference.

Suppose that instead of specifying a root object you want to specify a named variable and be able to access it from within your expression. The SpEL parser lets you provide it with variables against which expressions can be evaluated. In the following example, you provide it with a socialNetworkingSiteContext variable. Inside the expression, the variable is prefixed with a "#":

```
StandardEvaluationContext ctx1 = new StandardEvaluationContext ();
SocialNetworkingSiteContext socialNetworkingSiteContext =
     new SocialNetworkingSiteContext();
Friend myFriend = new Friend() ;
myFriend.setFirstName("Manuel");
socialNetworkingSiteContext.setLoggedInUser(myFriend);
ctx1.setVariable("socialNetworkingSiteContext",
socialNetworkingSiteContext );
Expression loggedInUserFirstNameExpression =
parser.parseExpression(
     "#socialNetworkingSiteContext.loggedInUser.firstName");
String loggedInUserFirstName = loggedInUserFirstName Expression.getValue(ctx1,
String.class);
```

Similarly, you can provide the expression language named functions that are available without any qualification inside an expression:

```
StandardEvaluationContext ctx1 = new StandardEvaluationContext();
ctx1.registerFunction("empty",
    StringUtils.class.getDeclaredMethod(
    "isEmpty", new Class[] { String.class }));
Expression functionEval =  parser.parseExpression(
     " #empty(null) ? 'empty' : 'not empty' ");
String result = functionEval.getValue(ctx1, String.class );
```

You can use the expression language parser infrastructure to template Strings. The returned value is a String, although within the String you can have the parser substitute the result of evaluated expressions. This could be useful in any number of scenarios—for example, in simple message preparation. You simply create an instance of org.springframework.expression.ParserContext. This class dictates to the parser which token is prefix (the prefix token is "${") and which is a suffix (the suffix token is "}"). The following example yields "The millisecond is 1246953975093".

```
ParserContext pc = new ParserContext() {
    public String getExpressionPrefix() {
            return "${";
    }
    public String getExpressionSuffix() {
            return "}";
    }
    public boolean isTemplate() {
            return true;
    }
};
String templatedExample = parser.parseExpression(
    "The millisecond is ${  T(System).currentTimeMillis() }.", pc).getValue(String.class);
```

2-5. My Code Doesn't Compile!

Problem
Perhaps you've happily updated to the latest and greatest Spring and waited for your workspace to refresh when—egad!—you encounter compilation errors!

Solution
There is none, as such. Some things are deprecated and have been removed. In the interim, your best bet is to upgrade or use alternatives to prepare for Spring 3.0.

How It Works
Besides the obvious elevation of the require baseline Java environment, most of the changes are backward compatible. Indeed, if anything, there's more added, and the coding conventions are the same. The new version is 95 percent backward compatible with regard to APIs and 99 percent backward compatible in the programming model. However, in order to embrace natural evolution, some APIs are being deprecated or removed in this release:

- Traditional Spring MVC controllers built on the older Spring MVC controller hierarchy. If you've been using the annotation-friendly version of Spring MVC introduced in Spring 2.5, you don't need to worry about it.

- Spring now officially supports Java 5, and with it Java 5 annotations. The support for the common attributes metadata (to enable solutions on Java 1.4) is no longer necessary.

- Traditional support for the object/relational mapping (ORM) layer TopLink is no longer available. This doesn't apply to the JPA provider support, of course, just to the original proprietary technology, including the TopLinkTemplate and the like.

- The testing support that debuted in the Spring 1.x series supporting JUnit 3.8 is no longer available, although there is a fantastic alternative in Spring's updated testing support based on JUnit 4 and TestNG as well as Spring's own testing framework.

2-6. Reducing XML Configuration with Java Config

Problem

You enjoy the power of the DI container but want to override some of the configuration, or you simply want to move more configuration out of the XML format and into Java where you can better benefit from refactoring and type safety.

Solution

You can use Java Config, a project which has been in incubation since early 2005—long before Google Guice hit the scene—and has recently been folded into the core framework.

How It Works

The JavaConfig support is powerful and represents a radically different way of doing things compared with the other configuration options, via XML or annotations. It is important to remember that the JavaConfig support can be used in tandem with the existing approaches. The simplest way to bootstrap Java configuration is with a simple XML configuration file. From there, Spring will take care of the rest.

```
ClassPathXmlApplicationContext classPathXmlApplicationContext =
new ClassPathXmlApplicationContext("myApplicationContext.xml");
```

The configuration for that file looks the same as you'd expect:

```
...
 <context:annotation-config />
 <context:component-scan base-package="com.my.base.package" />
...
```

This will let Spring find any classes marked with @Configuration. @Configuration is meta-annotated with @Component, which makes it eligible for annotation support. This means that it will honor injection using @Autowired, for example. Once your class is annotated with @Configuration, Spring will look for bean definitions in the class. (*Bean definitions* are Java methods annotated with @Bean.) Any definition is contributed to the ApplicationContext and takes its beanName from the method used to configure it.

Alternatively, you can explicitly specify the bean name in the @Bean annotation. A configuration with one bean definition might look like this:

```
import org.springframework.context.annotation.Bean;
import org.springframework.context.annotation.Configuration;

@Configuration
public class PersonConfiguration {
        @Bean
        public Person josh() {
                    Person josh = new Person();
                    josh.setName("Josh");
                    return josh ;
            }
}
```

This is equivalent to an XML application context with the following definition:

```
<bean id="josh" class="com.apress.springenterpriserecipes.➥
spring3.javaconfig.Person" p:name="Josh" />
```

You can access the bean from your Spring application context just as you would normally:

```
ApplicationContext context = … ;
Person person = context.getBean("josh", Person.class);
```

If you want to specify the id of the bean, you can do so by using the @Bean definitions id attribute:

```
@Bean(name="theArtistFormerlyKnownAsJosh")
        public Person josh() {
            //  …
            }
```

You can access this bean as follows:

```
ApplicationContext context = … ;
Person person = context.getBean("theArtistFormerlyKnownAsJosh", Person.class);
```

Now, I know what you're thinking: how is *that* an improvement? It's five times more lines of code! You mustn't dismiss the inherent readability of the Java example. Similarly, if the example compiles, you can be reasonably sure that your configuration was correct. The XML example doesn't afford you any of those benefits.

If you want to specify life cycle methods, you have choices. Life cycle methods in Spring were formerly implemented as callbacks against known interfaces, like InitializingBean and DisposableBean, which gets a callback after dependencies have been injected (public void afterPropertiesSet() throws Exception), and before the bean is destroyed and removed from the context (public void destroy() throws Exception), respectively. You may also configure the initialization and destruction methods manually in the XML configuration, using the init-method and destroy-method attributes of the bean xml element. Since Spring 2.5, you can also use JSR-250 annotations to designate methods as an initialization (@PostConstruct) and destruction method (@PreDestroy). In JavaConfig, you have yet one more option!

You can specify the life cycle methods using the @Bean annotation or you can simply call the method yourself! The first option, using the initMethod and destroyMethod attributes, is straightforward:

```
@Bean(  initMethod = "startLife", destroyMethod = "die")
        public Person companyLawyer() {
                    Person companyLawyer = new Person();
                    companyLawyer.setName("Alan Crane");
                    return companyLawyer;
            }
```

However, you can readily handle initialization on your own, too:

```
@Bean
public Person companyLawyer() {
    Person companyLawyer = new Person();
    companyLawyer.startLife() ;
    companyLawyer.setName("Alan Crane");
    return companyLawyer;
}
```

Referencing other beans is as simple and very similar:

```
@Configuration
public class PetConfiguration {
        @Bean
        public Cat cat(){
           return new Cat();
        }

        @Bean
        public Person master(){
         Person person = new Person() ;
         person.setPet( cat() );
         return person;
        }
// ...
}
```

It simply doesn't get any easier than that: if you need a reference to another bean, simply obtain the reference to the other bean just as you would in any other Java application. Spring will ensure that the bean is instantiated only once and that scope rules are applied if relevant.

The full gamut of configuration options for beans defined in XML is available to beans defined via JavaConfig.

The @Lazy, @Primary, and @DependsOn annotations work exactly like their XML counterparts. @Lazy defers construction of the bean until it's required to satisfy a dependency or it's explicitly accessed from the application context. @DependsOn specifies that the creation of a bean must come after the creation of some other bean, whose existence might be crucial to the correct creation of the bean. @Primary specifies that the bean on whose definition the annotation is placed is the one that should be returned when there are multiple beans of the same interface. Naturally, if you access beans by name from the container, this makes less sense.

The annotations sit above the bean configuration method to which it applies, like the other annotations. Here's an example:

```
@Bean @Lazy
public NetworkFileProcessor fileProcessor(){ … }
```

Often, you'll want to partition your bean configuration into multiple configuration classes, which leaves things more maintainable and modular. Pursuant to that, Spring lets you import other beans. In XML you do this using the import element (<import resource="someOtherElement.xml" />). In JavaConfig, similar functionality is available through the @Import annotation, which you place at the class level.

```
@Configuration
@Import(BusinessConfiguration.class)
public class FamilyConfiguration {
// ...
}
```

This has the effect of bringing into scope the beans defined in the BusinessConfiguration. From there, you can get access to the beans simply by using @Autowired or @Value if you want. If you inject the ApplicationContext using @Autowired, you can use it to obtain access to a bean. Here, the container imports the beans defined from the AttorneyConfiguration configuration class and then lets you inject them by name using the @Value annotation. Had there been only one instance of that type, you could have used @Autowired.

```java
package com.apress.springenterpriserecipes.spring3.javaconfig;

import static java.lang.System.*;

import java.util.Arrays;

import org.springframework.beans.factory.annotation.Value;
import org.springframework.context.annotation.Bean;
import org.springframework.context.annotation.Configuration;
import org.springframework.context.annotation.Import;
import org.springframework.context.support.ClassPathXmlApplicationContext;

@Configuration
@Import(AttorneyConfiguration.class)
public class LawFirmConfiguration {

        @Value("#{denny}")
        private Attorney denny;

        @Value("#{alan}")
        private Attorney alan;

        @Value("#{shirley}")
        private Attorney shirley;

        @Bean
        public LawFirm bostonLegal() {
                LawFirm lawFirm = new LawFirm();
                lawFirm.setLawyers(
                    Arrays.asList(denny, alan, shirley));
                lawFirm.setLocation("Boston");
                return lawFirm;
        }
}
```

This functionality is often overkill for defining simpler beans. For example, if you want to simply let Spring instantiate the bean, and you don't have anything to contribute to that process, you can either write an @Bean method, or you can fall back and configure it in XML. Which you do is up to you, as a matter of taste. If it were an object specific to my application, I'd handle it in the Java configuration, but I would leave Spring's many FactoryBean implementations inside the XML where they could be made quick work of or you could benefit from some of the schemas.

Summary

This chapter reviewed some of the major new features in Spring 3.0. You learned how to obtain the framework and how to include it in your application. The new Spring Expression Language (SpEL) was highlighted. It will be useful in the web tier as well as for your everyday configuration needs. You learned how to use Spring's TaskExecutor support to isolate your code from the platform's local thread pool implementation and inconsistencies. Finally, you were shown how to configure applications with a minimal of XML, relying instead on the JavaConfig option.

The next chapter will review working with data access in Spring, including JDBC access, ORM solutions (such as Hibernate and JPA), and more.

CHAPTER 3

■ ■ ■

Data Access

In this chapter, you will learn how Spring can simplify your database access tasks. Data access is a common requirement for most enterprise applications, which usually require accessing data stored in relational databases. As an essential part of Java SE, JDBC (Java Database Connectivity) defines a set of standard APIs for you to access relational databases in a vendor-independent fashion.

The purpose of JDBC is to provide APIs through which you can execute SQL statements against a database. However, when using JDBC, you have to manage database-related resources by yourself and handle database exceptions explicitly. To make JDBC easier to use, Spring provides an abstraction framework for interfacing with JDBC. As the heart of the Spring JDBC framework, JDBC templates are designed to provide template methods for different types of JDBC operations. Each template method is responsible for controlling the overall process and allows you to override particular tasks of the process.

If raw JDBC doesn't satisfy your requirement or you feel your application would benefit from something slightly higher level, then Spring's support for ORM solutions will interest you. In this chapter, you will also learn how to integrate *object/relational mapping (ORM)* frameworks into your Spring applications. Spring supports most of the popular ORM (or data mapper) frameworks, including Hibernate, JDO, iBATIS, and JPA (the Java Persistence API). Classic TopLink isn't supported starting from Spring 3.0 (the JPA implementation's still supported, of course). However, the JPA support is varied, and has support for many implementations of JPA, including the Hibernate and TopLink-based versions. The focus of this chapter will be on Hibernate and JPA. However, Spring's support for these ORM frameworks is consistent, so you can easily apply the techniques in this chapter to other ORM frameworks as well.

ORM is a modern technology for persisting objects into a relational database. An ORM framework persists your objects according to the mapping metadata you provide (XML or annotation-based), such as the mappings between classes and tables, properties and columns, and so on. It generates SQL statements for object persistence at runtime, so you needn't write database-specific SQL statements unless you want to take advantage of database-specific features or provide optimized SQL statements of your own. As a result, your application will be database independent, and it can be easily migrated to another database in the future. Compared to the direct use of JDBC, an ORM framework can significantly reduce the data access effort of your applications.

Hibernate is a popular open source and high-performance ORM framework in the Java community. Hibernate supports most JDBC-compliant databases and can use specific dialects to access particular databases. Beyond the basic ORM features, Hibernate supports more advanced features such as caching, cascading, and lazy loading. It also defines a querying language called *Hibernate Query Language (HQL)* for you to write simple but powerful object queries.

JPA defines a set of standard annotations and APIs for object persistence in both the Java SE and Java EE platforms. JPA is defined as part of the EJB 3.0 specification in JSR-220. JPA is just a set of standard APIs that require a JPA-compliant engine to provide persistence services. You can compare JPA with the JDBC API and a JPA engine with a JDBC driver. Hibernate can be configured as a JPA-compliant engine through an extension module called *Hibernate EntityManager*. This chapter will mainly demonstrate JPA with Hibernate as the underlying engine.

Problems with Direct JDBC

Suppose that you are going to develop an application for vehicle registration, whose major functions are the basic CRUD (create, read, update, and delete) operations on vehicle records. These records will be stored in a relational database and accessed with JDBC. First, you design the following Vehicle class, which represents a vehicle in Java:

```
package com.apress.springenterpriserecipes.vehicle;

public class Vehicle {

    private String vehicleNo;
    private String color;
    private int wheel;
    private int seat;

    // Constructors, Getters and Setters
    ...
}
```

Setting Up the Application Database

Before developing your vehicle registration application, you have to set up the database for it. For the sake of low memory consumption and easy configuration, I have chosen Apache Derby (http://db.apache.org/derby/) as my database engine. Derby is an open source relational database engine provided under the Apache License and implemented in pure Java.

■Note   You can download the Apache Derby binary distribution (e.g., v10.3) from the Apache Derby web site and extract it to a directory of your choice to complete the installation.

Derby can run in either the embedded mode or the client/server mode. For testing purposes, the client/server mode is more appropriate because it allows you to inspect and edit data with any visual database tools that support JDBC—for example, the Eclipse Data Tools Platform (DTP).

■Note   To start the Derby server in the client/server mode, just execute the startNetworkServer script for your platform (located in the bin directory of the Derby installation).

After starting up the Derby network server on localhost, you can connect to it with the JDBC properties shown in Table 3-1.

■Note   You require Derby's client JDBC driver derbyclient.jar (located in the lib directory of the Derby installation) to connect to the Derby server.

Table 3-1. JDBC Properties for Connecting to the Application Database

Property	Value
Driver class	org.apache.derby.jdbc.ClientDriver
URL	jdbc:derby://localhost:1527/vehicle;create=true
Username	app
Password	app

The first time you connect to this database, the database instance vehicle will be created, if it did not exist before, because you specified create=true in the URL. Note that the specification of this parameter will not cause the re-creation of the database if it already exists.

Follow these steps to connect to Derby:

1. Open a shell on your platform.

2. Type java -jar $DERBY_HOME/lib/derbyrun.jar ij on Unix variants or %DERBY_HOME%/lib/derbyrun.jar ij on Windows.

3. Issue the command CONNECT 'jdbc:derby://localhost:1527/ vehicle;create=true';.

You can provide any values for the username and password because Derby disables authentication by default. Next, you have to create the VEHICLE table for storing vehicle records with the following SQL statement. By default, this table will be created in the APP database schema.

```
CREATE TABLE VEHICLE (
    VEHICLE_NO    VARCHAR(10)    NOT NULL,
    COLOR         VARCHAR(10),
    WHEEL         INT,
    SEAT          INT,
    PRIMARY KEY (VEHICLE_NO)
);
```

Understanding the Data Access Object Design Pattern

A typical design mistake made by inexperienced developers is to mix different types of logic (e.g., presentation logic, business logic, and data access logic) in a single large module. This reduces the module's reusability and maintainability because of the tight coupling it introduces. The general purpose of the *Data Access Object (DAO)* pattern is to avoid these problems by separating data access logic from business logic and presentation logic. This pattern recommends that data access logic be encapsulated in independent modules called data access objects.

For your vehicle registration application, you can abstract the data access operations to insert, update, delete, and query a vehicle. These operations should be declared in a DAO interface to allow for different DAO implementation technologies.

```
package com.apress.springenterpriserecipes.vehicle;

public interface VehicleDao {

    public void insert(Vehicle vehicle);
    public void update(Vehicle vehicle);
    public void delete(Vehicle vehicle);
    public Vehicle findByVehicleNo(String vehicleNo);
}
```

Most parts of the JDBC APIs declare throwing java.sql.SQLException. But because this interface aims to abstract the data access operations only, it should not depend on the implementation technology. So, it's unwise for this general interface to declare throwing the JDBC-specific SQLException. A common practice when implementing a DAO interface is to wrap this kind of exception with a runtime exception (either your own business Exception subclass or a generic one).

Implementing the DAO with JDBC

To access the database with JDBC, you create an implementation for this DAO interface (e.g., JdbcVehicleDao). Because your DAO implementation has to connect to the database to execute SQL statements, you may establish database connections by specifying the driver class name, database URL, username, and password. However, in JDBC 2.0 or higher, you can obtain database connections from a preconfigured javax.sql.DataSource object without knowing about the connection details.

```
package com.apress.springenterpriserecipes.vehicle;

import java.sql.Connection;
import java.sql.PreparedStatement;
import java.sql.ResultSet;
import java.sql.SQLException;

import javax.sql.DataSource;

public class JdbcVehicleDao implements VehicleDao {

    private DataSource dataSource;

    public void setDataSource(DataSource dataSource) {
        this.dataSource = dataSource;
    }

    public void insert(Vehicle vehicle) {
        String sql = "INSERT INTO VEHICLE (VEHICLE_NO, COLOR, WHEEL, SEAT) "
                + "VALUES (?, ?, ?, ?)";
        Connection conn = null;
```

```java
        try {
            conn = dataSource.getConnection();
            PreparedStatement ps = conn.prepareStatement(sql);
            ps.setString(1, vehicle.getVehicleNo());
            ps.setString(2, vehicle.getColor());
            ps.setInt(3, vehicle.getWheel());
            ps.setInt(4, vehicle.getSeat());
            ps.executeUpdate();
            ps.close();
        } catch (SQLException e) {
            throw new RuntimeException(e);
        } finally {
            if (conn != null) {
                try {
                    conn.close();
                } catch (SQLException e) {}
            }
        }
    }

    public Vehicle findByVehicleNo(String vehicleNo) {
        String sql = "SELECT * FROM VEHICLE WHERE VEHICLE_NO = ?";
        Connection conn = null;
        try {
            conn = dataSource.getConnection();
            PreparedStatement ps = conn.prepareStatement(sql);
            ps.setString(1, vehicleNo);

            Vehicle vehicle = null;
            ResultSet rs = ps.executeQuery();
            if (rs.next()) {
                vehicle = new Vehicle(rs.getString("VEHICLE_NO"),
                        rs.getString("COLOR"), rs.getInt("WHEEL"),
                        rs.getInt("SEAT"));
            }
            rs.close();
            ps.close();
            return vehicle;
        } catch (SQLException e) {
            throw new RuntimeException(e);
        } finally {
            if (conn != null) {
                try {
                    conn.close();
                } catch (SQLException e) {}
            }
        }
    }

    public void update(Vehicle vehicle) {/* … */}

    public void delete(Vehicle vehicle) {/* … */}
}
```

The vehicle insert operation is a typical JDBC update scenario. Each time this method is called, you obtain a connection from the data source and execute the SQL statement on this connection. Your DAO interface doesn't declare throwing any checked exceptions, so if a SQLException occurs, you have to wrap it with an unchecked RuntimeException. (There is a detailed discussion on handling Exceptions in your DAOs later in this chapter). Finally, don't forget to release the connection in the finally block. Failing to do so may cause your application to run out of connections.

Here, the update and delete operations will be skipped because they are much the same as the insert operation from a technical point of view. For the query operation, you have to extract the data from the returned result set to build a vehicle object in addition to executing the SQL statement.

Configuring a Data Source in Spring

The javax.sql.DataSource interface is a standard interface defined by the JDBC specification that factories Connection instances. There are many data source implementations provided by different vendors and projects: C3PO and Apache Commons DBCP are popular open source options, and most applications servers will provide their own implementation. It is very easy to switch between different data source implementations because they implement the common DataSource interface. As a Java application framework, Spring also provides several convenient but less powerful data source implementations. The simplest one is DriverManagerDataSource, which opens a new connection every time it's requested.

■Note   To access a database instance running on the Derby server, you have to include derbyclient.jar (located in the lib directory of the Derby installation) in your classpath.

```
<beans xmlns="http://www.springframework.org/schema/beans"
    xmlns:xsi="http://www.w3.org/2001/XMLSchema-instance"
    xsi:schemaLocation="http://www.springframework.org/schema/beans
        http://www.springframework.org/schema/beans/spring-beans-3.0.xsd">

    <bean id="dataSource"
        class="org.springframework.jdbc.datasource.DriverManagerDataSource">
        <property name="driverClassName"
            value="org.apache.derby.jdbc.ClientDriver" />
        <property name="url"
            value="jdbc:derby://localhost:1527/vehicle;create=true" />
        <property name="username" value="app" />
        <property name="password" value="app" />
    </bean>

    <bean id="vehicleDao"
        class="com.apress.springenterpriserecipes.vehicle.JdbcVehicleDao">
        <property name="dataSource" ref="dataSource" />
    </bean>
</beans>
```

DriverManagerDataSource is not an efficient data source implementation because it opens a new connection for the client every time it's requested. Another data source implementation provided by Spring is SingleConnectionDataSource (a DriverManagerDataSource subclass). As its name indicates, this maintains only a single connection that's reused all the time and never closed. Obviously, it is not suitable in a multithreaded environment.

Spring's own data source implementations are mainly used for testing purposes. However, many production data source implementations support connection pooling. For example, the Database Connection Pooling Services (DBCP) module of the Apache Commons Library has several data source implementations that support connection pooling. Of these, BasicDataSource accepts the same connection properties as DriverManagerDataSource and allows you to specify the initial connection size and maximum active connections for the connection pool.

■Note   To use the data source implementations provided by DBCP, you have to include commons-dbcp.jar and commons-pool.jar (located in the lib/jakarta-commons directory of the Spring installation) in your classpath.

```
<bean id="dataSource"
    class="org.apache.commons.dbcp.BasicDataSource">
    <property name="driverClassName"
        value="org.apache.derby.jdbc.ClientDriver" />
    <property name="url"
        value="jdbc:derby://localhost:1527/vehicle;create=true" />
    <property name="username" value="app" />
    <property name="password" value="app" />
    <property name="initialSize" value="2" />
    <property name="maxActive" value="5" />
</bean>
```

Many Java EE application servers build in data source implementations that you can configure from the server console. If you have a data source configured in an application server and exposed for JNDI lookup, you can use JndiObjectFactoryBean to look it up.

```
<bean id="dataSource"
    class="org.springframework.jndi.JndiObjectFactoryBean">
    <property name="jndiName" value="jdbc/VehicleDS" />
</bean>
```

In Spring, a JNDI lookup can be simplified by the jndi-lookup element defined in the jee schema.

```
<beans xmlns="http://www.springframework.org/schema/beans"
    xmlns:xsi="http://www.w3.org/2001/XMLSchema-instance"
    xmlns:jee="http://www.springframework.org/schema/jee"
    xsi:schemaLocation="http://www.springframework.org/schema/beans
        http://www.springframework.org/schema/beans/spring-beans-3.0.xsd
        http://www.springframework.org/schema/jee
        http://www.springframework.org/schema/jee/spring-jee-2.5.xsd">

    <jee:jndi-lookup id="dataSource" jndi-name="jdbc/VehicleDS" />
    ...
</beans>
```

Running the DAO

The following `Main` class tests your DAO by using it to insert a new vehicle to the database. If it succeeds, you can query the vehicle from the database immediately.

```
package com.apress.springenterpriserecipes.vehicle;

import org.springframework.context.ApplicationContext;
import org.springframework.context.support.ClassPathXmlApplicationContext;

public class Main {

    public static void main(String[] args) {
        ApplicationContext context =
            new ClassPathXmlApplicationContext("beans.xml");

        VehicleDao vehicleDao = (VehicleDao) context.getBean("vehicleDao");
        Vehicle vehicle = new Vehicle("TEM0001", "Red", 4, 4);
        vehicleDao.insert(vehicle);

        vehicle = vehicleDao.findByVehicleNo("TEM0001");
        System.out.println("Vehicle No: " + vehicle.getVehicleNo());
        System.out.println("Color: " + vehicle.getColor());
        System.out.println("Wheel: " + vehicle.getWheel());
        System.out.println("Seat: " + vehicle.getSeat());
    }
}
```

Now you can implement a DAO using JDBC directly. However, as you can see from the preceding DAO implementation, most of the JDBC code is similar and needs to be repeated for each database operation. Such redundant code will make your DAO methods much longer and less readable.

3-1. Using a JDBC Template to Update a Database

Problem

To implement a JDBC update operation, you have to perform the following tasks, most of which are redundant:

1. Obtain a database connection from the data source.

2. Create a `PreparedStatement` object from the connection.

3. Bind the parameters to the `PreparedStatement` object.

4. Execute the `PreparedStatement` object.

5. Handle `SQLException`.

6. Clean up the statement object and connection.

Solution

The `org.springframework.jdbc.core.JdbcTemplate` class declares a number of overloaded `update()` template methods to control the overall update process. Different versions of the `update()` method allow you to override different task subsets of the default process. The Spring JDBC framework predefines several callback interfaces to encapsulate different task subsets. You can implement one of these callback interfaces and pass its instance to the corresponding `update()` method to complete the process.

How It Works

Updating a Database with a Statement Creator

The first callback interface to introduce is `PreparedStatementCreator`. You implement this interface to override the statement creation task (task 2) and the parameter binding task (task 3) of the overall update process. To insert a vehicle into the database, you implement the `PreparedStatementCreator` interface as follows:

```
package com.apress.springenterpriserecipes.vehicle;

import java.sql.Connection;
import java.sql.PreparedStatement;
import java.sql.SQLException;

import org.springframework.jdbc.core.PreparedStatementCreator;

public class InsertVehicleStatementCreator implements PreparedStatementCreator {

    private Vehicle vehicle;

    public InsertVehicleStatementCreator(Vehicle vehicle) {
        this.vehicle = vehicle;
    }

    public PreparedStatement createPreparedStatement(Connection conn)
            throws SQLException {
        String sql = "INSERT INTO VEHICLE (VEHICLE_NO, COLOR, WHEEL, SEAT) "
                + "VALUES (?, ?, ?, ?)";
        PreparedStatement ps = conn.prepareStatement(sql);
        ps.setString(1, vehicle.getVehicleNo());
        ps.setString(2, vehicle.getColor());
        ps.setInt(3, vehicle.getWheel());
        ps.setInt(4, vehicle.getSeat());
        return ps;
    }
}
```

When implementing the `PreparedStatementCreator` interface, you will get the database connection as the `createPreparedStatement()` method's argument. All you have to do in this method is to create a `PreparedStatement` object on this connection and bind your parameters to this object. Finally, you have to return the `PreparedStatement` object as the method's return value. Notice that the method signature declares throwing `SQLException`, which means that you don't need to handle this kind of exception yourself.

Now you can use this statement creator to simplify the vehicle insert operation. First of all, you have to create an instance of the JdbcTemplate class and pass in the data source for this template to obtain a connection from it. Then you just make a call to the update() method and pass in your statement creator for the template to complete the update process.

```
package com.apress.springenterpriserecipes.vehicle;
...
import org.springframework.jdbc.core.JdbcTemplate;

public class JdbcVehicleDao implements VehicleDao {
    ...
    public void insert(Vehicle vehicle) {
        JdbcTemplate jdbcTemplate = new JdbcTemplate(dataSource);
        jdbcTemplate.update(new InsertVehicleStatementCreator(vehicle));
    }
}
```

Typically, it is better to implement the PreparedStatementCreator interface and other callback interfaces as inner classes if they are used within one method only. This is because you can get access to the local variables and method arguments directly from the inner class, instead of passing them as constructor arguments. The only constraint on such variables and arguments is that they must be declared as final.

```
package com.apress.springenterpriserecipes.vehicle;
...
import org.springframework.jdbc.core.JdbcTemplate;
import org.springframework.jdbc.core.PreparedStatementCreator;

public class JdbcVehicleDao implements VehicleDao {
    ...
    public void insert(final Vehicle vehicle) {
        JdbcTemplate jdbcTemplate = new JdbcTemplate(dataSource);

        jdbcTemplate.update(new PreparedStatementCreator() {

            public PreparedStatement createPreparedStatement(Connection conn)
                    throws SQLException {
                String sql = "INSERT INTO VEHICLE "
                        + "(VEHICLE_NO, COLOR, WHEEL, SEAT) "
                        + "VALUES (?, ?, ?, ?)";
                PreparedStatement ps = conn.prepareStatement(sql);
                ps.setString(1, vehicle.getVehicleNo());
                ps.setString(2, vehicle.getColor());
                ps.setInt(3, vehicle.getWheel());
                ps.setInt(4, vehicle.getSeat());
                return ps;
            }
        });
    }
}
```

Now you can delete the preceding InsertVehicleStatementCreator class because it will not be used anymore.

Updating a Database with a Statement Setter

The second callback interface, PreparedStatementSetter, as its name indicates, performs only the parameter binding task (task 3) of the overall update process.

```
package com.apress.springenterpriserecipes.vehicle;
...
import org.springframework.jdbc.core.JdbcTemplate;
import org.springframework.jdbc.core.PreparedStatementSetter;

public class JdbcVehicleDao implements VehicleDao {
    ...
    public void insert(final Vehicle vehicle) {
        String sql = "INSERT INTO VEHICLE (VEHICLE_NO, COLOR, WHEEL, SEAT) "
            + "VALUES (?, ?, ?, ?)";
        JdbcTemplate jdbcTemplate = new JdbcTemplate(dataSource);

        jdbcTemplate.update(sql, new PreparedStatementSetter() {

            public void setValues(PreparedStatement ps)
                    throws SQLException {
                ps.setString(1, vehicle.getVehicleNo());
                ps.setString(2, vehicle.getColor());
                ps.setInt(3, vehicle.getWheel());
                ps.setInt(4, vehicle.getSeat());
            }
        });
    }
}
```

Another version of the update() template method accepts a SQL statement and a PreparedStatementSetter object as arguments. This method will create a PreparedStatement object for you from your SQL statement. All you have to do with this interface is to bind your parameters to the PreparedStatement object.

Updating a Database with a SQL Statement and Parameter Values

Finally, the simplest version of the update() method accepts a SQL statement and an object array as statement parameters. It will create a PreparedStatement object from your SQL statement and bind the parameters for you. Therefore, you don't have to override any of the tasks in the update process.

```
package com.apress.springenterpriserecipes.vehicle;
...
import org.springframework.jdbc.core.JdbcTemplate;

public class JdbcVehicleDao implements VehicleDao {
    ...
    public void insert(final Vehicle vehicle) {
        String sql = "INSERT INTO VEHICLE (VEHICLE_NO, COLOR, WHEEL, SEAT) "
                + "VALUES (?, ?, ?, ?)";
```

```
        JdbcTemplate jdbcTemplate = new JdbcTemplate(dataSource);

        jdbcTemplate.update(sql, new Object[] { vehicle.getVehicleNo(),
                vehicle.getColor(),vehicle.getWheel(), vehicle.getSeat() });
    }
}
```

Of the three different versions of the update() method introduced, the last is the simplest because you don't have to implement any callback interfaces. Additionally, we've managed to remove all setX (setInt, setString, etc.)-style methods for parameterizing the query. In contrast, the first is the most flexible because you can do any preprocessing of the PreparedStatement object before its execution. In practice, you should always choose the simplest version that meets all your needs.

There are also other overloaded update() methods provided by the JdbcTemplate class. Please refer javadoc for details.

Batch Updating a Database

Suppose that you want to insert a batch of vehicles into the database. If you call the insert() method multiple times, it will be very slow as the SQL statement will be compiled repeatedly. So, it would be better to add a new method to the DAO interface for inserting a batch of vehicles.

```
package com.apress.springenterpriserecipes.vehicle;
...
public interface VehicleDao {
    ...
    public void insertBatch(List<Vehicle> vehicles);
}
```

The JdbcTemplate class also offers the batchUpdate() template method for batch update operations. It requires a SQL statement and a BatchPreparedStatementSetter object as arguments. In this method, the statement is compiled (prepared) only once and executed multiple times. If your database driver supports JDBC 2.0, this method automatically makes use of the batch update features to increase performance.

```
package com.apress.springenterpriserecipes.vehicle;
...
import org.springframework.jdbc.core.BatchPreparedStatementSetter;
import org.springframework.jdbc.core.JdbcTemplate;

public class JdbcVehicleDao implements VehicleDao {
    ...
    public void insertBatch(final List<Vehicle> vehicles) {
        String sql = "INSERT INTO VEHICLE (VEHICLE_NO, COLOR, WHEEL, SEAT) "
                + "VALUES (?, ?, ?, ?)";
        JdbcTemplate jdbcTemplate = new JdbcTemplate(dataSource);

        jdbcTemplate.batchUpdate(sql, new BatchPreparedStatementSetter() {

                public int getBatchSize() {
                    return vehicles.size();
                }
```

```
        public void setValues(PreparedStatement ps, int i)
                throws SQLException {
            Vehicle vehicle = vehicles.get(i);
            ps.setString(1, vehicle.getVehicleNo());
            ps.setString(2, vehicle.getColor());
            ps.setInt(3, vehicle.getWheel());
            ps.setInt(4, vehicle.getSeat());
        }
    });
    }
}
```

You can test your batch insert operation with the following code snippet in the Main class:

```
package com.apress.springenterpriserecipes.vehicle;
...
public class Main {

    public static void main(String[] args) {
        ...
        VehicleDao vehicleDao = (VehicleDao) context.getBean("vehicleDao");
        Vehicle vehicle1 = new Vehicle("TEM0002", "Blue", 4, 4);
        Vehicle vehicle2 = new Vehicle("TEM0003", "Black", 4, 6);
        vehicleDao.insertBatch(
                Arrays.asList(new Vehicle[] { vehicle1, vehicle2 }));
    }
}
```

3-2. Using a JDBC Template to Query a Database

Problem

To implement a JDBC query operation, you have to perform the following tasks, two of which (task 5 and task 6) are additional as compared to an update operation:

1. Obtain a database connection from the data source.

2. Create a PreparedStatement object from the connection.

3. Bind the parameters to the PreparedStatement object.

4. Execute the PreparedStatement object.

5. Iterate the returned result set.

6. Extract data from the result set.

7. Handle SQLException.

8. Clean up the statement object and connection.

Solution

The JdbcTemplate class declares a number of overloaded query() template methods to control the overall query process. You can override the statement creation task (task 2) and the parameter binding task (task 3) by implementing the PreparedStatementCreator and PreparedStatementSetter interfaces, just as you did for the update operations. Moreover, the Spring JDBC framework supports multiple ways for you to override the data extraction task (task 6).

How It Works

Extracting Data with a Row Callback Handler

RowCallbackHandler is the primary interface that allows you to process the current row of the result set. One of the query() methods iterates the result set for you and calls your RowCallbackHandler for each row. So, the processRow() method will be called once for each row of the returned result set.

```
package com.apress.springenterpriserecipes.vehicle;
...
import org.springframework.jdbc.core.JdbcTemplate;
import org.springframework.jdbc.core.RowCallbackHandler;

public class JdbcVehicleDao implements VehicleDao {
    ...
    public Vehicle findByVehicleNo(String vehicleNo) {
        String sql = "SELECT * FROM VEHICLE WHERE VEHICLE_NO = ?";
        JdbcTemplate jdbcTemplate = new JdbcTemplate(dataSource);

        final Vehicle vehicle = new Vehicle();
        jdbcTemplate.query(sql, new Object[] { vehicleNo },
                new RowCallbackHandler() {
                    public void processRow(ResultSet rs) throws SQLException {
                        vehicle.setVehicleNo(rs.getString("VEHICLE_NO"));
                        vehicle.setColor(rs.getString("COLOR"));
                        vehicle.setWheel(rs.getInt("WHEEL"));
                        vehicle.setSeat(rs.getInt("SEAT"));
                    }
                });
        return vehicle;
    }
}
```

As there will be one row returned for the SQL query at maximum, you can create a vehicle object as a local variable and set its properties by extracting data from the result set. For a result set with more than one row, you should collect the objects as a list.

Extracting Data with a Row Mapper

The RowMapper<T> interface is more general than RowCallbackHandler. Its purpose is to map a single row of the result set to a customized object, so it can be applied to a single-row result set as well as a multiple-row result set. From the viewpoint of reuse, it's better to implement the RowMapper interface as a normal class than as an inner class. In the mapRow() method of this interface, you have to construct the object that represents a row and return it as the method's return value.

```
package com.apress.springenterpriserecipes.vehicle;

import java.sql.ResultSet;
import java.sql.SQLException;

import org.springframework.jdbc.core.RowMapper;

public class VehicleRowMapper implements RowMapper<Vehicle> {

    public Vehicle mapRow(ResultSet rs, int rowNum) throws SQLException {
        Vehicle vehicle = new Vehicle();
        vehicle.setVehicleNo(rs.getString("VEHICLE_NO"));
        vehicle.setColor(rs.getString("COLOR"));
        vehicle.setWheel(rs.getInt("WHEEL"));
        vehicle.setSeat(rs.getInt("SEAT"));
        return vehicle;
    }
}
```

As mentioned, RowMapper<T> can be used for either a single-row or multiple-row result set. When querying for a unique object like in findByVehicleNo(), you have to make a call to the queryForObject() method of JdbcTemplate.

```
package com.apress.springenterpriserecipes.vehicle;
...
import org.springframework.jdbc.core.JdbcTemplate;

public class JdbcVehicleDao implements VehicleDao {
    ...
    public Vehicle findByVehicleNo(String vehicleNo) {
        String sql = "SELECT * FROM VEHICLE WHERE VEHICLE_NO = ?";
        JdbcTemplate jdbcTemplate = new JdbcTemplate(dataSource);

        Vehicle vehicle = (Vehicle) jdbcTemplate.queryForObject(sql,
                new Object[] { vehicleNo }, new VehicleRowMapper());
        return vehicle;
    }
}
```

Spring comes with a convenient RowMapper implementation, BeanPropertyRowMappe<T>, which can automatically map a row to a new instance of the specified class. Note that the specified class must be a top-level class and must have a default or no-arg constructor. It first instantiates this class and then maps each column value to a property by matching their names. It supports matching a property name (e.g., vehicleNo) to the same column name or the column name with underscores (e.g., VEHICLE_NO).

```
package com.apress.springenterpriserecipes.vehicle;
...
import org.springframework.jdbc.core.BeanPropertyRowMapper;
import org.springframework.jdbc.core.JdbcTemplate;

public class JdbcVehicleDao implements VehicleDao {

    ...
```

```
    public Vehicle findByVehicleNo(String vehicleNo) {
        String sql = "SELECT * FROM VEHICLE WHERE VEHICLE_NO = ?";
        Vehicle vehicle = getSimpleJdbcTemplate().queryForObject(
            sql, Vehicle.class, vehicleNo);
        return vehicle;
    }
}
```

Querying for Multiple Rows

Now let's see how to query for a result set with multiple rows. For example, suppose that you need a findAll() method in the DAO interface to get all vehicles.

```
package com.apress.springenterpriserecipes.vehicle;
...
public interface VehicleDao {
    ...
    public List<Vehicle> findAll();
}
```

Without the help of RowMapper, you can still call the queryForList() method and pass in a SQL statement. The returned result will be a list of maps. Each map stores a row of the result set with the column names as the keys.

```
package com.apress.springenterpriserecipes.vehicle;
...
import org.springframework.jdbc.core.JdbcTemplate;

public class JdbcVehicleDao implements VehicleDao {
    ...
    public List<Vehicle> findAll() {
        String sql = "SELECT * FROM VEHICLE";
        JdbcTemplate jdbcTemplate = new JdbcTemplate(dataSource);

        List<Vehicle> vehicles = new ArrayList<Vehicle>();
        List<Map<String,Object>> rows = jdbcTemplate.queryForList(sql);
        for (Map<String, Object> row : rows) {
            Vehicle vehicle = new Vehicle();
            vehicle.setVehicleNo((String) row.get("VEHICLE_NO"));
            vehicle.setColor((String) row.get("COLOR"));
            vehicle.setWheel((Integer) row.get("WHEEL"));
            vehicle.setSeat((Integer) row.get("SEAT"));
            vehicles.add(vehicle);
        }
        return vehicles;
    }
}
```

You can test your findAll() method with the following code snippet in the Main class:

```
package com.apress.springenterpriserecipes.vehicle;
...
public class Main {

    public static void main(String[] args) {
        ...
        VehicleDao vehicleDao = (VehicleDao) context.getBean("vehicleDao");
        List<Vehicle> vehicles = vehicleDao.findAll();
        for (Vehicle vehicle : vehicles) {
            System.out.println("Vehicle No: " + vehicle.getVehicleNo());
            System.out.println("Color: " + vehicle.getColor());
            System.out.println("Wheel: " + vehicle.getWheel());
            System.out.println("Seat: " + vehicle.getSeat());
        }
    }
}
```

If you use a RowMapper<T> object to map the rows in a result set, you will get a list of mapped objects from the query() method.

```
package com.apress.springenterpriserecipes.vehicle;
...
import org.springframework.jdbc.core.BeanPropertyRowMapper;
import org.springframework.jdbc.core.JdbcTemplate;

public class JdbcVehicleDao implements VehicleDao {
    ...
  public List<Vehicle> findAll() {
     String sql = "SELECT * FROM VEHICLE";
     RowMapper<Vehicle> rm =
ParameterizedBeanPropertyRowMapper.newInstance(Vehicle.class);
     List<Vehicle> vehicles = getSimpleJdbcTemplate().query(sql, rm);
     return vehicles;
   }
}
```

Querying for a Single Value

Finally, let's see how to query for a single-row and single-column result set. As an example, add the following operations to the DAO interface:

```
package com.apress.springenterpriserecipes.vehicle;
...
public interface VehicleDao {
    ...
    public String getColor(String vehicleNo);
    public int countAll();
}
```

To query for a single string value, you can call the overloaded queryForObject() method, which requires an argument of java.lang.Class type. This method will help you to map the result value to the type you specified. For integer values, you can call the convenient method queryForInt().

```
package com.apress.springenterpriserecipes.vehicle;
...
import org.springframework.jdbc.core.JdbcTemplate;

public class JdbcVehicleDao implements VehicleDao {
    ...
    public String getColor(String vehicleNo) {
        String sql = "SELECT COLOR FROM VEHICLE WHERE VEHICLE_NO = ?";
        JdbcTemplate jdbcTemplate = new JdbcTemplate(dataSource);

        String color = (String) jdbcTemplate.queryForObject(sql,
                new Object[] { vehicleNo }, String.class);
        return color;
    }

    public int countAll() {
        String sql = "SELECT COUNT(*) FROM VEHICLE";
        JdbcTemplate jdbcTemplate = new JdbcTemplate(dataSource);

        int count = jdbcTemplate.queryForInt(sql);
        return count;
    }
}
```

You can test these two methods with the following code snippet in the Main class:

```
package com.apress.springenterpriserecipes.vehicle;
...
public class Main {

    public static void main(String[] args) {
        ...
        VehicleDao vehicleDao = (VehicleDao) context.getBean("vehicleDao");
        int count = vehicleDao.countAll();
        System.out.println("Vehicle Count: " + count);
        String color = vehicleDao.getColor("TEM0001");
        System.out.println("Color for [TEM0001]: " + color);
    }
}
```

3-3. Simplifying JDBC Template Creation

Problem

It's not efficient to create a new instance of JdbcTemplate every time you use it because you have to repeat the creation statement and incur the cost of creating a new object.

Solution

The JdbcTemplate class is designed to be thread-safe, so you can declare a single instance of it in the IoC container and inject this instance into all your DAO instances. Furthermore, the Spring JDBC framework offers a convenient class, org.springframework.jdbc.core.support.JdbcDaoSupport, to simplify your DAO implementation. This class declares a jdbcTemplate property, which can be injected from the IoC container or created automatically from a data source [e.g., JdbcTemplate jdbcTemplate = new JdbcTemplate(dataSource)]. Your DAO can extend this class to have this property inherited.

How It Works

Injecting a JDBC Template

Until now, you have created a new instance of JdbcTemplate in each DAO method. Actually, you can have it injected at the class level and use this injected instance in all DAO methods. For simplicity's sake, the following code shows only the change to the insert() method:

```
package com.apress.springenterpriserecipes.vehicle;
...
import org.springframework.jdbc.core.JdbcTemplate;

public class JdbcVehicleDao implements VehicleDao {

    private JdbcTemplate jdbcTemplate;

    public void setJdbcTemplate(JdbcTemplate jdbcTemplate) {
        this.jdbcTemplate = jdbcTemplate;
    }

    public void insert(final Vehicle vehicle) {
        String sql = "INSERT INTO VEHICLE (VEHICLE_NO, COLOR, WHEEL, SEAT) "
                + "VALUES (?, ?, ?, ?)";

        jdbcTemplate.update(sql, new Object[] { vehicle.getVehicleNo(),
                vehicle.getColor(), vehicle.getWheel(), vehicle.getSeat() });

    }
    ...
}
```

A JDBC template requires a data source to be set. You can inject this property by either a setter method or a constructor argument. Then, you can inject this JDBC template into your DAO.

```
<beans ...>
    ...
    <bean id="jdbcTemplate"
        class="org.springframework.jdbc.core.JdbcTemplate">
        <property name="dataSource" ref="dataSource" />
    </bean>

    <bean id="vehicleDao"
        class="com.apress.springenterpriserecipes.vehicle.JdbcVehicleDao">
        <property name="jdbcTemplate" ref="jdbcTemplate" />
    </bean>
</beans>
```

Extending the JdbcDaoSupport Class

The org.springframework.jdbc.core.support.JdbcDaoSupport class has a setDataSource() method and a setJdbcTemplate() method. Your DAO class can extend this class to have these methods inherited. Then you can either inject a JDBC template directly or inject a data source for it to create a JDBC template. The following code fragment is taken from Spring's JdbcDaoSupport class:

```
package org.springframework.jdbc.core.support;
...
public abstract class JdbcDaoSupport extends DaoSupport {

    private JdbcTemplate jdbcTemplate;

    public final void setDataSource(DataSource dataSource) {
        if( this.jdbcTemplate == null || dataSource != this.jdbcTemplate.➥
getDataSource() ){
            this.jdbcTemplate = createJdbcTemplate(dataSource);
            initTemplateConfig();
        }
    }

    public final void setJdbcTemplate(JdbcTemplate jdbcTemplate) {
        this.jdbcTemplate = jdbcTemplate;
        initTemplateConfig();
    }

    public final JdbcTemplate getJdbcTemplate() {
        return this.jdbcTemplate;
    }
    ...
}
```

In your DAO methods, you can simply call the getJdbcTemplate() method to retrieve the JDBC template. You also have to delete the dataSource and jdbcTemplate properties, as well as their setter methods, from your DAO class because they have already been inherited. Again, for simplicity's sake, only the change to the insert() method is shown.

```
package com.apress.springenterpriserecipes.vehicle;
...
import org.springframework.jdbc.core.support.JdbcDaoSupport;

public class JdbcVehicleDao extends JdbcDaoSupport implements VehicleDao {

    public void insert(final Vehicle vehicle) {
        String sql = "INSERT INTO VEHICLE (VEHICLE_NO, COLOR, WHEEL, SEAT) "
                + "VALUES (?, ?, ?, ?)";

        getJdbcTemplate().update(sql, new Object[] { vehicle.getVehicleNo(),
                vehicle.getColor(), vehicle.getWheel(), vehicle.getSeat() });
    }
    ...
}
```

By extending JdbcDaoSupport, your DAO class inherits the setDataSource() method. You can inject a data source into your DAO instance for it to create a JDBC template.

```
<beans ...>
    ...
    <bean id="vehicleDao"
        class="com.apress.springenterpriserecipes.vehicle.JdbcVehicleDao">
        <property name="dataSource" ref="dataSource" />
    </bean>
</beans>
```

3-4. Using the Simple JDBC Template with Java 1.5

Problem

The JdbcTemplate class works fine in most circumstances, but it can be further improved to take advantage of the Java 1.5 features.

Solution

org.springframework.jdbc.core.simple.SimpleJdbcTemplate is an evolution of JdbcTemplate that takes advantage of Java 1.5 features such as autoboxing, generics, and variable-length arguments to simplify its usage.

How It Works

Using a Simple JDBC Template to Update a Database

Many of the methods in the classic JdbcTemplate require statement parameters to be passed as an object array. In SimpleJdbcTemplate, they can be passed as variable-length arguments; this saves you the trouble of wrapping them in an array. To use SimpleJdbcTemplate, you can either instantiate it directly or retrieve its instance by extending the SimpleJdbcDaoSupport class.

```
package com.apress.springenterpriserecipes.vehicle;
...
import org.springframework.jdbc.core.simple.SimpleJdbcDaoSupport;

public class JdbcVehicleDao extends SimpleJdbcDaoSupport implements
        VehicleDao {

    public void insert(Vehicle vehicle) {
        String sql = "INSERT INTO VEHICLE (VEHICLE_NO, COLOR, WHEEL, SEAT) "
                + "VALUES (?, ?, ?, ?)";

        getSimpleJdbcTemplate().update(sql, vehicle.getVehicleNo(),
                vehicle.getColor(), vehicle.getWheel(), vehicle.getSeat());
    }
    ...
}
```

SimpleJdbcTemplate offers a convenient batch update method for you to specify a SQL statement and a batch of parameters in the form of List<Object[]> so that you don't need to implement the BatchPreparedStatementSetter interface. Note that SimpleJdbcTemplate requires either a DataSource or a JdbcTemplate.

```
package com.apress.springenterpriserecipes.vehicle;
...
import org.springframework.jdbc.core.simple.SimpleJdbcDaoSupport;

public class JdbcVehicleDao extends SimpleJdbcDaoSupport implements VehicleDao {
    ...
    public void insertBatch(List<Vehicle> vehicles) {
        String sql = "INSERT INTO VEHICLE (VEHICLE_NO, COLOR, WHEEL, SEAT) "
                + "VALUES (?, ?, ?, ?)";

        List<Object[]> parameters = new ArrayList<Object[]>();
        for (Vehicle vehicle : vehicles) {
            parameters.add(new Object[] { vehicle.getVehicleNo(),
                    vehicle.getColor(), vehicle.getWheel(), vehicle.getSeat() });
        }
        getSimpleJdbcTemplate().batchUpdate(sql, parameters);
    }
}
```

Using a Simple JDBC Template to Query a Database

When implementing the RowMapper<T> interface, the return type of the mapRow() method is java.lang.Object. ParameterizedRowMapper<T> is a subinterface that takes a type parameter as the return type of the mapRow() method.

```
package com.apress.springenterpriserecipes.vehicle;
...
import org.springframework.jdbc.core.simple.ParameterizedRowMapper;

public class VehicleRowMapper implements ParameterizedRowMapper<Vehicle> {

    public Vehicle mapRow(ResultSet rs, int rowNum) throws SQLException {
        Vehicle vehicle = new Vehicle();
        vehicle.setVehicleNo(rs.getString("VEHICLE_NO"));
        vehicle.setColor(rs.getString("COLOR"));
        vehicle.setWheel(rs.getInt("WHEEL"));
        vehicle.setSeat(rs.getInt("SEAT"));
        return vehicle;
    }
}
```

Using SimpleJdbcTemplate with ParameterizedRowMapper<T> can save you the trouble of casting the type of the returned result. For the queryForObject() method, the return type is determined by the ParameterizedRowMapper<T> object's type parameter, which is Vehicle in this case. Note that the statement parameters must be supplied at the end of the argument list since they are of variable length.

```
package com.apress.springenterpriserecipes.vehicle;
...
import org.springframework.jdbc.core.simple.SimpleJdbcDaoSupport;

public class JdbcVehicleDao extends SimpleJdbcDaoSupport implements
        VehicleDao {
    ...
    public Vehicle findByVehicleNo(String vehicleNo) {
        String sql = "SELECT * FROM VEHICLE WHERE VEHICLE_NO = ?";

        // No need to cast into Vehicle anymore.
        Vehicle vehicle = getSimpleJdbcTemplate().queryForObject(sql,
                new VehicleRowMapper(), vehicleNo);
        return vehicle;
    }
}
```

Spring also comes with a convenient ParameterizedRowMapper<T> implementation, ParameterizedBeanPropertyRowMapper<T>, which can automatically map a row to a new instance of the specified class.

```
package com.apress.springenterpriserecipes.vehicle;
...
import org.springframework.jdbc.core.simple.ParameterizedBeanPropertyRowMapper;
import org.springframework.jdbc.core.simple.SimpleJdbcDaoSupport;
```

```
public class JdbcVehicleDao extends SimpleJdbcDaoSupport implements
        VehicleDao {
    ...
    public Vehicle findByVehicleNo(String vehicleNo) {
        String sql = "SELECT * FROM VEHICLE WHERE VEHICLE_NO = ?";

        Vehicle vehicle = getSimpleJdbcTemplate().queryForObject(sql,
                ParameterizedBeanPropertyRowMapper.newInstance(Vehicle.class),
                vehicleNo);
        return vehicle;
    }
}
```

When using the classic JdbcTemplate, the findAll() method has a warning from the Java compiler because of an unchecked conversion from List to List<Vehicle>. This is because the return type of the query() method is List rather than the type-safe List<Vehicle>. After switching to SimpleJdbcTemplate and ParameterizedBeanPropertyRowMapper<T>, the warning will be eliminated immediately because the returned List is parameterized with the same type as the ParameterizedRowMapper<T> argument.

```
package com.apress.springenterpriserecipes.vehicle;
...
import org.springframework.jdbc.core.simple.ParameterizedBeanPropertyRowMapper;
import org.springframework.jdbc.core.simple.SimpleJdbcDaoSupport;

public class JdbcVehicleDao extends SimpleJdbcDaoSupport implements
        VehicleDao {
    ...
    public List<Vehicle> findAll() {
        String sql = "SELECT * FROM VEHICLE";

        List<Vehicle> vehicles = getSimpleJdbcTemplate().query(sql,
                ParameterizedBeanPropertyRowMapper.newInstance(Vehicle.class));
        return vehicles;
    }
}
```

When querying for a single value with SimpleJdbcTemplate, the return type of the queryForObject() method will be determined by the class argument (e.g., String.class). So, there's no need for you to perform type casting manually. Note that the statement parameters of variable length must also be supplied at the end of the argument list.

```
package com.apress.springenterpriserecipes.vehicle;
...
import org.springframework.jdbc.core.simple.SimpleJdbcDaoSupport;

public class JdbcVehicleDao extends SimpleJdbcDaoSupport implements
        VehicleDao {
    ...
    public String getColor(String vehicleNo) {
        String sql = "SELECT COLOR FROM VEHICLE WHERE VEHICLE_NO = ?";
```

```
    // No need to cast into String anymore.
    String color = getSimpleJdbcTemplate().queryForObject(sql,
            String.class, vehicleNo);
    return color;
    }
}
```

3-5. Using Named Parameters in a JDBC Template

Problem
In classic JDBC usage, SQL parameters are represented by the placeholder ? and are bound by position. The trouble with positional parameters is that whenever the parameter order is changed, you have to change the parameter bindings as well. For a SQL statement with many parameters, it is very cumbersome to match the parameters by position.

Solution
Another option when binding SQL parameters in the Spring JDBC framework is to use named parameters. As the term implies, named SQL parameters are specified by name (starting with a colon) rather than by position. Named parameters are easier to maintain and also improve readability. At runtime, the framework classes replace named parameters with placeholders. Named parameters are supported only in SimpleJdbcTemplate and NamedParameterJdbcTemplate.

How It Works
When using named parameters in your SQL statement, you can provide the parameter values in a map with the parameter names as the keys.

```
package com.apress.springenterpriserecipes.vehicle;
...
import org.springframework.jdbc.core.simple.SimpleJdbcDaoSupport;

public class JdbcVehicleDao extends SimpleJdbcDaoSupport implements
        VehicleDao {

    public void insert(Vehicle vehicle) {
        String sql = "INSERT INTO VEHICLE (VEHICLE_NO, COLOR, WHEEL, SEAT) "
                + "VALUES (:vehicleNo, :color, :wheel, :seat)";

        Map<String, Object> parameters = new HashMap<String, Object>();
        parameters.put("vehicleNo", vehicle.getVehicleNo());
        parameters.put("color", vehicle.getColor());
        parameters.put("wheel", vehicle.getWheel());
        parameters.put("seat", vehicle.getSeat());

        getSimpleJdbcTemplate().update(sql, parameters);
    }
    ...
}
```

You can also provide a SQL parameter source, whose responsibility is to offer SQL parameter values for named SQL parameters. There are three implementations of the SqlParameterSource interface. The basic one is MapSqlParameterSource, which wraps a map as its parameter source.

```java
package com.apress.springenterpriserecipes.vehicle;
...
import org.springframework.jdbc.core.namedparam.MapSqlParameterSource;
import org.springframework.jdbc.core.namedparam.SqlParameterSource;
import org.springframework.jdbc.core.simple.SimpleJdbcDaoSupport;

public class JdbcVehicleDao extends SimpleJdbcDaoSupport implements
        VehicleDao {

    public void insert(Vehicle vehicle) {
        String sql = "INSERT INTO VEHICLE (VEHICLE_NO, COLOR, WHEEL, SEAT) "
                + "VALUES (:vehicleNo, :color, :wheel, :seat)";

        Map<String, Object> parameters = new HashMap<String, Object>();
        ...
        SqlParameterSource parameterSource =
            new MapSqlParameterSource(parameters);

        getSimpleJdbcTemplate().update(sql, parameterSource);
    }
    ...
}
```

Another implementation of SqlParameterSource is BeanPropertySqlParameterSource, which wraps a normal Java object as a SQL parameter source. For each of the named parameters, the property with the same name will be used as the parameter value.

```java
package com.apress.springenterpriserecipes.vehicle;
...
import org.springframework.jdbc.core.namedparam.BeanPropertySqlParameterSource;
import org.springframework.jdbc.core.namedparam.SqlParameterSource;
import org.springframework.jdbc.core.simple.SimpleJdbcDaoSupport;

public class JdbcVehicleDao extends SimpleJdbcDaoSupport implements
        VehicleDao {

    public void insert(Vehicle vehicle) {
        String sql = "INSERT INTO VEHICLE (VEHICLE_NO, COLOR, WHEEL, SEAT) "
                + "VALUES (:vehicleNo, :color, :wheel, :seat)";

        SqlParameterSource parameterSource =
            new BeanPropertySqlParameterSource(vehicle);

        getSimpleJdbcTemplate().update(sql, parameterSource);
    }
    ...
}
```

Named parameters can also be used in batch update. You can provide either a Map array or a SqlParameterSource array for the parameter values.

```
package com.apress.springenterpriserecipes.vehicle;
...
import org.springframework.jdbc.core.namedparam.BeanPropertySqlParameterSource;
import org.springframework.jdbc.core.namedparam.SqlParameterSource;
import org.springframework.jdbc.core.simple.SimpleJdbcDaoSupport;

public class JdbcVehicleDao extends SimpleJdbcDaoSupport implements VehicleDao {
    ...
    public void insertBatch(List<Vehicle> vehicles) {
        String sql = "INSERT INTO VEHICLE (VEHICLE_NO, COLOR, WHEEL, SEAT) "
                + "VALUES (:vehicleNo, :color, :wheel, :seat)";

        List<SqlParameterSource> parameters = new ArrayList<SqlParameterSource>();
        for (Vehicle vehicle : vehicles) {
            parameters.add(new BeanPropertySqlParameterSource(vehicle));
        }

        getSimpleJdbcTemplate().batchUpdate(sql,
                parameters.toArray(new SqlParameterSource[0]));
    }
}
```

3-6. Handling Exceptions in the Spring JDBC Framework

Problem

Many of the JDBC APIs declare throwing java.sql.SQLException, a checked exception that must be caught. It's very troublesome to handle this kind of exception every time you perform a database operation. You often have to define your own policy to handle this kind of exception. Failure to do so may lead to inconsistent exception handling.

Solution

The Spring framework offers a consistent data access exception-handling mechanism for its data access module, including the JDBC framework. In general, all exceptions thrown by the Spring JDBC framework are subclasses of DataAccessException, a type of RuntimeException that you are not forced to catch. It's the root exception class for all exceptions in Spring's data access module.

Figure 3-1 shows only part of the DataAccessException hierarchy in Spring's data access module. In total, there are more than 30 exception classes defined for different categories of data access exceptions.

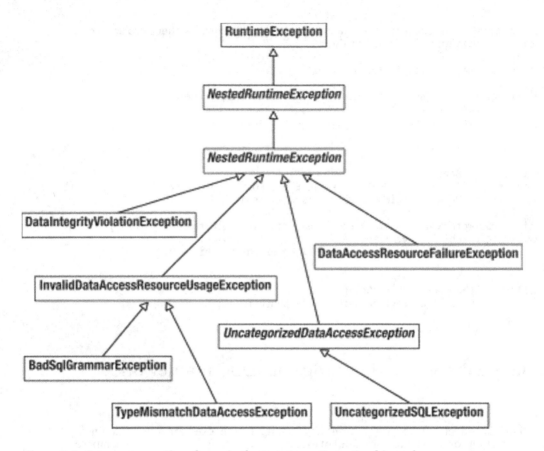

Figure 3-1. Common exception classes in the DataAccessException hierarchy

How It Works

Understanding Exception Handling in the Spring JDBC Framework

Until now, you haven't handled JDBC exceptions explicitly when using a JDBC template or JDBC operation objects. To help you understand the Spring JDBC framework's exception-handling mechanism, let's consider the following code fragment in the Main class, which inserts a vehicle. What happens if you insert a vehicle with a duplicate vehicle number?

```
package com.apress.springenterpriserecipes.vehicle;
...
public class Main {

    public static void main(String[] args) {
        ...
        VehicleDao vehicleDao = (VehicleDao) context.getBean("vehicleDao");
        Vehicle vehicle = new Vehicle("EX0001", "Green", 4, 4);
        vehicleDao.insert(vehicle);
    }
}
```

If you run the method twice, or the vehicle has already been inserted into the database, it will throw a DuplicateKeyException, a subclass of DataAccessException. In your DAO methods, you neither need to surround the code with a try/catch block nor declare throwing an exception in the method signature. This is because DataAccessException (and therefore its subclasses, including DuplicateKeyException) is an unchecked exception that you are not forced to catch. The direct parent class of DataAccessException is NestedRuntimeException, a core Spring exception class that wraps another exception in a RuntimeException.

When you use the classes of the Spring JDBC framework, they will catch SQLException for you and wrap it with one of the subclasses of DataAccessException. As this exception is a RuntimeException, you are not required to catch it.

But how does the Spring JDBC framework know which concrete exception in the DataAccessException hierarchy should be thrown? It's by looking at the errorCode and SQLState properties of the caught SQLException. As a DataAccessException wraps the under-lying SQLException as the root cause, you can inspect the errorCode and SQLState properties with the following catch block:

```
package com.apress.springenterpriserecipes.vehicle;
...
import java.sql.SQLException;

import org.springframework.dao.DataAccessException;

public class Main {

    public static void main(String[] args) {
        ...
        VehicleDao vehicleDao = (VehicleDao) context.getBean("vehicleDao");
        Vehicle vehicle = new Vehicle("EX0001", "Green", 4, 4);
        try {
            vehicleDao.insert(vehicle);
        } catch (DataAccessException e) {
            SQLException sqle = (SQLException) e.getCause();
            System.out.println("Error code: " + sqle.getErrorCode());
            System.out.println("SQL state: " + sqle.getSQLState());
        }
    }
}
```

When you insert the duplicate vehicle again, notice that Apache Derby returns the following error code and SQL state:

```
Error code : -1
SQL state : 23505
```

If you refer to the Apache Derby reference manual, you will find the error code description shown in Table 3-2.

Table 3-2. Apache Derby's Error Code Description

SQL State	Message Text
23505	The statement was aborted because it would have caused a duplicate key value in a unique or primary key constraint or unique index identified by '*<value>*' defined on '*<value>*'.

How does the Spring JDBC framework know that state 23505 should be mapped to DuplicateKeyException? The error code and SQL state are database specific, which means different database products may return different codes for the same kind of error. Moreover, some database products will specify the error in the errorCode property, while others (like Derby) will do so in the SQLState property.

As an open Java application framework, Spring understands the error codes of most popular database products. Because of the large number of error codes, however, it can only maintain mappings for the most frequently encountered errors. The mapping is defined in the sql-error-codes.xml file, located in the org.springframework.jdbc.support package. The following snippet for Apache Derby is taken from this file:

```
<?xml version="1.0" encoding="UTF-8"?>
<!DOCTYPE beans PUBLIC "-//SPRING//DTD BEAN 3.0//EN"
    "http://www.springframework.org/dtd/spring-beans-3.0.dtd">

<beans>
    ...

<bean id="Derby" class="org.springframework.jdbc.support.SQLErrorCodes">
                    <property name="databaseProductName">
                                  <value>Apache Derby</value>
                    </property>
                    <property name="useSqlStateForTranslation">
                                  <value>true</value>
                    </property>
                    <property name="badSqlGrammarCodes">
          <value>42802,42821,42X01,42X02,42X03,42X04,42X05,42X06,➥
42X07,42X08</value>
                    </property>
```

```
                    <property name="duplicateKeyCodes">
                            <value>23505</value>
                    </property>
                    <property name="dataIntegrityViolationCodes">
                            <value>22001,22005,23502,23503,23513,➥
X0Y32</value>
                    </property>
                    <property name="dataAccessResourceFailureCodes">
                            <value>04501,08004,42Y07</value>
                    </property>
                    <property name="cannotAcquireLockCodes">
                            <value>40XL1</value>
                    </property>
                    <property name="deadlockLoserCodes">
                            <value>40001</value>
                    </property>
            </bean>
</beans>
```

Note that the databaseProductName property is used to match the database product name returned by Connection.getMetaData().getDatabaseProductName(). This enables Spring to know which type of database is currently connecting. The useSqlStateForTranslation property means that the SQLState property, rather than the errorCode property, should be used to match the error code. Finally, the SQLErrorCodes class defines several categories for you to map database error codes. The code 23505 lies in the dataIntegrityViolationCodes category.

Customizing Data Access Exception Handling

The Spring JDBC framework only maps well-known error codes. Sometimes you may wish to customize the mapping yourself. For example, you might decide to add more codes to an existing category or define a custom exception for particular error codes.

In Table 3-2, the error code 23505 indicates a duplicate key error in Apache Derby. It is mapped by default to DataIntegrityViolationException. Suppose that you want to create a custom exception type, MyDuplicateKeyException, for this kind of error. It should extend DataIntegrityViolationException because it is also a kind of data integrity violation error. Remember that for an exception to be thrown by the Spring JDBC framework, it must be compatible with the root exception class DataAccessException.

```
package com.apress.springenterpriserecipes.vehicle;

import org.springframework.dao.DataIntegrityViolationException;

public class MyDuplicateKeyException extends DataIntegrityViolationException {

    public MyDuplicateKeyException(String msg) {
        super(msg);
    }

    public MyDuplicateKeyException(String msg, Throwable cause) {
        super(msg, cause);
    }
}
```

By default, Spring will look up an exception from the sql-error-codes.xml file located in the org.springframework.jdbc.support package. However, you can override some of the mappings by providing a file with the same name in the root of the classpath. If Spring can find your custom file, it will look up an exception from your mapping first. However, if it does not find a suitable exception there, Spring will look up the default mapping.

For example, suppose that you want to map your custom DuplicateKeyException type to error code 23505. You have to add the binding via a CustomSQLErrorCodesTranslation bean, and then add this bean to the customTranslations category.

```xml
<?xml version="1.0" encoding="UTF-8"?>
<!DOCTYPE beans PUBLIC "-//SPRING//DTD BEAN 2.0//EN"
    "http://www.springframework.org/dtd/spring-beans-2.0.dtd">

<beans>
    <bean id="Derby"
        class="org.springframework.jdbc.support.SQLErrorCodes">
        <property name="databaseProductName">
            <value>Apache Derby</value>
        </property>
        <property name="useSqlStateForTranslation">
            <value>true</value>
        </property>
        <property name="customTranslations">
            <list>
                <ref local="myDuplicateKeyTranslation" />
            </list>
        </property>
    </bean>

    <bean id=" myDuplicateKeyTranslation"
        class="org.springframework.jdbc.support.CustomSQLErrorCodesTranslation">
        <property name="errorCodes">
            <value>23505</value>
        </property>
        <property name="exceptionClass">
            <value>
                com.apress.springenterpriserecipes.vehicle.DuplicateKeyException
            </value>
        </property>
    </bean>
</beans>
```

Now if you remove the try/catch block surrounding the vehicle insert operation and insert a duplicate vehicle, the Spring JDBC framework will throw a MyDuplicateKeyException instead.

However, if you are not satisfied with the basic code-to-exception mapping strategy used by the SQLErrorCodes class, you may further implement the SQLExceptionTranslator interface and inject its instance into a JDBC template via the setExceptionTranslator() method.

3-7. Problems with Using ORM Frameworks Directly

Suppose you are developing a course management system for a training center. The first class you create for this system is Course. This class is called an *entity class* or a *persistent class* because it represents a real-world entity and its instances will be persisted to a database. Remember that for each entity class to be persisted by an ORM framework, a default constructor with no argument is required.

```
package com.apress.springenterpriserecipes.course;
...
public class Course {

    private Long id;
    private String title;
    private Date beginDate;
    private Date endDate;
    private int fee;

    // Constructors, Getters and Setters
    ...
}
```

For each entity class, you must define an identifier property to uniquely identify an entity. It's a best practice to define an auto-generated identifier because this has no business meaning and thus won't be changed under any circumstances. Moreover, this identifier will be used by the ORM framework to determine an entity's state. If the identifier value is null, this entity will be treated as a new and unsaved entity. When this entity is persisted, an insert SQL statement will be issued; otherwise an update statement will. To allow the identifier to be null, you should choose a primitive wrapper type like java.lang.Integer and java.lang.Long for the identifier.

In your course management system, you need a DAO interface to encapsulate the data access logic. Let's define the following operations in the CourseDao interface:

```
package com.apress.springenterpriserecipes.course;
...
public interface CourseDao {

    public void store(Course course);
    public void delete(Long courseId);
    public Course findById(Long courseId);
    public List<Course> findAll();
}
```

Usually, when using ORM for persisting objects, the insert and update operations are combined into a single operation (e.g., store). This is to let the ORM framework (not you) decide whether an object should be inserted or updated.

In order for an ORM framework to persist your objects to a database, it must know the mapping metadata for the entity classes. You have to provide mapping metadata to it in its supported format. The native format for Hibernate is XML. However because each ORM framework may have its own format for defining mapping metadata, JPA defines a set of persistent annotations for you to define mapping metadata in a standard format that is more likely to be reusable in other ORM frameworks.

Hibernate also supports the use of JPA annotations to define mapping metadata, so there are essentially three different strategies for mapping and persisting your objects with Hibernate and JPA:

- Using the Hibernate API to persist objects with Hibernate XML mappings

- Using the Hibernate API to persist objects with JPA annotations

- Using JPA to persist objects with JPA annotations

The core programming elements of Hibernate, JPA, and other ORM frameworks resemble those of JDBC. They are summarized in Table 3-3.

Table 3-3. Core Programming Elements for Different Data Access Strategies

Concept	JDBC	Hibernate	JPA
Resource	Connection	Session	EntityManager
Resource factory	DataSource	SessionFactory	EntityManagerFactory
Exception	SQLException	HibernateException	PersistenceException

In Hibernate, the core interface for object persistence is Session, whose instances can be obtained from a SessionFactory instance. In JPA, the corresponding interface is EntityManager, whose instances can be obtained from an EntityManagerFactory instance. The exceptions thrown by Hibernate are of type HibernateException, while those thrown by JPA may be of type PersistenceException or other Java SE exceptions like IllegalArgumentException and IllegalStateException. Note that all these exceptions are subclasses of RuntimeException, which you are not forced to catch and handle.

Persisting Objects Using the Hibernate API with Hibernate XML Mappings

To map entity classes with Hibernate XML mappings, you can provide a single mapping file for each class or a large file for several classes. Practically, you should define one for each class by joining the class name with .hbm.xml as the file extension for ease of maintenance. The middle extension hbm stands for Hibernate metadata.

The mapping file for the Course class should be named Course.hbm.xml and put in the same package as the entity class.

```
<!DOCTYPE hibernate-mapping
    PUBLIC "-//Hibernate/Hibernate Mapping DTD 3.0//EN"
    "http://hibernate.sourceforge.net/hibernate-mapping-3.0.dtd">

<hibernate-mapping package="com.apress.springenterpriserecipes.course">
    <class name="Course" table="COURSE">
        <id name="id" type="long" column="ID">
            <generator class="identity" />
        </id>
        <property name="title" type="string">
            <column name="TITLE" length="100" not-null="true" />
        </property>
        <property name="beginDate" type="date" column="BEGIN_DATE" />
        <property name="endDate" type="date" column="END_DATE" />
        <property name="fee" type="int" column="FEE" />
    </class>
</hibernate-mapping>
```

In the mapping file, you can specify a table name for this entity class and a table column for each simple property. You can also specify the column details such as column length, not-null constraints, and unique constraints. In addition, each entity must have an identifier defined, which can be generated automatically or assigned manually. In this example, the identifier will be generated using a table identity column.

Each application that uses Hibernate requires a global configuration file to configure properties such as the database settings (either JDBC connection properties or a data source's JNDI name), the database dialect, the mapping metadata's locations, and so on. When using XML mapping files to define mapping metadata, you have to specify the locations of the XML files. By default, Hibernate will read the hibernate.cfg.xml file from the root of the classpath. The middle extension cfg stands for configuration. If there is a hibernate.properties file on the classpath, that file will be consulted first.

```
<!DOCTYPE hibernate-configuration PUBLIC
    "-//Hibernate/Hibernate Configuration DTD 3.0//EN"
    "http://hibernate.sourceforge.net/hibernate-configuration-3.0.dtd">

<hibernate-configuration>
    <session-factory>
        <property name="connection.driver_class">
            org.apache.derby.jdbc.ClientDriver
        </property>
        <property name="connection.url">
            jdbc:derby://localhost:1527/course;create=true
        </property>
        <property name="connection.username">app</property>
        <property name="connection.password">app</property>
        <property name="dialect">org.hibernate.dialect.DerbyDialect</property>
        <property name="show_sql">true</property>
        <property name="hbm2ddl.auto">update</property>

        <mapping resource="com/apress/springenterpriserecipes/course/➥
Course.hbm.xml" />
    </session-factory>
</hibernate-configuration>
```

Before you can persist your objects, you have to create tables in a database schema to store the object data. When using an ORM framework like Hibernate, you usually needn't design the tables by yourself. If you set the hbm2ddl.auto property to update, Hibernate can help you to update the database schema and create the tables when necessary. Naturally, you shouldn't enable this in production, but it can be a great speed boost for development.

Now let's implement the DAO interface in the hibernate subpackage using the plain Hibernate API. Before you call the Hibernate API for object persistence, you have to initialize a Hibernate session factory (e.g., in the constructor).

```
package com.apress.springenterpriserecipes.course.hibernate;
...
import org.hibernate.Query;
import org.hibernate.Session;
import org.hibernate.SessionFactory;
import org.hibernate.Transaction;
import org.hibernate.cfg.Configuration;
```

```java
public class HibernateCourseDao implements CourseDao {

    private SessionFactory sessionFactory;

    public HibernateCourseDao() {
        Configuration configuration = new Configuration().configure();
        sessionFactory = configuration.buildSessionFactory();
    }

    public void store(Course course) {
        Session session = sessionFactory.openSession();
        Transaction tx = session.getTransaction();
        try {
            tx.begin();
            session.saveOrUpdate(course);
            tx.commit();
        } catch (RuntimeException e) {
            tx.rollback();
            throw e;
        } finally {
            session.close();
        }
    }

    public void delete(Long courseId) {
        Session session = sessionFactory.openSession();
        Transaction tx = session.getTransaction();
        try {
            tx.begin();
            Course course = (Course) session.get(Course.class, courseId);
            session.delete(course);
            tx.commit();
        } catch (RuntimeException e) {
            tx.rollback();
            throw e;
        } finally {
            session.close();
        }
    }

    public Course findById(Long courseId) {
        Session session = sessionFactory.openSession();
        try {
            return (Course) session.get(Course.class, courseId);
        } finally {
            session.close();
        }
    }
}
```

```
    public List<Course> findAll() {
        Session session = sessionFactory.openSession();
        try {
            Query query = session.createQuery("from Course");
            return query.list();
        } finally {
            session.close();
        }
    }
}
```

The first step in using Hibernate is to create a `Configuration` object and ask it to load the Hibernate configuration file. By default, it loads `hibernate.cfg.xml` from the classpath root when you call the `configure()` method. Then you build a Hibernate session factory from this `Configuration` object. The purpose of a session factory is to produce sessions for you to persist your objects.

In the preceding DAO methods, you first open a session from the session factory. For any operation that involves database update, such as `saveOrUpdate()` and `delete()`, you must start a Hibernate transaction on that session. If the operation completes successfully, you commit the transaction. Otherwise, you roll it back if any `RuntimeException` happens. For read-only operations such as `get()` and HQL queries, there's no need to start a transaction. Finally, you must remember to close a session to release the resources held by this session.

You can create the following `Main` class to test run all the DAO methods. It also demonstrates an entity's typical life cycle.

```
package com.apress.springenterpriserecipes.course;
...
public class Main {

    public static void main(String[] args) {
        CourseDao courseDao = new HibernateCourseDao();

        Course course = new Course();
        course.setTitle("Core Spring");
        course.setBeginDate(new GregorianCalendar(2007, 8, 1).getTime());
        course.setEndDate(new GregorianCalendar(2007, 9, 1).getTime());
        course.setFee(1000);
        courseDao.store(course);

        List<Course> courses = courseDao.findAll();
        Long courseId = courses.get(0).getId();

        course = courseDao.findById(courseId);
        System.out.println("Course Title: " + course.getTitle());
        System.out.println("Begin Date: " + course.getBeginDate());
        System.out.println("End Date: " + course.getEndDate());
        System.out.println("Fee: " + course.getFee());

        courseDao.delete(courseId);
    }
}
```

Persisting Objects Using the Hibernate API with JPA Annotations

JPA annotations are standardized in the JSR-220 specification, so they're supported by all JPA-compliant ORM frameworks, including Hibernate. Moreover, the use of annotations will be more convenient for you to edit mapping metadata in the same source file.

The following Course class illustrates the use of JPA annotations to define mapping metadata:

```java
package com.apress.springenterpriserecipes.course;
...
import javax.persistence.Column;
import javax.persistence.Entity;
import javax.persistence.GeneratedValue;
import javax.persistence.GenerationType;
import javax.persistence.Id;
import javax.persistence.Table;

@Entity
@Table(name = "COURSE")
public class Course {

    @Id
    @GeneratedValue(strategy = GenerationType.IDENTITY)
    @Column(name = "ID")
    private Long id;

    @Column(name = "TITLE", length = 100, nullable = false)
    private String title;

    @Column(name = "BEGIN_DATE")
    private Date beginDate;

    @Column(name = "END_DATE")
    private Date endDate;

    @Column(name = "FEE")
    private int fee;

    // Constructors, Getters and Setters
    ...
}
```

Each entity class must be annotated with the @Entity annotation. You can assign a table name for an entity class in this annotation. For each property, you can specify a column name and column details using the @Column annotation. Each entity class must have an identifier defined by the @Id annotation. You can choose a strategy for identifier generation using the @GeneratedValue annotation. Here, the identifier will be generated by a table identity column.

Hibernate supports both native XML mapping files and JPA annotations as ways of defining mapping metadata. For JPA annotations, you have to specify the fully qualified names of the entity classes in hibernate.cfg.xml for Hibernate to read the annotations.

```
<hibernate-configuration>
    <session-factory>
        ...
        <!-- For Hibernate XML mappings -->
        <!--
        <mapping resource="com/apress/springenterpriserecipes/course/➥
Course.hbm.xml" />
        -->

        <!-- For JPA annotations -->
        <mapping class="com.apress.springenterpriserecipes.course.Course" />
    </session-factory>
</hibernate-configuration>
```

In the Hibernate DAO implementation, the Configuration class you used is for reading XML mappings. If you use JPA annotations to define mapping metadata for Hibernate, you have to use its subclass, AnnotationConfiguration, instead.

```
package com.apress.springenterpriserecipes.course.hibernate;
...
import org.hibernate.SessionFactory;
import org.hibernate.cfg.AnnotationConfiguration;

public class HibernateCourseDao implements CourseDao {

    private SessionFactory sessionFactory;

    public HibernateCourseDao() {
        // For Hibernate XML mapping
        // Configuration configuration = new Configuration().configure();

        // For JPA annotation
        Configuration configuration = new AnnotationConfiguration().configure();

        sessionFactory = configuration.buildSessionFactory();
    }
    ...
}
```

Persisting Objects Using JPA with Hibernate as the Engine

In addition to persistent annotations, JPA defines a set of programming interfaces for object persistence. However, JPA is not a persistence implementation; you have to pick up a JPA-compliant engine to provide persistence services. Hibernate can be JPA-compliant through the Hibernate EntityManager extension module. With this extension, Hibernate can work as an underlying JPA engine to persist objects. This lets you retain both the valuable investment in Hibernate (perhaps it's faster or handles certain operations more to your satisfaction) and write code that is JPA-compliant and portable among other JPA engines. This can also be a useful way to transition a code base to JPA. New code is written strictly against the JPA APIs, and older code is transitioned to the JPA interfaces.

In a Java EE environment, you can configure the JPA engine in a Java EE container. But in a Java SE application, you have to set up the engine locally. The configuration of JPA is through the central XML file persistence.xml, located in the META-INF directory of the classpath root. In this file, you can set any vendor-specific properties for the underlying engine configuration.

Now let's create the JPA configuration file persistence.xml in the META-INF directory of the classpath root. Each JPA configuration file contains one or more <persistence-unit> elements. A *persistence unit* defines a set of persistent classes and how they should be persisted. Each persistence unit requires a name for identification. Here, you assign the name course to this persistence unit.

```
<persistence xmlns="http://java.sun.com/xml/ns/persistence"
    xmlns:xsi="http://www.w3.org/2001/XMLSchema-instance"
    xsi:schemaLocation="http://java.sun.com/xml/ns/persistence
        http://java.sun.com/xml/ns/persistence/persistence_1_0.xsd"
    version="1.0">

    <persistence-unit name="course">
        <properties>
            <property name="hibernate.ejb.cfgfile" value="/hibernate.cfg.xml" />
        </properties>
    </persistence-unit>
</persistence>
```

In this JPA configuration file, you configure Hibernate as your underlying JPA engine by referring to the Hibernate configuration file located in the classpath root. However, because Hibernate EntityManager will automatically detect XML mapping files and JPA annotations as mapping metadata, you have no need to specify them explicitly. Otherwise, you will encounter an org.hibernate.DuplicateMappingException. Pick a strategy_annotations or XML_and stay with it. You don't need to maintain both.

```
<hibernate-configuration>
    <session-factory>
        ...
        <!-- Don't need to specify mapping files and annotated classes -->
        <!--
        <mapping resource="com/apress/springenterpriserecipes/course/➥
Course.hbm.xml" />
        <mapping class="com.apress.springenterpriserecipes.course.Course" />
        -->
    </session-factory>
</hibernate-configuration>
```

As an alternative to referring to the Hibernate configuration file, you can also centralize all the Hibernate configurations in persistence.xml.

```
<persistence ...>
    <persistence-unit name="course">
        <properties>
            <property name="hibernate.connection.driver_class"
                value="org.apache.derby.jdbc.ClientDriver" />
            <property name="hibernate.connection.url"
                value="jdbc:derby://localhost:1527/course;create=true" />
            <property name="hibernate.connection.username" value="app" />
            <property name="hibernate.connection.password" value="app" />
```

```
            <property name="hibernate.dialect"
                value="org.hibernate.dialect.DerbyDialect" />
            <property name="hibernate.show_sql" value="true" />
            <property name="hibernate.hbm2ddl.auto" value="update" />
        </properties>
    </persistence-unit>
</persistence>'
```

In a Java EE environment, a Java EE container is able to manage the entity manager for you and inject it into your EJB components directly. But when you use JPA outside of a Java EE container (e.g., in a Java SE application), you have to create and maintain the entity manager by yourself.

Now let's implement the CourseDao interface in the jpa subpackage using JPA in a Java SE application. Before you call JPA for object persistence, you have to initialize an entity manager factory. The purpose of an entity manager factory is to produce entity managers for you to persist your objects.

■Note   To use Hibernate as the underlying JPA engine, you have to include hibernate-entitymanager.jar and jboss-archive-browsing.jar (located in the lib/hibernate directory of the Spring installation) in your classpath. Because Hibernate EntityManager depends on Javassist (http://www.jboss.org/javassist/), you also have to include javassist.jar in your classpath. If you have Hibernate installed, you should find it in the lib directory of the Hibernate installation. Otherwise, you have to download it from its web site.

```
package com.apress.springenterpriserecipes.course.jpa;
...
import javax.persistence.EntityManager;
import javax.persistence.EntityManagerFactory;
import javax.persistence.EntityTransaction;
import javax.persistence.Persistence;
import javax.persistence.Query;

public class JpaCourseDao implements CourseDao {

    private EntityManagerFactory entityManagerFactory;

    public JpaCourseDao() {
        entityManagerFactory = Persistence.createEntityManagerFactory("course");
    }

    public void store(Course course) {
        EntityManager manager = entityManagerFactory.createEntityManager();
        EntityTransaction tx = manager.getTransaction();
        try {
            tx.begin();
            manager.merge(course);
            tx.commit();
        } catch (RuntimeException e) {
            tx.rollback();
```

```
            throw e;
        } finally {
            manager.close();
        }
    }

    public void delete(Long courseId) {
        EntityManager manager = entityManagerFactory.createEntityManager();
        EntityTransaction tx = manager.getTransaction();
        try {
            tx.begin();
            Course course = manager.find(Course.class, courseId);
            manager.remove(course);
            tx.commit();
        } catch (RuntimeException e) {
            tx.rollback();
            throw e;
        } finally {
            manager.close();
        }
    }

    public Course findById(Long courseId) {
        EntityManager manager = entityManagerFactory.createEntityManager();
        try {
            return manager.find(Course.class, courseId);
        } finally {
            manager.close();
        }
    }

    public List<Course> findAll() {
        EntityManager manager = entityManagerFactory.createEntityManager();
        try {
            Query query = manager.createQuery(
                "select course from Course course");
            return query.getResultList();
        } finally {
            manager.close();
        }
    }
}
```

The entity manager factory is built by the static method createEntityManagerFactory() of the javax.persistence.Persistence class. You have to pass in a persistence unit name defined in persistence.xml for an entity manager factory.

In the preceding DAO methods, you first create an entity manager from the entity manager factory. For any operation that involves database update, such as merge() and remove(), you must start a JPA transaction on the entity manager. For read-only operations such as find() and JPA queries, there's no need to start a transaction. Finally, you must close an entity manager to release the resources.

You can test this DAO with the similar `Main` class, but this time you instantiate the JPA DAO implementation instead.

```
package com.apress.springenterpriserecipes.course;
...
public class Main {

    public static void main(String[] args) {
        CourseDao courseDao = new JpaCourseDao();
        ...
    }
}
```

In the preceding DAO implementations for both Hibernate and JPA, there are only one or two lines that are different for each DAO method. The rest of the lines are boilerplate routine tasks that you have to repeat. Moreover, each ORM framework has its own API for local transaction management.

3-8. Configuring ORM Resource Factories in Spring

Problem

When using an ORM framework on its own, you have to configure its resource factory with its API. For Hibernate and JPA, you have to build a session factory and an entity manager factory from the native Hibernate API and JPA. You have no choice but to manage these objects manually, without Spring's support.

Solution

Spring provides several factory beans for you to create a Hibernate session factory or a JPA entity manager factory as a singleton bean in the IoC container. These factories can be shared between multiple beans via dependency injection. Moreover, this allows the session factory and the entity manager factory to integrate with other Spring data access facilities, such as data sources and transaction managers.

How It Works

Configuring a Hibernate Session Factory in Spring

First of all, let's modify `HibernateCourseDao` to accept a session factory via dependency injection, instead of creating it directly with the native Hibernate API in the constructor.

```
package com.apress.springenterpriserecipes.course.hibernate;
...
import org.hibernate.SessionFactory;

public class HibernateCourseDao implements CourseDao {

    private SessionFactory sessionFactory;
```

```
    public void setSessionFactory(SessionFactory sessionFactory) {
        this.sessionFactory = sessionFactory;
    }
    ...
}
```

Now let's see how to declare a session factory that uses XML mapping files in Spring. For this purpose, you have to enable the XML mapping file definition in hibernate.cfg.xml again.

```
<hibernate-configuration>
    <session-factory>
        ...
        <!-- For Hibernate XML mappings -->
        <mapping resource="com/apress/springenterpriserecipes/course/➥
Course.hbm.xml" />
    </session-factory>
</hibernate-configuration>
```

Then you create a bean configuration file for using Hibernate as the ORM framework (e.g., beans-hibernate.xml in the classpath root). You can declare a session factory that uses XML mapping files with the factory bean LocalSessionFactoryBean. You can also declare a HibernateCourseDao instance under Spring's management.

```
<beans xmlns="http://www.springframework.org/schema/beans"
    xmlns:xsi="http://www.w3.org/2001/XMLSchema-instance"
    xsi:schemaLocation="http://www.springframework.org/schema/beans
        http://www.springframework.org/schema/beans/spring-beans-3.0.xsd">

    <bean id="sessionFactory"
        class="org.springframework.orm.hibernate3.LocalSessionFactoryBean">
        <property name="configLocation" value="classpath:hibernate.cfg.xml" />
    </bean>

    <bean id="courseDao"
        class="com.apress.springenterpriserecipes.course.hibernate. ➥
HibernateCourseDao">
        <property name="sessionFactory" ref="sessionFactory" />
    </bean>
</beans>
```

Note that you can specify the configLocation property for this factory bean to load the Hibernate configuration file. The configLocation property is of type Resource, but you can assign a string value to it. The built-in property editor ResourceEditor will convert it into a Resource object. The preceding factory bean loads the configuration file from the root of the classpath.

Now you can modify the Main class to retrieve the HibernateCourseDao instance from the Spring IoC container.

```
package com.apress.springenterpriserecipes.course;
...
import org.springframework.context.ApplicationContext;
import org.springframework.context.support.ClassPathXmlApplicationContext;
```

```
public class Main {

    public static void main(String[] args) {
        ApplicationContext context =
            new ClassPathXmlApplicationContext("beans-hibernate.xml");

        CourseDao courseDao = (CourseDao) context.getBean("courseDao");
        ...
    }
}
```

The preceding factory bean creates a session factory by loading the Hibernate configuration file, which includes the database settings (either JDBC connection properties or a data source's JNDI name). Now, suppose that you have a data source defined in the Spring IoC container. If you want to use this data source for your session factory, you can inject it into the dataSource property of LocalSessionFactoryBean. The data source specified in this property will override the database settings in the Hibernate configuration file. If this is set, the Hibernate settings should not define a connection provider to avoid meaningless double configuration.

```
<beans ...>
    ...
    <bean id="dataSource"
        class="org.springframework.jdbc.datasource.DriverManagerDataSource">
        <property name="driverClassName"
            value="org.apache.derby.jdbc.ClientDriver" />
        <property name="url"
            value="jdbc:derby://localhost:1527/course;create=true" />
        <property name="username" value="app" />
        <property name="password" value="app" />
    </bean>

    <bean id="sessionFactory"
        class="org.springframework.orm.hibernate3.LocalSessionFactoryBean">
        <property name="dataSource" ref="dataSource" />
        <property name="configLocation" value="classpath:hibernate.cfg.xml" />
    </bean>
</beans>
```

Or you can even ignore the Hibernate configuration file by merging all the configurations into LocalSessionFactoryBean. For example, you can specify the locations of the XML mapping files in the mappingResources property and other Hibernate properties such as the database dialect in the hibernateProperties property.

```
<bean id="sessionFactory"
    class="org.springframework.orm.hibernate3.LocalSessionFactoryBean">
    <property name="dataSource" ref="dataSource" />
    <property name="mappingResources">
        <list>
            <value>com/apress/springenterpriserecipes/course/Course.hbm.xml</value>
        </list>
    </property>
```

```
    <property name="hibernateProperties">
        <props>
            <prop key="hibernate.dialect">org.hibernate.dialect.DerbyDialect</prop>
            <prop key="hibernate.show_sql">true</prop>
            <prop key="hibernate.hbm2ddl.auto">update</prop>
        </props>
    </property>
</bean>
```

The mappingResources property's type is String[], so you can specify a set of mapping files in the classpath. LocalSessionFactoryBean also allows you take advantage of Spring's resource-loading support to load mapping files from various types of locations. You can specify the resource paths of the mapping files in the mappingLocations property, whose type is Resource[].

```
<bean id="sessionFactory"
    class="org.springframework.orm.hibernate3.LocalSessionFactoryBean">
    ...
    <property name="mappingLocations">
        <list>
            <value>classpath:com/apress/springenterpriserecipes/course/➥
Course.hbm.xml</value>
        </list>
    </property>
    ...
</bean>
```

With Spring's resource-loading support, you can also use wildcards in a resource path to match multiple mapping files so that you don't need to configure their locations every time you add a new entity class. Spring's preregistered ResourceArrayPropertyEditor will convert this path into a Resource array.

```
<bean id="sessionFactory"
    class="org.springframework.orm.hibernate3.LocalSessionFactoryBean">
    ...
    <property name="mappingLocations"
        value="classpath:com/apress/springenterpriserecipes/course/*.hbm.xml" />
    ...
</bean>
```

If your mapping metadata is provided through JPA annotations, you have to make use of AnnotationSessionFactoryBean instead. You have to specify the persistent classes in the annotatedClasses property of AnnotationSessionFactoryBean.

```
<bean id="sessionFactory" class="org.springframework.orm.hibernate3.➥
    annotation.AnnotationSessionFactoryBean">
    <property name="dataSource" ref="dataSource" />
    <property name="annotatedClasses">
        <list>
            <value>com.apress.springenterpriserecipes.course.Course</value>
        </list>
    </property>
```

```
        <property name="hibernateProperties">
            <props>
                <prop key="hibernate.dialect">org.hibernate.dialect.DerbyDialect</prop>
                <prop key="hibernate.show_sql">true</prop>
                <prop key="hibernate.hbm2ddl.auto">update</prop>
            </props>
        </property>
</bean>
```

Now you can delete the Hibernate configuration file (i.e., `hibernate.cfg.xml`) because its configurations have been ported to Spring.

Configuring a JPA Entity Manager Factory in Spring

First of all, let's modify `JpaCourseDao` to accept an entity manager factory via dependency injection, instead of creating it directly in the constructor.

```
package com.apress.springenterpriserecipes.course.jpa;
...
import javax.persistence.EntityManagerFactory;
import javax.persistence.Persistence;

public class JpaCourseDao implements CourseDao {

    private EntityManagerFactory entityManagerFactory;

    public void setEntityManagerFactory(
            EntityManagerFactory entityManagerFactory) {
        this.entityManagerFactory = entityManagerFactory;
    }
    ...
}
```

The JPA specification defines how you should obtain an entity manager factory in Java SE and Java EE environments. In a Java SE environment, an entity manager factory is created manually by calling the `createEntityManagerFactory()` static method of the `Persistence` class.

Now let's create a bean configuration file for using JPA (e.g., `beans-jpa.xml` in the classpath root). Spring provides a factory bean, `LocalEntityManagerFactoryBean`, for you to create an entity manager factory in the IoC container. You must specify the persistence unit name defined in the JPA configuration file. You can also declare a `JpaCourseDao` instance under Spring's management.

```
<beans xmlns="http://www.springframework.org/schema/beans"
    xmlns:xsi="http://www.w3.org/2001/XMLSchema-instance"
    xsi:schemaLocation="http://www.springframework.org/schema/beans
        http://www.springframework.org/schema/beans/spring-beans-3.0.xsd">

    <bean id="entityManagerFactory"
        class="org.springframework.orm.jpa.LocalEntityManagerFactoryBean">
        <property name="persistenceUnitName" value="course" />
    </bean>
```

```
    <bean id="courseDao"
        class="com.apress.springenterpriserecipes.course.jpa.JpaCourseDao">
        <property name="entityManagerFactory" ref="entityManagerFactory" />
    </bean>
</beans>
```

Now you can test this JpaCourseDao instance with the Main class by retrieving it from the Spring IoC container.

```
package com.apress.springenterpriserecipes.course;
...
import org.springframework.context.ApplicationContext;
import org.springframework.context.support.ClassPathXmlApplicationContext;

public class Main {

    public static void main(String[] args) {
        ApplicationContext context =
            new ClassPathXmlApplicationContext("beans-jpa.xml");

        CourseDao courseDao = (CourseDao) context.getBean("courseDao");
        ...
    }
}
```

In a Java EE environment, you can look up an entity manager factory from a Java EE container with JNDI. In Spring, you can perform a JNDI lookup by using the <jee:jndi-lookup> element.

```
<jee:jndi-lookup id="entityManagerFactory" jndi-name="jpa/coursePU" />
```

LocalEntityManagerFactoryBean creates an entity manager factory by loading the JPA configuration file (i.e., persistence.xml). Spring supports a more flexible way to create an entity manager factory by another factory bean, LocalContainerEntityManagerFactoryBean. It allows you to override some of the configurations in the JPA configuration file, such as the data source and database dialect. So, you can take advantage of Spring's data access facilities to configure the entity manager factory.

```
<beans ...>
    ...
    <bean id="dataSource"
        class="org.springframework.jdbc.datasource.DriverManagerDataSource">
        <property name="driverClassName"
            value="org.apache.derby.jdbc.ClientDriver" />
        <property name="url"
            value="jdbc:derby://localhost:1527/course;create=true" />
        <property name="username" value="app" />
        <property name="password" value="app" />
    </bean>
```

```
<bean id="entityManagerFactory" class="org.springframework.orm.jpa.➡
    LocalContainerEntityManagerFactoryBean">
    <property name="persistenceUnitName" value="course" />
    <property name="dataSource" ref="dataSource" />
    <property name="jpaVendorAdapter">
        <bean class="org.springframework.orm.jpa.vendor.➡
            HibernateJpaVendorAdapter">
            <property name="databasePlatform"
                value="org.hibernate.dialect.DerbyDialect" />
            <property name="showSql" value="true" />
            <property name="generateDdl" value="true" />
        </bean>
    </property>
</bean>
</beans>
```

In the preceding bean configurations, you inject a data source into this entity manager factory. It will override the database settings in the JPA configuration file. You can set a JPA vendor adapter to LocalContainerEntityManagerFactoryBean to specify JPA engine–specific properties. With Hibernate as the underlying JPA engine, you should choose HibernateJpaVendorAdapter. Other properties that are not supported by this adapter can be specified in the jpaProperties property.

Now your JPA configuration file (i.e., persistence.xml) can be simplified as follows because its configurations have been ported to Spring:

```
<persistence ...>
    <persistence-unit name="course" />
</persistence>
```

3-9. Persisting Objects with Spring's ORM Templates

Problem

When using an ORM framework on its own, you have to repeat certain routine tasks for each DAO operation. For example, in a DAO operation implemented with Hibernate or JPA, you have to open and close a session or an entity manager, and begin, commit, and roll back a transaction with the native API.

Solution

Spring's approach to simplifying an ORM framework's usage is the same as JDBC's—by defining template classes and DAO support classes. Also, Spring defines an abstract layer on top of different transaction management APIs. For different ORM frameworks, you only have to pick up a corresponding transaction manager implementation. Then you can manage transactions for them in a similar way.

In Spring's data access module, the support for different data access strategies is consistent. Table 3-4 compares the support classes for JDBC, Hibernate, and JPA.

Table 3-4. *Spring's Support Classes for Different Data Access Strategies*

Support Class	JDBC	Hibernate	JPA
Template class	JdbcTemplate	HibernateTemplate	JpaTemplate
DAO support	JdbcDaoSupport	HibernateDaoSupport	JpaDaoSupport
Transaction	DataSourceTransaction	HibernateTransaction	JpaTransactionManager

Spring defines the HibernateTemplate and JpaTemplate classes to provide template methods for different types of Hibernate and JPA operations to minimize the effort involved in using them. The template methods in HibernateTemplate and JpaTemplate ensure that Hibernate sessions and JPA entity managers will be opened and closed properly. They will also have native Hibernate and JPA transactions participate in Spring-managed transactions. As a result, you will be able to manage transactions declaratively for your Hibernate and JPA DAOs without any boilerplate transaction code.

How It Works

Using a Hibernate Template and a JPA Template
First, the HibernateCourseDao class can be simplified as follows with the help of Spring's HibernateTemplate:

```
package com.apress.springenterpriserecipes.course.hibernate;
...
import org.springframework.orm.hibernate3.HibernateTemplate;
import org.springframework.transaction.annotation.Transactional;

public class HibernateCourseDao implements CourseDao {

    private HibernateTemplate hibernateTemplate;

    public void setHibernateTemplate(HibernateTemplate hibernateTemplate) {
        this.hibernateTemplate = hibernateTemplate;
    }

    @Transactional
    public void store(Course course) {
        hibernateTemplate.saveOrUpdate(course);
    }

    @Transactional
    public void delete(Long courseId) {
        Course course = (Course) hibernateTemplate.get(Course.class, courseId);
        hibernateTemplate.delete(course);
    }
```

```
    @Transactional(readOnly = true)
    public Course findById(Long courseId) {
        return (Course) hibernateTemplate.get(Course.class, courseId);
    }

    @Transactional(readOnly = true)
    public List<Course> findAll() {
        return hibernateTemplate.find("from Course");
    }
}
```

In this DAO implementation, you declare all the DAO methods to be transactional with the
@Transactional annotation. Among these methods, findById() and findAll() are read-only. The
template methods in HibernateTemplate are responsible for managing the sessions and transactions.
If there are multiple Hibernate operations in a transactional DAO method, the template methods will
ensure that they will run within the same session and transaction. As a result, you have no need to deal
with the Hibernate API for session and transaction management.

The HibernateTemplate class is thread-safe, so you can declare a single instance of it in the bean
configuration file for Hibernate (i.e., beans-hibernate.xml) and inject this instance into all Hibernate
DAOs. A HibernateTemplate instance requires the sessionFactory property to be set. You can inject this
property by either setter method or constructor argument.

```
<beans xmlns="http://www.springframework.org/schema/beans"
    xmlns:xsi="http://www.w3.org/2001/XMLSchema-instance"
    xmlns:tx="http://www.springframework.org/schema/tx"
    xsi:schemaLocation="http://www.springframework.org/schema/beans
        http://www.springframework.org/schema/beans/spring-beans-3.0.xsd
        http://www.springframework.org/schema/tx
        http://www.springframework.org/schema/tx/spring-tx-3.0.xsd">
    ...
    <tx:annotation-driven />

    <bean id="transactionManager"
        class="org.springframework.orm.hibernate3.HibernateTransactionManager">
        <property name="sessionFactory" ref="sessionFactory" />
    </bean>

    <bean id="hibernateTemplate"
        class="org.springframework.orm.hibernate3.HibernateTemplate">
        <property name="sessionFactory" ref="sessionFactory" />
    </bean>

    <bean name="courseDao"
        class="com.apress.springenterpriserecipes.course.hibernate. ➥
HibernateCourseDao">
        <property name="hibernateTemplate" ref="hibernateTemplate" />
    </bean>
</beans>
```

To enable declarative transaction management for the methods annotated with @Transactional, you have to enable the <tx:annotation-driven> element in your bean configuration file. By default, it will look for a transaction manager with the name transactionManager, so you have to declare a HibernateTransactionManager instance with that name. HibernateTransactionManager requires the session factory property to be set. It will manage transactions for sessions opened through this session factory.

Similarly, you can simplify the JpaCourseDao class as follows with the help of Spring's JpaTemplate. You also declare all the DAO methods to be transactional.

```
package com.apress.springenterpriserecipes.course.jpa;
...
import org.springframework.orm.jpa.JpaTemplate;
import org.springframework.transaction.annotation.Transactional;

public class JpaCourseDao implements CourseDao {

    private JpaTemplate jpaTemplate;

    public void setJpaTemplate(JpaTemplate jpaTemplate) {
        this.jpaTemplate = jpaTemplate;
    }

    @Transactional
    public void store(Course course) {
        jpaTemplate.merge(course);
    }

    @Transactional
    public void delete(Long courseId) {
        Course course = jpaTemplate.find(Course.class, courseId);
        jpaTemplate.remove(course);
    }

    @Transactional(readOnly = true)
    public Course findById(Long courseId) {
        return jpaTemplate.find(Course.class, courseId);
    }

    @Transactional(readOnly = true)
    public List<Course> findAll() {
        return jpaTemplate.find("from Course");
    }
}
```

In the bean configuration file for JPA (i.e., beans-jpa.xml), you can declare a JpaTemplate instance and inject it into all JPA DAOs. Also, you have to declare a JpaTransactionManager instance for managing JPA transactions.

```
<beans xmlns="http://www.springframework.org/schema/beans"
    xmlns:xsi="http://www.w3.org/2001/XMLSchema-instance"
    xmlns:tx="http://www.springframework.org/schema/tx"
    xsi:schemaLocation="http://www.springframework.org/schema/beans
        http://www.springframework.org/schema/beans/spring-beans-3.0.xsd
```

```
        http://www.springframework.org/schema/tx
        http://www.springframework.org/schema/tx/spring-tx-3.0.xsd">
    ...
    <tx:annotation-driven />

    <bean id="transactionManager"
        class="org.springframework.orm.jpa.JpaTransactionManager">
        <property name="entityManagerFactory" ref="entityManagerFactory" />
    </bean>

    <bean id="jpaTemplate"
        class="org.springframework.orm.jpa.JpaTemplate">
        <property name="entityManagerFactory" ref="entityManagerFactory" />
    </bean>

    <bean name="courseDao"
        class="com.apress.springenterpriserecipes.course.jpa.JpaCourseDao">
        <property name="jpaTemplate" ref="jpaTemplate" />
    </bean>
</beans>
```

Another advantage of HibernateTemplate and JpaTemplate is that they will translate native Hibernate and JPA exceptions into exceptions in Spring's DataAccessException hierarchy. This allows consistent exception handling for all the data access strategies in Spring. For instance, if a database constraint is violated when persisting an object, Hibernate will throw an org.hibernate.exception.ConstraintViolationException while JPA will throw a javax.persistence.EntityExistsException. These exceptions will be translated by HibernateTemplate and JpaTemplate into DataIntegrityViolationException, which is a subclass of Spring's DataAccessException.

If you want to get access to the underlying Hibernate session or JPA entity manager in HibernateTemplate or JpaTemplate in order to perform native Hibernate or JPA operations, you can implement the HibernateCallback or JpaCallback interface and pass its instance to the execute() method of the template. This will give you a chance to use any implementation-specific features directly if there's not sufficient support already available from the template implementations.

```
hibernateTemplate.execute(new HibernateCallback() {
    public Object doInHibernate(Session session) throws HibernateException,
            SQLException {
        // ... anything you can imagine doing can be done here. ➡
  Cache invalidation, for example…
    }
};

jpaTemplate.execute(new JpaCallback() {
    public Object doInJpa(EntityManager em) throws PersistenceException {
// ... anything you can imagine doing can be done here.    }
};
```

Extending the Hibernate and JPA DAO Support Classes

Your Hibernate DAO can extend HibernateDaoSupport to have the setSessionFactory() and setHibernateTemplate() methods inherited. Then, in your DAO methods, you can simply call the getHibernateTemplate() method to retrieve the template instance.

```
package com.apress.springenterpriserecipes.course.hibernate;
...
import org.springframework.orm.hibernate3.support.HibernateDaoSupport;
import org.springframework.transaction.annotation.Transactional;

public class HibernateCourseDao extends HibernateDaoSupport implements
        CourseDao {

    @Transactional
    public void store(Course course) {
        getHibernateTemplate().saveOrUpdate(course);
    }

    @Transactional
    public void delete(Long courseId) {
        Course course = (Course) getHibernateTemplate().get(Course.class,
                courseId);
        getHibernateTemplate().delete(course);
    }

    @Transactional(readOnly = true)
    public Course findById(Long courseId) {
        return (Course) getHibernateTemplate().get(Course.class, courseId);
    }

    @Transactional(readOnly = true)
    public List<Course> findAll() {
        return getHibernateTemplate().find("from Course");
    }
}
```

Because HibernateCourseDao inherits the setSessionFactory() and setHibernateTemplate() methods, you can inject either of them into your DAO so that you can retrieve the HibernateTemplate instance. If you inject a session factory, you will be able to delete the HibernateTemplate declaration.

```
<bean name="courseDao"
    class="com.apress.springenterpriserecipes.course.hibernate.HibernateCourseDao">
    <property name="sessionFactory" ref="sessionFactory" />
</bean>
```

Similarly, your JPA DAO can extend JpaDaoSupport to have setEntityManagerFactory() and setJpaTemplate() inherited. In your DAO methods, you can simply call the getJpaTemplate() method to retrieve the template instance. This instance will contain the pre-initialized EntityManagerFactory.

```
package com.apress.springenterpriserecipes.course.jpa;
...
import org.springframework.orm.jpa.support.JpaDaoSupport;
import org.springframework.transaction.annotation.Transactional;
```

```
public class JpaCourseDao extends JpaDaoSupport implements CourseDao {

    @Transactional
    public void store(Course course) {
        getJpaTemplate().merge(course);
    }

    @Transactional
    public void delete(Long courseId) {
        Course course = getJpaTemplate().find(Course.class, courseId);
        getJpaTemplate().remove(course);
    }

    @Transactional(readOnly = true)
    public Course findById(Long courseId) {
        return getJpaTemplate().find(Course.class, courseId);
    }

    @Transactional(readOnly = true)
    public List<Course> findAll() {
        return getJpaTemplate().find("from Course");
    }
}
```

Because JpaCourseDao inherits both setEntityManagerFactory() and setJpaTemplate(), you can inject either of them into your DAO. If you inject an entity manager factory, you will be able to delete the JpaTemplate declaration.

```
<bean name="courseDao"
    class="com.apress.springenterpriserecipes.course.jpa.JpaCourseDao">
    <property name="entityManagerFactory" ref="entityManagerFactory" />
</bean>
```

3-10. Persisting Objects with Hibernate's Contextual Sessions

Problem
Spring's HibernateTemplate can simplify your DAO implementation by managing sessions and transactions for you. However, using HibernateTemplate means your DAO has to depend on Spring's API.

Solution
An alternative to Spring's HibernateTemplate is to use Hibernate's contextual sessions. In Hibernate 3, a session factory can manage contextual sessions for you and allows you to retrieve them by the getCurrentSession() method on org.hibernate.SessionFactory. Within a single transaction, you will get the same session for each getCurrentSession() method call. This ensures that there will be only one Hibernate session per transaction, so it works nicely with Spring's transaction management support.

How It Works

To use the contextual session approach, your DAO methods require access to the session factory, which can be injected via a setter method or a constructor argument. Then, in each DAO method, you get the contextual session from the session factory and use it for object persistence.

```java
package com.apress.springenterpriserecipes.course.hibernate;
...
import org.hibernate.Query;
import org.hibernate.SessionFactory;
import org.springframework.transaction.annotation.Transactional;

public class HibernateCourseDao implements CourseDao {

    private SessionFactory sessionFactory;

    public void setSessionFactory(SessionFactory sessionFactory) {
        this.sessionFactory = sessionFactory;
    }

    @Transactional
    public void store(Course course) {
        sessionFactory.getCurrentSession().saveOrUpdate(course);
    }

    @Transactional
    public void delete(Long courseId) {
        Course course = (Course) sessionFactory.getCurrentSession().get(
                Course.class, courseId);
        sessionFactory.getCurrentSession().delete(course);
    }

    @Transactional(readOnly = true)
    public Course findById(Long courseId) {
        return (Course) sessionFactory.getCurrentSession().get(
                Course.class, courseId);
    }

    @Transactional(readOnly = true)
    public List<Course> findAll() {
        Query query = sessionFactory.getCurrentSession().createQuery(
                "from Course");
        return query.list();
    }
}
```

Note that all your DAO methods must be made transactional. This is required because Spring wraps the SessionFactory with a proxy that expects that Spring's transaction management is in play when methods on a session are made. It will attempt to find a transaction and then fail, complaining that no Hibernate session's been bound to the thread. You can achieve this by annotating each method or the entire class with @Transactional. This ensures that the persistence operations within a DAO method will be executed in the same transaction and hence by the same session. Moreover, if a service layer component's method calls multiple DAO methods, and it propagates its own transaction to these methods, then all these DAO methods will run within the same session as well.

In the bean configuration file for Hibernate (i.e., beans-hibernate.xml), you have to declare a HibernateTransactionManager instance for this application and enable declarative transaction management via <tx:annotation-driven>.

```xml
<beans xmlns="http://www.springframework.org/schema/beans"
    xmlns:xsi="http://www.w3.org/2001/XMLSchema-instance"
    xmlns:tx="http://www.springframework.org/schema/tx"
    xsi:schemaLocation="http://www.springframework.org/schema/beans
        http://www.springframework.org/schema/beans/spring-beans-3.0.xsd
        http://www.springframework.org/schema/tx
        http://www.springframework.org/schema/tx/spring-tx-3.0.xsd">
    ...
    <tx:annotation-driven />

    <bean id="transactionManager"
        class="org.springframework.orm.hibernate3.HibernateTransactionManager">
        <property name="sessionFactory" ref="sessionFactory" />
    </bean>

    <bean name="courseDao"
        class="com.apress.springenterpriserecipes.course.hibernate. ➥
HibernateCourseDao">
        <property name="sessionFactory" ref="sessionFactory" />
    </bean>
</beans>
```

Remember that HibernateTemplate will translate the native Hibernate exceptions into exceptions in Spring's DataAccessException hierarchy. This allows consistent exception handling for different data access strategies in Spring. However, when calling the native methods on a Hibernate session, the exceptions thrown will be of native type HibernateException. If you want the Hibernate exceptions to be translated into Spring's DataAccessException for consistent exception handling, you have to apply the @Repository annotation to your DAO class that requires exception translation.

```java
package com.apress.springenterpriserecipes.course.hibernate;
...
import org.springframework.stereotype.Repository;

@Repository
public class HibernateCourseDao implements CourseDao {
    ...
}
```

Then register a PersistenceExceptionTranslationPostProcessor instance to translate the native Hibernate exceptions into data access exceptions in Spring's DataAccessException hierarchy. This bean post processor will only translate exceptions for beans annotated with @Repository.

```xml
<beans ...>
    ...
    <bean class="org.springframework.dao.annotation.➥
        PersistenceExceptionTranslationPostProcessor" />
</beans>
```

In Spring, @Repository is a stereotype annotation. By annotating it, a component class can be auto-detected through component scanning. You can assign a component name in this annotation and have the session factory auto-wired by the Spring IoC container with @Autowired.

```
package com.apress.springenterpriserecipes.course.hibernate;
...
import org.hibernate.SessionFactory;
import org.springframework.beans.factory.annotation.Autowired;
import org.springframework.stereotype.Repository;

@Repository("courseDao")
public class HibernateCourseDao implements CourseDao {

    private SessionFactory sessionFactory;

    @Autowired
    public void setSessionFactory(SessionFactory sessionFactory) {
        this.sessionFactory = sessionFactory;
    }
    ...
}
```

Then you can simply enable the <context:component-scan> element and delete the original HibernateCourseDao bean declaration.

```
<beans xmlns="http://www.springframework.org/schema/beans"
    xmlns:xsi="http://www.w3.org/2001/XMLSchema-instance"
    xmlns:context="http://www.springframework.org/schema/context"
    xmlns:tx="http://www.springframework.org/schema/tx"
    xsi:schemaLocation="http://www.springframework.org/schema/beans
        http://www.springframework.org/schema/beans/spring-beans-3.0.xsd
        http://www.springframework.org/schema/context
        http://www.springframework.org/schema/context/spring-context-3.0.xsd
        http://www.springframework.org/schema/tx
        http://www.springframework.org/schema/tx/spring-tx-3.0.xsd">

    <context:component-scan
        base-package="com.apress.springenterpriserecipes.course.hibernate" />
    ...
</beans>
```

3-11. Persisting Objects with JPA's Context Injection

Problem

In a Java EE environment, a Java EE container can manage entity managers for you and inject them into your EJB components directly. An EJB component can simply perform persistence operations on an injected entity manager without caring much about the entity manager creation and transaction management.

Similarly, Spring provides JpaTemplate to simplify your DAO implementation by managing entity managers and transactions for you. However, using Spring's JpaTemplate means your DAO is dependent on Spring's API.

Solution

An alternative to Spring's JpaTemplate is to use JPA's context injection. Originally, the @PersistenceContext annotation is used for entity manager injection in EJB components. Spring can also interpret this annotation by means of a bean post processor. It will inject an entity manager into a property with this annotation. Spring ensures that all your persistence operations within a single transaction will be handled by the same entity manager.

How It Works

To use the context injection approach, you can declare an entity manager field in your DAO and annotate it with the @PersistenceContext annotation. Spring will inject an entity manager into this field for you to persist your objects.

```
package com.apress.springenterpriserecipes.course.jpa;
...
import javax.persistence.EntityManager;
import javax.persistence.PersistenceContext;
import javax.persistence.Query;

import org.springframework.transaction.annotation.Transactional;

public class JpaCourseDao implements CourseDao {

    @PersistenceContext
    private EntityManager entityManager;

    @Transactional
    public void store(Course course) {
        entityManager.merge(course);
    }

    @Transactional
    public void delete(Long courseId) {
        Course course = entityManager.find(Course.class, courseId);
        entityManager.remove(course);
    }

    @Transactional(readOnly = true)
    public Course findById(Long courseId) {
        return entityManager.find(Course.class, courseId);
    }
```

```
    @Transactional(readOnly = true)
    public List<Course> findAll() {
        Query query = entityManager.createQuery("from Course");
        return query.getResultList();
    }
}
```

You can annotate each DAO method or the entire DAO class with @Transactional to make all these methods transactional. It ensures that the persistence operations within a DAO method will by executed in the same transaction and hence by the same entity manager.

In the bean configuration file for JPA (i.e., beans-jpa.xml), you have to declare a JpaTransactionManager instance and enable declarative transaction management via <tx:annotation-driven>. You have to register a PersistenceAnnotationBeanPostProcessor instance to inject entity managers into properties annotated with @PersistenceContext.

```
<beans xmlns="http://www.springframework.org/schema/beans"
    xmlns:xsi="http://www.w3.org/2001/XMLSchema-instance"
    xmlns:tx="http://www.springframework.org/schema/tx"
    xsi:schemaLocation="http://www.springframework.org/schema/beans
        http://www.springframework.org/schema/beans/spring-beans-2.5.xsd
        http://www.springframework.org/schema/tx
        http://www.springframework.org/schema/tx/spring-tx-2.5.xsd">

    ...
    <tx:annotation-driven />

    <bean id="transactionManager"
        class="org.springframework.orm.jpa.JpaTransactionManager">
        <property name="entityManagerFactory" ref="entityManagerFactory" />
    </bean>

    <bean name="courseDao"
        class="com.apress.springenterpriserecipes.course.jpa.JpaCourseDao" />

    <bean class="org.springframework.orm.jpa.support.➥
        PersistenceAnnotationBeanPostProcessor" />
</beans>
```

A PersistenceAnnotationBeanPostProcessor instance will be registered automatically once you enable the <context:annotation-config> element. So, you can delete its explicit bean declaration.

```
<beans xmlns="http://www.springframework.org/schema/beans"
    xmlns:xsi="http://www.w3.org/2001/XMLSchema-instance"
    xmlns:context="http://www.springframework.org/schema/context"
    xmlns:tx="http://www.springframework.org/schema/tx"
    xsi:schemaLocation="http://www.springframework.org/schema/beans
        http://www.springframework.org/schema/beans/spring-beans-3.0.xsd
        http://www.springframework.org/schema/context
        http://www.springframework.org/schema/context/spring-context-2.5.xsd
        http://www.springframework.org/schema/tx
        http://www.springframework.org/schema/tx/spring-tx-3.0.xsd">
```

```xml
    <context:annotation-config />
    ...
</beans>
```

This bean post processor can also inject the entity manager factory into a property with the @PersistenceUnit annotation. This allows you to create entity managers and manage transactions by yourself. It's no different from injecting the entity manager factory via a setter method.

```java
package com.apress.springenterpriserecipes.course.jpa;
...
import javax.persistence.EntityManagerFactory;
import javax.persistence.PersistenceUnit;

public class JpaCourseDao implements CourseDao {
    @PersistenceContext
    private EntityManager entityManager;

    @PersistenceUnit
    private EntityManagerFactory entityManagerFactory;
    ...
}
```

Remember that JpaTemplate will translate the native JPA exceptions into exceptions in Spring's DataAccessException hierarchy. However, when calling native methods on a JPA entity manager, the exceptions thrown will be of native type PersistenceException, or other Java SE exceptions like IllegalArgumentException and IllegalStateException. If you want JPA exceptions to be translated into Spring's DataAccessException, you have to apply the @Repository annotation to your DAO class.

```java
package com.apress.springenterpriserecipes.course.jpa;
...
import org.springframework.stereotype.Repository;

@Repository("courseDao")
public class JpaCourseDao implements CourseDao {
    ...
}
```

Then register a PersistenceExceptionTranslationPostProcessor instance to translate the native JPA exceptions into exceptions in Spring's DataAccessException hierarchy. You can also enable <context:component-scan> and delete the original JpaCourseDao bean declaration because @Repository is a stereotype annotation in Spring 2.5 and beyond.

```xml
<beans ...>
    ...
    <context:component-scan
        base-package="com.apress.springenterpriserecipes.course.jpa" />

    <bean class="org.springframework.dao.annotation.PersistenceException➥
Translation PostProcessor" />
</beans>
```

Summary

This chapter discussed how to use Spring's support for JDBC, Hibernate, and JPA. You learned how to configure a DataSource to connect to a database, and also how to use Spring's `JdbcTemplate`, `HibernateTemplate`, and `JpaTemplate` to rid your code of tedious boilerplate handling. You saw how to use the utility base classes to build DAO classes with JDBC, Hibernate, and JPA, and also how to use Spring's support for stereotype annotations and component scanning to easily build new DAOs and Services with a minimum of XML.

In the next chapter, you will learn how to use transactions (i.e., for JMS or a `DataSource`) with Spring to help ensure consistent state.

CHAPTER 4

■ ■ ■

Transaction Management in Spring

In this chapter, you will learn about the basic concept of transactions and Spring's capabilities in the area of transaction management. Transaction management is an essential technique in enterprise applications to ensure data integrity and consistency. Spring, as an enterprise application framework, provides an abstract layer on top of different transaction management APIs. As an application developer, you can use Spring's transaction management facilities without having to know much about the underlying transaction management APIs.

Like the *bean-managed transaction (BMT)* and *container-managed transaction (CMT)* approaches in EJB, Spring supports both programmatic and declarative transaction management. The aim of Spring's transaction support is to provide an alternative to EJB transactions by adding transaction capabilities to POJOs.

Programmatic transaction management is achieved by embedding transaction management code in your business methods to control the commit and rollback of transactions. You usually commit a transaction if a method completes normally and roll back a transaction if a method throws certain types of exceptions. With programmatic transaction management, you can define your own rules to commit and roll back transactions.

However, when managing transactions programmatically, you have to include transaction management code in each transactional operation. As a result, the boilerplate transaction code is repeated in each of these operations. Moreover, it's hard for you to enable and disable transaction management for different applications. If you have a solid understanding of AOP, you may already have noticed that transaction management is a kind of crosscutting concern.

Declarative transaction management is preferable to programmatic transaction management in most cases. It's achieved by separating transaction management code from your business methods via declarations. Transaction management, as a kind of crosscutting concern, can be modularized with the AOP approach. Spring supports declarative transaction management through the Spring AOP framework. This can help you to enable transactions for your applications more easily and define a consistent transaction policy. Declarative transaction management is less flexible than programmatic transaction management. Programmatic transaction management allows you to control transactions through your code_explicitly starting, committing, and joining them as you see fit. You can specify a set of transaction attributes to define your transactions at a fine level of granularity. The transaction attributes supported by Spring include the propagation behavior, isolation level, rollback rules, transaction timeout, and whether or not the transaction is read-only. These attributes allow you to further customize the behavior of your transactions.

Upon finishing this chapter, you will be able to apply different transaction management strategies in your application. Moreover, you will be familiar with different transaction attributes to finely define your transactions.

Programmatic and Declarative Transaction Management

Programmatic transaction management is a good idea in certain cases where you don't feel the addition of Spring proxies is worth the trouble or negligible performance loss. Here, you might access the native transaction yourself and control the transaction manually. A more convenient option that avoids the overhead of Spring proxies is the TransactionTemplate class, which provides a template method around which a transactional boundary is started and then committed.

4-1. Problems with Transaction Management

Transaction management is an essential technique in enterprise application development to ensure data integrity and consistency. Without transaction management, your data and resources may be corrupted and left in an inconsistent state. Transaction management is particularly important in a concurrent and distributed environment for recovering from unexpected errors.

In simple words, a *transaction* is a series of actions that are treated as a single unit of work. These actions should either complete entirely or take no effect at all. If all the actions go well, the transaction should be committed permanently. In contrast, if any of them goes wrong, the transaction should be rolled back to the initial state as if nothing had happened.

The concept of transactions can be described with four key properties: *atomicity, consistency, isolation, and durability (ACID).*

Atomicity: A transaction is an atomic operation that consists of a series of actions. The atomicity of a transaction ensures that the actions either complete entirely or take no effect at all.

Consistency: Once all actions of a transaction have completed, the transaction is committed. Then your data and resources will be in a consistent state that conforms to business rules.

Isolation: Because there may be many transactions processing with the same data set at the same time, each transaction should be isolated from others to prevent data corruption.

Durability: Once a transaction has completed, its result should be durable to survive any system failure (imagine if the power to your machine was cut right in the middle of a transaction's commit). Usually, the result of a transaction is written to persistent storage.

To understand the importance of transaction management, let's begin with an example about purchasing books from an online book shop. First, you have to create a new schema for this application in your database. If you are choosing Apache Derby as your database engine, you can connect to it with the JDBC properties shown in Table 4-1. For the examples in this book, we're using Derby 10.4.2.0.

Table 4-1. JDBC Properties for Connecting to the Application Database

Property	Value
Driver class	org.apache.derby.jdbc.ClientDriver
URL	jdbc:derby://localhost:1527/bookshop;create=true
Username	app
Password	app

With the preceding configuration, the database will be created for you because of the parameter on the JDBC URL: create=true. You should remove this for production, however. For your book shop application, you need a place to store the data. You'll create a simple database to manage books and accounts for.

The entity relational (ER) diagram for the tables looks like Figure 4-1.

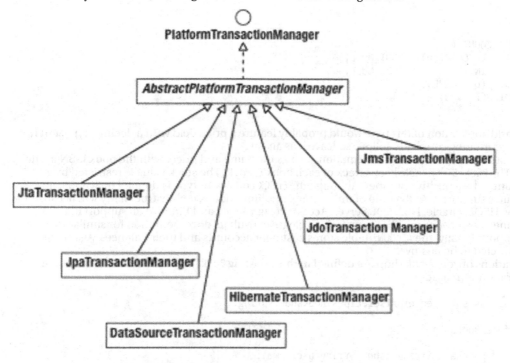

Figure 4-1. BOOK_STOCK describes how many given BOOKs exist.

Now, let's create the SQL for the preceding model. You'll use the ij tool that ships with Derby. On a command line, proceed to the directory where Derby is installed (usually just where you unzipped it when you downloaded it.). Descend to the bin directory. If Derby's not already started, run startNetworkServer (or startNetworkServer.bat on Windows). Now you need to log in and execute the SQL DDL. Background the Derby Server process or open up a second shell and return to the same bin directory in the Derby installation directory. Execute ij. In the shell, execute the following:

```
connect jdbc:derby://localhost:1527/bookshop;create=true ;
```

Paste the following SQL into the shell and verify its success:

```
CREATE TABLE BOOK (
    ISBN            VARCHAR(50)     NOT NULL,
    BOOK_NAME       VARCHAR(100)    NOT NULL,
    PRICE           INT,
    PRIMARY KEY (ISBN)
);
```

155

```sql
CREATE TABLE BOOK_STOCK (
    ISBN      VARCHAR(50)      NOT NULL,
    STOCK     INT              NOT NULL,
    PRIMARY KEY (ISBN),
    CHECK (STOCK >= 0)
);

CREATE TABLE ACCOUNT (
    USERNAME    VARCHAR(50)     NOT NULL,
    BALANCE     INT             NOT NULL,
    PRIMARY KEY (USERNAME),
    CHECK (BALANCE >= 0)
);
```

A real-world application of this type would probably feature a price field with a decimal type, but it makes the programming simpler to follow, so leave it as an int.

The BOOK table stores basic book information such as the name and price, with the book ISBN as the primary key. The BOOK_STOCK table keeps track of each book's stock. The stock value is restricted by a CHECK constraint to be a positive number. Although the CHECK constraint type is defined in SQL-99, not all database engines support it. At the time of this writing, this limitation is mainly true of MySQL because Sybase, Derby, HSQL, Oracle, DB2, SQL Server, Access, PostgresSQL, and FireBird all support it. If your database engine doesn't support CHECK constraints, please consult its documentation for similar constraint support. Finally, the ACCOUNT table stores customer accounts and their balances. Again, the balance is restricted to be positive.

The operations of your book shop are defined in the following BookShop interface. For now, there is only one operation: purchase().

```
package com.apress.springenterpriserecipes.bookshop.spring;

public interface BookShop {

    public void purchase(String isbn, String username);
}
```

Because you will implement this interface with JDBC, you create the following JdbcBookShop class. To better understand the nature of transactions, let's implement this class without the help of Spring's JDBC support.

```java
package com.apress.springenterpriserecipes.bookshop.spring;

import java.sql.Connection;
import java.sql.PreparedStatement;
import java.sql.ResultSet;
import java.sql.SQLException;

import javax.sql.DataSource;
```

```java
public class JdbcBookShop implements BookShop {

    private DataSource dataSource;

    public void setDataSource(DataSource dataSource) {
        this.dataSource = dataSource;
    }

    public void purchase(String isbn, String username) {
        Connection conn = null;
        try {
            conn = dataSource.getConnection();

            PreparedStatement stmt1 = conn.prepareStatement(
                    "SELECT PRICE FROM BOOK WHERE ISBN = ?");
            stmt1.setString(1, isbn);
            ResultSet rs = stmt1.executeQuery();
            rs.next();
            int price = rs.getInt("PRICE");
            stmt1.close();

            PreparedStatement stmt2 = conn.prepareStatement(
                    "UPDATE BOOK_STOCK SET STOCK = STOCK - 1 "+
                    "WHERE ISBN = ?");
            stmt2.setString(1, isbn);
            stmt2.executeUpdate();
            stmt2.close();

            PreparedStatement stmt3 = conn.prepareStatement(
                    "UPDATE ACCOUNT SET BALANCE = BALANCE - ? "+
                    "WHERE USERNAME = ?");
            stmt3.setInt(1, price);
            stmt3.setString(2, username);
            stmt3.executeUpdate();
            stmt3.close();
        } catch (SQLException e) {
            throw new RuntimeException(e);
        } finally {
            if (conn != null) {
                try {
                    conn.close();
                } catch (SQLException e) {}
            }
        }
    }
}
```

For the purchase() operation, you have to execute three SQL statements in total. The first is to query the book price. The second and third update the book stock and account balance accordingly.

Then you can declare a book shop instance in the Spring IoC container to provide purchasing services. For simplicity's sake, you can use DriverManagerDataSource, which opens a new connection to the database for every request.

■Note   To access a database running on the Derby server, you have to include derbyclient.jar (located in the lib directory of the Derby installation) in your classpath. Alternatively, if you're using Maven, you can add a dependency element:

```
<dependency>
    <groupId>org.apache.derby</groupId>
    <artifactId>derbyclient</artifactId>
    <version>10.4.2.0</version>
</dependency>
```

```
<beans xmlns="http://www.springframework.org/schema/beans"
    xmlns:xsi="http://www.w3.org/2001/XMLSchema-instance"
    xsi:schemaLocation="http://www.springframework.org/schema/beans
        http://www.springframework.org/schema/beans/spring-beans-3.0.xsd">

    <bean id="dataSource"
        class="org.springframework.jdbc.datasource.DriverManagerDataSource">
        <property name="driverClassName"
            value="org.apache.derby.jdbc.ClientDriver"/>
        <property name="url"
            value="jdbc:derby://localhost:1527/bookshop;create=true"/>
        <property name="username"value="app"/>
        <property name="password"value="app"/>
    </bean>

    <bean id="bookShop"➥
class="com.apress.springenterpriserecipes.bookshop.spring.JdbcBookShop">
        <property name="dataSource"ref="dataSource"/>
    </bean>
</beans>
```

To demonstrate the problems that can arise without transaction management, suppose you have the data shown in Tables 4-2, 4-3, and 4-4 entered in your bookshop database.

Table 4-2. Sample Data in the BOOK Table for Testing Transactions

ISBN	BOOK_NAME	PRICE
0001	The First Book	30

Table 4-3. Sample Data in the BOOK_STOCK Table for Testing Transactions

ISBN	STOCK
0001	10

Table 4-4. Sample Data in the ACCOUNT Table for Testing Transactions

USERNAME	BALANCE
user1	20

Then write the following Main class for purchasing the book with ISBN 0001 by the user user1. Because that user's account has only $20, it is not sufficient to purchase the book.

```
package com.apress.springenterpriserecipes.bookshop.spring;

import org.springframework.context.ApplicationContext;
import org.springframework.context.support.ClassPathXmlApplicationContext;

public class Main {

    public static void main(String[] args) {
        ApplicationContext context =
            new ClassPathXmlApplicationContext("beans.xml");

        BookShop bookShop = (BookShop) context.getBean("bookShop");
        bookShop.purchase("0001", "user1");
    }
}
```

When you run this application, you will encounter a SQLException because the CHECK constraint of the ACCOUNT table has been violated. This is an expected result because you were trying to debit more than the account balance. However, if you check the stock for this book in the BOOK_STOCK table, you will find that it was accidentally deducted by this unsuccessful operation! The reason is that you executed the second SQL statement to deduct the stock before you got an exception in the third statement.

As you can see, the lack of transaction management causes your data to be left in an inconsistent state. To avoid this inconsistency, your three SQL statements for the purchase() operation should be executed within a single transaction. Once any of the actions in a transaction fail, the entire transaction should be rolled back to undo all changes made by the executed actions.

Managing Transactions with JDBC Commit and Rollback

When using JDBC to update a database, by default each SQL statement will be committed immediately after its execution. This behavior is known as *auto-commit*. However, it does not allow you to manage transactions for your operations.

JDBC supports the primitive transaction management strategy of explicitly calling the commit() and rollback() methods on a connection. But before you can do that, you must turn off auto-commit, which is turned on by default.

```
package com.apress.springenterpriserecipes.bookshop.spring;
...
public class JdbcBookShop implements BookShop {
    ...
    public void purchase(String isbn, String username) {
        Connection conn = null;
        try {
            conn = dataSource.getConnection();
            conn.setAutoCommit(false);
            ...
            conn.commit();
        } catch (SQLException e) {
            if (conn != null) {
                try {
                    conn.rollback();
                } catch (SQLException e1) {}
            }
            throw new RuntimeException(e);
        } finally {
            if (conn != null) {
                try {
                    conn.close();
                } catch (SQLException e) {}
            }
        }
    }
}
```

The auto-commit behavior of a database connection can be altered by calling the setAutoCommit() method. By default, auto-commit is turned on to commit each SQL statement immediately after its execution. To enable transaction management, you must turn off this default behavior and commit the connection only when all the SQL statements have been executed successfully. If any of the statements go wrong, you must roll back all changes made by this connection.

Now, if you run your application again, the book stock will not be deducted when the user's balance is insufficient to purchase the book.

Although you can manage transactions by explicitly committing and rolling back JDBC connections, the code required for this purpose is boilerplate code that you have to repeat for different methods. Moreover, this code is JDBC specific, so once you have chosen another data access technology, it needs to be changed also. Spring's transaction support offers a set of technology-independent facilities, including transaction managers (e.g., `org.springframework.transaction.PlatformTransactionManager`), a transaction template (e.g., `org.springframework.transaction.support.TransactionTemplate`), and transaction declaration support to simplify your transaction management tasks.

4-2. Choosing a Transaction Manager Implementation

Problem

Typically, if your application involves only a single data source, you can simply manage transactions by calling the `commit()` and `rollback()` methods on a database connection. However, if your transactions extend across multiple data sources or you prefer to make use of the transaction management capabilities provided by your Java EE application server, you may choose the Java Transaction API (JTA). Besides, you may have to call different proprietary transaction APIs for different object/relational mapping frameworks such as Hibernate and JPA.

As a result, you have to deal with different transaction APIs for different technologies. It would be hard for you to switch from one set of APIs to another.

Solution

Spring abstracts a general set of transaction facilities from different transaction management APIs. As an application developer, you can simply utilize Spring's transaction facilities without having to know much about the underlying transaction APIs. With these facilities, your transaction management code will be independent of any specific transaction technology.

Spring's core transaction management abstraction is `PlatformTransactionManager`. It encapsulates a set of technology-independent methods for transaction management. Remember that a transaction manager is needed no matter which transaction management strategy (programmatic or declarative) you choose in Spring. The `PlatformTransactionManager` interface provides three methods for working with transactions:

- `TransactionStatus getTransaction(TransactionDefinition definition) throws TransactionException`

- `void commit(TransactionStatus status) throws TransactionException;`

- `void rollback(TransactionStatus status) throws TransactionException;`

How It Works

PlatformTransactionManager is a general interface for all Spring transaction managers. Spring has several built-in implementations of this interface for use with different transaction management APIs:

- If you have to deal with only a single data source in your application and access it with JDBC, DataSourceTransactionManager should meet your needs.

- If you are using JTA for transaction management on a Java EE application server, you should use JtaTransactionManager to look up a transaction from the application server. Additionally, JtaTransactionManager is appropriate for distributed transactions (transactions that span multiple resources). Note that while it's common to use a JTA transaction manager to integrate the application servers' transaction manager, there's nothing stopping you from using a stand-alone JTA transaction manager such as Atomikos.

- If you are using an object/relational mapping framework to access a database, you should choose a corresponding transaction manager for this framework, such as HibernateTransactionManager and JpaTransactionManager.

Figure 4-2 shows the common implementations of the PlatformTransactionManager interface in Spring.

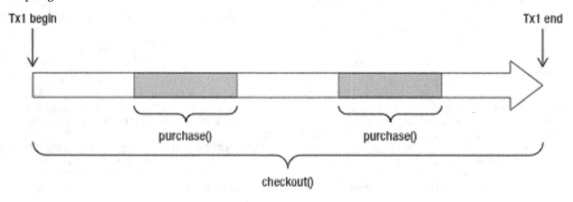

Figure 4-2. Common implementations of the PlatformTransactionManager interface

A transaction manager is declared in the Spring IoC container as a normal bean. For example, the following bean configuration declares a DataSourceTransactionManager instance. It requires the dataSource property to be set so that it can manage transactions for connections made by this data source.

```
<bean id="transactionManager"
    class="org.springframework.jdbc.datasource.DataSourceTransactionManager">
    <property name="dataSource"ref="dataSource"/>
</bean>
```

4-3. Managing Transactions Programmatically with the Transaction Manager API

Problem

You need to precisely control when to commit and roll back transactions in your business methods, but you don't want to deal with the underlying transaction API directly.

Solution

Spring's transaction manager provides a technology-independent API that allows you to start a new transaction (or obtain the currently active transaction) by calling the getTransaction() method and manage it by calling the commit() and rollback() methods. Because PlatformTransactionManager is an abstract unit for transaction management, the methods you called for transaction management are guaranteed to be technology independent.

How It Works

To demonstrate how to use the transaction manager API, let's create a new class, TransactionalJdbcBookShop, which will make use of the Spring JDBC template. Because it has to deal with a transaction manager, you add a property of type PlatformTransactionManager and allow it to be injected via a setter method.

```
package com.apress.springenterpriserecipes.bookshop.spring;

import org.springframework.dao.DataAccessException;
import org.springframework.jdbc.core.support.JdbcDaoSupport;
import org.springframework.transaction.PlatformTransactionManager;
import org.springframework.transaction.TransactionDefinition;
import org.springframework.transaction.TransactionStatus;
import org.springframework.transaction.support.DefaultTransactionDefinition;

public class TransactionalJdbcBookShop extends JdbcDaoSupport implements
        BookShop {

    private PlatformTransactionManager transactionManager;

    public void setTransactionManager(
            PlatformTransactionManager transactionManager) {
        this.transactionManager = transactionManager;
    }

    public void purchase(String isbn, String username) {
        TransactionDefinition def = new DefaultTransactionDefinition();
        TransactionStatus status = transactionManager.getTransaction(def);

        try {
            int price = getJdbcTemplate().queryForInt(
                    "SELECT PRICE FROM BOOK WHERE ISBN = ?",
                    new Object[] { isbn });
```

```
        getJdbcTemplate().update(
                "UPDATE BOOK_STOCK SET STOCK = STOCK - 1 "+
                "WHERE ISBN = ?", new Object[] { isbn });

        getJdbcTemplate().update(
                "UPDATE ACCOUNT SET BALANCE = BALANCE - ? "+
                "WHERE USERNAME = ?",
                new Object[] { price, username });

        transactionManager.commit(status);
    } catch (DataAccessException e) {
        transactionManager.rollback(status);
        throw e;
    }
  }
}
```

Before you start a new transaction, you have to specify the transaction attributes in a transaction definition object of type TransactionDefinition. For this example, you can simply create an instance of DefaultTransactionDefinition to use the default transaction attributes.

Once you have a transaction definition, you can ask the transaction manager to start a new transaction with that definition by calling the getTransaction() method. Then it will return a TransactionStatus object to keep track of the transaction status. If all the statements execute successfully, you ask the transaction manager to commit this transaction by passing in the transaction status. Because all exceptions thrown by the Spring JDBC template are subclasses of DataAccessException, you ask the transaction manager to roll back the transaction when this kind of exception is caught.

In this class, you have declared the transaction manager property of the general type PlatformTransactionManager. Now you have to inject an appropriate transaction manager implementation. Because you are dealing with only a single data source and accessing it with JDBC, you should choose DataSourceTransactionManager. Here you also wire a dataSource because the class is a subclass of Spring's JdbcDaoSupport, which requires it.

```
<beans ...>
    ...
    <bean id="transactionManager"
        class="org.springframework.jdbc.datasource.DataSourceTransactionManager">
        <property name="dataSource"ref="dataSource"/>
    </bean>

    <bean id="bookShop"
        class="com.apress.springenterpriserecipes.bookshop.spring.➥
TransactionalJdbcBookShop">
        <property name="dataSource"ref="dataSource"/>
        <property name="transactionManager"ref="transactionManager"/>
    </bean>
</beans>
```

4-4. Managing Transactions Programmatically with a Transaction Template

Problem

Suppose that you have a code block, but not the entire body, of a business method that has the following transaction requirements:

- Start a new transaction at the beginning of the block.
- Commit the transaction after the block completes successfully.
- Roll back the transaction if an exception is thrown in the block.

If you call Spring's transaction manager API directly, the transaction management code can be generalized in a technology-independent manner. However, you may not want to repeat the boilerplate code for each similar code block.

Solution

As with the JDBC template, Spring also provides a TransactionTemplate to help you control the overall transaction management process and transaction exception handling. You just have to encapsulate your code block in a callback class that implements the `TransactionCallback<T>` interface and pass it to the `TransactionTemplate`'s execute method for execution. In this way, you don't need to repeat the boilerplate transaction management code for this block. The template objects that Spring provides are lightweight, and usually can be discarded or re-created with no performance impact. A JDBC template can be re-created on-the-fly with a `DataSource` reference, for example, and so too can a `TransactionTemplate` be re-created by providing a reference to a transaction manager. You can, of course, simply create one in your Spring application context, too.

How It Works

A `TransactionTemplate` is created on a transaction manager just as a JDBC template is created on a data source. A transaction template executes a transaction callback object that encapsulates a transactional code block. You can implement the callback interface either as a separate class or as an inner class. If it's implemented as an inner class, you have to make the method arguments final for it to access.

```
package com.apress.springenterpriserecipes.bookshop.spring;
...
import org.springframework.transaction.PlatformTransactionManager;
import org.springframework.transaction.TransactionStatus;
import org.springframework.transaction.support.TransactionCallbackWithoutResult;
import org.springframework.transaction.support.TransactionTemplate;

public class TransactionalJdbcBookShop extends JdbcDaoSupport implements
        BookShop {

    private PlatformTransactionManager transactionManager;

    public void setTransactionManager(
```

```
            PlatformTransactionManager transactionManager) {
        this.transactionManager = transactionManager;
    }

    public void purchase(final String isbn, final String username) {
        TransactionTemplate transactionTemplate =
            new TransactionTemplate(transactionManager);

        transactionTemplate.execute(new TransactionCallbackWithoutResult() {

            protected void doInTransactionWithoutResult(
                    TransactionStatus status) {

                int price = getJdbcTemplate().queryForInt(
                        "SELECT PRICE FROM BOOK WHERE ISBN = ?",
                        new Object[] { isbn });

                getJdbcTemplate().update(
                        "UPDATE BOOK_STOCK SET STOCK = STOCK - 1 "+
                        "WHERE ISBN = ?", new Object[] { isbn });

                getJdbcTemplate().update(
                        "UPDATE ACCOUNT SET BALANCE = BALANCE - ? "+
                        "WHERE USERNAME = ?",
                        new Object[] { price, username });
            }
        });
    }
}
```

A TransactionTemplate can accept a transaction callback object that implements either the TransactionCallback<T> or an instance of the one implementor of that interface provided by the framework, the TransactionCallbackWithoutResult class. For the code block in the purchase() method for deducting the book stock and account balance, there's no result to be returned, so TransactionCallbackWithoutResult is fine. For any code blocks with return values, you should implement the TransactionCallback<T> interface instead. The return value of the callback object will finally be returned by the template's T execute() method. The main benefit is that the responsibility of starting, rolling back, or commiting the transaction has been removed.

During the execution of the callback object, if it throws an unchecked exception (e.g., RuntimeException and DataAccessException fall into this category), or if you explicitly called setRollbackOnly() on the TransactionStatus argument in the doInTransaction method, the transaction will be rolled back. Otherwise, it will be committed after the callback object completes.

In the bean configuration file, the bookshop bean still requires a transaction manager to create a TransactionTemplate.

```
<beans ...>
    ...
    <bean id="transactionManager"
        class="org.springframework.jdbc.datasource.DataSourceTransactionManager">
        <property name="dataSource"ref="dataSource"/>
    </bean>
```

```
<bean id="bookShop"
    class="com.apress.springenterpriserecipes.bookshop.spring. ➥
TransactionalJdbcBookShop">
    <property name="dataSource"ref="dataSource"/>
    <property name="transactionManager"ref="transactionManager"/>
</bean>
</beans>
```

You can also have the IoC container inject a transaction template instead of creating it directly. Because a transaction template handles all transactions, there's no need for your class to refer to the transaction manager any more.

```
package com.apress.springenterpriserecipes.bookshop.spring;
...
import org.springframework.transaction.support.TransactionTemplate;

public class TransactionalJdbcBookShop extends JdbcDaoSupport implements
        BookShop {

    private TransactionTemplate transactionTemplate;

    public void setTransactionTemplate(
            TransactionTemplate transactionTemplate) {
        this.transactionTemplate = transactionTemplate;
    }

    public void purchase(final String isbn, final String username) {
        transactionTemplate.execute(new TransactionCallbackWithoutResult() {
            protected void doInTransactionWithoutResult(TransactionStatus status) {
                ...
            }
        });
    }
}
```

Then you define a transaction template in the bean configuration file and inject it, instead of the transaction manager, into your book shop bean. Notice that the transaction template instance can be used for more than one transactional bean because it is a thread-safe object. Finally, don't forget to set the transaction manager property for your transaction template.

```
<beans ...>
    ...
    <bean id="transactionManager"
        class="org.springframework.jdbc.datasource.DataSourceTransactionManager">
        <property name="dataSource"ref="dataSource"/>
    </bean>

    <bean id="transactionTemplate"
        class="org.springframework.transaction.support.TransactionTemplate">
        <property name="transactionManager"ref="transactionManager"/>
    </bean>
```

```
    <bean id="bookShop"
        class="com.apress.springenterpriserecipes.bookshop.spring.➦
TransactionalJdbcBookShop">
        <property name="dataSource"ref="dataSource"/>
        <property name="transactionTemplate"ref="transactionTemplate"/>
    </bean>
</beans>
```

4-5. Managing Transactions Declaratively with Transaction Advices

Problem

Because transaction management is a kind of crosscutting concern, you should manage transactions declaratively with the AOP approach available from Spring 2.x onward.

Solution

Spring (since version 2.0) offers a transaction advice that can be easily configured via the `<tx:advice>` element defined in the tx schema. This advice can be enabled with the AOP configuration facilities defined in the aop schema.

How It Works

To enable declarative transaction management, you can declare a transaction advice via the `<tx:advice>` element defined in the tx schema, so you have to add this schema definition to the `<beans>` root element beforehand. Once you have declared this advice, you need to associate it with a pointcut. Because a transaction advice is declared outside the `<aop:config>` element, it cannot link with a pointcut directly. You have to declare an advisor in the `<aop:config>` element to associate an advice with a pointcut.

■Note   Because Spring AOP uses the AspectJ pointcut expressions to define pointcuts, you have to include `aspectjweaver.jar` (located in the `lib/aspectj` directory of the Spring installation) in your classpath. If you're using Maven, then the dependency is as follows:

```
<dependency>
        <groupId>org.aspectj</groupId>
        <artifactId>aspectjweaver</artifactId>
        <version>1.6.2</version>
</dependency>
```

```
<beans xmlns="http://www.springframework.org/schema/beans"
    xmlns:xsi="http://www.w3.org/2001/XMLSchema-instance"
    xmlns:tx="http://www.springframework.org/schema/tx"
    xmlns:aop="http://www.springframework.org/schema/aop"
    xsi:schemaLocation="http://www.springframework.org/schema/beans
        http://www.springframework.org/schema/beans/spring-beans-3.0.xsd
        http://www.springframework.org/schema/tx
        http://www.springframework.org/schema/tx/spring-tx-3.0.xsd
        http://www.springframework.org/schema/aop
        http://www.springframework.org/schema/aop/spring-aop-3.0.xsd">

    <tx:advice id="bookShopTxAdvice"
        transaction-manager="transactionManager">
        <tx:attributes>
            <tx:method name="purchase"/>
        </tx:attributes>
    </tx:advice>

    <aop:config>
        <aop:pointcut id="bookShopOperation"expression=
            "execution(* com.apress.springenterpriserecipes.bookshop.spring. ➥
BookShop.*(..))"/>
        <aop:advisor advice-ref="bookShopTxAdvice"
            pointcut-ref="bookShopOperation"/>
    </aop:config>
    ...
    <bean id="transactionManager"
        class="org.springframework.jdbc.datasource.DataSourceTransactionManager">
        <property name="dataSource"ref="dataSource"/>
    </bean>

    <bean id="bookShop"
        class="com.apress.springenterpriserecipes.bookshop.spring.JdbcBookShop">
        <property name="dataSource"ref="dataSource"/>
    </bean>
</beans>
```

The preceding AspectJ pointcut expression matches all the methods declared in the BookShop interface. However, because Spring AOP is based on proxies, it can apply only to public methods. Thus only public methods can be made transactional with Spring AOP.

Each transaction advice requires an identifier and a reference to a transaction manager in the IoC container. If you don't specify a transaction manager explicitly, Spring will search the application context for a TransactionManager with a bean name of transactionManager. The methods that require transaction management are specified with multiple <tx:method> elements inside the <tx:attributes> element. The method name supports wildcards for you to match a group of methods. You can also define transaction attributes for each group of methods, but let's use the default attributes for simplicity's sake. The defaults are shown in Table 4-5.

Table 4-5. Attributes Used with tx:attributes

Attribute	Required	Default	Description
name	Yes	n/a	The name of the methods against which the advice will be applied. You can use wildcards (*).
propagation	No	REQUIRED	The propagation specification for the transaction.
isolation	No	DEFAULT	The isolation level specification for the transaction.
timeout	No	-1	How long the transaction will try to commit before it times out.
			Continued
read-only	No	False	Tells the container whether the transaction is read-only or not. This is a Spring-specific setting. If you're used to standard Java EE transaction configuration, you won't have seen this setting before. Its meaning is different for different resources (e.g., databases have a different notion of "read-only"than a JMS queue does).
rollback-for	No	N/A	Comma-delimited list of fully qualified Exception types that, when thrown from the method, the transaction should rollback for.
no-rollback-for	No	N/A	A comma-delimited list of Exception types that, when thrown from the method, the transaction should ignore and not roll back for.

Now you can retrieve the bookShop bean from the Spring IoC container to use. Because this bean's methods are matched by the pointcut, Spring will return a proxy that has transaction management enabled for this bean.

```
package com.apress.springenterpriserecipes.bookshop.aspectj;
...
public class Main {

    public static void main(String[] args) {
        ...
        BookShop bookShop = (BookShop) context.getBean("bookShop");
        bookShop.purchase("0001", "user1");
    }
}
```

4-6. Managing Transactions Declaratively with the @Transactional Annotation

Problem

Declaring transactions in the bean configuration file requires knowledge of AOP concepts such as pointcuts, advices, and advisors. Developers who lack this knowledge might find it hard to enable declarative transaction management.

Solution

In addition to declaring transactions in the bean configuration file with pointcuts, advices, and advisors, Spring allows you to declare transactions simply by annotating your transactional methods with @Transactional and enabling the <tx:annotation-driven> element. However, Java 1.5 or higher is required to use this approach. Note that although you could apply the annotation to an interface method, it's not a recommended practice.

How It Works

To define a method as transactional, you can simply annotate it with @Transactional. Note that you should only annotate public methods due to the proxy-based limitations of Spring AOP.

```
package com.apress.springenterpriserecipes.bookshop.spring;
...
import org.springframework.transaction.annotation.Transactional;

public class JdbcBookShop extends JdbcDaoSupport implements BookShop {

    @Transactional
    public void purchase(String isbn, String username) {

        int price = getJdbcTemplate().queryForInt(
            "SELECT PRICE FROM BOOK WHERE ISBN = ?",
            new Object[] { isbn });

        getJdbcTemplate().update(
            "UPDATE BOOK_STOCK SET STOCK = STOCK - 1 "+
            "WHERE ISBN = ?", new Object[] { isbn });

        getJdbcTemplate().update(
            "UPDATE ACCOUNT SET BALANCE = BALANCE - ? "+
            "WHERE USERNAME = ?",
            new Object[] { price, username });
    }
}
```

You may apply the @Transactional annotation at the method level or the class level. When applying this annotation to a class, all of the public methods within this class will be defined as transactional. Although you can apply @Transactional to interfaces or method declarations in an interface, it's not recommended because it may not work properly with class-based proxies (i.e., CGLIB proxies).

In the bean configuration file, you only have to enable the <tx:annotation-driven> element and specify a transaction manager for it. That's all you need to make it work. Spring will advise methods with @Transactional, or methods in a class with @Transactional, from beans declared in the IoC container. As a result, Spring can manage transactions for these methods.

```
<beans xmlns="http://www.springframework.org/schema/beans"
  xmlns:xsi="http://www.w3.org/2001/XMLSchema-instance"
  xmlns:tx="http://www.springframework.org/schema/tx"
  xsi:schemaLocation="http://www.springframework.org/schema/beans
 http://www.springframework.org/schema/beans/spring-beans-3.0.xsd
    http://www.springframework.org/schema/tx
http://www.springframework.org/schema/tx/spring-tx-3.0.xsd">
    <tx:annotation-driven transaction-manager="transactionManager"/>
    ...
    <bean id="transactionManager"
        class="org.springframework.jdbc.datasource.DataSourceTransactionManager">
        <property name="dataSource"ref="dataSource"/>
    </bean>

    <bean id="bookShop"
        class="com.apress.springenterpriserecipes.bookshop.spring.JdbcBookShop">
        <property name="dataSource"ref="dataSource"/>
    </bean>
</beans>
```

In fact, you can omit the transaction-manager attribute in the <tx:annotation-driven> element if your transaction manager has the name transactionManager. This element will automatically detect a transaction manager with this name. You have to specify a transaction manager only when it has a different name.

```
<beans ...>
    <tx:annotation-driven />
    ...
</beans>
```

4-7. Setting the Propagation Transaction Attribute

Problem

When a transactional method is called by another method, it is necessary to specify how the transaction should be propagated. For example, the method may continue to run within the existing transaction, or it may start a new transaction and run within its own transaction.

Solution

A transaction's propagation behavior can be specified by the *propagation* transaction attribute. Spring defines seven propagation behaviors, as shown in Table 4-6. These behaviors are defined in the `org.springframework.transaction.TransactionDefinition` interface. Note that not all types of transaction managers support all of these propagation behaviors. Their behavior is contingent on the underlying resource. Databases, for example, may support varying isolation levels, which constrains what propagation behaviors the transaction manager can support.

Table 4-6. Propagation Behaviors Supported by Spring

Propagation	Description
REQUIRED	If there's an existing transaction in progress, the current method should run within this transaction. Otherwise, it should start a new transaction and run within its own transaction.
REQUIRES_NEW	The current method must start a new transaction and run within its own transaction. If there's an existing transaction in progress, it should be suspended.
SUPPORTS	If there's an existing transaction in progress, the current method can run within this transaction. Otherwise, it is not necessary to run within a transaction.
NOT_SUPPORTED	The current method should not run within a transaction. If there's an existing transaction in progress, it should be suspended.
MANDATORY	The current method must run within a transaction. If there's no existing transaction in progress, an exception will be thrown.
NEVER	The current method should not run within a transaction. If there's an existing transaction in progress, an exception will be thrown.
NESTED	If there's an existing transaction in progress, the current method should run within the nested transaction (supported by the JDBC 3.0 save point feature) of this transaction. Otherwise, it should start a new transaction and run within its own transaction. This feature is unique to Spring (whereas the previous propagation behaviors have analogs in Java EE transaction propagation). The behavior is useful for situations such as batch processing, in which you've got a long running process (imagine processing 1 million records) and you want to chunk the commits on the batch. So you commit every 10,000 records. If something goes wrong, you roll back the nested transaction and you've lost only 10,000 records' worth of work (as opposed to the entire 1 million).

How It Works

Transaction propagation happens when a transactional method is called by another method. For example, suppose that a customer would like to check out all books to purchase at the book shop cashier. To support this operation, you define the Cashier interface as follows:

```
package com.apress.springenterpriserecipes.bookshop.spring;
...
public interface Cashier {

    public void checkout(List<String> isbns, String username);
}
```

You can implement this interface by delegating the purchases to a book shop bean by calling its purchase() method multiple times. Note that the checkout() method is made transactional by applying the @Transactional annotation.

```
package com.apress.springenterpriserecipes.bookshop.spring;
...
import org.springframework.transaction.annotation.Transactional;

public class BookShopCashier implements Cashier {

    private BookShop bookShop;

    public void setBookShop(BookShop bookShop) {
        this.bookShop = bookShop;
    }

    @Transactional
    public void checkout(List<String> isbns, String username) {
        for (String isbn : isbns) {
            bookShop.purchase(isbn, username);
        }
    }
}
```

Then define a cashier bean in your bean configuration file and refer to the book shop bean for purchasing books.

```
<bean id="cashier"
    class="com.apress.springenterpriserecipes.bookshop.spring.BookShopCashier">
    <property name="bookShop"ref="bookShop"/>
</bean>
```

To illustrate the propagation behavior of a transaction, enter the data shown in Tables 4-7, 4-8, and 4-9 in your bookshop database.

Table 4-7. Sample Data in the BOOK Table for Testing Propagation Behaviors

ISBN	BOOK_NAME	PRICE
0001	The First Book	30
0002	The Second Book	50

Table 4-8. Sample Data in the BOOK_STOCK Table for Testing Propagation Behaviors

ISBN	STOCK
0001	10
0002	10

Table 4-9. Sample Data in the ACCOUNT Table for Testing Propagation Behaviors

USERNAME	BALANCE
user1	40

The REQUIRED Propagation Behavior

When the user user1 checks out the two books from the cashier, the balance is sufficient to purchase the first book, but not the second.

```
package com.apress.springenterpriserecipes.bookshop.spring;
...
public class Main {

    public static void main(String[] args) {
        ...
        Cashier cashier = (Cashier) context.getBean("cashier");
        List<String> isbnList =
                Arrays.asList(new String[] { "0001", "0002"});
        cashier.checkout(isbnList, "user1");
    }
}
```

When the book shop's purchase() method is called by another transactional method, such as checkout(), it will run within the existing transaction by default. This default propagation behavior is called REQUIRED. That means there will be only one transaction whose boundary is the beginning and ending of the checkout() method. This transaction will be committed only at the end of the checkout() method. As a result, the user can purchase none of the books. Figure 4-3 illustrates the REQUIRED propagation behavior.

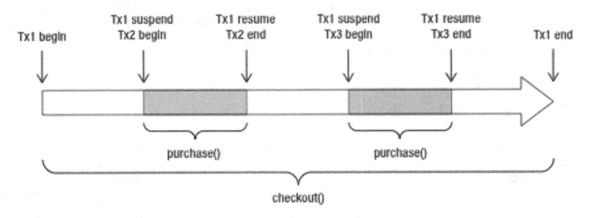

Figure 4-3. The REQUIRED transaction propagation behavior

However, if the purchase() method is called by a non-transactional method and there's no existing transaction in progress, it will start a new transaction and run within its own transaction.

The propagation transaction attribute can be defined in the @Transactional annotation. For example, you can set the REQUIRED behavior for this attribute as follows. In fact, this is unnecessary, because it's the default behavior.

```
package com.apress.springenterpriserecipes.bookshop.spring;
...
import org.springframework.transaction.annotation.Propagation;
import org.springframework.transaction.annotation.Transactional;

public class JdbcBookShop extends JdbcDaoSupport implements BookShop {
    ...
    @Transactional(propagation = Propagation.REQUIRED)
    public void purchase(String isbn, String username) {
        ...
    }
}
```

```
package com.apress.springenterpriserecipes.bookshop.spring;
...
import org.springframework.transaction.annotation.Propagation;
import org.springframework.transaction.annotation.Transactional;

public class BookShopCashier implements Cashier {
    ...
    @Transactional(propagation = Propagation.REQUIRED)
    public void checkout(List<String> isbns, String username) {
        ...
    }
}
```

The REQUIRES_NEW Propagation Behavior

Another common propagation behavior is REQUIRES_NEW. It indicates that the method must start a new transaction and run within its new transaction. If there's an existing transaction in progress, it should be suspended first (as, for example, with the checkout method on BookShopCashier, with a propagation of REQUIRED).

```
package com.apress.springenterpriserecipes.bookshop.spring;
...
import org.springframework.transaction.annotation.Propagation;
import org.springframework.transaction.annotation.Transactional;

public class JdbcBookShop extends JdbcDaoSupport implements BookShop {
    ...
    @Transactional(propagation = Propagation.REQUIRES_NEW)
    public void purchase(String isbn, String username) {
        ...
    }
}
```

In this case, there will be three transactions started in total. The first transaction is started by the checkout() method, but when the first purchase() method is called, the first transaction will be suspended and a new transaction will be started. At the end of the first purchase() method, the new transaction completes and commits. When the second purchase() method is called, another new transaction will be started. However, this transaction will fail and roll back. As a result, the first book will be purchased successfully while the second will not. Figure 4-4 illustrates the REQUIRES_NEW propagation behavior.

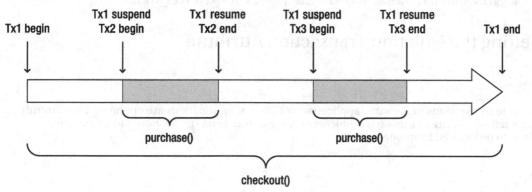

Figure 4-4. The REQUIRES_NEW transaction propagation behavior

Setting the Propagation Attribute in Transaction Advices, Proxies, and APIs

In a Spring transaction advice, the propagation transaction attribute can be specified in the `<tx:method>` element as follows:

```
<tx:advice ...>
    <tx:attributes>
        <tx:method name="..."
            propagation="REQUIRES_NEW"/>
    </tx:attributes>
</tx:advice>
```

In classic Spring AOP, the propagation transaction attribute can be specified in the transaction attributes of `TransactionInterceptor` and `TransactionProxyFactoryBean` as follows:

```
<property name="transactionAttributes">
    <props>
        <prop key="...">PROPAGATION_REQUIRES_NEW</prop>
    </props>
</property>
```

In Spring's transaction management API, the propagation transaction attribute can be specified in a `DefaultTransactionDefinition` object and then passed to a transaction manager's `getTransaction()` method or a transaction template's constructor.

```
DefaultTransactionDefinition def = new DefaultTransactionDefinition();
def.setPropagationBehavior(TransactionDefinition.PROPAGATION_REQUIRES_NEW);
```

4-8. Setting the Isolation Transaction Attribute

Problem

When multiple transactions of the same application or different applications are operating concurrently on the same dataset, many unexpected problems may arise. You must specify how you expect your transactions to be isolated from one another.

Solution

The problems caused by concurrent transactions can be categorized into four types:

Dirty read: For two transactions T1 and T2, T1 reads a field that has been updated by T2 but not yet committed. Later, if T2 rolls back, the field read by T1 will be temporary and invalid.

Non-repeatable read: For two transactions T1 and T2, T1 reads a field and then T2 updates the field. Later, if T1 reads the same field again, the value will be different.

Phantom read: For two transactions T1 and T2, T1 reads some rows from a table and then T2 inserts new rows into the table. Later, if T1 reads the same table again, there will be additional rows.

Lost Updates: For two transactions T1 and T2, they both select a row for update and, based on the state of that row, make an update to it. Thus, one overwrites the other when what should've happened is that the second transaction to commit should have waited until the first one committed before it performed its selection.

In theory, transactions should be completely isolated from each other (i.e., serializable) to avoid all the mentioned problems. However, this isolation level will have great impact on performance because transactions have to run in serial order. In practice, transactions can run in lower isolation levels in order to improve performance.

A transaction's isolation level can be specified by the *isolation* transaction attribute. Spring supports five isolation levels, as shown in Table 4-10. These levels are defined in the `org.springframework.transaction.TransactionDefinition` interface.

Table 4-10. *Isolation Levels Supported by Spring*

Isolation	Description
DEFAULT	Uses the default isolation level of the underlying database. For most databases, the default isolation level is READ_COMMITTED.
READ_UNCOMMITTED	Allows a transaction to read uncommitted changes by other transactions. The dirty read, non-repeatable read, and phantom read problems may occur.
READ_COMMITTED	Allows a transaction to read only those changes that have been committed by other transactions. The dirty read problem can be avoided, but the non-repeatable read and phantom read problems may still occur.
REPEATABLE_READ	Ensures that a transaction can read identical values from a field multiple times. For the duration of this transaction, updates made by other transactions to this field are prohibited. The dirty read and non-repeatable read problems can be avoided, but the phantom read problem may still occur.
SERIALIZABLE	Ensures that a transaction can read identical rows from a table multiple times. For the duration of this transaction, inserts, updates, and deletes made by other transactions to this table are prohibited. All the concurrency problems can be avoided, but the performance will be low.

Note that transaction isolation is supported by the underlying database engine but not an application or a framework. However, not all database engines support all these isolation levels. You can change the isolation level of a JDBC connection by calling the `setTransactionIsolation()` method on the `java.sql.Connection` interface.

How It Works

To illustrate the problems caused by concurrent transactions, let's add two new operations to your book shop for increasing and checking the book stock.

```
package com.apress.springenterpriserecipes.bookshop.spring;

public interface BookShop {
    ...
    public void increaseStock(String isbn, int stock);
    public int checkStock(String isbn);
}
```

Then you implement these operations as follows. Note that these two operations should also be declared as transactional.

```
package com.apress.springenterpriserecipes.bookshop.spring;
...
import org.springframework.transaction.annotation.Transactional;

public class JdbcBookShop extends JdbcDaoSupport implements BookShop {
    ...
    @Transactional
    public void increaseStock(String isbn, int stock) {
        String threadName = Thread.currentThread().getName();
        System.out.println(threadName + "- Prepare to increase book stock");

        getJdbcTemplate().update(
                "UPDATE BOOK_STOCK SET STOCK = STOCK + ? "+
                "WHERE ISBN = ?",
                new Object[] { stock, isbn });

        System.out.println(threadName + "- Book stock increased by "+ stock);
        sleep(threadName);

        System.out.println(threadName + "- Book stock rolled back");
        throw new RuntimeException("Increased by mistake");
    }

    @Transactional
    public int checkStock(String isbn) {
        String threadName = Thread.currentThread().getName();
        System.out.println(threadName + "- Prepare to check book stock");

        int stock = getJdbcTemplate().queryForInt(
                "SELECT STOCK FROM BOOK_STOCK WHERE ISBN = ?",
                new Object[] { isbn });
```

```
        System.out.println(threadName + "- Book stock is "+ stock);
        sleep(threadName);

        return stock;
    }

    private void sleep(String threadName) {
        System.out.println(threadName + "- Sleeping");
        try {
            Thread.sleep(10000);
        } catch (InterruptedException e) {}
        System.out.println(threadName + "- Wake up");
    }
}
```

To simulate concurrency, your operations need to be executed by multiple threads. You can track the current status of the operations through the `println` statements. For each operation, you print a couple of messages to the console around the SQL statement's execution. The messages should include the thread name for you to know which thread is currently executing the operation.

After each operation executes the SQL statement, you ask the thread to sleep for 10 seconds. As you know, the transaction will be committed or rolled back immediately once the operation completes. Inserting a sleep statement can help to postpone the commit or rollback. For the `increase()` operation, you eventually throw a `RuntimeException` to cause the transaction to roll back.

Before you start with the isolation level examples, enter the data from Tables 4-11 and 4-12 into your bookshop database. (Note that the `ACCOUNT` table isn't needed in this example.)

Table 4-11. Sample Data in the BOOK Table for Testing Isolation Levels

ISBN	BOOK_NAME	PRICE
0001	The First Book	30

Table 4-12. Sample Data in the BOOK_STOCK Table for Testing Isolation Levels

ISBN	STOCK
0001	10

The READ_UNCOMMITTED and READ_COMMITTED Isolation Levels

`READ_UNCOMMITTED` is the lowest isolation level that allows a transaction to read uncommitted changes made by other transactions. You can set this isolation level in the `@Transaction` annotation of your `checkStock()` method.

```
package com.apress.springenterpriserecipes.bookshop.spring;
...
import org.springframework.transaction.annotation.Isolation;
import org.springframework.transaction.annotation.Transactional;

public class JdbcBookShop extends JdbcDaoSupport implements BookShop {
    ...
    @Transactional(isolation = Isolation.READ_UNCOMMITTED)
    public int checkStock(String isbn) {
        ...
    }
}
```

You can create some threads to experiment on this transaction isolation level. In the following Main class, there are two threads you are going to create. Thread 1 increases the book stock, while thread 2 checks the book stock. Thread 1 starts 5 seconds before thread 2.

```
package com.apress.springenterpriserecipes.bookshop.spring;
...
public class Main {

    public static void main(String[] args) {
        ...
        final BookShop bookShop = (BookShop) context.getBean("bookShop");

        Thread thread1 = new Thread(new Runnable() {
            public void run() {
                try {
                    bookShop.increaseStock("0001", 5);
                } catch (RuntimeException e) {}
            }
        }, "Thread 1");

        Thread thread2 = new Thread(new Runnable() {
            public void run() {
                bookShop.checkStock("0001");
            }
        }, "Thread 2");

        thread1.start();
        try {
            Thread.sleep(5000);
        } catch (InterruptedException e) {}
        thread2.start();
    }
}
```

If you run the application, you will get the following result:

```
Thread 1_Prepare to increase book stock
Thread 1_Book stock increased by 5
Thread 1_Sleeping
Thread 2_Prepare to check book stock
Thread 2_Book stock is 15
Thread 2_Sleeping
Thread 1_Wake up
Thread 1_Book stock rolled back
Thread 2_Wake up
```

First, thread 1 increased the book stock and then went to sleep. At that time, thread 1's transaction had not yet been rolled back. While thread 1 was sleeping, thread 2 started and attempted to read the book stock. With the READ_UNCOMMITTED isolation level, thread 2 would be able to read the stock value that had been updated by an uncommitted transaction.

However, when thread 1 wakes up, its transaction will be rolled back due to a RuntimeException, so the value read by thread 2 is temporary and invalid. This problem is known as *dirty read*, because a transaction may read values that are "dirty."

To avoid the dirty read problem, you should raise the isolation level of checkStock() to READ_COMMITTED.

```java
package com.apress.springenterpriserecipes.bookshop.spring;
...
import org.springframework.transaction.annotation.Isolation;
import org.springframework.transaction.annotation.Transactional;

public class JdbcBookShop extends JdbcDaoSupport implements BookShop {
    ...
    @Transactional(isolation = Isolation.READ_COMMITTED)
    public int checkStock(String isbn) {
        ...
    }
}
```

If you run the application again, thread 2 won't be able to read the book stock until thread 1 has rolled back the transaction. In this way, the dirty read problem can be avoided by preventing a transaction from reading a field that has been updated by another uncommitted transaction.

```
Thread 1_Prepare to increase book stock
Thread 1_Book stock increased by 5
Thread 1_Sleeping
Thread 2_Prepare to check book stock
Thread 1_Wake up
Thread 1_Book stock rolled back
Thread 2_Book stock is 10
Thread 2_Sleeping
Thread 2_Wake up
```

In order that the underlying database can support the READ_COMMITTED isolation level, it may acquire an *update lock* on a row that was updated but not yet committed. Then other transactions must wait to read that row until the update lock is released, which happens when the locking transaction commits or rolls back.

The REPEATABLE_READ Isolation Level

Now let's restructure the threads to demonstrate another concurrency problem. Swap the tasks of the two threads so that thread 1 checks the book stock before thread 2 increases the book stock.

```java
package com.apress.springenterpriserecipes.bookshop.spring;
...
public class Main {

    public static void main(String[] args) {
        ...
        final BookShop bookShop = (BookShop) context.getBean("bookShop");

        Thread thread1 = new Thread(new Runnable() {
            public void run() {
                bookShop.checkStock("0001");
            }
        }, "Thread 1");

        Thread thread2 = new Thread(new Runnable() {
            public void run() {
                try {
                    bookShop.increaseStock("0001", 5);
                } catch (RuntimeException e) {}
            }
        }, "Thread 2");
```

```
        thread1.start();
        try {
            Thread.sleep(5000);
        } catch (InterruptedException e) {}
        thread2.start();
    }
}
```

If you run the application, you will get the following result:

```
Thread 1_Prepare to check book stock
Thread 1_Book stock is 10
Thread 1_Sleeping
Thread 2_Prepare to increase book stock
Thread 2_Book stock increased by 5
Thread 2_Sleeping
Thread 1_Wake up
Thread 2_Wake up
Thread 2_Book stock rolled back
```

First, thread 1 read the book stock and then went to sleep. At that time, thread 1's transaction had not yet been committed. While thread 1 was sleeping, thread 2 started and attempted to increase the book stock. With the READ_COMMITTED isolation level, thread 2 would be able to update the stock value that was read by an uncommitted transaction.

However, if thread 1 reads the book stock again, the value will be different from its first read. This problem is known as *non-repeatable read* because a transaction may read different values for the same field.

To avoid the non-repeatable read problem, you should raise the isolation level of checkStock() to REPEATABLE_READ.

```
package com.apress.springenterpriserecipes.bookshop.spring;
...
import org.springframework.transaction.annotation.Isolation;
import org.springframework.transaction.annotation.Transactional;

public class JdbcBookShop extends JdbcDaoSupport implements BookShop {
    ...
    @Transactional(isolation = Isolation.REPEATABLE_READ)
    public int checkStock(String isbn) {
        ...
    }
}
```

If you run the application again, thread 2 won't be able to update the book stock until thread 1 has committed the transaction. In this way, the non-repeatable read problem can be avoided by preventing a transaction from updating a value that has been read by another uncommitted transaction.

```
Thread 1-Prepare to check book stock
Thread 1-Book stock is 10
Thread 1-Sleeping
Thread 2-Prepare to increase book stock
Thread 1-Wake up
Thread 2-Book stock increased by 5
Thread 2-Sleeping
Thread 2-Wake up
Thread 2-Book stock rolled back
```

In order that the underlying database can support the REPEATABLE_READ isolation level, it may acquire a *read lock* on a row that was read but not yet committed. Then other transactions must wait to update the row until the read lock is released, which happens when the locking transaction commits or rolls back.

The SERIALIZABLE Isolation Level

After a transaction has read several rows from a table, another transaction inserts new rows into the same table. If the first transaction reads the same table again, it will find additional rows that are different from the first read. This problem is known as *phantom read*. Actually, phantom read is very similar to non-repeatable read, but involves multiple rows.

To avoid the phantom read problem, you should raise the isolation level to the highest: SERIALIZABLE. Notice that this isolation level is the slowest because it may acquire a read lock on the full table. In practice, you should always choose the lowest isolation level that can satisfy your requirements.

Setting the Isolation Level Attribute in Transaction Advices, Proxies, and APIs

In a Spring xxxtransaction advice, the isolation level can be specified in the `<tx:method>` element as follows:

```
<tx:advice ...>
    <tx:attributes>
        <tx:method name="*"
            isolation="REPEATABLE_READ"/>
    </tx:attributes>
</tx:advice>
```

In classic Spring AOP, the isolation level can be specified in the transaction attributes of `TransactionInterceptor` and `TransactionProxyFactoryBean` as follows:

```
<property name="transactionAttributes">
    <props>
        <prop key="...">
            PROPAGATION_REQUIRED, ISOLATION_REPEATABLE_READ
        </prop>
    </props>
</property>
```

In Spring's transaction management API, the isolation level can be specified in a
DefaultTransactionDefinition object and then passed to a transaction manager's getTransaction()
method or a transaction template's constructor.

```
DefaultTransactionDefinition def = new DefaultTransactionDefinition();
def.setIsolationLevel(TransactionDefinition.ISOLATION_REPEATABLE_READ);
```

4-9. Setting the Rollback Transaction Attribute

Problem

By default, only unchecked exceptions (i.e., of type RuntimeException and Error) will cause a transaction
to roll back, while checked exceptions will not. Sometimes you may wish to break this rule and set your
own exceptions for rolling back.

Solution

The exceptions that cause a transaction to roll back or not can be specified by the *rollback* transaction
attribute. Any exceptions not explicitly specified in this attribute will be handled by the default rollback
rule (i.e., rolling back for unchecked exceptions and not rolling back for checked exceptions).

How It Works

A transaction's rollback rule can be defined in the @Transactional annotation via the rollbackFor and
noRollbackFor attributes. These two attributes are declared as Class[], so you can specify more than one
exception for each attribute.

```
package com.apress.springenterpriserecipes.bookshop.spring;
...
import org.springframework.transaction.annotation.Propagation;
import org.springframework.transaction.annotation.Transactional;
import java.io.IOException;

public class JdbcBookShop extends JdbcDaoSupport implements BookShop {
    ...
    @Transactional(
            propagation = Propagation.REQUIRES_NEW,
            rollbackFor = IOException.class,
            noRollbackFor = ArithmeticException.class)
    public void purchase(String isbn, String username) throws Exception{
    throw new ArithmeticException();
            //throw new IOException();
    }
}
```

In a Spring transaction advice, the rollback rule can be specified in the <tx:method> element. You
can separate the exceptions with commas if there's more than one exception.

```
<tx:advice ...>
    <tx:attributes>
        <tx:method name="..."
            rollback-for="java.io.IOException"
            no-rollback-for="java.lang.ArithmeticException"/>
        ...
    </tx:attributes>
</tx:advice>
```

In classic Spring AOP, the rollback rule can be specified in the transaction attributes of TransactionInterceptor and TransactionProxyFactoryBean. The minus sign indicates an exception to cause a transaction to roll back, while the plus sign indicates an exception to cause a transaction to commit.

```
<property name="transactionAttributes">
    <props>
        <prop key="...">
            PROPAGATION_REQUIRED, -java.io.IOException,
            +java.lang.ArithmeticException
        </prop>
    </props>
</property>
```

In Spring's transaction management API, the rollback rule can be specified in a RuleBasedTransactionAttribute object. Because it implements the TransactionDefinition interface, it can be passed to a transaction manager's getTransaction() method or a transaction template's constructor.

```
RuleBasedTransactionAttribute attr = new RuleBasedTransactionAttribute();
attr.getRollbackRules().add(
    new RollbackRuleAttribute(IOException.class));
attr.getRollbackRules().add(
    new NoRollbackRuleAttribute(SendFailedException.class));
```

4-10. Setting the Timeout and Read-Only Transaction Attributes

Problem

Because a transaction may acquire locks on rows and tables, a long transaction will tie up resources and have an impact on overall performance. Besides, if a transaction only reads but does not update data, the database engine could optimize this transaction. You can specify these attributes to increase the performance of your application.

Solution

The *timeout* transaction attribute (an integer that describes seconds) indicates how long your transaction can survive before it is forced to roll back. This can prevent a long transaction from tying up resources. The *read-only* attribute indicates that this transaction will only read but not update data. The read-only flag is just a hint to enable a resource to optimize the transaction, and a resource might not necessarily cause a failure if a write is attempted.

How It Works

The timeout and read-only transaction attributes can be defined in the @Transactional annotation. Note that timeout is measured in seconds.

```
package com.apress.springenterpriserecipes.bookshop.spring;
...
import org.springframework.transaction.annotation.Isolation;
import org.springframework.transaction.annotation.Transactional;

public class JdbcBookShop extends JdbcDaoSupport implements BookShop {
    ...
    @Transactional(
            isolation = Isolation.REPEATABLE_READ,
            timeout = 30,
            readOnly = true)
    public int checkStock(String isbn) {
        ...
    }
}
```

In a Spring 2.0 transactional advice, the timeout and read-only transaction attributes can be specified in the <tx:method> element.

```
<tx:advice ...>
    <tx:attributes>
        <tx:method name="checkStock"
            timeout="30"
            read-only="true"/>
    </tx:attributes>
</tx:advice>
```

In classic Spring AOP, the timeout and read-only transaction attributes can be specified in the transaction attributes of TransactionInterceptor and TransactionProxyFactoryBean.

```
<property name="transactionAttributes">
    <props>
        <prop key="...">
            PROPAGATION_REQUIRED, timeout_30, readOnly
        </prop>
    </props>
</property>
```

In Spring's transaction management API, the timeout and read-only transaction attributes can be specified in a DefaultTransactionDefinition object and then passed to a transaction manager's getTransaction() method or a transaction template's constructor.

```
DefaultTransactionDefinition def = new DefaultTransactionDefinition();
def.setTimeout(30);
def.setReadOnly(true);
```

4-11. Managing Transactions with Load-Time Weaving

Problem

By default, Spring's declarative transaction management is enabled via its AOP framework. However, as Spring AOP can only advise public methods of beans declared in the IoC container, you are restricted to managing transactions within this scope using Spring AOP. Sometimes you may wish to manage transactions for non-public methods, or methods of objects created outside the Spring IoC container (e.g., domain objects).

Solution

Spring 2.5 also provides an AspectJ aspect named AnnotationTransactionAspect that can manage transactions for any methods of any objects, even if the methods are non-public or the objects are created outside the Spring IoC container. This aspect will manage transactions for any methods with the @Transactional annotation. You can choose either AspectJ's compile-time weaving or load-time weaving to enable this aspect.

How It Works

First of all, let's create a domain class Book, whose instances (i.e., domain objects) may be created outside the Spring IoC container.

```
package com.apress.springenterpriserecipes.bookshop.aspectj;

import org.springframework.beans.factory.annotation.Autowired;
import org.springframework.beans.factory.annotation.Configurable;
import org.springframework.jdbc.core.JdbcTemplate;

@Configurable
public class Book {

    private String isbn;
    private String name;
    private int price;

    // Constructors, Getters and Setters
    ...
```

```
private JdbcTemplate jdbcTemplate;

@Autowired
public void setJdbcTemplate(JdbcTemplate jdbcTemplate) {
    this.jdbcTemplate = jdbcTemplate;
}

public void purchase(String username) {
    jdbcTemplate.update(
            "UPDATE BOOK_STOCK SET STOCK = STOCK - 1 "+
            "WHERE ISBN = ?",
            new Object[] { isbn });

    jdbcTemplate.update(
            "UPDATE ACCOUNT SET BALANCE = BALANCE - ? "+
            "WHERE USERNAME = ?",
            new Object[] { price, username });
    }
}
```

This domain class has a purchase() method that will deduct the current book instance's stock and the user account's balance from the database. To utilize Spring's powerful JDBC support features, you can inject the JDBC template via setter injection.

You can use Spring's load-time weaving support to inject a JDBC template into book domain objects. You have to annotate this class with @Configurable to declare that this type of object is configurable in the Spring IoC container. Moreover, you can annotate the JDBC template's setter method with @Autowired to have it auto-wired.

Spring includes an AspectJ aspect, AnnotationBeanConfigurerAspect, in its aspect library for configuring object dependencies even if these objects are created outside the IoC container. To enable this aspect, you just define the <context:spring-configured> element in your bean configuration file. To weave this aspect into your domain classes at load time, you also have to define <context:load-time-weaver>. Finally, to auto-wire the JDBC template into book domain objects via @Autowired, you need <context:annotation-config> also.

■Note   To use the Spring aspect library for AspectJ in Spring 2.0 and 2.5, you have to include spring-aspects.jar (located in the dist/weaving directory of the Spring installation) in your classpath. In Spring 3.0, the jar's been renamed spring-instruments.jar. If you're using Maven, the following configuration will work. Replace ${spring.version} with the 3.0 series version you want:

```
<dependency>
<groupId>org.springframework</groupId>
<artifactId>spring-instrument</artifactId>
<version>${spring3.version}</version>
</dependency>
```

```xml
<beans xmlns="http://www.springframework.org/schema/beans"
    xmlns:xsi="http://www.w3.org/2001/XMLSchema-instance"
    xmlns:context="http://www.springframework.org/schema/context"
    xsi:schemaLocation="http://www.springframework.org/schema/beans
        http://www.springframework.org/schema/beans/spring-beans-3.0xsd
        http://www.springframework.org/schema/context
        http://www.springframework.org/schema/context/spring-context-3.0.xsd">

    <context:load-time-weaver />

    <context:annotation-config />

    <context:spring-configured />

    <bean id="dataSource"
        class="org.springframework.jdbc.datasource.DriverManagerDataSource">
        <property name="driverClassName"
            value="org.apache.derby.jdbc.ClientDriver"/>
        <property name="url"
            value="jdbc:derby://localhost:1527/bookshop;create=true"/>
        <property name="username"value="app"/>
        <property name="password"value="app"/>
    </bean>

    <bean id="jdbcTemplate"
        class="org.springframework.jdbc.core.JdbcTemplate">
        <property name="dataSource"ref="dataSource"/>
    </bean>
</beans>
```

In this bean configuration file, you can define a JDBC template on a data source and then it will be auto-wired into book domain objects for them to access the database.

Now you can create the following Main class to test this domain class. Of course, there's no transaction support at this moment.

```java
package com.apress.springenterpriserecipes.bookshop.aspectj;

import org.springframework.context.ApplicationContext;
import org.springframework.context.support.ClassPathXmlApplicationContext;

public class Main {

    public static void main(String[] args) {
        ApplicationContext context =
            new ClassPathXmlApplicationContext("beans.xml");

        Book book = new Book("0001", "My First Book", 30);
        book.purchase("user1");
    }
}
```

For a simple Java application, you can weave this aspect into your classes at load time with the Spring agent specified as a VM argument.

```
java -javaagent: spring-instrument.jar
com.apress.springenterpriserecipes.bookshop.aspectj.Main
```

To enable transaction management for a domain object's method, you can simply annotate it with @Transactional, just as you did for methods of Spring beans.

```
package com.apress.springenterpriserecipes.bookshop.aspectj;
...
import org.springframework.beans.factory.annotation.Configurable;
import org.springframework.transaction.annotation.Transactional;

@Configurable
public class Book {
    ...
    @Transactional
    public void purchase(String username) {
        ...
    }
}
```

Finally, to enable Spring's AnnotationTransactionAspect for transaction management, you just define the <tx:annotation-driven> element and set its mode to aspectj. The <tx:annotation-driven> element takes two values for the mode attribute: aspectj and proxy. aspect stipulates that the container should use load-time or compile-time weaving to enable the transaction advice. This requires the spring-aspects jar to be on the classpath, as well as the appropriate configuration at load time or compile time. Alternatively, proxy stipulates that the container should use the Spring AOP mechanisms. It's important to note that the aspect mode doesn't support configuration of the @Transactional annotation on interfaces. Then the transaction aspect will automatically get enabled. You also have to provide a transaction manager for this aspect. By default, it will look for a transaction manager whose name is transactionManager.

```
<beans xmlns="http://www.springframework.org/schema/beans"
    xmlns:xsi="http://www.w3.org/2001/XMLSchema-instance"
    xmlns:context="http://www.springframework.org/schema/context"
    xmlns:tx="http://www.springframework.org/schema/tx"
    xsi:schemaLocation="http://www.springframework.org/schema/beans
        http://www.springframework.org/schema/beans/spring-beans-3.0.xsd
        http://www.springframework.org/schema/context
        http://www.springframework.org/schema/context/spring-context-3.0.xsd
        http://www.springframework.org/schema/tx
        http://www.springframework.org/schema/tx/spring-tx-3.0.xsd">
    ...
    <tx:annotation-driven mode="aspectj"/>

    <bean id="transactionManager"
        class="org.springframework.jdbc.datasource.DataSourceTransactionManager">
        <property name="dataSource"ref="dataSource"/>
    </bean>
</beans>
```

Summary

This chapter discussed transactions and why you should use them. You explored the approach taken for transaction management historically in Java EE and then learned how the approach the Spring framework offers differs. You explored explicit use of transactions in your code as well as implicit use with annotation-driven aspects. You set up a database and used transactions to enforce valid state in the database.

In the next chapter, you will explore Spring's remoting support. Spring provides a layer to isolate your POJOs from the protocol and platform over which they are exposed to remote clients. You will explore the approach in general as well as see it applied to a few key technologies on the Java EE and Spring platforms.

CHAPTER 5

■ ■ ■

EJB, Spring Remoting, and Web Services

In this chapter, you will learn about Spring's support for various remoting technologies, such as EJB, RMI, Hessian, Burlap, HTTP Invoker, and Web Services. *Remoting* is a key technology in developing distributed applications, especially multitier enterprise applications. It allows different applications or components, running in different JVMs or on different machines, to communicate with each other using a specific protocol.

Spring's remoting support is consistent across different remoting technologies. On the server side, Spring allows you to expose an arbitrary bean as a remote service through a service exporter. On the client side, Spring provides various proxy factory beans for you to create a local proxy for a remote service so that you can use the remote service as if it were a local bean.

Nowadays, there are two main approaches to developing web services: *contract-first* and *contract-last*. Automatically exposing a bean from the IoC container as a web service means that the service is contract-last because the service contract is generated from an existing bean. The Spring team has created a subproject called Spring Web Services (Spring-WS), which focuses on the development of contract-first web services. In this approach, a service contract is defined first, and code is then written to fulfill this contract.

5-1. Exposing and Invoking Services Through RMI

Problem

You want to expose a service from your Java application for other Java-based clients to invoke remotely. Because both parties are running on the Java platform, you can choose a pure Java-based solution without considering cross-platform portability.

Solution

Remote Method Invocation (RMI) is a Java-based remoting technology that allows two Java applications running in different JVMs to communicate with each other. With RMI, an object can invoke the methods of a remote object. RMI relies on object serialization to marshal and unmarshal method arguments and return values.

Considering the typical RMI usage scenario, to expose a service through RMI, you have to create the service interface that extends `java.rmi.Remote` and whose methods declare throwing `java.rmi.RemoteException`. Then you create the service implementation for this interface. After that, you start an RMI registry and register your service to it. As you can see, there are quite a lot of steps required for exposing a simple service.

To invoke a service through RMI, you first look up the remote service reference in an RMI registry, and then you can call the methods on it. However, to call the methods on a remote service, you must handle `java.rmi.RemoteException` in case of any exception thrown by the remote service.

Fortunately, Spring's remoting facilities can significantly simplify the RMI usage on both the server and client sides. On the server side, you can use `RmiServiceExporter` to export a Spring bean as an RMI service, whose methods can be invoked remotely. It's just several lines of bean configuration without any programming. Beans exported in this way don't need to implement `java.rmi.Remote` or throw `java.rmi.RemoteException`. On the client side, you can simply use `RmiProxyFactoryBean` to create a proxy for the remote service. It allows you to use the remote service as if it were a local bean. Again, it requires no additional programming at all.

How It Works

Suppose you are going to build a weather web service for clients running on different platforms to invoke. This service includes an operation for querying a city's temperatures on multiple dates. First, you create the `TemperatureInfo` class representing the minimum, maximum, and average temperatures of a particular city and date.

```
package com.apress.springenterpriserecipes.weather;
...
public class TemperatureInfo implements Serializable {

    private String city;
    private Date date;
    private double min;
    private double max;
    private double average;

    // Constructors, Getters and Setters
    ...
}
```

Next, you define the service interface that includes the `getTemperatures()` operation, which returns a city's temperatures on multiple dates as requested.

```
package com.apress.springenterpriserecipes.weather;
...
public interface WeatherService {

    public List<TemperatureInfo> getTemperatures(String city, List<Date> dates);
}
```

You have to provide an implementation for this interface. In a production application, you probably want to implement this service interface by querying the database. Here, you may hard-code the temperatures for testing purposes.

```
package com.apress.springenterpriserecipes.weather;
...
public class WeatherServiceImpl implements WeatherService {

    public List<TemperatureInfo> getTemperatures(String city, List<Date> dates) {
        List<TemperatureInfo> temperatures = new ArrayList<TemperatureInfo>();
        for (Date date : dates) {
            temperatures.add(new TemperatureInfo(city, date, 5.0, 10.0, 8.0));
        }
        return temperatures;
    }
}
```

Exposing an RMI Service

Suppose you want to expose the weather service as an RMI service. To use Spring's remoting facilities for this purpose, create a bean configuration file such as rmi-server.xml in the classpath root to define the service. In this file, you declare a bean for the weather service implementation and export it as an RMI service by using RmiServiceExporter.

```
<beans xmlns="http://www.springframework.org/schema/beans"
    xmlns:xsi="http://www.w3.org/2001/XMLSchema-instance"
    xsi:schemaLocation="http://www.springframework.org/schema/beans
        http://www.springframework.org/schema/beans/spring-beans-3.0.xsd">

    <bean id="weatherService"
        class="com.apress.springenterpriserecipes.weather.WeatherServiceImpl" />

    <bean class="org.springframework.remoting.rmi.RmiServiceExporter">
        <property name="serviceName" value="WeatherService" />
        <property name="serviceInterface"
            value="com.apress.springenterpriserecipes.weather.WeatherService" />
        <property name="service" ref="weatherService" />
    </bean>
</beans>
```

There are several properties you must configure for an RmiServiceExporter instance, including the service name, the service interface, and the service object to export. You can export any bean configured in the IoC container as an RMI service. RmiServiceExporter will create an RMI proxy to wrap this bean and bind it to the RMI registry. When the proxy receives an invocation request from the RMI registry, it will invoke the corresponding method on the bean.

By default, RmiServiceExporter attempts to look up an RMI registry at localhost port 1099. If it can't find the RMI registry, it will start a new one. However, if you want to bind your service to another running RMI registry, you can specify the host and port of that registry in the registryHost and registryPort properties. Note that once you specify the registry host, RmiServiceExporter will not start a new registry, even if the specified registry doesn't exist.

To start a server that provides the RMI weather service, run the following class to create an application context for the preceding bean configuration file:

```
package com.apress.springenterpriserecipes.weather;

import org.springframework.context.support.ClassPathXmlApplicationContext;
```

```
public class RmiServer {

    public static void main(String[] args) {
        new ClassPathXmlApplicationContext("rmi-server.xml");
    }
}
```

In this configuration, the server will launch; among the output you should see a message indicating that an existing RMI registry could not be found.

Invoking an RMI Service

By using Spring's remoting facilities, you can invoke a remote service just like a local bean. For example, you can create a client that refers to the weather service by its interface.

```
package com.apress.springenterpriserecipes.weather;
...
public class WeatherServiceClient {

    private WeatherService weatherService;

    public void setWeatherService(WeatherService weatherService) {
        this.weatherService = weatherService;
    }

    public TemperatureInfo getTodayTemperature(String city) {
        List<Date> dates = Arrays.asList(new Date[] { new Date() });
        List<TemperatureInfo> temperatures =
            weatherService.getTemperatures(city, dates);
        return temperatures.get(0);
    }
}
```

In a client bean configuration file, such as client.xml located in the classpath root, you can use RmiProxyFactoryBean to create a proxy for the remote service. Then you can use this service as if it were a local bean (e.g., inject it into the weather service client).

```
<beans xmlns="http://www.springframework.org/schema/beans"
    xmlns:xsi="http://www.w3.org/2001/XMLSchema-instance"
    xsi:schemaLocation="http://www.springframework.org/schema/beans
        http://www.springframework.org/schema/beans/spring-beans-3.0.xsd">

    <bean id="client"
        class="com.apress.springenterpriserecipes.weather.WeatherServiceClient">
        <property name="weatherService" ref="weatherService" />
    </bean>
```

```
<bean id="weatherService"
      class="org.springframework.remoting.rmi.RmiProxyFactoryBean">
    <property name="serviceUrl"
        value="rmi://localhost:1099/WeatherService" />
    <property name="serviceInterface"
        value="com.apress.springenterpriserecipes.weather.WeatherService" />
</bean>
</beans>
```

There are two properties you must configure for an `RmiProxyFactoryBean` instance. The service URL property specifies the host and port of the RMI registry, as well as the service name. The service interface allows this factory bean to create a proxy for the remote service. The proxy will transfer the invocation requests to the remote service transparently. You can test this service with the following `Client` main class:

```
package com.apress.springenterpriserecipes.weather;

import org.springframework.context.ApplicationContext;
import org.springframework.context.support.ClassPathXmlApplicationContext;

public class Client {

    public static void main(String[] args) {
        ApplicationContext context =
            new ClassPathXmlApplicationContext("client.xml");
        WeatherServiceClient client =
            (WeatherServiceClient) context.getBean("client");

        TemperatureInfo temperature = client.getTodayTemperature("Houston");
        System.out.println("Min temperature : " + temperature.getMin());
        System.out.println("Max temperature : " + temperature.getMax());
        System.out.println("Average temperature : " + temperature.getAverage());
    }
}
```

5-2. Creating EJB 2.x Components with Spring

Problem

In EJB 2.x, each EJB component requires a remote/local interface, a remote/local home interface, and a bean implementation class, in which you must implement all EJB life cycle callback methods even if you don't need them.

Solution

Spring's remoting support can't completely remove the burden of all these requirements, but it does provide powerful support for building EJB2.x components with Spring. The Spring support classes facilitate building session beans—*stateful session beans (SFSBs)* and *stateless session beans (SLSBs)*—and *message-driven beans (MDBs)* with Spring. Classic entity beans have no direct support in Spring, presumably because they map more usefully to something like Hibernate or JDO. These classes provide empty implementation for all EJB life cycle callback methods.

Your EJB classes can extend these classes to inherit the methods. Table 5-1 shows Spring's EJB support classes for different types of EJB.

Table 5-1. Spring's EJB Support Classes for Different Types of EJB

EJB Support Class	EJB Type
AbstractStatelessSessionBean	Stateless session bean
AbstractStatefulSessionBean	Stateful session bean
AbstractMessageDrivenBean	General message-driven bean that may not use JMS
AbstractJmsMessageDrivenBean	Message-driven bean that uses JMS

Moreover, the EJB support classes provide access to the Spring IoC container for you to implement your business logic in POJOs and wrap them with EJB components. Because POJOs are easier to develop and test, implementing business logic in POJOs can accelerate your EJB development. For more on messaging, please see Chapter 7.

How It Works

Suppose you are going to develop a system for a post office. You are asked to develop a stateless session bean for calculating postage based on the destination country and the weight. The target runtime environment is an application server that supports EJB 2.x only, so you have to develop the EJB component that will work with this version.

Compared with lightweight POJOs, EJB 2.x components are more difficult to build, deploy, and test. A good practice for developing EJB 2.x components is to implement business logic in POJOs and then wrap them with EJB components. First, you define the following business interface for postage calculation:

```
package com.apress.springenterpriserecipes.post;

public interface PostageService {

    public double calculatePostage(String country, double weight);
}
```

Then you have to implement this interface. Typically, it should query the database for the postage and perform some calculation. Here, you may hard-code the result for testing purposes.

```
package com.apress.springenterpriserecipes.post;

public class PostageServiceImpl implements PostageService {

    public double calculatePostage(String country, double weight) {
        return 1.0;
    }
}
```

Before you start creating your EJB component, you might like to have a simple EJB container for testing purposes. For simplicity's sake, we have chosen Apache OpenEJB (http://openejb.apache.org/) as the EJB container, which is very easy to install, configure, and deploy. OpenEJB is an open source EJB container. OpenEJB was designed for the Apache Geronimo server project (http://geronimo.apache.org/), but you don't need Apache Geronimo to run OpenEJB.

■Note   You can download OpenEJB Standalone Server (e.g., v3.1.1) from the OpenEJB web site and extract it to a directory of your choice to complete the installation.

Creating EJB 2.x Components Without Spring's Support

First, let's create the EJB component without Spring's support. To allow remote access to this EJB component, you expose the following remote interface to clients.

■Note   To compile and build your EJB component, you have to include the library that contains standard EJB classes and interfaces in your classpath. For OpenEJB 3.1.1, it's javaee-api-5.0-2.jar (located in the lib directory of the OpenEJB installation).

```
package com.apress.springenterpriserecipes.post;

import java.rmi.RemoteException;

import javax.ejb.EJBObject;

public interface PostageServiceRemote extends EJBObject {

    public double calculatePostage(String country, double weight)
        throws RemoteException;
}
```

This calculatePostage() method has a signature similar to that in the business interface, except it declares throwing RemoteException.

Also, you need a remote home interface for clients to retrieve a remote reference to this EJB component, whose methods must declare throwing RemoteException and CreateException.

```
package com.apress.springenterpriserecipes.post;

import java.rmi.RemoteException;

import javax.ejb.CreateException;
import javax.ejb.EJBHome;
```

```
public interface PostageServiceHome extends EJBHome {

    public PostageServiceRemote create() throws RemoteException, CreateException;
}
```

If you want to expose this EJB component for local access within an enterprise application, the preceding two interfaces should extend EJBLocalObject and EJBLocalHome instead, whose methods don't need to throw RemoteException. For simplicity's sake, I'm omitting the local and local home interfaces here.

Note that the following EJB implementation class also implements the PostageService business interface so that you can delegate requests to the POJO service implementation.

```
package com.apress.springenterpriserecipes.post;

import javax.ejb.SessionBean;
import javax.ejb.SessionContext;

public class PostageServiceBean implements SessionBean, PostageService {

    private PostageService postageService;
    private SessionContext sessionContext;
  // this isn't part of the interface, but is required
    public void ejbCreate() {
        postageService = new PostageServiceImpl();
    }

    public void ejbActivate() {}
    public void ejbPassivate() {}
    public void ejbRemove() {}

    public void setSessionContext(SessionContext sessionContext) {
        this.sessionContext = sessionContext;
    }

    public double calculatePostage(String country, double weight) {
        return postageService.calculatePostage(country, weight);
    }
}
```

In the ejbCreate() life cycle method, you instantiate the POJO service implementation class. It's up to this object to perform the actual postage calculation. The EJB component just delegates requests to this object.

The astute reader will note that the ejbCreate() method is nowhere to be found on the SessionBean interface. Instead, it's a convention. Stateless session beans can contain one version of ejbCreate(). If the method has any arguments, the corresponding create method on the EJBHome bean must have the same arguments. The ejbCreate() method is the EJB hook for initialization of state, much as a JSR-250 annotated @PostConstruct() method or afterPropertiesSet() method work in Java EE 5 and Spring. If you have a stateful session bean, then there may be multiple overloaded ejbCreate() methods. Similarly, for each overloaded form of ejbCreate() on the SessionBean, there must be a create method with the same arguments on the EJBHome. We mention all this (which, if we're honest, doesn't even begin to cover the nuances involved) to put in stark relief the Spring container's lightweight approach *and* to show that even the Spring abstractions for EJB 2.x are incredible improvements.

Finally, you require an EJB deployment descriptor for your EJB component. You create the file
ejb-jar.xml in the META-INF directory of your classpath and add the following contents to describe your
EJB component:

```
<ejb-jar>
    <enterprise-beans>
        <session>
            <display-name>PostageService</display-name>
            <ejb-name>PostageService</ejb-name>
        <home>com.apress.springenterpriserecipes.post.PostageServiceHome</home>
        <remote>com.apress.springenterpriserecipes. ➥
post.PostageServiceRemote</remote>
            <ejb-class>
                com.apress.springenterpriserecipes.post.PostageServiceBean
            </ejb-class>
            <session-type>Stateless</session-type>
            <transaction-type>Bean</transaction-type>
        </session>
    </enterprise-beans>
</ejb-jar>
```

Now your EJB component is finished, and you should pack your interfaces, classes, and deployment
descriptors in a JAR file. Then start up your EJB container and deploy this EJB component to it.

■Note   To start the OpenEJB container, you first set the OPENEJB_HOME environment variable to point to your
OpenEJB installation directory. Then execute the OpenEJB startup script (located in the bin directory) with the
parameter start (e.g., openejb start). In another shell, to deploy an EJB component, you also execute the
OpenEJB startup script, but this time you pass deploy and the location of your EJB JAR file as parameters. (e.g.,
openejb deploy PostService.jar).

For OpenEJB, the default JNDI name for a remote home interface of an EJB 2.x component is the
EJB name with RemoteHome as its suffix (PostageServiceRemoteHome in this case). If the deployment is
successful, you should see the following output:

```
Application deployed successfully at "c:\PostageService.jar"
App(id=C:\openejb-3.1.1\apps\PostageService.jar)
    EjbJar(id=PostageService.jar, path=C:\openejb-3.1.1\apps\PostageService.jar)
        Ejb(ejb-name=PostageService, id=PostageService)
            Jndi(name=PostageServiceRemoteHome)
            Jndi(name=PostageServiceLocal)
```

Creating EJB 2.x Components with Spring's Support

As you can see, your EJB implementation class needs to implement all EJB life cycle methods even if you don't need them. It should extend Spring's EJB support class to get the life cycle methods implemented by default. The support class for stateless session beans is `AbstractStatelessSessionBean`.

■Note   To use Spring's EJB support for your EJB implementation classes, you have to include a few Spring framework jars, including `spring-beans`, `spring-core`, `spring-context`, `spring-context-support`, `spring-asm`, and `spring-expression` in the classpath of your EJB container. For OpenEJB, you can copy these JAR files to the `lib` directory of the OpenEJB installation directory. If your OpenEJB container is running, you will have to restart it. In our testing, there was a conflict between the Spring 3 milestone releases we were using and the `openejb-cxf` jar in the lib directory of the OpenEJB installation. You may simply remove that jar or ignore the stack trace in the console at startup.

```
package com.apress.springenterpriserecipes.post;

import javax.ejb.CreateException;

import org.springframework.ejb.support.AbstractStatelessSessionBean;

public class PostageServiceBean extends AbstractStatelessSessionBean
        implements PostageService {

    private PostageService postageService;

    protected void onEjbCreate() throws CreateException {
        postageService = (PostageService)
                getBeanFactory().getBean("postageService");
    }

    public double calculatePostage(String country, double weight) {
        return postageService.calculatePostage(country, weight);
    }
}
```

When you extend the `AbstractStatelessSessionBean` class, your EJB class no longer needs to implement any EJB life cycle methods, but you can still override them if necessary. Note that this class has an `onEjbCreate()` method that you must implement to perform initialization tasks. Here, you just retrieve the `postageService` bean from the Spring IoC container for this EJB component to use. Of course, you must define it in a bean configuration file. This file can have an arbitrary name, but must be located in the classpath. For example, you can create it as `beans-ejb.xml` in the root of the classpath.

```
    xmlns:xsi="http://www.w3.org/2001/XMLSchema-instance"
    xsi:schemaLocation="http://www.springframework.org/schema/beans
        http://www.springframework.org/schema/beans/spring-beans-3.0.xsd">

    <bean id="postageService"
        class="com.apress.springenterpriserecipes.post.PostageServiceImpl" />
</beans>
```

The final step is to tell the EJB support class where your bean configuration is. By default, it looks at the JNDI environment variable java:comp/env/ejb/BeanFactoryPath for the file location. So, you add an environment entry to your EJB deployment descriptor for this location.

```
<ejb-jar>
    <enterprise-beans>
        <session>
            <display-name>PostageService</display-name>
            <ejb-name>PostageService</ejb-name>
            <home>com.apress.springenterpriserecipes.post.PostageServiceHome</home>
            <remote>com.apress.springenterpriserecipes.post.PostageServiceRemote➥
</remote>
            <ejb-class>
                com.apress.springenterpriserecipes.post.PostageServiceBean
            </ejb-class>
            <session-type>Stateless</session-type>
            <transaction-type>Bean</transaction-type>
            <env-entry>
                <env-entry-name>ejb/BeanFactoryPath</env-entry-name>
                <env-entry-type>java.lang.String</env-entry-type>
                <env-entry-value>beans-ejb.xml</env-entry-value>
            </env-entry>
        </session>
    </enterprise-beans>
</ejb-jar>
```

The EJB support classes instantiate the Spring IoC container using BeanFactoryLocator. The default BeanFactoryLocator they use is ContextJndiBeanFactoryLocator, which instantiates the IoC (a regular BeanFactory implementation such as ApplicationContext) container using a bean configuration file specified by the JNDI environment variable java:comp/env/ejb/BeanFactoryPath. You can override this variable name by calling the setBeanFactoryLocatorKey() method in a constructor or in the setSessionContext() method.

Now you can repack your EJB JAR file to include the preceding bean configuration file and redeploy it to your EJB container. In OpenEJB, this is a simple undeploy and redeploy sequence. It will vary from container to container.

5-3. Accessing EJB 2.x Components in Spring

Problem

In EJB 2.x, you have to perform the following tasks to invoke a method on a remote EJB component. Invoking a method on a local EJB component is very similar, except that you have no need to handle RemoteException.

- Initialize the JNDI lookup context, which may throw a NamingException.

- Look up the home interface from JNDI, which may throw a NamingException.

- Retrieve a remote EJB reference from the home interface, which may throw a CreateException or a RemoteException.

- Invoke the method on the remote interface, which may throw a RemoteException.

As you can see, it requires a lot of coding to invoke a method on an EJB component. The exceptions NamingException, CreateException, and RemoteException are all checked exceptions that you must handle. Moreover, your client is bound to EJB and would require a lot of changes if you ever switched the service implementation from EJB to another technology.

Solution

Spring offers two factory beans, SimpleRemoteStatelessSessionProxyFactoryBean and LocalStatelessSessionProxyFactoryBean, for creating a proxy for a remote/local stateless session bean respectively. They allow EJB clients to invoke an EJB component by the business interface as if it were a simple local object. The proxy handles the JNDI context initialization, home interface lookup, and invocation of local/remote EJB methods behind the scenes.

The EJB proxy also converts exceptions such as NamingException, CreateException, and RemoteException into runtime exceptions, so the client code is not required to handle them. For example, if a RemoteException is thrown when accessing a remote EJB component, the EJB proxy will convert it into Spring's runtime exception RemoteAccessException.

How It Works

Suppose that there's a front desk subsystem in your post office system that requires postage calculation. First, let's define the FrontDesk interface as follows:

```
package com.apress.springenterpriserecipes.post;

public interface FrontDesk {

    public double calculatePostage(String country, double weight);
}
```

Because there's an EJB 2.x remote stateless session bean for calculating postage, you only have to access it in your front desk subsystem. To talk to the remote service, you interface in terms of the EJBHome and the EJB Remote (PostageServiceRemote) interface. It is against these interfaces that a client-side proxy will be created. You are given the following remote interface and home interface for this EJB component:

```
package com.apress.springenterpriserecipes.post;

import java.rmi.RemoteException;

import javax.ejb.EJBObject;

public interface PostageServiceRemote extends EJBObject {

    public double calculatePostage(String country, double weight)
        throws RemoteException;
}
```

```
package com.apress.springenterpriserecipes.post;

import java.rmi.RemoteException;

import javax.ejb.CreateException;
import javax.ejb.EJBHome;

public interface PostageServiceHome extends EJBHome {

    public PostageServiceRemote create() throws RemoteException, CreateException;
}
```

Suppose this EJB component has already been deployed in an EJB container (e.g., an OpenEJB container started up on localhost). The JNDI name of this EJB component is PostageServiceRemoteHome.

■Note   To access an EJB component deployed in an EJB container, you have to include the EJB container's client library in your classpath. For OpenEJB 3.1.1, it is openejb-client-3.1.1.jar (located in the lib directory of the OpenEJB installation).

Accessing EJB 2.x Components

With Spring's support, accessing an EJB component can be significantly simplified. You can access an EJB component by its business interface. A business interface differs from an EJB remote interface in that it doesn't extend EJBObject, and its method declarations don't throw RemoteException, which means that the client doesn't have to handle this type of exception, and it doesn't know that the service is implemented by an EJB component. The business interface for postage calculation is shown following:

```
package com.apress.springenterpriserecipes.post;

public interface PostageService {
    public double calculatePostage(String country, double weight);
}
```

Now, in FrontDeskImpl, you can define a setter method for the PostageService business interface to let Spring inject the service implementation so that your FrontDeskImpl will no longer be EJB specific. Later, if you reimplement the PostageService interface with another technology (SOAP, RMI, Hessian/Burlap, Flash AMF, etc), you won't need to modify a single line of code.

```
package com.apress.springenterpriserecipes.post;

public class FrontDeskImpl implements FrontDesk {

    private PostageService postageService;

    public void setPostageService(PostageService postageService) {
        this.postageService = postageService;
    }

    public double calculatePostage(String country, double weight) {
        return postageService.calculatePostage(country, weight);
    }
}
```

Spring offers the proxy factory bean SimpleRemoteStatelessSessionProxyFactoryBean to create a local proxy for a remote stateless session bean.

```
<beans xmlns="http://www.springframework.org/schema/beans"
    xmlns:xsi="http://www.w3.org/2001/XMLSchema-instance"
    xsi:schemaLocation="http://www.springframework.org/schema/beans
        http://www.springframework.org/schema/beans/spring-beans-3.0.xsd">

    <bean id="postageService"
class="org.springframework.ejb.access.SimpleRemoteStatelessSession➥
ProxyFactoryBean">
        <property name="jndiEnvironment">
            <props>
                <prop key="java.naming.factory.initial">
                    org.apache.openejb.client.RemoteInitialContextFactory
                </prop>
                <prop key="java.naming.provider.url">
                    ejbd://localhost:4201
                </prop>
            </props>
        </property>
        <property name="jndiName" value="PostageServiceRemoteHome" />
        <property name="businessInterface"
            value="com.apress.springenterpriserecipes.post.PostageService" />
    </bean>
```

```
        <bean id="frontDesk"
            class="com.apress.springenterpriserecipes.post.FrontDeskImpl">
            <property name="postageService" ref="postageService" />
        </bean>
</beans>
```

You have to configure the JNDI details for this EJB proxy in the jndiEnvironment and jndiName properties. The most important is to specify the business interface for this proxy to implement. The calls to methods declared in this interface will be translated into remote method calls to the remote EJB component. You can inject this proxy into FrontDeskImpl in the same way as a normal bean.

EJB proxies can also be defined using the <jee:remote-slsb> and <jee:local-slsb> elements in the jee schema. You must add the jee schema definition to the <beans> root element beforehand.

```
<beans xmlns="http://www.springframework.org/schema/beans"
    xmlns:xsi="http://www.w3.org/2001/XMLSchema-instance"
    xmlns:jee="http://www.springframework.org/schema/jee"
    xsi:schemaLocation="http://www.springframework.org/schema/beans
        http://www.springframework.org/schema/beans/spring-beans-3.0.xsd
        http://www.springframework.org/schema/jee
        http://www.springframework.org/schema/jee/spring-jee-3.0.xsd">

    <jee:remote-slsb id="postageService"
        jndi-name="PostageServiceRemoteHome"
        business-interface="com.apress.springenterpriserecipes.post.PostageService">
        <jee:environment>
            java.naming.factory.initial=➥
                org.apache.openejb.client.RemoteInitialContextFactory
            java.naming.provider.url=ejbd://localhost:4201
        </jee:environment>
    </jee:remote-slsb>
    ...
</bean>
```

To access the EJB from a client, your code looks like almost any example demonstrating accessing beans from a Spring context. It describes the instantiation of a Spring ApplicationContext and the use of a bean that's interface-compatible with your service's POJO interface.

```
import org.springframework.context.ApplicationContext;

public class FrontDeskMain {

    public static void main(String[] args) {
        ApplicationContext context =
            new ClassPathXmlApplicationContext("beans-front.xml");

        FrontDesk frontDesk = (FrontDesk) context.getBean("frontDesk");
        double postage = frontDesk.calculatePostage("US", 1.5);
        System.out.println(postage);
    }
}
```

5-4. Creating EJB 3.0 Components in Spring

Problem

Happily, creating EJB 3.0 components is much simpler than with EJB 2.x. Indeed, an EJB can be as simple as a business interface and a POJO implementation class. In EJB 3.1, even this restriction is lifted, so that_like Spring_you can simply specify a POJO and expose that a service. However, writing EJB 3 beans could be unpleasant if you need access to beans in a Spring application context. Without special support, there is no way to have beans auto-wired into the EJB.

Solution

Use the org.springframework.ejb.interceptor.SpringBeanAutowiringInterceptor interceptor to let Spring configure @Autowired elements on your EJB.

How It Works

First, build an EJB component. You will need to specify an implementation and at minimum a remote interface. The business interface for our EJB 3.0 stateless session bean will be the same as for the EJB 2.0 example. The bean implementation class can be a simple Java class that implements this interface and is annotated with the EJB annotations. A remote stateless session bean requires the @Stateless and @Remote annotations. In the @Remote annotation, you have to specify the remote interface for this EJB component.

```
package com.apress.springenterpriserecipes.post;

public interface PostageService {
    public double calculatePostage(String country, double weight);
}
```

Next, we must create an implementation.

```
package com.apress.springenterpriserecipes.post;

import javax.ejb.Remote;
import javax.ejb.Stateless;

@Stateless
@Remote( { PostageService.class })
public class PostageServiceBean implements PostageService {

    public double calculatePostage(String country, double weight) {
        return 1.0;
    }
}
```

You specify the remote interface for the session bean using the @Remote annotation that decorates the class. That is all that's required for the coding to create a working EJB3 bean. Compile and then package these classes into a .jar. Then, deploy them to OpenEJB in the same manner as for the EJB 2.x example.

■Note   To compile an EJB component against OpenEJB, you'll need the `javaee-api-5.0-2` jar from the `lib` folder on your classpath.

Thus far, you've created a very simple working service in almost no code, and haven't needed to use Spring. Let's have Spring inject a resource, which might be useful for a host of reasons: proxying Spring services with EJB3s, injecting custom resources configured in Spring, or even using Spring to isolate your EJBs from acquiring references to other distributed resources such as a REST endpoint or an RMI endpoint.

To do this, use Spring's `SpringBeanAutowiringInterceptor` class to provide configuration for the EJB. Here is the implementation class (PostageServiceBean) with a few extra lines. First: an @Interceptors annotation decorates the `PostageServiceBean`. This tells Spring to handle @Autowired injection points in the class. The interceptor obtains beans, by default, from a `ContextSingletonBeanFactoryLocation`, which in turn looks for an XML application context named beanRefContext.xml, which is presumed to be on the classpath. The second new line of interest here is an example injection of a Spring `JdbcTemplate` instance.

```java
package com.apress.springenterpriserecipes.post;

import javax.ejb.Remote;
import javax.ejb.Stateless;
import javax.interceptor.Interceptors;

import org.springframework.jdbc.core.JdbcTemplate;
import org.springframework.ejb.interceptor.SpringBeanAutowiringInterceptor;

@Stateless
@Remote( { PostageService.class })
@Interceptors(SpringBeanAutowiringInterceptor.class)
public class PostageServiceBean implements PostageService {

        @Autowired
        private JdbcTemplate jdbcTemplate;

        public double calculatePostage(String country, double weight) {
                // use the jdbcTemplate …
                return 1.0;
        }
}
```

5-5. Accessing EJB 3.0 Components in Spring

Problem

EJB 3.0 offers some improvements on EJB 2.x. First, the EJB interface is a simple Java interface whose methods don't throw RemoteException, while the implementation class is a simple Java class annotated with EJB annotations. Moreover, the concept of home interface has been eliminated in order to simplify the EJB lookup process. You can look up an EJB reference from JNDI directly in EJB 3.0. However, the JNDI lookup code is still complex, and you also have to handle NamingException.

Solution

By using Spring's `JndiObjectFactoryBean`, you can easily declare a JNDI object reference in the Spring IoC container. You can use this factory bean to declare a reference to an EJB 3.0 component.

How It Works

Now that you've created and deployed an EJB component, you can create a client. If you have chosen OpenEJB as your EJB container, the default JNDI name for a remote EJB 3.0 component is the EJB class name with `Remote` as its suffix (`PostageServiceBeanRemote`, in this case). Note that the JNDI name isn't specified in the standard in EJB 3.0, so this may change from container to container. In EJB 3.1, this is remedied, and beans are prescribed a predictable naming scheme so that bean JNDI names are portable across implementations.

Accessing EJB 3.0 Components with Spring's Support

Accessing EJB 3.0 components is simpler than EJB 2.x. You can look up an EJB reference from JNDI directly without looking up its home interface first, so you don't need to handle `CreateException`. Moreover, the EJB interface is a business interface that doesn't throw a `RemoteException`.

Although accessing EJB 3.0 components is simpler than EJB 2.x, the JNDI lookup code is still too complex, and you have to handle `NamingException`. With Spring's support, your `FrontDeskImpl` class can define a setter method for this EJB component's business interface for Spring to inject the EJB reference that is looked up from JNDI.

```
package com.apress.springenterpriserecipes.post;

public class FrontDeskImpl implements FrontDesk {

    private PostageService postageService;

    public void setPostageService(PostageService postageService) {
        this.postageService = postageService;
    }

    public double calculatePostage(String country, double weight) {
        return postageService.calculatePostage(country, weight);
    }
}
```

Spring offers the factory bean `JndiObjectFactoryBean` to declare a JNDI object reference in its IoC container. You declare this bean in the front desk system's bean configuration file.

```
<beans xmlns="http://www.springframework.org/schema/beans"
    xmlns:xsi="http://www.w3.org/2001/XMLSchema-instance"
    xsi:schemaLocation="http://www.springframework.org/schema/beans
        http://www.springframework.org/schema/beans/spring-beans-3.0.xsd">
```

```
    <bean id="postageService"
        class="org.springframework.jndi.JndiObjectFactoryBean">
        <property name="jndiEnvironment">
            <props>
                <prop key="java.naming.factory.initial">
                    org.apache.openejb.client.RemoteInitialContextFactory
                </prop>
                <prop key="java.naming.provider.url">
                    ejbd://localhost:4201
                </prop>
            </props>
        </property>
        <property name="jndiName" value="PostageServiceBeanRemote" />
    </bean>

    <bean id="frontDesk"
        class="com.apress.springenterpriserecipes.post.FrontDeskImpl">
        <property name="postageService" ref="postageService" />
    </bean>
</beans>
```

You can configure the JNDI details for this factory bean in the jndiEnvironment and jndiName properties. Then you can inject this proxy into FrontDeskImpl in the same way as a normal bean.

In Spring, JNDI objects can also be defined using the <jee:jndi-lookup> element in the jee schema.

```
<beans xmlns="http://www.springframework.org/schema/beans"
    xmlns:xsi="http://www.w3.org/2001/XMLSchema-instance"
    xmlns:jee="http://www.springframework.org/schema/jee"
    xsi:schemaLocation="http://www.springframework.org/schema/beans
        http://www.springframework.org/schema/beans/spring-beans-3.0.xsd
        http://www.springframework.org/schema/jee
        http://www.springframework.org/schema/jee/spring-jee-3.0.xsd">

    <jee:jndi-lookup id="postageService"
        jndi-name="PostageServiceBeanRemote">
        <jee:environment>
            java.naming.factory.initial=➥
                org.apache.openejb.client.RemoteInitialContextFactory
            java.naming.provider.url=ejbd://localhost:4201
        </jee:environment>
    </jee:jndi-lookup>
    ...
</beans>
```

5-6. Exposing and Invoking Services Through HTTP

Problem

RMI and EJB communicate through their own protocol which may not pass through firewalls. Ideally, you'd like to communicate over HTTP.

Solution

Hessian and *Burlap* are two simple lightweight remoting technologies developed by Caucho Technology (http://www.caucho.com/). They both communicate using proprietary messages over HTTP and have their own serialization mechanism, but they are much simpler than web services. The only difference between them is that Hessian communicates using binary messages while Burlap communicates using XML messages. The message formats of both Hessian and Burlap are also supported on other platforms besides Java, such as PHP, Python, C#, and Ruby. This allows your Java applications to communicate with applications running on the other platforms.

In addition to the preceding two technologies, the Spring framework itself also offers a remoting technology called *HTTP Invoker*. It also communicates over HTTP, but uses Java's object serialization mechanism to serialize objects. Unlike Hessian and Burlap, HTTP Invoker requires both sides of a service to be running on the Java platform and using the Spring framework. However, it can serialize all kinds of Java objects, some of which may not be serialized by Hessian/Burlap's proprietary mechanism.

Spring's remoting facilities are consistent in exposing and invoking remote services with these technologies. On the server side, you can create a service exporter such as HessianServiceExporter, BurlapServiceExporter, or HttpInvokerServiceExporter to export a Spring bean as a remote service whose methods can be invoked remotely. It's just several lines of bean configurations without any programming. On the client side, you can simply configure a proxy factory bean such as HessianProxyFactoryBean, BurlapProxyFactoryBean, or HttpInvokerProxyFactoryBean to create a proxy for a remote service. It allows you to use the remote service as if it were a local bean. Again, it requires no additional programming at all.

How It Works

Exposing a Hessian Service

To expose a Hessian service with Spring, you have to create a web application using Spring MVC. First, you create the following directory structure for your web application context.

■Note To expose a Hessian or Burlap service, you have to copy hessian-3.2.1.jar (located in the lib/caucho directory of the Spring installation) to the WEB-INF/lib directory.

```
weather/
    WEB-INF/
        classes/
        lib/*jar
        weather-servlet.xml
        web.xml
```

In the web deployment descriptor (i.e., web.xml), you have to configure Spring MVC's DispatcherServlet.

```xml
<web-app version="2.4" xmlns="http://java.sun.com/xml/ns/j2ee"
    xmlns:xsi="http://www.w3.org/2001/XMLSchema-instance"
    xsi:schemaLocation="http://java.sun.com/xml/ns/j2ee
        http://java.sun.com/xml/ns/j2ee/web-app_2_4.xsd">

    <servlet>
        <servlet-name>weather</servlet-name>
        <servlet-class>
            org.springframework.web.servlet.DispatcherServlet
        </servlet-class>
        <load-on-startup>1</load-on-startup>
    </servlet>

    <servlet-mapping>
        <servlet-name>weather</servlet-name>

        <url-pattern>/services/*</url-pattern>
    </servlet-mapping>
</web-app>
```

In the preceding servlet mapping definition, you map all URLs under the services path to DispatcherServlet. Because the name of this servlet is weather, you create the following Spring MVC configuration file, weather-servlet.xml, in the root of WEB-INF. In this file, you declare a bean for the weather service implementation and export it as a Hessian service using HessianServiceExporter.

```xml
<beans xmlns="http://www.springframework.org/schema/beans"
    xmlns:xsi="http://www.w3.org/2001/XMLSchema-instance"
    xsi:schemaLocation="http://www.springframework.org/schema/beans
        http://www.springframework.org/schema/beans/spring-beans-3.0.xsd">

    <bean id="weatherService"
        class="com.apress.springenterpriserecipes.weather.WeatherServiceImpl" />

    <bean name="/WeatherService"
        class="org.springframework.remoting.caucho.HessianServiceExporter">
        <property name="service" ref="weatherService" />
        <property name="serviceInterface"
            value="com.apress.springenterpriserecipes.weather.WeatherService" />
    </bean>
</beans>
```

For a HessianServiceExporter instance, you have to configure a service object to export and its service interface. You can export any bean configured in the IoC container as a Hessian service, and then HessianServiceExporter will create a proxy to wrap this bean. When the proxy receives an invocation request, it will invoke the corresponding method on that bean. By default, BeanNameUrlHandlerMapping is preconfigured for a Spring MVC application. It maps requests to handlers according to the URL patterns specified as bean names. The preceding configuration maps the URL pattern /WeatherService to this exporter.

Now you can deploy this web application to a web container (e.g., Apache Tomcat 6.0). By default, Tomcat listens on port 8080, so if you deploy your application to the weather context path, you can access this service with the following URL:

```
http://localhost:8080/weather/services/WeatherService
```

Invoking a Hessian Service

By using Spring's remoting facilities, you can invoke a remote service just like a local bean. In the client bean configuration file client.xml, you can use HessianProxyFactoryBean to create a proxy for the remote Hessian service. Then you can use this service as if it were a local bean.

■Note   To invoke a Hessian or Burlap service, you have to include caucho-3.2.1.jar (located in the lib/caucho directory of the Spring installation) in your classpath.

```xml
<bean id="weatherService"
    class="org.springframework.remoting.caucho.HessianProxyFactoryBean">
    <property name="serviceUrl"
        value="http://localhost:8080/weather/services/WeatherService" />
    <property name="serviceInterface"
        value="com.apress.springenterpriserecipes.weather.WeatherService" />
</bean>
```

You have to configure two properties for a HessianProxyFactoryBean instance. The service URL property specifies the URL for the target service. The service interface property is for this factory bean to create a local proxy for the remote service. The proxy will send the invocation requests to the remote service transparently.

Exposing a Burlap Service

The configuration for exposing a Burlap service is similar to that for Hessian, except you should use BurlapServiceExporter instead.

```xml
<bean name="/WeatherService"
    class="org.springframework.remoting.caucho.BurlapServiceExporter">
    <property name="service" ref="weatherService" />
    <property name="serviceInterface"
        value="com.apress.springenterpriserecipes.weather.WeatherService" />
</bean>
```

Invoking a Burlap Service

Invoking a Burlap service is very similar to Hessian. The only difference is that you should use
BurlapProxyFactoryBean.

```
<bean id="weatherService"
    class="org.springframework.remoting.caucho.BurlapProxyFactoryBean">
    <property name="serviceUrl"
        value="http://localhost:8080/weather/services/WeatherService" />
    <property name="serviceInterface"
        value="com.apress.springenterpriserecipes.weather.WeatherService" />
</bean>
```

Exposing an HTTP Invoker Service

Again, the configuration for exposing a service using HTTP Invoker is similar to that for Hessian and
Burlap, except you have to use HttpInvokerServiceExporter instead.

```
<bean name="/WeatherService"
    class="org.springframework.remoting.httpinvoker.HttpInvokerServiceExporter">
    <property name="service" ref="weatherService" />
    <property name="serviceInterface"
        value="com.apress.springenterpriserecipes.weather.WeatherService" />
</bean>
```

Invoking an HTTP Invoker Service

Invoking a service exposed by HTTP Invoker is also similar to Hessian and Burlap. This time you have to
use HttpInvokerProxyFactoryBean.

```
<bean id="weatherService"
    class="org.springframework.remoting.httpinvoker.HttpInvokerProxyFactoryBean">
    <property name="serviceUrl"
        value="http://localhost:8080/weather/services/WeatherService" />
    <property name="serviceInterface"
        value="com.apress.springenterpriserecipes.weather.WeatherService" />
</bean>
```

5-7. Choosing a Web Service Development Approach

Problem

When you are asked to develop a web service, you first have to consider which web service development
approach you are going to use.

Solution

There are two approaches to developing a web service, depending on whether you define the contract
first or last. A web service contract is described using *Web Services Description Language (WSDL)*. In
contract-last, you expose an existing service interface as a web service whose service contract is
generated automatically. In contract-first, you design the service contract in terms of XML and then
write code to fulfill it.

How It Works

Contract-Last Web Services

In contract-last web service development, you expose an existing service interface as a web service. There are many tools and libraries that can help expose a Java class/interface as a web service. They can generate the WSDL file for the class/interface by applying rules, such as turning the class/interface into a port type, turning the methods into operations, and generating the request/response message formats according to the method arguments and return value. All in all, everything is generated from a service interface like the following:

```
package com.apress.springenterpriserecipes.weather;
...
public interface WeatherService {

    public List<TemperatureInfo> getTemperatures(String city, List<Date> dates);
}
```

This approach is called contract-last because you define the contract for this web service as the last step in the development process by generating it from Java code. In other words, you are designing the service with Java, not with WSDL or XML.

Contract-First Web Services

In contrast, the contract-first approach encourages you to think of the service contract first, in terms of XML including XSD and WSDL. In this approach, you design the request and response messages for your service first. The messages are designed with XML, which is very good at representing complex data structures in a platform- and language-independent way. The next step is to implement this contract in a particular platform and programming language.

For example, the request message of your weather service contains a city element and multiple date elements. Note that you should specify the namespace for your messages to avoid naming conflicts with other XML documents.

```
<GetTemperaturesRequest
    xmlns="http://springenterpriserecipes.apress.com/weather/schemas">
    <city>Houston</city>
    <date>2007-12-01</date>
    <date>2007-12-08</date>
    <date>2007-12-15</date>
</GetTemperaturesRequest>
```

Then the response message would contain multiple Temperature elements in response to the requested city and dates.

```
<GetTemperaturesResponse
    xmlns="http://springenterpriserecipes.apress.com/weather/schemas">
    <TemperatureInfo city="Houston" date="2007-12-01">
        <min>5.0</min>
        <max>10.0</max>
        <average>8.0</average>
    </TemperatureInfo>
```

```
<TemperatureInfo city="Houston" date="2007-12-08">
    <min>4.0</min>
    <max>13.0</max>
    <average>7.0</average>
</TemperatureInfo>
<TemperatureInfo city="Houston" date="2007-12-15">
    <min>10.0</min>
    <max>18.0</max>
    <average>15.0</average>
</TemperatureInfo>
</GetTemperaturesResponse>
```

After designing the sample request and response messages, you can start creating the contract for this web service using XSD and WSDL. There are many tools and IDEs that can help generate the default XSD and WSDL files for an XML document. You only need to carry out a few optimizations to have it fit your requirements.

Comparison

When developing a contract-last web service, you are actually exposing the internal API of your application to clients. But this API is likely to be changed—and after it's changed, you will also have to change the contract of your web service, which may involve changing all the clients. However, if you design the contract first, it reflects the external API that you want to expose. It's not as likely to need changing as the internal API.

Although many tools and libraries can expose a Java class/interface as a web service, the fact is that the contract generated from Java is not always portable to other platforms. For example, a Java map may not be portable to other programming languages without a similar data structure. Sometimes you have to change the method signature in order to make a service contract portable. In some cases, it's also hard to map an object to XML (e.g., an object graph with cyclic references) because there's actually an *impedance mismatch* between an object model and an XML model, just like that between an object model and a relational model.

XML is good at representing complex data structures in a platform- and language-independent way. A service contract defined with XML is 100 percent portable to any platform. In addition, you can define constraints in the XSD file for your messages so that they can be validated automatically. For these reasons, it's more efficient to design a service contract with XML and implement it with a programming language such as Java. There are many libraries in Java for processing XML efficiently.

From a performance viewpoint, generating a service contract from Java code may lead to an inefficient design. This is because you might not consider the message granularity carefully, as it's derived from the method signature directly. In contrast, defining the service contract first is more likely to lead to an efficient design.

Finally, the biggest reason for choosing the contract-last approach is its simplicity. Exposing a Java class/interface as a web service doesn't require you to know much about XML, WSDL, SOAP, and so on. You can expose a web service very quickly.

5-8. Exposing and Invoking Web Services Using XFire

Problem

Because Web Services is a standard and cross-platform application communication technology, you want to expose a web service from your Java application for clients on different platforms to invoke.

Solution

Spring comes with several service exporters that can export a bean as a remote service based on the RMI, Hessian, Burlap, or HTTP Invoker remoting technologies, but Spring doesn't come with a service exporter that can export a bean as a web service. However, there's an external framework called *XFire* (http://xfire.codehaus.org/) that supplies one. XFire is an open source Java SOAP framework that can export a simple Java object as a web service. XFire supports Spring by providing facilities such as a service exporter and a client proxy factory bean, whose usage is consistent with those provided by Spring for other remoting technologies.

How It Works

Exposing a Web Service Using XFire

To expose a web service using XFire in Spring, you first create the following directory structure for your web application context.

■Note   To expose a web service using XFire, you have to download and install XFire (e.g., v1.2.6). Then copy xfire-all-1.2.6.jar (located in the root of the XFire installation), activation-1.1.jar, jdom-1.0.jar, stax-api-1.0.1.jar, wsdl4j-1.6.1.jar, and wstx-asl-3.2.0.jar (all located in the lib directory) to the WEB-INF/lib directory.

```
weather/
    WEB-INF/
        classes/
        lib/*jar
        weather-servlet.xml
        web.xml
```

In web.xml, you configure Spring MVC's DispatcherServlet and map all the URLs under the services path to it.

```
<web-app version="2.4" xmlns="http://java.sun.com/xml/ns/j2ee"
    xmlns:xsi="http://www.w3.org/2001/XMLSchema-instance"
    xsi:schemaLocation="http://java.sun.com/xml/ns/j2ee
        http://java.sun.com/xml/ns/j2ee/web-app_2_4.xsd">

    <servlet>
        <servlet-name>weather</servlet-name>
        <servlet-class>
            org.springframework.web.servlet.DispatcherServlet
        </servlet-class>
        <load-on-startup>1</load-on-startup>
    </servlet>
```

```
    <servlet-mapping>
        <servlet-name>weather</servlet-name>
        <url-pattern>/services/*</url-pattern>
    </servlet-mapping>
</web-app>
```

In the Spring MVC configuration file, weather-servlet.xml, you declare a bean for the weather service implementation and export it as a web service by using XFireExporter.

```
<beans xmlns="http://www.springframework.org/schema/beans"
    xmlns:xsi="http://www.w3.org/2001/XMLSchema-instance"
    xsi:schemaLocation="http://www.springframework.org/schema/beans
        http://www.springframework.org/schema/beans/spring-beans-3.0.xsd ">

    <bean id="weatherService"
        class="com.apress.springenterpriserecipes.weather.WeatherServiceImpl" />

    <bean name="/WeatherService"
        class="org.codehaus.xfire.spring.remoting.XFireExporter">
        <property name="xfire" ref="xfire" />
        <property name="serviceBean" ref="weatherService" />
        <property name="serviceInterface"
            value="com.apress.springenterpriserecipes.weather.WeatherService" />
    </bean>
</beans>
```

For an XFireExporter instance, you have to configure a service object to export and its service interface. Note that this exporter requires a reference to the core xfire bean for actual web service processing. The xfire bean is defined in the bean configuration file bundled with the XFire library. You only have to configure ContextLoaderListener in your web.xml to load this file from the classpath.

```
<web-app ...>
    <context-param>
        <param-name>contextConfigLocation</param-name>
        <param-value>
            classpath:org/codehaus/xfire/spring/xfire.xml
        </param-value>
    </context-param>

    <listener>
        <listener-class>
            org.springframework.web.context.ContextLoaderListener
        </listener-class>
    </listener>
    ...
</web-app>
```

Now you can deploy your web application to a web container such as Apache Tomcat 6.0. Then you can access this web service with the following URL:

```
http://localhost:8080/weather/services/WeatherService
```

Inspecting the Generated WSDL File

Each web service requires a WSDL file for describing the service contract. XFire can generate the WSDL file for your service dynamically. For the weather service, you can access the WSDL file through the following URL:

```
http://localhost:8080/weather/services/WeatherService?wsdl
```

The generated WSDL file for your weather service is shown following. For simplicity, the less important parts are omitted.

```xml
<?xml version="1.0" encoding="UTF-8" ?>
<wsdl:definitions targetNamespace="http://weather.springenterprise➥
recipes.apress.com"
    xmlns:tns="http://weather.springenterpriserecipes.apress.com"
    ...>
    <wsdl:types>
        <xsd:schema xmlns:xsd="http://www.w3.org/2001/XMLSchema"
            attributeFormDefault="qualified" elementFormDefault="qualified"
            targetNamespace="http://weather.springenterpriserecipes.apress.com">
            <xsd:complexType name="ArrayOfDateTime">
                <xsd:sequence>
                    <xsd:element maxOccurs="unbounded" minOccurs="0"
                        name="dateTime" type="xsd:dateTime" />
                </xsd:sequence>
            </xsd:complexType>
            <xsd:element name="getTemperatures">
                <xsd:complexType>
                    <xsd:sequence>
                        <xsd:element maxOccurs="1" minOccurs="1" name="in0"
                            nillable="true" type="xsd:string" />
                        <xsd:element maxOccurs="1" minOccurs="1" name="in1"
                            nillable="true" type="tns:ArrayOfDateTime" />
                    </xsd:sequence>
                </xsd:complexType>
            </xsd:element>
            <xsd:complexType name="ArrayOfTemperatureInfo">
                <xsd:sequence>
                    <xsd:element maxOccurs="unbounded" minOccurs="0"
                        name="TemperatureInfo" nillable="true"
                        type="tns:TemperatureInfo" />
                </xsd:sequence>
            </xsd:complexType>
            <xsd:complexType name="TemperatureInfo">
                <xsd:sequence>
                    <xsd:element minOccurs="0" name="average" type="xsd:double" />
                    <xsd:element minOccurs="0" name="city"
                        nillable="true" type="xsd:string" />
                    <xsd:element minOccurs="0" name="date" type="xsd:dateTime" />
                    <xsd:element minOccurs="0" name="max" type="xsd:double" />
                    <xsd:element minOccurs="0" name="min" type="xsd:double" />
                </xsd:sequence>
            </xsd:complexType>
```

```
            <xsd:element name="getTemperaturesResponse">
                <xsd:complexType>
                    <xsd:sequence>
                        <xsd:element maxOccurs="1" minOccurs="1" name="out"
                            nillable="true" type="tns:ArrayOfTemperatureInfo" />
                    </xsd:sequence>
                </xsd:complexType>
            </xsd:element>
        </xsd:schema>
    </wsdl:types>
    <wsdl:message name="getTemperaturesRequest">
        <wsdl:part name="parameters" element="tns:getTemperatures" />
    </wsdl:message>
    <wsdl:message name="getTemperaturesResponse">
        <wsdl:part name="parameters" element="tns:getTemperaturesResponse" />
    </wsdl:message>
    <wsdl:portType name="WeatherServicePortType">
        <wsdl:operation name="getTemperatures">
            <wsdl:input name="getTemperaturesRequest"
                message="tns:getTemperaturesRequest" />
            <wsdl:output name="getTemperaturesResponse"
                message="tns:getTemperaturesResponse" />
        </wsdl:operation>
    </wsdl:portType>
    ...
    <wsdl:service name="WeatherService">
        <wsdl:port name="WeatherServiceHttpPort"
            binding="tns:WeatherServiceHttpBinding">
            <wsdlsoap:address location=
                "http://localhost:8080/weather/services/WeatherService" />
        </wsdl:port>
    </wsdl:service>
</wsdl:definitions>
```

From the preceding WSDL file, you can see that XFire generates this file by making the following conversions:

- The package com.apress.springenterpriserecipes.weather is turned into the target namespace (targetNamespace) http://weather.springenterpriserecipes.apress.com.

- The class WeatherService is turned into the port type WeatherServicePortType.

- The method getTemperatures() is turned into the operation getTemperatures.

- The method arguments are turned into the getTemperatures element, including two subelements, in0 and in1, whose types are string and the ArrayOfDateTime complex type.

- The return value is turned into the getTemperaturesResponse element, including the subelement out, whose type is the ArrayOfTemperatureInfo complex type. It's an array of another complex type, TemperatureInfo, which has five elements: average, city, date, max, and min.

Invoking a Web Service Using XFire

By using XFire's client factory bean, you can invoke a web service just like a local bean. In the client bean configuration file, client.xml, you can use XFireClientFactoryBean to create a proxy for the web service. Then you can use this service as if it were a local bean.

```
<bean id="weatherService"
    class="org.codehaus.xfire.spring.remoting.XFireClientFactoryBean">
    <property name="wsdlDocumentUrl"
        value="http://localhost:8080/weather/services/WeatherService?wsdl" />
    <property name="serviceInterface"
        value="com.apress.springenterpriserecipes.weather.WeatherService" />
</bean>
```

Two properties have to be configured for an XFireClientFactoryBean instance. The WSDL URL property specifies the URL for the WSDL file. The service interface property is for this factory bean to create a proxy for the web service. The proxy will transfer the invocation requests to the web service transparently.

Exposing an Annotation-Based Web Service Using XFire

XFire also supports the web service annotations defined by JSR-181: Web Services Metadata for the Java Platform. It can automatically export your beans annotated with the web service annotations without manual configuration. First of all, you have to annotate your web service implementation class with these annotations.

■Note   To use the JSR-181 web service annotations, you have to copy xfire-jsr181-api-1.0-M1.jar (located in the lib directory of the XFire installation) to the WEB-INF/lib directory.

```
package com.apress.springenterpriserecipes.weather;
...
import javax.jws.WebMethod;
import javax.jws.WebService;

@WebService(serviceName = "WeatherService")
public class WeatherServiceImpl implements WeatherService {

    @WebMethod(operationName = "getTemperatures")
    public List<TemperatureInfo> getTemperatures(String city, List<Date> dates) {
        ...
    }
}
```

Then you can simply define a `Jsr181HandlerMapping` bean to map the web service requests to appropriate service beans according to the JSR-181 annotations. To make the mappings consistent with before, you should set the `urlPrefix` property to `/`, so that it will be added in front of the service names specified in the annotation. Remember that you also have to inject the core `xfire` bean into this handler mapping.

```
<beans ...>
    <bean id="weatherService"
        class="com.apress.springenterpriserecipes.weather.WeatherServiceImpl" />

    <bean class="org.codehaus.xfire.spring.remoting.Jsr181HandlerMapping">
        <property name="xfire" ref="xfire" />
        <property name="webAnnotations">
            <bean class="org.codehaus.xfire.annotations.jsr181.Jsr181➡
WebAnnotations" />
        </property>
        <property name="urlPrefix" value="/" />
    </bean>
</beans>
```

5-9. Defining the Contract of Web Services

Problem

According to the contract-first web service approach, the first step of developing a web service is to define the service contract.

Solution

A web service's contract consists of two parts: the data contract and the service contract. They are both defined with the XML technology in a platform- and language-independent way.

Data contract: Describes the complex data types and request and response messages of this web service. A data contract is typically defined with XSD, although you can also use DTDs, RELAX NG, or Schematron.

Service contract: Describes the operations of this web service. A web service may have multiple operations. A service contract is defined with WSDL.

When using a comprehensive web service development framework like Spring-WS, the service contract can usually be generated automatically. But you must create the data contract yourself.

To create the data contract for your web service, you can start by creating the XSD file. Because there are many powerful XML tools available in the community, this won't be too hard. However, most developers prefer to start by creating some sample XML messages, and then generate the XSD file from them. Of course, you need to optimize the generated XSD file yourself, as it may not fit your requirements entirely, and sometimes you may wish to add more constraints to it.

How It Works

Creating Sample XML Messages

For your weather service, you can represent the temperature of a particular city and date as in the following XML message:

```
<TemperatureInfo city="Houston" date="2007-12-01">
    <min>5.0</min>
    <max>10.0</max>
    <average>8.0</average>
</TemperatureInfo>
```

Then, you can define the data contract for your weather service. Suppose you want to define an operation that allows clients to query the temperatures of a particular city for multiple dates. Each request consists of a `city` element and multiple date elements. You should also specify the namespace for this request to avoid naming conflicts with other XML documents. Let's save this XML message to `request.xml`.

```
<GetTemperaturesRequest
    xmlns="http://springenterpriserecipes.apress.com/weather/schemas">
    <city>Houston</city>
    <date>2007-12-01</date>
    <date>2007-12-08</date>
    <date>2007-12-15</date>
</GetTemperaturesRequest>
```

The response consists of multiple `TemperatureInfo` elements, each of which represents the temperature of a particular city and date, in accordance with the requested dates. Let's save this XML message to `response.xml`.

```
<GetTemperaturesResponse
    xmlns="http://springenterpriserecipes.apress.com/weather/schemas">
    <TemperatureInfo city="Houston" date="2007-12-01">
        <min>5.0</min>
        <max>10.0</max>
        <average>8.0</average>
    </TemperatureInfo>
    <TemperatureInfo city="Houston" date="2007-12-08">
        <min>4.0</min>
        <max>13.0</max>
        <average>7.0</average>
    </TemperatureInfo>
    <TemperatureInfo city="Houston" date="2007-12-15">
        <min>10.0</min>
        <max>18.0</max>
        <average>15.0</average>
    </TemperatureInfo>
</GetTemperaturesResponse>
```

Generating an XSD File from Sample XML Messages

Now you can generate the XSD file from the preceding sample XML messages. Most popular XML tools and enterprise Java IDEs can generate an XSD file from a couple of XML files. Here, I have chosen Apache XMLBeans (http://xmlbeans.apache.org/) to generate my XSD file.

■Note   You can download Apache XMLBeans (e.g., v2.4.0) from the Apache XMLBeans web site and extract it to a directory of your choice to complete the installation.

Apache XMLBeans provides a tool called inst2xsd for generating XSD files from XML instance files. It supports several design types for generating XSD files. The simplest is called *Russian doll design*, which generates local elements and local types for the target XSD file. Because there's no enumeration type used in your XML messages, you should also disable the enumeration generation feature. You can execute the following command to generate the XSD file for your data contract:

```
inst2xsd -design rd -enumerations never request.xml response.xml
```

The generated XSD file will have the default name schema0.xsd, located in the same directory. Let's rename it to temperature.xsd.

```
<?xml version="1.0" encoding="UTF-8"?>
<xs:schema attributeFormDefault="unqualified"
    elementFormDefault="qualified"
    targetNamespace="http://springenterpriserecipes.apress.com/weather/schemas"
    xmlns:xs="http://www.w3.org/2001/XMLSchema">

    <xs:element name="GetTemperaturesRequest">
        <xs:complexType>
            <xs:sequence>
                <xs:element type="xs:string" name="city" />
                <xs:element type="xs:date" name="date"
                    maxOccurs="unbounded" minOccurs="0" />
            </xs:sequence>
        </xs:complexType>
    </xs:element>

    <xs:element name="GetTemperaturesResponse">
        <xs:complexType>
            <xs:sequence>
                <xs:element name="TemperatureInfo"
                    maxOccurs="unbounded" minOccurs="0">
                    <xs:complexType>
                        <xs:sequence>
                            <xs:element type="xs:float" name="min" />
                            <xs:element type="xs:float" name="max" />
                            <xs:element type="xs:float" name="average" />
```

```
                    </xs:sequence>
                    <xs:attribute type="xs:string" name="city"
                            use="optional" />
                    <xs:attribute type="xs:date" name="date"
                            use="optional" />
                </xs:complexType>
            </xs:element>
        </xs:sequence>
    </xs:complexType>
</xs:element>
</xs:schema>
```

Optimizing the Generated XSD File

As you can see, the generated XSD file allows clients to query temperatures of unlimited dates. If you want to add a constraint on the maximum and minimum query dates, you can modify the maxOccurs and minOccurs attributes.

```
<?xml version="1.0" encoding="UTF-8"?>
<xs:schema attributeFormDefault="unqualified"
    elementFormDefault="qualified"
    targetNamespace="http://springenterpriserecipes.apress.com/weather/schemas"
    xmlns:xs="http://www.w3.org/2001/XMLSchema">

    <xs:element name="GetTemperaturesRequest">
        <xs:complexType>
            <xs:sequence>
                <xs:element type="xs:string" name="city" />
                <xs:element type="xs:date" name="date"
                    maxOccurs="5" minOccurs="1" />
            </xs:sequence>
        </xs:complexType>
    </xs:element>

    <xs:element name="GetTemperaturesResponse">
        <xs:complexType>
            <xs:sequence>
                <xs:element name="TemperatureInfo"
                    maxOccurs="5" minOccurs="1">
                    ...
                </xs:element>
            </xs:sequence>
        </xs:complexType>
    </xs:element>
</xs:schema>
```

Previewing the Generated WSDL File

As you will learn later, Spring-WS can automatically generate the service contract for you, based on the data contract and some conventions that you can override. Here, you can preview the generated WSDL file to better understand the service contract. For simplicity's sake, the less-important parts are omitted.

```
<?xml version="1.0" encoding="UTF-8" ?>
<wsdl:definitions ...
    targetNamespace="http://springenterpriserecipes.apress.com/weather/schemas">
    <wsdl:types>
        <!-- Copied from the XSD file -->
        ...
    </wsdl:types>
    <wsdl:message name="GetTemperaturesResponse">
        <wsdl:part element="schema:GetTemperaturesResponse"
            name="GetTemperaturesResponse">
        </wsdl:part>
    </wsdl:message>
    <wsdl:message name="GetTemperaturesRequest">
        <wsdl:part element="schema:GetTemperaturesRequest"
            name="GetTemperaturesRequest">
        </wsdl:part>
    </wsdl:message>
    <wsdl:portType name="Weather">
        <wsdl:operation name="GetTemperatures">
            <wsdl:input message="schema:GetTemperaturesRequest"
                name="GetTemperaturesRequest">
            </wsdl:input>
            <wsdl:output message="schema:GetTemperaturesResponse"
                name="GetTemperaturesResponse">
            </wsdl:output>
        </wsdl:operation>
    </wsdl:portType>
    ...
    <wsdl:service name="WeatherService">
        <wsdl:port binding="schema:WeatherBinding" name="WeatherPort">
            <soap:address
                location="http://localhost:8080/weather/services" />
        </wsdl:port>
    </wsdl:service>
</wsdl:definitions>
```

In the Weather port type, a GetTemperatures operation is defined, whose name is derived from the prefix of the input and output messages (i.e., <GetTemperaturesRequest> and <GetTemperaturesResponse>). The definitions of these two elements are included in the <wsdl:types> part, as defined in the data contract.

5-10. Implementing Web Services Using Spring-WS

Problem

Once you have defined the contract for your web service, you can start implementing the service itself according to this contract. You want to use Spring-WS to implement this service.

Solution

Spring-WS provides a set of facilities for you to develop contract-first web services. The essential tasks for building a Spring-WS web service include the following:

- Setting up and configuring a Spring MVC application for Spring-WS

- Mapping web service requests to endpoints

- Creating service endpoints to handle the request messages and return the response messages

- Publishing the WSDL file for this web service

The concept of an *endpoint* in web services is much like that of a controller in web applications. The difference is that a web controller deals with HTTP requests and HTTP responses, while a service endpoint deals with XML request messages and XML response messages. They both need to invoke other back-end services to handle the requests.

Spring-WS provides various abstract endpoint classes for you to process the request and response XML messages using different XML processing technologies/APIs. These classes are all located in the `org.springframework.ws.server.endpoint` package. You can simply extend one of them to process the XML messages with a particular technology/API. Table 5-2 lists these endpoint classes.

Table 5-2. Endpoint Classes for Different XML Processing Technologies/APIs

Technology/API	Endpoint Class
DOM	AbstractDomPayloadEndpoint
JDOM	AbstractJDomPayloadEndpoint
dom4j	AbstractDom4jPayloadEndpoint
XOM	AbstractXomPayloadEndpoint
SAX	AbstractSaxPayloadEndpoint
Event-based StAX	AbstractStaxEventPayloadEndpoint
Streaming StAX	AbstractStaxStreamPayloadEndpoint
XML marshalling	AbstractMarshallingPayloadEndpoint

Note that the preceding endpoint classes are all for creating payload endpoints. That means you can access only the payloads of the request and response messages (i.e., the contents in the SOAP body, but not other parts of the messages like the SOAP headers). If you need to get access to the entire SOAP message, you should write an endpoint class by implementing the `org.springframework.ws.server.endpoint.MessageEndpoint` interface.

How It Works

Setting Up a Spring-WS Application

To implement a web service using Spring-WS, you first create the following directory structure for your web application context. Ensure that your `lib` directory contains the latest version of Spring-WS.

```
weather/
    WEB-INF/
        classes/
        lib/*jar
        temperature.xsd
        weather-servlet.xml
        web.xml
```

In `web.xml`, you have to configure the `MessageDispatcherServlet` servlet of Spring-WS, which is different from `DispatcherServlet` for a typical Spring MVC application. This servlet specializes in dispatching web service messages to appropriate endpoints and detecting the framework facilities of Spring-WS.

```xml
<web-app version="2.4" xmlns="http://java.sun.com/xml/ns/j2ee"
    xmlns:xsi="http://www.w3.org/2001/XMLSchema-instance"
    xsi:schemaLocation="http://java.sun.com/xml/ns/j2ee
        http://java.sun.com/xml/ns/j2ee/web-app_2_4.xsd">

    <servlet>
        <servlet-name>weather</servlet-name>
        <servlet-class>
            org.springframework.ws.transport.http.MessageDispatcherServlet
        </servlet-class>
        <load-on-startup>1</load-on-startup>
    </servlet>

    <servlet-mapping>
        <servlet-name>weather</servlet-name>
        <url-pattern>/services/*</url-pattern>
    </servlet-mapping>
</web-app>
```

In the Spring MVC configuration file, `weather-servlet.xml`, you first declare a bean for the weather service implementation. Later, you will define endpoints and mappings to handle the web service requests.

```xml
<beans xmlns="http://www.springframework.org/schema/beans"
    xmlns:xsi="http://www.w3.org/2001/XMLSchema-instance"
    xsi:schemaLocation="http://www.springframework.org/schema/beans
        http://www.springframework.org/schema/beans/spring-beans-3.0.xsd">

    <bean id="weatherService"
        class="com.apress.springenterpriserecipes.weather.WeatherServiceImpl" />
</beans>
```

Mapping Web Service Requests to Endpoints

In a Spring MVC application, you use handler mapping to map web requests to handlers. But in a Spring-WS application, you should use endpoint mapping to map web service requests to endpoints.

The most common endpoint mapping is PayloadRootQNameEndpointMapping. It maps web service requests to endpoints according to the name of the request payload's root element. The name used by this endpoint mapping is the qualified name (i.e., including the namespace). So you must include the namespace in the mapping keys, which is presented inside a brace.

```
<bean class="org.springframework.ws.server.endpoint.mapping. ➥
    PayloadRootQNameEndpointMapping">
    <property name="mappings">
        <props>
            <prop key="{http://springenterpriserecipes.apress.com/weather/schemas}➥
                GetTemperaturesRequest">
                temperatureEndpoint
            </prop>
        </props>
    </property>
</bean>
```

Creating Service Endpoints

Spring-WS supports various XML parsing APIs, including DOM, JDOM, dom4j, SAX, StAX, and XOM. As an example, I will use dom4j (http://www.dom4j.org) to create a service endpoint. Creating an endpoint using other XML parsing APIs is very similar.

You can create a dom4j endpoint by extending the AbstractDom4jPayloadEndpoint class. The core method defined in this class that you must override is invokeInternal(). In this method, you can access the request XML element, whose type is org.dom4j.Element, and the response document, whose type is org.dom4j.Document, as method arguments. The purpose of the response document is for you to create the response element from it. Now all you have to do in this method is handle the request message and return the response message.

■Note   To create a service endpoint using dom4j with XPath, you have to copy dom4j-1.6.1.jar (located in the lib/dom4j directory of the Spring-WS installation) and jaxen-1.1.1.jar (located in lib/jaxen) to the WEB-INF/lib directory.

```
package com.apress.springenterpriserecipes.weather;
...
import org.dom4j.Document;
import org.dom4j.Element;
import org.dom4j.XPath;
import org.dom4j.xpath.DefaultXPath;
import org.springframework.ws.server.endpoint.AbstractDom4jPayloadEndpoint;
```

```java
public class TemperatureDom4jEndpoint extends AbstractDom4jPayloadEndpoint {

    private static final String namespaceUri =
        "http://springenterpriserecipes.apress.com/weather/schemas";

    private XPath cityPath;
    private XPath datePath;
    private DateFormat dateFormat;
    private WeatherService weatherService;

    public TemperatureDom4jEndpoint() {

        // Create the XPath objects, including the namespace
        Map<String, String> namespaceUris = new HashMap<String, String>();
        namespaceUris.put("weather", namespaceUri);
        cityPath = new DefaultXPath(
            "/weather:GetTemperaturesRequest/weather:city");
        cityPath.setNamespaceURIs(namespaceUris);
        datePath = new DefaultXPath(
            "/weather:GetTemperaturesRequest/weather:date");
        datePath.setNamespaceURIs(namespaceUris);

        dateFormat = new SimpleDateFormat("yyyy-MM-dd");
    }

    public void setWeatherService(WeatherService weatherService) {
        this.weatherService = weatherService;
    }

    protected Element invokeInternal(Element requestElement,
            Document responseDocument) throws Exception {

        // Extract the service parameters from the request message
        String city = cityPath.valueOf(requestElement);
        List<Date> dates = new ArrayList<Date>();
        for (Object node : datePath.selectNodes(requestElement)) {
            Element element = (Element) node;
            dates.add(dateFormat.parse(element.getText()));
        }

        // Invoke the back-end service to handle the request
        List<TemperatureInfo> temperatures =
            weatherService.getTemperatures(city, dates);

        // Build the response message from the result of back-end service
        Element responseElement = responseDocument.addElement(
                "GetTemperaturesResponse", namespaceUri);
        for (TemperatureInfo temperature : temperatures) {
            Element temperatureElement = responseElement.addElement(
                    "TemperatureInfo");
            temperatureElement.addAttribute("city", temperature.getCity());
            temperatureElement.addAttribute(
                    "date", dateFormat.format(temperature.getDate()));
```

```
            temperatureElement.addElement("min").setText(
                    Double.toString(temperature.getMin()));
            temperatureElement.addElement("max").setText(
                    Double.toString(temperature.getMax()));
            temperatureElement.addElement("average").setText(
                    Double.toString(temperature.getAverage()));
        }
        return responseElement;
    }
}
```

In the preceding invokeInternal() method, you first extract the service parameters from the request message. Here, you use XPath to help locate the elements. The XPath objects are created in the constructor so that they can be reused for subsequent request handling. Note that you must also include the namespace in the XPath expressions, or else they will not be able to locate the elements correctly.

After extracting the service parameters, you invoke the back-end service to handle the request. Because this endpoint is configured in the Spring IoC container, it can easily refer to other beans through dependency injection.

Finally, you build the response message from the back-end service's result. The dom4j library provides a rich set of APIs for you to build an XML message. Remember that you must include the default namespace in your response element.

With the service endpoint written, you can declare it in weather-servlet.xml. Because this endpoint needs the weather service bean's help to query temperatures, you have to make a reference to it.

```
<bean id="temperatureEndpoint"
    class="com.apress.springenterpriserecipes.weather.TemperatureDom4jEndpoint">
    <property name="weatherService" ref="weatherService" />
</bean>
```

Publishing the WSDL File

The last step to complete your web service is to publish the WSDL file. In Spring-WS, it's not necessary for you to write the WSDL file manually, although you may still supply a manually written WSDL file. You only declare a DynamicWsdl11Definition bean in the web application context, and then it can generate the WSDL file dynamically. MessageDispatcherServlet can also detect this bean by the WsdlDefinition interface.

```
<bean id="temperature"
    class="org.springframework.ws.wsdl.wsdl11.DynamicWsdl11Definition">
    <property name="builder">
        <bean class="org.springframework.ws.wsdl.wsdl11.builder.➥
            XsdBasedSoap11Wsdl4jDefinitionBuilder">
            <property name="schema" value="/WEB-INF/temperature.xsd" />
            <property name="portTypeName" value="Weather" />
            <property name="locationUri"
                    value="http://localhost:8080/weather/services" />
        </bean>
    </property>
</bean>
```

The only property you must configure for this WSDL definition bean is a builder that builds the WSDL file from your XSD file. XsdBasedSoap11Wsdl4jDefinitionBuilder builds the WSDL file using the WSDL4J library. Suppose that you have put your XSD file in the WEB-INF directory—you specify this location in the schema property. This builder scans the XSD file for elements that end with the Request or Response suffix. Then it generates WSDL operations using these elements as input and output messages, inside a WSDL port type specified by the portTypeName property.

Because you have defined <GetTemperaturesRequest> and <GetTemperaturseResponse> in your XSD file, and you have specified the port type name as Weather, the WSDL builder will generate the following WSDL port type and operation for you. The following snippet is taken from the generated WSDL file:

```
<wsdl:portType name="Weather">
    <wsdl:operation name="GetTemperatures">
        <wsdl:input message="schema:GetTemperaturesRequest"
            name="GetTemperaturesRequest" />
        <wsdl:output message="schema:GetTemperaturesResponse"
            name="GetTemperaturesResponse" />
    </wsdl:operation>
</wsdl:portType>
```

The last property, locationUri, is for you to include this web service's deployed location in the WSDL file. To allow an easy switch to a production URI, you should externalize this URI in a properties file and use Spring's PropertyPlaceholderConfigurer to read the properties from it.

Finally, you can access this WSDL file by joining its definition's bean name and the .wsdl suffix. Supposing that your service is deployed in http://localhost:8080/weather/services, this WSDL file's URL would be http://localhost:8080/weather/services/temperature.wsdl, given that the bean name of the WSDL definition is temperature.

5-11. Invoking Web Services Using Spring-WS

Problem

Given the contract of a web service, you can start creating a service client to invoke this service according to the contract. You want to use Spring-WS to create the service client.

Solution

When using Spring-WS on the client side, web services can be invoked through the core template class org.springframework.ws.client.core.WebServiceTemplate. It's very like the JdbcTemplate class and other data access templates in that it defines template methods for sending and receiving request and response messages.

How It Works

Now let's create a Spring-WS client to invoke the weather service according to the contract it publishes. You can create a Spring-WS client by parsing the request and response XML messages. As an example, I will use dom4j to implement it. You are free to choose other XML parsing APIs for it, however.

To shield the client from the low-level invocation details, you can create a local proxy for the remote web service. This proxy also implements the WeatherService interface, and it will translate local method calls into remote web service calls.

■Note   To invoke a web service using Spring-WS, you have to include spring-ws-1.5.8.jar (located in the dist directory of the Spring-WS installation), stax-api-1.0.2.jar (located in lib/stax), activation-1.1.1.jar and saaj-api-1.3.jar (located in lib/java-ee), and saaj-impl-1.3.jar (located in lib/saaj) in your classpath. To use dom4j, you also have to include dom4j-1.6.1.jar (located in lib/dom4j).

```java
package com.apress.springenterpriserecipes.weather;
...
import org.dom4j.Document;
import org.dom4j.DocumentHelper;
import org.dom4j.Element;
import org.dom4j.io.DocumentResult;
import org.dom4j.io.DocumentSource;
import org.springframework.ws.client.core.WebServiceTemplate;

public class WeatherServiceProxy implements WeatherService {

    private static final String namespaceUri =
        "http://springenterpriserecipes.apress.com/weather/schemas";

    private DateFormat dateFormat;
    private WebServiceTemplate webServiceTemplate;

    public WeatherServiceProxy() throws Exception {
        dateFormat = new SimpleDateFormat("yyyy-MM-dd");
    }

    public void setWebServiceTemplate(WebServiceTemplate webServiceTemplate) {
        this.webServiceTemplate = webServiceTemplate;
    }

    public List<TemperatureInfo> getTemperatures(String city, List<Date> dates) {

        // Build the request document from the method arguments
        Document requestDocument = DocumentHelper.createDocument();
        Element requestElement = requestDocument.addElement(
                "GetTemperaturesRequest", namespaceUri);
        requestElement.addElement("city").setText(city);
        for (Date date : dates) {
            requestElement.addElement("date").setText(dateFormat.format(date));
        }

        // Invoke the remote web service
        DocumentSource source = new DocumentSource(requestDocument);
        DocumentResult result = new DocumentResult();
        webServiceTemplate.sendSourceAndReceiveToResult(source, result);
```

```
// Extract the result from the response document
Document responsetDocument = result.getDocument();
Element responseElement = responsetDocument.getRootElement();
List<TemperatureInfo> temperatures = new ArrayList<TemperatureInfo>();
for (Object node : responseElement.elements("TemperatureInfo")) {
    Element element = (Element) node;
    try {
        Date date = dateFormat.parse(element.attributeValue("date"));
        double min = Double.parseDouble(element.elementText("min"));
        double max = Double.parseDouble(element.elementText("max"));
        double average = Double.parseDouble(
                element.elementText("average"));
        temperatures.add(
                new TemperatureInfo(city, date, min, max, average));
    } catch (ParseException e) {
        throw new RuntimeException(e);
    }
}
        return temperatures;
    }
}
```

In the getTemperatures() method, you first build the request message using the dom4j
API. WebServiceTemplate provides a sendSourceAndReceiveToResult() method that accepts a
java.xml.transform.Source and a java.xml.transform.Result object as arguments. You have to build a
dom4j DocumentSource object to wrap your request document, and create a new dom4j DocumentResult
object for the method to write the response document to it. Finally, you get the response message and
extract the results from it.

With the service proxy written, you can declare it in a client bean configuration file such as
client.xml. Because this proxy requires an instance of WebServiceTemplate for sending and receiving the
messages, you have to instantiate it and inject this instance into the proxy. Also, you specify the default
service URI for the template so that all the requests will be sent to this URI by default.

```
<beans xmlns="http://www.springframework.org/schema/beans"
    xmlns:xsi="http://www.w3.org/2001/XMLSchema-instance"
    xsi:schemaLocation="http://www.springframework.org/schema/beans
        http://www.springframework.org/schema/beans/spring-beans-3.0.xsd">

    <bean id="client"
        class="com.apress.springenterpriserecipes.weather.WeatherServiceClient">
        <property name="weatherService" ref="weatherServiceProxy" />
    </bean>

    <bean id="weatherServiceProxy"
        class="com.apress.springenterpriserecipes.weather.WeatherServiceProxy">
        <property name="webServiceTemplate" ref="webServiceTemplate" />
    </bean>

    <bean id="webServiceTemplate"
        class="org.springframework.ws.client.core.WebServiceTemplate">
        <property name="defaultUri"
            value="http://localhost:8080/weather/services" />
    </bean>
</beans>
```

Now you can inject this manually written proxy into WeatherServiceClient and run it with the Client main class.

Because your DAO class can extend JdbcDaoSupport to get a precreated JdbcTemplate instance, your web service client can similarly extend the WebServiceGatewaySupport class to retrieve a WebServiceTemplate instance without explicit injection. At this point, you can comment out the webServiceTemplate variable and setter method.

```
package com.apress.springenterpriserecipes.weather;
...
import org.springframework.ws.client.core.support.WebServiceGatewaySupport;

public class WeatherServiceProxy extends WebServiceGatewaySupport
        implements WeatherService {

    public List<TemperatureInfo> getTemperatures(String city, List<Date> dates) {
        ...
        // Invoke the remote web service
        DocumentSource source = new DocumentSource(requestDocument);
        DocumentResult result = new DocumentResult();
        getWebServiceTemplate().sendSourceAndReceiveToResult(source, result);
        ...
    }
}
```

However, without a WebServiceTemplate bean declared explicitly, you have to inject the default URI to the proxy directly. The setter method for this property is inherited from the WebServiceGatewaySupport class.

```
<beans ...>
    ...
    <bean id="weatherServiceProxy"
        class="com.apress.springenterpriserecipes.weather.WeatherServiceProxy">
        <property name="defaultUri"
            value="http://localhost:8080/weather/services" />
    </bean>
</beans>
```

5-12. Developing Web Services with XML Marshalling

Problem
To develop web services with the contract-first approach, you have to process request and response XML messages. If you parse the XML messages with XML parsing APIs directly, you'll have to deal with the XML elements one by one with low-level APIs, which is a cumbersome and inefficient task.

Solution
Spring-WS supports using XML marshalling technology to marshal/unmarshal objects to/from XML documents. In this way, you can deal with object properties instead of XML elements. This technology is also known as *object/XML mapping (OXM)*, because you are actually mapping objects to and from XML documents.

To implement endpoints with an XML marshalling technology, you have to extend the `AbstractMarshallingPayloadEndpoint` class and configure an XML marshaller for it. Table 5-3 lists the marshallers provided by Spring-WS for different XML marshalling APIs.

Table 5-3. Marshallers for Different XML Marshalling APIs

API	Marshaller
JAXB 1.0	`org.springframework.oxm.jaxb.Jaxb1Marshaller`
JAXB 2.0	`org.springframework.oxm.jaxb.Jaxb2Marshaller`
Castor	`org.springframework.oxm.castor.CastorMarshaller`
XMLBeans	`org.springframework.oxm.xmlbeans.XmlBeansMarshaller`
JiBX	`org.springframework.oxm.jibx.JibxMarshaller`
XStream	`org.springframework.oxm.xstream.XStreamMarshaller`

To invoke a web service, `WebServiceTemplate` also allows you to choose an XML marshalling technology to process the request and response XML messages.

How It Works

Creating Service Endpoints with XML Marshalling

Spring-WS supports various XML marshalling APIs, including JAXB 1.0, JAXB 2.0, Castor, XMLBeans, JiBX, and XStream. As an example, I will create a service endpoint using Castor (http://www.castor.org/) as the marshaller. Using other XML marshalling APIs is very similar.

The first step in using XML marshalling is creating the object model according to the XML message formats. This model can usually be generated by the marshalling API. For some marshalling APIs, the object model must be generated by them so that they can insert marshalling-specific information. Because Castor supports marshalling between XML messages and arbitrary Java objects, you can start creating the following classes by yourself.

```
package com.apress.springenterpriserecipes.weather;
...
public class GetTemperaturesRequest {

    private String city;
    private List<Date> dates;

    // Constructors, Getters and Setters
    ...
}
```

```
package com.apress.springenterpriserecipes.weather;
...
public class GetTemperaturesResponse {

    private List<TemperatureInfo> temperatures;

    // Constructors, Getters and Setters
    ...
}
```

With the object model created, you can write a marshalling endpoint by extending the AbstractMarshallingPayloadEndpoint class. The core method defined in this class that you must override is invokeInternal(). In this method, you can access the request object, which is unmarshalled from the request message, as the method argument. Now all you have to do in this method is handle the request object and return the response object. Then it will be marshalled to the response XML message.

■Note To create a service endpoint using Castor, you have to copy castor-1. 2.jar (located in the lib/castor directory of the Spring-WS installation) and xercesImpl-2.8.1.jar (located in lib/xerces) to the WEB-INF/lib directory.

```
package com.apress.springenterpriserecipes.weather;
...
import org.springframework.ws.server.endpoint.AbstractMarshallingPayloadEndpoint;

public class TemperatureMarshallingEndpoint extends
        AbstractMarshallingPayloadEndpoint {

    private WeatherService weatherService;

    public void setWeatherService(WeatherService weatherService) {
        this.weatherService = weatherService;
    }

    protected Object invokeInternal(Object requestObject) throws Exception {
        GetTemperaturesRequest request = (GetTemperaturesRequest) requestObject;

        List<TemperatureInfo> temperatures =
            weatherService.getTemperatures(request.getCity(), request.getDates());

        return new GetTemperaturesResponse(temperatures);
    }
}
```

A marshalling endpoint requires both the marshaller and unmarshaller properties to be set. Usually, you can specify a single marshaller for both properties. For Castor, you declare a CastorMarshaller bean as the marshaller.

```
<beans ...>
    ...
    <bean id="temperatureEndpoint"
        class="com.apress.springenterpriserecipes.weather.Temperature➡
MarshallingEndpoint">
        <property name="marshaller" ref="marshaller" />
        <property name="unmarshaller" ref="marshaller" />
        <property name="weatherService" ref="weatherService" />
    </bean>

    <bean id="marshaller"
        class="org.springframework.oxm.castor.CastorMarshaller">
        <property name="mappingLocation" value="classpath:mapping.xml" />
    </bean>
</beans>
```

Note that Castor requires a mapping configuration file to know how to map objects to and from XML documents. You can create this file in the classpath root and specify it in the mappingLocation property (e.g., mapping.xml). The following Castor mapping file defines the mappings for the GetTemperaturesRequest, GetTemperaturesResponse, and TemperatureInfo classes:

```
<!DOCTYPE mapping PUBLIC "-//EXOLAB/Castor Mapping DTD Version 1.0//EN"
    "http://castor.org/mapping.dtd">

<mapping>
    <class name="com.apress.springenterpriserecipes.weather.GetTemperaturesRequest">
        <map-to xml="GetTemperaturesRequest"
            ns-uri="http://springenterpriserecipes.apress.com/weather/schemas" />
        <field name="city" type="string">
            <bind-xml name="city" node="element" />
        </field>
        <field name="dates" collection="arraylist" type="string"
            handler="com.apress.springenterpriserecipes.weather.DateFieldHandler">
            <bind-xml name="date" node="element" />
        </field>
    </class>

    <class name="com.apress.springenterpriserecipes.weather.➡
GetTemperaturesResponse">
        <map-to xml="GetTemperaturesResponse"
            ns-uri="http://springenterpriserecipes.apress.com/weather/schemas" />
        <field name="temperatures" collection="arraylist"
            type="com.apress.springenterpriserecipes.weather.TemperatureInfo">
            <bind-xml name="TemperatureInfo" node="element" />
        </field>
    </class>
```

```xml
    <class name="com.apress.springenterpriserecipes.weather.TemperatureInfo">
        <map-to xml="TemperatureInfo"
            ns-uri="http://springenterpriserecipes.apress.com/weather/schemas" />
        <field name="city" type="string">
            <bind-xml name="city" node="attribute" />
        </field>
        <field name="date" type="string"
            handler="com.apress.springenterpriserecipes.weather.DateFieldHandler">
            <bind-xml name="date" node="attribute" />
        </field>
        <field name="min" type="double">
            <bind-xml name="min" node="element" />
        </field>
        <field name="max" type="double">
            <bind-xml name="max" node="element" />
        </field>
        <field name="average" type="double">
            <bind-xml name="average" node="element" />
        </field>
    </class>
</mapping>
```

Remember that for each class mapping, you must specify the namespace URI for the element. Besides, for all the date fields, you have to specify a handler to convert the dates with a particular date format. The handler is implemented as shown following:

```java
package com.apress.springenterpriserecipes.weather;
...
import org.exolab.castor.mapping.GeneralizedFieldHandler;

public class DateFieldHandler extends GeneralizedFieldHandler {

    private DateFormat format = new SimpleDateFormat("yyyy-MM-dd");

    public Object convertUponGet(Object value) {
        return format.format((Date) value);
    }

    public Object convertUponSet(Object value) {
        try {
            return format.parse((String) value);
        } catch (ParseException e) {
            throw new RuntimeException(e);
        }
    }

    public Class getFieldType() {
        return Date.class;
    }
}
```

Invoking Web Services with XML Marshalling

A Spring-WS client can also marshal/unmarshal the request and response objects to/from XML messages. As an example, I will create a client using Castor as the marshaller so that you can reuse the object models GetTemperaturesRequest, GetTemperaturesResponse, and TemperatureInfo, and also the mapping configuration file, mapping.xml, from the service endpoint.

Let's implement the service proxy with XML marshalling. WebServiceTemplate provides a marshalSendAndReceive() method that accepts a request object as the method argument, which will be marshalled to the request message. This method has to return a response object that will be unmarshalled from the response message.

■Note   To create a service client using Castor, you have to include castor-1.2.jar (located in the lib/castor directory of the Spring-WS installation) and xercesImpl-2.8.1.jar (located in lib/xerces) in your classpath.

```
package com.apress.springenterpriserecipes.weather;
...
import org.springframework.ws.client.core.support.WebServiceGatewaySupport;

public class WeatherServiceProxy extends WebServiceGatewaySupport
        implements WeatherService {

    public List<TemperatureInfo> getTemperatures(String city, List<Date> dates) {
        GetTemperaturesRequest request = new GetTemperaturesRequest(city, dates);
        GetTemperaturesResponse response = (GetTemperaturesResponse)
            getWebServiceTemplate().marshalSendAndReceive(request);
        return response.getTemperatures();
    }
}
```

When using XML marshalling, WebServiceTemplate requires both the marshaller and unmarshaller properties to be set. You can also set them to WebServiceGatewaySupport if you extend this class to have WebServiceTemplate auto-created. Usually, you can specify a single marshaller for both properties. For Castor, you declare a CastorMarshaller bean as the marshaller.

```
<beans ...>
    <bean id="client"
        class="com.apress.springenterpriserecipes.weather.WeatherServiceClient">
        <property name="weatherService" ref="weatherServiceProxy" />
    </bean>

    <bean id="weatherServiceProxy"
        class="com.apress.springenterpriserecipes.weather.WeatherServiceProxy">
        <property name="defaultUri"
            value="http://localhost:8080/weather/services" />
        <property name="marshaller" ref="marshaller" />
        <property name="unmarshaller" ref="marshaller" />
    </bean>
```

```
    <bean id="marshaller"
        class="org.springframework.oxm.castor.CastorMarshaller">
        <property name="mappingLocation" value="classpath:mapping.xml" />
    </bean>
</beans>
```

5-13. Creating Service Endpoints with Annotations

Problem

By extending a Spring-WS base endpoint class, your endpoint class will be bound to the Spring-WS class hierarchy, and each endpoint class will only be able to handle one type of web service request.

Solution

Spring-WS supports annotating an arbitrary class as a service endpoint by the @Endpoint annotation, without extending a framework-specific class. You can also group multiple handler methods in an endpoint class so that it can handle multiple types of web service requests.

How It Works

For example, you can annotate your temperature endpoint with the @Endpoint annotation so that it doesn't need to extend a Spring-WS base endpoint class. The signature of the handler methods can also be more flexible.

```
package com.apress.springenterpriserecipes.weather;
...
import org.springframework.ws.server.endpoint.annotation.Endpoint;
import org.springframework.ws.server.endpoint.annotation.PayloadRoot;

@Endpoint
public class TemperatureMarshallingEndpoint {

    private static final String namespaceUri =
        "http://springenterpriserecipes.apress.com/weather/schemas";

    private WeatherService weatherService;

    public void setWeatherService(WeatherService weatherService) {
        this.weatherService = weatherService;
    }

    @PayloadRoot(
            localPart = "GetTemperaturesRequest",
            namespace = namespaceUri)
```

```
    public GetTemperaturesResponse getTemperature(GetTemperaturesRequest request) {
        List<TemperatureInfo> temperatures =
            weatherService.getTemperatures(request.getCity(), request.getDates());
        return new GetTemperaturesResponse(temperatures);
    }
}
```

Besides the @Endpoint annotation, you have to annotate each handler method with the @PayloadRoot annotation for mapping a service request. In this annotation, you specify the local name (localPort) and namespace of the payload root element to be handled. Then you just declare a PayloadRootAnnotationMethodEndpointMapping bean, and it will be able to detect the mapping from the @PayloadRoot annotation automatically.

```
<beans ...>
    ...
    </bean class="org.springframework.ws.server.endpoint.➥
mapping.PayloadRootAnnotationMethodEndpointMapping" />

    <bean id="temperatureEndpoint"
        class="com.apress.springenterpriserecipes.weather.Temperature➥
MarshallingEndpoint">
        <property name="weatherService" ref="weatherService" />
    </bean>

    <bean class="org.springframework.ws.server.endpoint.adapter.➥
GenericMarshallingMethodEndpointAdapter">
        <property name="marshaller" ref="marshaller" />
        <property name="unmarshaller" ref="marshaller" />
    </bean>

    <bean id="marshaller"
        class="org.springframework.oxm.castor.CastorMarshaller">
        <property name="mappingLocation" value="classpath:mapping.xml" />
    </bean>
</beans>
```

Because your endpoint class no longer extends a base endpoint class, it doesn't inherit the capabilities of marshalling and unmarshalling XML messages. You have to configure a GenericMarshallingMethodEndpointAdapter to do so.

Summary

This chapter discussed how to use Spring's remoting support. You learned how to set up an RMI service and about Spring's support for classic EJB and EJB3 services. Spring-WS, Spring's excellent support for web service creation, was also discussed.

In the next chapter, you will see some Spring framework tools for everyday requirements such as scheduling and sending e-mail.

CHAPTER 6

■ ■ ■

Spring in the Enterprise

In this chapter, you will learn about Spring's support for three common technologies on the Java EE platform: *Java Management Extensions (JMX)*, sending e-mail, and scheduling tasks.

JMX is a technology for managing and monitoring system resources such as devices, applications, objects, and service-driven networks. The specification is powerful for the management of systems at runtime and for adapting legacy systems. These resources are represented by *managed beans (MBeans)*. Originally, JMX was distributed separately, but it has been part of Java SE since version 5.0. JMX has seen many improvements, but the original specification for JMX_JSR 03_is very old! Spring supports JMX by allowing you to export any Spring beans as *model MBeans* (a kind of *dynamic MBean*), without programming against the JMX API. In addition, Spring enables you to access remote MBeans easily.

JavaMail is the standard API and implementation for sending e-mail in Java. Spring further provides an abstract layer for you to send e-mail in an implementation-independent fashion.

There are two main options for scheduling tasks on the Java platform: JDK Timer and Quartz Scheduler (http://www.opensymphony.com/quartz/). JDK Timer offers simple task scheduling features that you can use conveniently because the features are bundled with JDK. Compared with JDK Timer, Quartz offers more powerful job scheduling features. For both options, Spring supplies utility classes for you to configure scheduling tasks in the bean configuration file, without programming against their APIs.

Upon finishing this chapter, you will be able to export and access MBeans in a Spring application. You will also be able to utilize Spring's supporting features to simplify sending e-mail and scheduling tasks.

6-1. Exporting Spring Beans as JMX MBeans

Problem

You want to register an object from your Java application as a JMX MBean to allow management and monitoring. In this sense, management is the capability to look at services that are running and manipulate their runtime state on the fly. Imagine being able to do these tasks from a web page: rerun batch jobs, invoke methods, and change configuration metadata that you'd normally be able to do only at runtime. However, if you use the JMX API for this purpose, a lot of coding will be required, and you'll have to deal with JMX's complexity.

Solution

Spring supports JMX by allowing you to export any beans in its IoC container as model MBeans. This can be done simply by declaring an MBeanExporter instance. With Spring's JMX support, you no longer need to deal with the JMX API directly, so you can write code that is not JMX specific. In addition, Spring enables you to declare JSR-160 (Java Management Extensions Remote API) connectors to expose your MBeans for remote access over a specific protocol by using a factory bean. Spring provides factory beans for both servers and clients.

Spring's JMX support comes with other mechanisms by which you can assemble an MBean's management interface. These options include using exporting beans by method names, interfaces, and annotations. Spring can also detect and export your MBeans automatically from beans declared in the IoC container and annotated with JMX-specific annotations defined by Spring. The MBeanExporter class exports beans, delegating to an instance of MBeanInfoAssembler to do the heavy lifting.

How It Works

Suppose that you are developing a utility for replicating files from a source directory to a destination directory. Let's design the interface for this utility as follows:

```
package com.apress.springenterpriserecipes.replicator;
...
public interface FileReplicator {

    public String getSrcDir();
    public void setSrcDir(String srcDir);

    public String getDestDir();
    public void setDestDir(String destDir);

    public void replicate() throws IOException;
}
```

The source and destination directories are designed as properties of a replicator object, not method arguments. That means each file replicator instance replicates files only for a particular source and destination directory. You can create multiple replicator instances in your application.

Before you implement this replicator, you need another class that copies a file from one directory to another, given its name.

```
package com.apress.springenterpriserecipes.replicator;
...
public interface FileCopier {

    public void copyFile(String srcDir, String destDir, String filename)
            throws IOException;
}
```

There are many strategies for implementing this file copier. For instance, you can make use of the FileCopyUtils class provided by Spring.

```
package com.apress.springenterpriserecipes.replicator;
...
import org.springframework.util.FileCopyUtils;
```

```java
public class FileCopierJMXImpl implements FileCopier {

    public void copyFile(String srcDir, String destDir, String filename)
            throws IOException {
        File srcFile = new File(srcDir, filename);
        File destFile = new File(destDir, filename);
        FileCopyUtils.copy(srcFile, destFile);
    }
}
```

With the help of a file copier, you can implement your file replicator, as shown following. Each time you call the replicate() method, all files in the source directory will be replicated to the destination directory. To avoid unexpected problems caused by concurrent replication, you declare this method as synchronized.

```java
package com.apress.springenterpriserecipes.replicator;

import java.io.File;
import java.io.IOException;

public class FileReplicatorImpl implements FileReplicator {

    private String srcDir;
    private String destDir;
    private FileCopier fileCopier;

    // accessors …
    // mutators …

    public void setSrcDir(String srcDir) {
        this.srcDir = srcDir;
        revaluateDirectories();
    }

    public void setDestDir(String destDir) {
        this.destDir = destDir;
        revaluateDirectories();
    }

    public void setFileCopier(FileCopier fileCopier) {

            this.fileCopier = fileCopier;

    }


    public synchronized void replicate() throws IOException {
        File[] files = new File(srcDir).listFiles();
        for (File file : files) {
            if (file.isFile()) {
                fileCopier.copyFile(srcDir, destDir, file.getName());
            }
        }
    }
}
```

```java
    private void revaluateDirectories() {
        File src = new File(srcDir);
        File dest = new File(destDir);
        if (!src.exists())
            src.mkdirs();
        if (!dest.exists())
            dest.mkdirs();
    }
}
```

Now you can configure one or more file replicator instances in the bean configuration file for your needs (in the example, this file is called beans-jmx.xml). The documentReplicator instance needs references to two directories: a source directory from which files are read and a target directory to which files are backed up. The code in this example attempts to read from a directory called docs in your operating system user's home directory and then copy to a folder called docs_backup in your operating system user's home directory. When this bean starts up, it creates the two directories if they don't already exist there.

■Tip   The "home directory" is different for each operating system, but typically on Unix it's the directory that ~ resolves to. On a Linux box, the folder might be /home/user. On Mac OS X, the folder might be /Users/user, and on Windows it might similar to C:\Documents and Settings\user.

```xml
<beans xmlns="http://www.springframework.org/schema/beans"
    xmlns:xsi="http://www.w3.org/2001/XMLSchema-instance"
    xsi:schemaLocation="http://www.springframework.org/schema/beans
        http://www.springframework.org/schema/beans/spring-beans-3.0.xsd">

    <bean id="fileCopier"
        class="com.apress.springenterpriserecipes.replicator.FileJMXCopierImpl" />

    <bean id="documentReplicator"
        class="com.apress.springenterpriserecipes.replicator. ➥
FileJMXcReplicatorImpl">
        <property name="srcDir" value="#{systemProperties['user.home']}/docs" />
        <property name="destDir" value="#{systemProperties['user.home']}➥
/docs_backup" />
        <property name="fileCopier" ref="fileCopier" />
    </bean>
</beans>
```

Registering MBeans Without Spring's Support

First, let's see how to register a model MBean using the JMX API directly. In the following Main class, you get the documentReplicator bean from the IoC container and register it as an MBean for management and monitoring. All properties and methods are included in the MBean's management interface.

```java
package com.apress.springenterpriserecipes.replicator;
...
import java.lang.management.ManagementFactory;
```

```java
import javax.management.Descriptor;
import javax.management.JMException;
import javax.management.MBeanServer;
import javax.management.ObjectName;
import javax.management.modelmbean.DescriptorSupport;
import javax.management.modelmbean.InvalidTargetObjectTypeException;
import javax.management.modelmbean.ModelMBeanAttributeInfo;
import javax.management.modelmbean.ModelMBeanInfo;
import javax.management.modelmbean.ModelMBeanInfoSupport;
import javax.management.modelmbean.ModelMBeanOperationInfo;
import javax.management.modelmbean.RequiredModelMBean;

import org.springframework.context.ApplicationContext;
import org.springframework.context.support.ClassPathXmlApplicationContext;

public class Main {

    public static void main(String[] args) throws IOException {
        ApplicationContext context =
            new ClassPathXmlApplicationContext("beans.xml");

        FileReplicator documentReplicator =
            (FileReplicator) context.getBean("documentReplicator");

        try {
            MBeanServer mbeanServer = ManagementFactory.getPlatformMBeanServer();
            ObjectName objectName = new ObjectName("bean:name=documentReplicator");

            RequiredModelMBean mbean = new RequiredModelMBean();
            mbean.setManagedResource(documentReplicator, "objectReference");

            Descriptor srcDirDescriptor = new DescriptorSupport(new String[] {
                    "name=SrcDir", "descriptorType=attribute",
                    "getMethod=getSrcDir", "setMethod=setSrcDir" });
            ModelMBeanAttributeInfo srcDirInfo = new ModelMBeanAttributeInfo(
                    "SrcDir", "java.lang.String", "Source directory",
                    true, true, false, srcDirDescriptor);

            Descriptor destDirDescriptor = new DescriptorSupport(new String[] {
                    "name=DestDir", "descriptorType=attribute",
                    "getMethod=getDestDir", "setMethod=setDestDir" });
            ModelMBeanAttributeInfo destDirInfo = new ModelMBeanAttributeInfo(
                    "DestDir", "java.lang.String", "Destination directory",
                    true, true, false, destDirDescriptor);

            ModelMBeanOperationInfo getSrcDirInfo = new ModelMBeanOperationInfo(
                    "Get source directory",
                    FileReplicator.class.getMethod("getSrcDir"));
            ModelMBeanOperationInfo setSrcDirInfo = new ModelMBeanOperationInfo(
                    "Set source directory",
                    FileReplicator.class.getMethod("setSrcDir", String.class));
```

251

```
        ModelMBeanOperationInfo getDestDirInfo = new ModelMBeanOperationInfo(
                "Get destination directory",
                FileReplicator.class.getMethod("getDestDir"));
        ModelMBeanOperationInfo setDestDirInfo = new ModelMBeanOperationInfo(
                "Set destination directory",
                FileReplicator.class.getMethod("setDestDir", String.class));
        ModelMBeanOperationInfo replicateInfo = new ModelMBeanOperationInfo(
                "Replicate files",
                FileReplicator.class.getMethod("replicate"));

        ModelMBeanInfo mbeanInfo = new ModelMBeanInfoSupport(
                "FileReplicator", "File replicator",
                new ModelMBeanAttributeInfo[] { srcDirInfo, destDirInfo },
                null,
                new ModelMBeanOperationInfo[] { getSrcDirInfo, setSrcDirInfo,
                        getDestDirInfo, setDestDirInfo, replicateInfo },
                null);
        mbean.setModelMBeanInfo(mbeanInfo);

        mbeanServer.registerMBean(mbean, objectName);
    } catch (JMException e) {
        ...
    } catch (InvalidTargetObjectTypeException e) {
        ...
    } catch (NoSuchMethodException e) {
        ...
    }

    System.in.read();
    }
}
```

To register an MBean, you need an instance of the interface javax.managment.MBeanServer. In JDK 1.5, you can call the static method ManagementFactory.getPlatformMBeanServer() to locate a platform MBean server. It will create an MBean server if none exists, and then register this server instance for future use. Each MBean requires an MBean *object name* that includes a domain. The preceding MBean is registered under the domain bean with the name documentReplicator.

From the preceding code, you can see that for each MBean attribute and MBean operation, you need to create a ModelMBeanAttributeInfo object and a ModelMBeanOperationInfo object for describing it. After those, you have to create a ModelMBeanInfo object for describing the MBean's management interface by assembling the preceding information. For details about using these classes, you can consult their javadocs.

Moreover, you have to handle the JMX-specific exceptions when calling the JMX API. These exceptions are checked exceptions that you must handle.

Note that you must prevent your application from terminating before you look inside it with a JMX client tool. Requesting a key from the console using System.in.read() would be a good choice.

Finally, you have to add the VM argument -Dcom.sun.management.jmxremote to enable local monitoring of this application. You should also include all other options for your command, such as the classpath, as necessary.

```
java -Dcom.sun.management.jmxremote com.apress.➥
springenterpriserecipes.replicator.Main
```

Now you can use any JMX client tools to monitor your MBeans locally. The simplest one may be JConsole, which comes with JDK 1.5.

■Note   To start JConsole, just execute the `jconsole` executable file (located in the `bin` directory of the JDK installation).

When JConsole starts, you can see a list of JMX-enabled applications on the Local tab of the connection window. After connecting to the replicator application, you can see your `documentReplicator` MBean under the bean domain. If you want to invoke `replicate()`, simply click the button "replicate."

Exporting Spring Beans as MBeans

To export beans configured in the Spring IoC container as MBeans, you simply declare an `MBeanExporter` instance and specify the beans to export, with their MBean object names as the keys.

```
<bean id="mbeanExporter"
    class="org.springframework.jmx.export.MBeanExporter">
    <property name="beans">
        <map>
            <entry key="bean:name=documentReplicator"
                value-ref="documentReplicator" />
        </map>
    </property>
</bean>
```

The preceding configuration exports the `documentReplicator` bean as an MBean, under the domain bean and with the name `documentReplicator`. By default, all public properties are included as attributes and all public methods (with the exception of those from `java.lang.Object`) are included as operations in the MBean's management interface.

`MBeanExporter` attempts to locate an MBean server instance and register your MBeans with it implicitly. If your application is running in an environment that provides an MBean server (e.g., most Java EE application servers), `MBeanExporter` will be able to locate this MBean server instance.

However, in an environment with no MBean server available, you have to create one explicitly using Spring's `MBeanServerFactoryBean`. To make your application portable to different runtime environments, you should enable the `locateExistingServerIfPossible` property so that this factory bean will create an MBean server only if none is available.

■Note   JDK 1.5 will create an MBean server for the first time when you locate it. So, if you're using JDK 1.5 or above, you needn't create an MBean server explicitly.

```
<bean id="mbeanServer"
    class="org.springframework.jmx.support.MBeanServerFactoryBean">
    <property name="locateExistingServerIfPossible" value="true" />
</bean>
```

If, on the other hand, you have multiple MBeans servers running, you need to tell the mbeanServer bean to which server it should bind. You do this by specifying the agentId of the server. To figure out the agentId of a given server, browse to the JMImplementation/MBeanServerDelegate/Attributes/MBeanServerId node of the server you're inspecting in JConsole. There, you'll see the string value. On this author's local machine, the value is workstation_1253860476443. To enable it, configure the agentId property of the MBeanServer.

```
<bean id="mbeanServer"
    class="org.springframework.jmx.support.MBeanServerFactoryBean">
    <property name="locateExistingServerIfPossible" value="true" />
    <property name="agentId" value="workstation_1253860476443" />
</bean>
```

If you have multiple MBean server instances in your context, you can explicitly specify a specific MBean server for MBeanExporter to export your MBeans to. In this case, MBeanExporter will not locate an MBean server; it will use the specified MBean server instance. This property is for you to specify a particular MBean server when more than one is available.

```
<beans ...>
    ...
    <bean id="mbeanServer"
        class="org.springframework.jmx.support.MBeanServerFactoryBean">
        <property name="locateExistingServerIfPossible" value="true" />
    </bean>

    <bean id="mbeanExporter"
        class="org.springframework.jmx.export.MBeanExporter">
        ...
        <property name="server" ref="mbeanServer" />
    </bean>
</beans>
```

The Main class for exporting an MBean can be simplified as shown following. You have to retain the key-requesting statement to prevent your application from terminating.

```
package com.apress.springenterpriserecipes.replicator;
...
import org.springframework.context.support.ClassPathXmlApplicationContext;

public class Main {

    public static void main(String[] args) throws IOException {
        new ClassPathXmlApplicationContext("beans.xml");
        System.in.read();
    }
}
```

Exposing MBeans for Remote Access

If you want your MBeans to be accessed remotely, you need to enable a remoting protocol for JMX. JSR-160 defines a standard for JMX remoting through a JMX connector. Spring allows you to create a JMX connector server through ConnectorServerFactoryBean.

By default, `ConnectorServerFactoryBean` creates and starts a JMX connector server bound to the service URL `service:jmx:jmxmp://localhost:9875`, which exposes the JMX connector through the JMX Messaging Protocol (JMXMP). However, most JMX implementations, including JDK 1.5's, don't support JMXMP. Therefore, you should choose a widely supported remoting protocol for your JMX connector, such as RMI. To expose your JMX connector through a specific protocol, you just provide the service URL for it.

```
<beans ...>
    ...
    <bean id="rmiRegistry"
        class="org.springframework.remoting.rmi.RmiRegistryFactoryBean" />

    <bean id="connectorServer"
        class="org.springframework.jmx.support.ConnectorServerFactoryBean"
        depends-on="rmiRegistry">
        <property name="serviceUrl" value=
            "service:jmx:rmi://localhost/jndi/rmi://localhost:1099/replicator" />
    </bean>
</beans>
```

You specify the preceding URL to bind your JMX connector to an RMI registry listening on port 1099 of localhost. If no RMI registry has been created externally, you should create one by using `RmiRegistryFactoryBean`. The default port for this registry is 1099, but you can specify another one in its `port` property. Note that `ConnectorServerFactoryBean` must create the connector server after the RMI registry is created and ready. You can set the `depends-on` attribute for this purpose.

Now your MBeans can be accessed remotely via RMI. When JConsole starts, you can enter the following service URL on the Advanced tab of the connection window.

```
service:jmx:rmi://localhost/jndi/rmi://localhost:1099/replicator
```

Assembling the Management Interface of MBeans

Recall that by default, the Spring `MBeanExporter` exports all public properties of a bean as MBean attributes and all public methods as MBean operations. In fact, you can assemble the management interface of your MBeans using an MBean assembler. The simplest MBean assembler in Spring is `MethodNameBasedMBeanInfoAssembler`, which allows you to specify the names of the methods to export.

```
<beans ...>
    ...
    <bean id="mbeanExporter"
        class="org.springframework.jmx.export.MBeanExporter">
        ...
        <property name="assembler" ref="assembler" />
    </bean>

    <bean id="assembler" class="org.springframework.jmx.export.assembler.
        MethodNameBasedMBeanInfoAssembler">
        <property name="managedMethods">
            <list>
                <value>getSrcDir</value>
                <value>setSrcDir</value>
                <value>getDestDir</value>
                <value>setDestDir</value>
```

```
            <value>replicate</value>
        </list>
    </property>
</bean>
</beans>
```

Another MBean assembler is `InterfaceBasedMBeanInfoAssembler`, which exports all methods defined in the interfaces you specified.

```
<bean id="assembler" class="org.springframework.jmx.export.assembler.➥
InterfaceBasedMBeanInfoAssembler">
    <property name="managedInterfaces">
        <list>
            <value>com.apress.springenterpriserecipes.replicator. ➥
FileReplicator</value>
        </list>
    </property>
</bean>
```

Spring also provides `MetadataMBeanInfoAssembler` to assemble an MBean's management interface based on the metadata in the bean class. It supports two types of metadata: JDK annotations and Apache Commons Attributes (behind the scenes, this is accomplished using a strategy interface `JmxAttributeSource`). For a bean class annotated with JDK annotations, you specify an `AnnotationJmxAttributeSource` instance as the attribute source of `MetadataMBeanInfoAssembler`.

```
<bean id="assembler" class="org.springframework.jmx.export.assembler. ➥
    MetadataMBeanInfoAssembler">
    <property name="attributeSource">
        <bean class="org.springframework.jmx.export.annotation. ➥
            AnnotationJmxAttributeSource" />
    </property>
</bean>
```

Then you annotate your bean class and methods with the annotations `@ManagedResource`, `@ManagedAttribute`, and `@ManagedOperation` for `MetadataMBeanInfoAssembler` to assemble the management interface for this bean. The annotations are easily interpreted. They expose the element that they annotate. If you have a JavaBeans-compliant property, JMX will use the term *attribute*. Classes themselves are referred to as *resources*. In JMX, methods will be called *operations*. Knowing that, it's easy to see what the following code does:

```
package com.apress.springenterpriserecipes.replicator;
...
import org.springframework.jmx.export.annotation.ManagedAttribute;
import org.springframework.jmx.export.annotation.ManagedOperation;
import org.springframework.jmx.export.annotation.ManagedResource;

@ManagedResource(description = "File replicator")
public class FileReplicatorImpl implements FileReplicator {
    ...
    @ManagedAttribute(description = "Get source directory")
    public String getSrcDir() {
        ...
    }
```

```
@ManagedAttribute(description = "Set source directory")
public void setSrcDir(String srcDir) {
    ...
}

@ManagedAttribute(description = "Get destination directory")
public String getDestDir() {
    ...
}

@ManagedAttribute(description = "Set destination directory")
public void setDestDir(String destDir) {
    ...
}

    ...

@ManagedOperation(description = "Replicate files")
public synchronized void replicate() throws IOException {
    ...
}
}
```

Auto-Detecting MBeans by Annotations

In addition to exporting a bean explicitly with MBeanExporter, you can simply configure its subclass AnnotationMBeanExporter to auto-detect MBeans from beans declared in the IoC container. You needn't configure an MBean assembler for this exporter because it uses MetadataMBeanInfoAssembler with AnnotationJmxAttributeSource by default. You can delete the previous beans and assembler properties for this exporter.

```
<bean id="mbeanExporter"
    class="org.springframework.jmx.export.annotation.AnnotationMBeanExporter">
    ...
</bean>
```

AnnotationMBeanExporter detects any beans configured in the IoC container with the @ManagedResource annotation and exports them as MBeans. By default, this exporter exports a bean to the domain whose name is the same as its package name. Also, it uses the bean's name in the IoC container as its MBean name, and the bean's short class name as its type. So your documentReplicator bean will be exported under the following MBean object name:

```
com.apress.springenterpriserecipes.replicator:name=documentReplicator, ➡
type=FileReplicatorJMXImpl
```

If you don't want to use the package name as the domain name, you can set the default domain for this exporter.

```
<bean id="mbeanExporter"
    class="org.springframework.jmx.export.annotation.AnnotationMBeanExporter">
    ...
    <property name="defaultDomain" value="bean" />
</bean>
```

After setting the default domain to bean, the documentReplicator bean will be exported under the following MBean object name:

```
bean:name=documentReplicator,type=FileReplicatorJMXImpl
```

Moreover, you can specify a bean's MBean object name in the objectName attribute of the @ManagedResource annotation. For example, you can export your file copier as an MBean by annotating it with the following annotations:

```
package com.apress.springenterpriserecipes.replicator;
...
import org.springframework.jmx.export.annotation.ManagedOperation;
import org.springframework.jmx.export.annotation.ManagedOperationParameter;
import org.springframework.jmx.export.annotation.ManagedOperationParameters;
import org.springframework.jmx.export.annotation.ManagedResource;

@ManagedResource(
    objectName = "bean:name=fileCopier,type=FileCopierImpl",
    description = "File Copier")
public class FileCopierImpl implements FileCopier {

    @ManagedOperation(
        description = "Copy file from source directory to destination directory")
    @ManagedOperationParameters( {
        @ManagedOperationParameter(
            name = "srcDir", description = "Source directory"),
        @ManagedOperationParameter(
            name = "destDir", description = "Destination directory"),
        @ManagedOperationParameter(
            name = "filename", description = "File to copy") })
    public void copyFile(String srcDir, String destDir, String filename)
            throws IOException {
        ...
    }
}
```

However, specifying the object name in this way works only for classes that you're going to create a single instance of in the IoC container (e.g., file copier), not for classes that you may create multiple instances of (e.g., file replicator). This is because you can only specify a single object name for a class. As a result, you shouldn't try and run the same server multiple times without changing the names.

You can simply declare a <context:mbean-export> element in your bean configuration file, instead of the AnnotationMBeanExporter declaration, which you can omit.

```
<beans xmlns="http://www.springframework.org/schema/beans"
    xmlns:xsi="http://www.w3.org/2001/XMLSchema-instance"
    xmlns:context="http://www.springframework.org/schema/context"
    xsi:schemaLocation="http://www.springframework.org/schema/beans
        http://www.springframework.org/schema/beans/spring-beans-3.0.xsd
        http://www.springframework.org/schema/context
        http://www.springframework.org/schema/context/spring-context-3.0.xsd">

    <context:mbean-export server="mbeanServer" default-domain="bean" />
    ...
</beans>
```

You can specify an MBean server and a default domain name for this element through the server and default-domain attributes. However, you won't be able to set other MBean exporter properties such as notification listener mappings. Whenever you have to set these properties, you need to declare an AnnotationMBeanExporter instance explicitly.

6-2. Publishing and Listening to JMX Notifications

Problem
You want to publish JMX notifications from your MBeans and listen to them with JMX notification listeners.

Solution
Spring allows your beans to publish JMX notifications through the NotificationPublisher interface. You can also register standard JMX notification listeners in the IoC container to listen to JMX notifications.

How It Works

Publishing JMX Notifications
The Spring IoC container supports the beans that are going to be exported as MBeans to publish JMX notifications. These beans must implement the NotificationPublisherAware interface (as you might implement ApplicationContextAware to receive a reference to the current bean's containing ApplicatonContext instance) to get access to NotificationPublisher so that they can publish notifications.

```
package com.apress.springenterpriserecipes.replicator;
...
import javax.management.Notification;

import org.springframework.jmx.export.notification.NotificationPublisher;
import org.springframework.jmx.export.notification.NotificationPublisherAware;

@ManagedResource(description = "File replicator")
public class FileReplicatorJMXImpl implements FileReplicator,
        NotificationPublisherAware {
    ...
    private int sequenceNumber;
    private NotificationPublisher notificationPublisher;

    public void setNotificationPublisher(
            NotificationPublisher notificationPublisher) {
        this.notificationPublisher = notificationPublisher;
    }
```

```
@ManagedOperation(description = "Replicate files")
  public void replicate() throws IOException {
      notificationPublisher.sendNotification(
              new Notification("replication.start", this, sequenceNumber));
      ...
      notificationPublisher.sendNotification(
              new Notification("replication.complete", this, sequenceNumber));
      sequenceNumber++;
  }
}
```

In this file replicator, you send a JMX notification whenever a replication starts or completes. The notification is visible both in the standard output in the console as well as in the Notifications node for your service in JConsole. To see them, you must click Subscribe. Then invoke the replicate() method, and you'll see two new notifications arrive, much like your e-mail's inbox. The first argument in the Notification constructor is the notification type, while the second is the notification source. Each notification requires a sequence number. You can use the same sequence for a notification pair to keep track of them.

Listening to JMX Notifications

Now let's create a notification listener to listen to JMX notifications. Because a listener will be notified of many different types of notifications, such as javax.management.AttributeChangeNotification when an MBean's attribute has changed, you have to filter those notifications that you are interested in handling.

```
package com.apress.springenterpriserecipes.replicator;

import javax.management.Notification;
import javax.management.NotificationListener;

public class ReplicationNotificationListener implements NotificationListener {

    public void handleNotification(Notification notification, Object handback) {
        if (notification.getType().startsWith("replication")) {
            System.out.println(
                    notification.getSource() + " " +
                    notification.getType() + " #" +
                    notification.getSequenceNumber());
        }
    }
}
```

Then you can register this notification listener with your MBean exporter to listen to notifications emitted from certain MBeans.

```
<bean id="mbeanExporter"
    class="org.springframework.jmx.export.annotation.AnnotationMBeanExporter">
    <property name="defaultDomain" value="bean" />
    <property name="notificationListenerMappings">
        <map>
```

```
            <entry key="bean:name=documentReplicator,type=FileReplicatorJMXImpl">
                    <bean class="com.apress.springenterpriserecipes.replicator. ➥
ReplicationNotificationListener" />
            </entry>
        </map>
    </property>
</bean>
```

6-3. Accessing Remote JMX MBeans in Spring

Problem

You want to access JMX MBeans running on a remote MBean server exposed by a JMX connector. When accessing remote MBeans directly with the JMX API, you have to write complex JMX-specific code.

Solution

Spring offers two approaches to simplify your remote MBean access. First, it provides a factory bean for you to create an MBean server connection declaratively. With this server connection, you can query and update an MBean's attributes, as well as invoke its operations. Second, Spring provides another factory bean that allows you to create a proxy for a remote MBean. With this proxy, you can operate a remote MBean as if it were a local bean.

How It Works

Accessing Remote MBeans Through an MBean Server Connection

A JMX client requires an MBean server connection to access MBeans running on a remote MBean server. Spring provides org.springframework.jmx.support.MBeanServerConnectionFactoryBean for you to create a connection to a remote JSR-160–enabled MBean server declaratively. You only have to provide the service URL for it to locate the MBean server. Now let's declare this factory bean in your client bean configuration file (e.g., beans-jmx-client.xml).

```xml
<beans xmlns="http://www.springframework.org/schema/beans"
    xmlns:xsi="http://www.w3.org/2001/XMLSchema-instance"
    xsi:schemaLocation="http://www.springframework.org/schema/beans
        http://www.springframework.org/schema/beans/spring-beans-3.0.xsd">

    <bean id="mbeanServerConnection"
        class="org.springframework.jmx.support.MBeanServerConnectionFactoryBean">
        <property name="serviceUrl" value=
                "service:jmx:rmi://localhost/jndi/rmi://localhost:1099/replicator" />
    </bean>
</beans>
```

With the MBean server connection created by this factory bean, you can access and operate the MBeans running on this server. For example, you can query and update an MBean's attributes through the getAttribute() and setAttribute() methods, giving the MBean's object name and attribute name. You can also invoke an MBean's operations by using the invoke() method.

```
package com.apress.springenterpriserecipes.replicator;

import javax.management.Attribute;
import javax.management.MBeanServerConnection;
import javax.management.ObjectName;

import org.springframework.context.ApplicationContext;
import org.springframework.context.support.ClassPathXmlApplicationContext;

public class Client {

    public static void main(String[] args) throws Exception {
        ApplicationContext context =
            new ClassPathXmlApplicationContext("beans-client.xml");

        MBeanServerConnection mbeanServerConnection =
            (MBeanServerConnection) context.getBean("mbeanServerConnection");

        ObjectName mbeanName = new ObjectName(
                "bean:name=documentReplicator,type=FileReplicatorJMXImpl");

        String srcDir = (String) mbeanServerConnection.getAttribute(
                mbeanName, "SrcDir");

        mbeanServerConnection.setAttribute(
                mbeanName, new Attribute("DestDir", srcDir + "_1"));

        mbeanServerConnection.invoke(
                mbeanName, "replicate", new Object[] {}, new String[] {});
    }
}
```

Suppose that you've created the following JMX notification listener, which listens to file replication notifications:

```
package com.apress.springenterpriserecipes.replicator;

import javax.management.Notification;
import javax.management.NotificationListener;

public class ReplicationNotificationListener implements NotificationListener {

    public void handleNotification(Notification notification, Object handback) {
        if (notification.getType().startsWith("replication")) {
            System.out.println(
                    notification.getSource() + " " +
                    notification.getType() + " #" +
                    notification.getSequenceNumber());
        }
    }
}
```

You can register this notification listener to the MBean server connection to listen to notifications emitted from this MBean server.

```
package com.apress.springenterpriserecipes.replicator;
...
import javax.management.MBeanServerConnection;
import javax.management.ObjectName;

public class Client {

    public static void main(String[] args) throws Exception {
        ...
        MBeanServerConnection mbeanServerConnection =
            (MBeanServerConnection) context.getBean("mbeanServerConnection");

        ObjectName mbeanName = new ObjectName(
                "bean:name=documentReplicator,type=FileReplicatorImpl");

        mbeanServerConnection.addNotificationListener(
                mbeanName, new ReplicationNotificationListener(), null, null);
        ...
    }
}
```

After you run this, check JConsole again under the Notifications node. You'll see the same two notifications as before and an interesting, new notification of type jmx.attribute.change.

Accessing Remote MBeans Through an MBean Proxy

Another approach that Spring offers for remote MBean access is through MBeanProxy, which can be created by MBeanProxyFactoryBean.

```
<beans ...>
    <bean id="mbeanServerConnection"
        class="org.springframework.jmx.support.MBeanServerConnectionFactoryBean">
        <property name="serviceUrl" value=
            "service:jmx:rmi://localhost/jndi/rmi://localhost:1099/replicator" />
    </bean>

    <bean id="fileReplicatorProxy"
        class="org.springframework.jmx.access.MBeanProxyFactoryBean">
        <property name="server" ref="mbeanServerConnection" />
        <property name="objectName"
            value="bean:name=documentReplicator,type=FileReplicatorImpl" />
        <property name="proxyInterface"
            value="com.apress.springenterpriserecipes.replicator.FileReplicator" />
    </bean>
</beans>
```

You need to specify the object name and the server connection for the MBean you are going to proxy. The most important is the proxy interface, whose local method calls will be translated into remote MBean calls behind the scenes.

Now you can operate the remote MBean through this proxy as if it were a local bean. The preceding MBean operations invoked on the MBean server connection directly can be simplified as follows:

```
package com.apress.springenterpriserecipes.replicator;
...
public class Client {

    public static void main(String[] args) throws Exception {
        ...
        FileReplicator fileReplicatorProxy =
            (FileReplicator) context.getBean("fileReplicatorProxy");

        String srcDir = fileReplicatorProxy.getSrcDir();
        fileReplicatorProxy.setDestDir(srcDir + "_1");
        fileReplicatorProxy.replicate();
    }
}
```

6-4. Sending E-mail with Spring's E-mail Support

Problem

Many applications need to send e-mail. In a Java application, you can send e-mail with the JavaMail API. However, when using JavaMail, you have to handle the JavaMail-specific mail sessions and exceptions. As a result, your application becomes JavaMail dependent and hard to switch to another e-mail API.

Solution

Spring's e-mail support makes it easier to send e-mail by providing an abstract and implementation-independent API for sending e-mail. The core interface of Spring's e-mail support is MailSender.

The JavaMailSender interface is a subinterface of MailSender that includes specialized JavaMail features such as *Multipurpose Internet Mail Extensions (MIME)* message support. To send an e-mail message with HTML content, inline images, or attachments, you have to send it as a MIME message.

How It Works

Suppose that you want your file replicator application to notify the administrator of any error. First, you create the following ErrorNotifier interface, which includes a method for notifying of a file copy error:

```
package com.apress.springenterpriserecipes.replicator;

public interface ErrorNotifier {

    public void notifyCopyError(String srcDir, String destDir, String filename);
}
```

■Note   Invoking this notifier in case of error is left for you to accomplish. As you can consider error handling a crosscutting concern, AOP would be an ideal solution to this problem. You can write an after throwing advice to invoke this notifier.

Next, you can implement this interface to send a notification in a way of your choice. The most common way is to send e-mail. Before you implement the interface in this way, you may need a local e-mail server that supports the *Simple Mail Transfer Protocol (SMTP)* for testing purposes. We recommend installing Apache James Server (http://james.apache.org/server/index.html), which is very easy to install and configure.

■Note   You can download Apache James Server (e.g., version 2.3.2) from the Apache James web site and extract it to a directory of your choice to complete the installation. To start it, just execute the run script (located in the bin directory).

Let's create two user accounts for sending and receiving e-mail with this server. By default, the remote manager service of James listens on port 4555. You can telnet, using a console, to this port and run the following commands (displayed in bold) to add the users system and admin, whose passwords are 12345:

```
JAMES Remote Administration Tool 2.3.1
Please enter your login and password
Login id:
root
Password:
root
Welcome root. HELP for a list of commands
adduser system 12345
User system added
adduser admin 12345
User admin added
listusers
Existing accounts 2
user: admin
user: system
quit
Bye
```

Sending E-mail Using the JavaMail API

Now let's take a look at how to send e-mail using the JavaMail API. You can implement the
ErrorNotifier interface to send e-mail notifications in case of errors.

■Note   To use JavaMail in your application, you have to include mail.jar and activation.jar (located in the
lib/j2ee directory of the Spring installation) in your classpath.

```java
package com.apress.springenterpriserecipes.replicator;

import java.util.Properties;

import javax.mail.Message;
import javax.mail.MessagingException;
import javax.mail.Session;
import javax.mail.Transport;
import javax.mail.internet.InternetAddress;
import javax.mail.internet.MimeMessage;

public class EmailErrorNotifier implements ErrorNotifier {

    public void notifyCopyError(String srcDir, String destDir, String filename) {
        Properties props = new Properties();
        props.put("mail.smtp.host", "localhost");
        props.put("mail.smtp.port", "25");
        props.put("mail.smtp.username", "system");
        props.put("mail.smtp.password", "12345");
        Session session = Session.getDefaultInstance(props, null);
        try {
            Message message = new MimeMessage(session);
            message.setFrom(new InternetAddress("system@localhost"));
            message.setRecipients(Message.RecipientType.TO,
                    InternetAddress.parse("admin@localhost"));
            message.setSubject("File Copy Error");
            message.setText(
                "Dear Administrator,\n\n" +
                "An error occurred when copying the following file :\n" +
                "Source directory : " + srcDir + "\n" +
                "Destination directory : " + destDir + "\n" +
                "Filename : " + filename);
            Transport.send(message);
        } catch (MessagingException e) {
            throw new RuntimeException(e);
        }
    }
}
```

You first open a mail session connecting to an SMTP server by defining the properties. Then you create a message from this session for constructing your e-mail. After that, you send the e-mail by making a call to `Transport.send()`. When dealing with the JavaMail API, you have to handle the checked exception `MessagingException`. Note that all these classes, interfaces, and exceptions are defined by JavaMail.

Next, declare an instance of `EmailErrorNotifier` in the Spring IoC container for sending e-mail notifications in case of file replication errors.

```
<bean id="errorNotifier"
    class="com.apress.springenterpriserecipes.replicator.EmailErrorNotifier" />
```

You can write the following `Main` class to test `EmailErrorNotifier`. After running it, you can configure your e-mail application to receive the e-mail from your James Server via POP3.

```
package com.apress.springenterpriserecipes.replicator;

import org.springframework.context.ApplicationContext;
import org.springframework.context.support.ClassPathXmlApplicationContext;

public class Main {

    public static void main(String[] args) {
        ApplicationContext context =
            new ClassPathXmlApplicationContext("beans.xml");

        ErrorNotifier errorNotifier =
            (ErrorNotifier) context.getBean("errorNotifier");
        errorNotifier.notifyCopyError(
            "c:/documents", "d:/documents", "spring.doc");
    }
}
```

Sending E-mail with Spring's MailSender

Now let's see how to send e-mail with the help of Spring's `MailSender` interface, which can send `SimpleMailMessage` in its `send()` method. With this interface, your code is no longer JavaMail specific, and now it's easier to test.

```
package com.apress.springenterpriserecipes.replicator;

import org.springframework.mail.MailSender;
import org.springframework.mail.SimpleMailMessage;

public class EmailErrorNotifier implements ErrorNotifier {

    private MailSender mailSender;

    public void setMailSender(MailSender mailSender) {
        this.mailSender = mailSender;
    }
```

```java
    public void notifyCopyError(String srcDir, String destDir, String filename) {
        SimpleMailMessage message = new SimpleMailMessage();
        message.setFrom("system@localhost");
        message.setTo("admin@localhost");
        message.setSubject("File Copy Error");
        message.setText(
                "Dear Administrator,\n\n" +
                "An error occurred when copying the following file :\n" +
                "Source directory : " + srcDir + "\n" +
                "Destination directory : " + destDir + "\n" +
                "Filename : " + filename);
        mailSender.send(message);
    }
}
```

Next, you have to configure a `MailSender` implementation in the bean configuration file and inject it into `EmailErrorNotifier`. In Spring, the unique implementation of this interface is `JavaMailSenderImpl`, which uses JavaMail to send e-mail.

```xml
<beans ...>
    ...
    <bean id="mailSender"
        class="org.springframework.mail.javamail.JavaMailSenderImpl">
        <property name="host" value="localhost" />
        <property name="port" value="25" />
        <property name="username" value="system" />
        <property name="password" value="12345" />
    </bean>

    <bean id="errorNotifier"
        class="com.apress.springenterpriserecipes.replicator.EmailErrorNotifier">
        <property name="mailSender" ref="mailSender" />
    </bean>
</beans>
```

The default port used by `JavaMailSenderImpl` is the standard SMTP port 25, so if your e-mail server listens on this port for SMTP, you can simply omit this property. Also, if your SMTP server doesn't require user authentication, you needn't set the username and password.

If you have a JavaMail session configured in your Java EE application server, you can first look it up with the help of `JndiObjectFactoryBean`.

```xml
<bean id="mailSession"
    class="org.springframework.jndi.JndiObjectFactoryBean">
    <property name="jndiName" value="mail/Session" />
</bean>
```

Or you can look up a JavaMail session through the `<jee:jndi-lookup>` element if you are using Spring 2.0 or later.

```xml
<jee:jndi-lookup id="mailSession" jndi-name="mail/Session" />
```

You can inject the JavaMail session into `JavaMailSenderImpl` for its use. In this case, you no longer need to set the host, port, username, or password.

```
<bean id="mailSender"
    class="org.springframework.mail.javamail.JavaMailSenderImpl">
    <property name="session" ref="mailSession" />
</bean>
```

Defining an E-mail Template

Constructing an e-mail message from scratch in the method body is not efficient because you have to hard-code the e-mail properties. Also, you may have difficulty in writing the e-mail text in terms of Java strings. You can consider defining an e-mail message template in the bean configuration file and construct a new e-mail message from it.

```
<beans ...>
    ...
    <bean id="copyErrorMailMessage"
        class="org.springframework.mail.SimpleMailMessage">
        <property name="from" value="system@localhost" />
        <property name="to" value="admin@localhost" />
        <property name="subject" value="File Copy Error" />
        <property name="text">
            <value>
<![CDATA[
Dear Administrator,

An error occurred when copying the following file :
Source directory : %s
Destination directory : %s
Filename : %s
]]>
            </value>
        </property>
    </bean>

    <bean id="errorNotifier"
        class="com.apress.springenterpriserecipes.replicator.EmailErrorNotifier">
        <property name="mailSender" ref="mailSender" />
        <property name="copyErrorMailMessage" ref="copyErrorMailMessage" />
    </bean>
</beans>
```

Note that in the preceding message text, you include the placeholders %s, which will be replaced by message parameters through String.format(). Of course, you can also use a powerful templating language such as Velocity or FreeMarker to generate the message text according to a template. It's also a good practice to separate mail message templates from bean configuration files.

Each time you send e-mail, you can construct a new SimpleMailMessage instance from this injected template. Then you can generate the message text using String.format() to replace the %s placeholders with your message parameters.

```
package com.apress.springenterpriserecipes.replicator;
...
import org.springframework.mail.SimpleMailMessage;
```

```java
public class EmailErrorNotifier implements ErrorNotifier {
    ...
    private SimpleMailMessage copyErrorMailMessage;

    public void setCopyErrorMailMessage(SimpleMailMessage copyErrorMailMessage) {
        this.copyErrorMailMessage = copyErrorMailMessage;
    }

    public void notifyCopyError(String srcDir, String destDir, String filename) {
        SimpleMailMessage message = new SimpleMailMessage(copyErrorMailMessage);
        message.setText(String.format(
                copyErrorMailMessage.getText(), srcDir, destDir, filename));
        mailSender.send(message);
    }
}
```

Sending MIME Messages

So far, the `SimpleMailMessage` class you used can send only a simple plain text e-mail message. To send e-mail that contains HTML content, inline images, or attachments, you have to construct and send a MIME message instead. MIME is supported by JavaMail through the `javax.mail.internet.MimeMessage` class.

First of all, you have to use the `JavaMailSender` interface instead of its parent interface `MailSender`. The `JavaMailSenderImpl` instance you injected does implement this interface, so you needn't modify your bean configurations. The following notifier sends Spring's bean configuration file as an e-mail attachment to the administrator:

```java
package com.apress.springenterpriserecipes.replicator;

import javax.mail.MessagingException;
import javax.mail.internet.MimeMessage;

import org.springframework.core.io.ClassPathResource;
import org.springframework.mail.MailParseException;
import org.springframework.mail.SimpleMailMessage;
import org.springframework.mail.javamail.JavaMailSender;
import org.springframework.mail.javamail.MimeMessageHelper;

public class EmailErrorNotifier implements ErrorNotifier {

    private JavaMailSender mailSender;
    private SimpleMailMessage copyErrorMailMessage;

    public void setMailSender(JavaMailSender mailSender) {
        this.mailSender = mailSender;
    }

    public void setCopyErrorMailMessage(SimpleMailMessage copyErrorMailMessage) {
        this.copyErrorMailMessage = copyErrorMailMessage;
    }
```

```
    public void notifyCopyError(String srcDir, String destDir, String filename) {
        MimeMessage message = mailSender.createMimeMessage();
        try {
            MimeMessageHelper helper = new MimeMessageHelper(message, true);
            helper.setFrom(copyErrorMailMessage.getFrom());
            helper.setTo(copyErrorMailMessage.getTo());
            helper.setSubject(copyErrorMailMessage.getSubject());
            helper.setText(String.format(
                    copyErrorMailMessage.getText(), srcDir, destDir, filename));

            ClassPathResource config = new ClassPathResource("beans.xml");
            helper.addAttachment("beans.xml", config);
        } catch (MessagingException e) {
            throw new MailParseException(e);
        }
        mailSender.send(message);
    }
}
```

Unlike SimpleMailMessage, the MimeMessage class is defined by JavaMail, so you can only instantiate it by calling mailSender.createMimeMessage(). Spring provides the helper class MimeMessageHelper to simplify the operations of MimeMessage. It allows you to add an attachment from a Spring Resource object. However, the operations of this helper class still throw JavaMail's MessagingException. You have to convert this exception into Spring's mail runtime exception for consistency.

Spring offers another method for you to construct a MIME message, which is through implementing the MimeMessagePreparator interface.

```
package com.apress.springenterpriserecipes.replicator;
...
import javax.mail.internet.MimeMessage;

import org.springframework.mail.javamail.MimeMessagePreparator;

public class EmailErrorNotifier implements ErrorNotifier {
    ...
    public void notifyCopyError(
            final String srcDir, final String destDir, final String filename) {
        MimeMessagePreparator preparator = new MimeMessagePreparator() {

            public void prepare(MimeMessage mimeMessage) throws Exception {
                MimeMessageHelper helper =
                    new MimeMessageHelper(mimeMessage, true);
                helper.setFrom(copyErrorMailMessage.getFrom());
                helper.setTo(copyErrorMailMessage.getTo());
                helper.setSubject(copyErrorMailMessage.getSubject());
                helper.setText(String.format(
                    copyErrorMailMessage.getText(), srcDir, destDir, filename));

                ClassPathResource config = new ClassPathResource("beans.xml");
                helper.addAttachment("beans.xml", config);
            }
        };
```

```
        mailSender.send(preparator);
    }
}
```

In the `prepare()` method, you can prepare the `MimeMessage` object, which is precreated for `JavaMailSender`. If there's any exception thrown, it will be converted into Spring's mail runtime exception automatically.

6-5. Scheduling with Spring's JDK Timer Support

Problem

Your application has a basic scheduling requirement that you want to fulfill using JDK Timer. Moreover, you want to configure your scheduling tasks in a declarative way.

Solution

Spring provides utility classes for JDK Timer to enable you to configure scheduling tasks in the bean configuration file, without programming against the JDK Timer API.

How It Works

Creating a Timer Task

To use JDK Timer for scheduling, first create your task by extending the abstract class `TimerTask`. For example, the following timer task executes the `replicate()` method of a file replicator:

```
package com.apress.springenterpriserecipes.replicator;
...
import java.util.TimerTask;

public class FileReplicationTask extends TimerTask {

    private FileReplicator fileReplicator;

    public void setFileReplicator(FileReplicator fileReplicator) {
        this.fileReplicator = fileReplicator;
    }

    public void run() {
        try {
            fileReplicator.replicate();
        } catch (IOException e) {
            throw new RuntimeException(e);
        }
    }
}
```

Then you define this task in the bean configuration file referring to the file replicator documentReplicator.

```
<bean id="documentReplicationTask"
    class="com.apress.springenterpriserecipes.replicator.FileReplicationTask">
    <property name="fileReplicator" ref="documentReplicator" />
</bean>
```

Using JDK Timer Without Spring's Support

After creating a timer task, you can schedule it by calling one of the overloaded schedule() methods of Timer. For example, the following timer runs the file replication task every 60 seconds with a 5-second delay for the first time of execution.

```
package com.apress.springenterpriserecipes.replicator;

import java.util.Timer;
import java.util.TimerTask;

import org.springframework.context.ApplicationContext;
import org.springframework.context.support.ClassPathXmlApplicationContext;

public class Main {

    public static void main(String[] args) throws Exception {
        ApplicationContext context =
            new ClassPathXmlApplicationContext("beans.xml");

        TimerTask documentReplicationTask =
            (TimerTask) context.getBean("documentReplicationTask");

        Timer timer = new Timer();
        timer.schedule(documentReplicationTask, 5000, 60000);
    }
}
```

Using JDK Timer with Spring's Support

First, Spring offers MethodInvokingTimerTaskFactoryBean for you to define a timer task that executes a single method of a particular object. This saves you the trouble of extending TimerTask. You can use the following task definition to replace the previous:

```
<bean id="documentReplicationTask" class="org.springframework.scheduling.
    timer.MethodInvokingTimerTaskFactoryBean">
    <property name="targetObject" ref="documentReplicator" />
    <property name="targetMethod" value="replicate" />
</bean>
```

Next, Spring allows you to configure the scheduling details of your task in the bean configuration file, through a ScheduledTimerTask instance that wraps a TimerTask instance.

```
<bean id="scheduledDocumentReplicationTask"
    class="org.springframework.scheduling.timer.ScheduledTimerTask">
    <property name="timerTask" ref="documentReplicationTask" />
    <property name="delay" value="5000" />
    <property name="period" value="60000" />
</bean>
```

Finally, you can configure a TimerFactoryBean instance to create and set up a Timer to run your ScheduledTimerTask instance. You can specify multiple tasks in this factory bean.

```
<bean class="org.springframework.scheduling.timer.TimerFactoryBean">
    <property name="scheduledTimerTasks">
        <list>
            <ref local="scheduledDocumentReplicationTask" />
        </list>
    </property>
</bean>
```

Now you can simply start your timer with the following Main class. In this way, you don't require a single line of code for scheduling tasks.

```
package com.apress.springenterpriserecipes.replicator;

import org.springframework.context.support.ClassPathXmlApplicationContext;

public class Main {

    public static void main(String[] args) throws Exception {
        new ClassPathXmlApplicationContext("beans.xml");
    }
}
```

6-6. Scheduling with Spring's Quartz Support

Problem
Your application has an advanced scheduling requirement that you want to fulfill using Quartz Scheduler. Such a requirement might be something seemingly complex like the ability to run at arbitrary times, or at strange intervals ("every other Thursday, but only after 10 am and before 2 pm"). Moreover, you want to configure your scheduling jobs in a declarative way.

Solution
Spring provides utility classes for Quartz to enable you to configure scheduling jobs in the bean configuration file, without programming against the Quartz API.

How It Works

Using Quartz Without Spring's Support

To use Quartz for scheduling, first create your job by implementing the Job interface. For example, the following job executes the replicate() method of a file replicator, retrieved from the job data map through the JobExecutionContext object that's passed in.

■Note   To use Quartz in your application, you must include quartz-all-1.6.0.jar (located in the lib/quartz directory of the Spring installation), commons-collections.jar (located in lib/jakarta-commons), and jta.jar (located in lib/j2ee) in your classpath.

```
package com.apress.springenterpriserecipes.replicator;
...
import org.quartz.Job;
import org.quartz.JobExecutionContext;
import org.quartz.JobExecutionException;

public class FileReplicationJob implements Job {

    public void execute(JobExecutionContext context)
            throws JobExecutionException {
        Map dataMap = context.getJobDetail().getJobDataMap();
        FileReplicator fileReplicator =
            (FileReplicator) dataMap.get("fileReplicator");
        try {
            fileReplicator.replicate();
        } catch (IOException e) {
            throw new JobExecutionException(e);
        }
    }
}
```

After creating the job, you configure and schedule it with the Quartz API. For instance, the following scheduler runs your file replication job every 60 seconds with a 5-second delay for the first time of execution:

```
package com.apress.springenterpriserecipes.replicator;
...
import org.quartz.JobDetail;
import org.quartz.Scheduler;
import org.quartz.SimpleTrigger;
import org.quartz.impl.StdSchedulerFactory;
import org.springframework.context.ApplicationContext;
import org.springframework.context.support.ClassPathXmlApplicationContext;
```

```
public class Main {

    public static void main(String[] args) throws Exception {
        ApplicationContext context =
            new ClassPathXmlApplicationContext("beans.xml");

        FileReplicator documentReplicator =
            (FileReplicator) context.getBean("documentReplicator");

        JobDetail job = new JobDetail();
        job.setName("documentReplicationJob");
        job.setJobClass(FileReplicationJob.class);
        Map dataMap = job.getJobDataMap();
        dataMap.put("fileReplicator", documentReplicator);

        SimpleTrigger trigger = new SimpleTrigger();
        trigger.setName("documentReplicationJob");
        trigger.setStartTime(new Date(System.currentTimeMillis() + 5000));
        trigger.setRepeatCount(SimpleTrigger.REPEAT_INDEFINITELY);
        trigger.setRepeatInterval(60000);

        Scheduler scheduler = new StdSchedulerFactory().getScheduler();
        scheduler.start();
        scheduler.scheduleJob(job, trigger);
    }
}
```

In the Main class, you first configure the job details for your file replication job in a JobDetail object and prepare job data in its jobDataMap property. Next, you create a SimpleTrigger object to configure the scheduling properties. Finally, you create a scheduler to run your job using this trigger.

Quartz supports two types of triggers: SimpleTrigger and CronTrigger. SimpleTrigger allows you to set trigger properties such as start time, end time, repeat interval, and repeat count. CronTrigger accepts a Unix *cron* expression for you to specify the times to run your job. For example, you can replace the preceding SimpleTrigger with the following CronTrigger to run your job at 17:30 every day:

```
CronTrigger trigger = new CronTrigger();
trigger.setName("documentReplicationJob");
trigger.setCronExpression("0 30 17 * * ?");
```

A cron expression is made up of seven fields (the last field is optional), separated by spaces. Table 6-1 shows the field description for a cron expression.

Table 6-1. Field Description for a Cron Expression

Position	Field Name	Range
1	Second	0–59
2	Minute	0–59
3	Hour	0–23

Position	Field Name	Range
4	Day of month	1–31
5	Month	1–12 or JAN–DEC
6	Day of week	1–7 or SUN–SAT
7	Year (optional)	1970–2099

Each part of a cron expression can be assigned a specific value (e.g., 3), a range (e.g., 1–5), a list (e.g., 1,3,5), a wildcard (*; matches all values), or a question mark (?; used in either of the "Day of month" and "Day of week" fields for matching one of these fields but not both). For more information on the cron expressions supported by CronTrigger, refer to its javadoc (http://quartz.sourceforge.net/javadoc/org/quartz/CronTrigger.html).

Using Quartz with Spring's Support

When using Quartz, you can create a job by implementing the Job interface and retrieve job data from the job data map through JobExecutionContext. To decouple your job class from the Quartz API, Spring provides QuartzJobBean, which you can extend to retrieve job data through setter methods. QuartzJobBean converts the job data map into properties and injects them via the setter methods.

```
package com.apress.springenterpriserecipes.replicator;
...
import org.quartz.JobExecutionContext;
import org.quartz.JobExecutionException;
import org.springframework.scheduling.quartz.QuartzJobBean;

public class FileReplicationJob extends QuartzJobBean {

    private FileReplicator fileReplicator;

    public void setFileReplicator(FileReplicator fileReplicator) {
        this.fileReplicator = fileReplicator;
    }

    protected void executeInternal(JobExecutionContext context)
            throws JobExecutionException {
        try {
            fileReplicator.replicate();
        } catch (IOException e) {
            throw new JobExecutionException(e);
        }
    }
}
```

Then you can configure a Quartz JobDetail object in Spring's bean configuration file through JobDetailBean. By default, Spring uses this bean's name as the job name. You can modify it by setting the name property.

```
<bean name="documentReplicationJob"
    class="org.springframework.scheduling.quartz.JobDetailBean">
    <property name="jobClass"
        value="com.apress.springenterpriserecipes.replicator.FileReplicationJob" />
    <property name="jobDataAsMap">
        <map>
            <entry key="fileReplicator" value-ref="documentReplicator" />
        </map>
    </property>
</bean>
```

Spring also offers MethodInvokingJobDetailFactoryBean for you to define a job that executes a single method of a particular object. This saves you the trouble of creating a job class. You can use the following job detail to replace the previous:

```
<bean id="documentReplicationJob" class="org.springframework. ➥
    scheduling.quartz.MethodInvokingJobDetailFactoryBean">
    <property name="targetObject" ref="documentReplicator" />
    <property name="targetMethod" value="replicate" />
</bean>
```

You can configure a Quartz SimpleTrigger object in Spring's bean configuration file through SimpleTriggerBean, which requires a reference to a JobDetail object. This bean provides common default values for certain trigger properties, such as using the bean name as the job name, setting indefinite repeat count, and so on.

```
<bean id="documentReplicationTrigger"
    class="org.springframework.scheduling.quartz.SimpleTriggerBean">
    <property name="jobDetail" ref="documentReplicationJob" />
    <property name="repeatInterval" value="60000" />
    <property name="startDelay" value="5000" />
</bean>
```

You can also configure a Quartz CronTrigger object in the bean configuration file through CronTriggerBean.

```
<bean id="documentReplicationTrigger"
    class="org.springframework.scheduling.quartz.CronTriggerBean">
    <property name="jobDetail" ref="documentReplicationJob" />
    <property name="cronExpression" value=" 0 * * * * ? " />
</bean>
```

Finally, you can configure a SchedulerFactoryBean instance to create a Scheduler object for running your trigger. You can specify multiple triggers in this factory bean.

```
<bean class="org.springframework.scheduling.quartz.SchedulerFactoryBean">
    <property name="triggers">
        <list>
            <ref bean="documentReplicationTrigger" />
            <!-- other triggers you have may be included here -->
        </list>
    </property>
</bean>
```

Now you can simply start your scheduler with the following Main class. In this way, you don't require a single line of code for scheduling jobs.

```
package com.apress.springenterpriserecipes.replicator;

import org.springframework.context.support.ClassPathXmlApplicationContext;

public class Main {

    public static void main(String[] args) throws Exception {
        new ClassPathXmlApplicationContext("beans.xml");
    }
}
```

Summary

This chapter discussed JMX and a few of the surrounding specifications. You learned how to export Spring beans as JMX MBeans, and how to use those MBeans from a client, both remotely and locally by using Spring's proxies. You published and listened to notification events on a JMX server from Spring. You built a simple replicator and exposed its configuration through JMX. You learned how to schedule the replication using the JDK's Timer support, and to use the Quartz Scheduler.

In the next chapter, you will learn about messaging using Spring's support for JMS.

CHAPTER 7

■■■

Messaging

In this chapter, you will learn about Spring's support for *Java Message Service (JMS)*. JMS defines a set of standard APIs for message-oriented communication (using "message-oriented middleware," a.k.a MOM) in the Java EE platform. With JMS, different applications can communicate in a loosely coupled way compared with other remoting technologies such as RMI. However, when using the JMS API to send and receive messages, you have to manage the JMS resources yourself and handle the JMS API's exceptions, which results in many lines of JMS-specific code. Spring simplifies JMS's usage with a template-based approach, just as it does for JDBC. Moreover, Spring enables beans declared in its IoC container to listen for JMS messages and react to them.

By the end of this chapter, you will be able to create and access message-based middleware using Spring and JMS. This chapter will also provide you with a working knowledge of messaging in general, which will help you in chapter 8, where we discuss Spring Integration. You will also know how to use Spring's JMS support to simplify sending, receiving, and listening for JMS messages.

7-1. Sending and Receiving JMS Messages with Spring

Problem

In the Java EE platform, applications often need to communicate using JMS. However, to send or receive a JMS message, you have to perform the following tasks:

- Create a JMS connection factory on a message broker.
- Create a JMS destination, which can be either a queue or a topic.
- Open a JMS connection from the connection factory.
- Obtain a JMS session from the connection.
- Send/receive the JMS message with a message producer/consumer.
- Handle JMSException, which is a checked exception that must be handled.
- Close the JMS session and connection.

As you can see, it requires a lot of coding to send or receive a simple JMS message. In fact, most of these tasks are boilerplate and require you to repeat them each time when dealing with JMS.

On the Topic of Topics...

In this chapter, we'll refer quite a bit to *topics* and *queues*. Messaging solutions are designed to solve two types of architecture requirements: messaging from one point in an application to another known point, and messaging from one point in an application to many other unknown points. These patterns are the middleware equivalents of telling somebody something face to face and saying something over a loud speaker to a room of people, respectively.

If you want messages sent on a message queue to be broadcast to an unknown set of clients who are "listening" for the message (as in the loud speaker analogy), send the message on a *topic*. If you want the message sent to a single, known client, then you send it over a *queue*.

Solution

Spring offers a template-based solution for simplifying your JMS code. With a JMS template (Spring framework class JmsTemplate), you can send and receive JMS messages with much less code. The template handles the boilerplate tasks for you and also converts the JMS API's JMSException hierarchy into Spring's runtime exception org.springframework.jms.JmsException hierarchy. The translation converts exceptions to a mirrored hierarchy of unchecked exceptions.

In JMS 1.0.2, topics and queues are known as *domains* and are handled with a different API that is provided for legacy reasons, so you'll find jars or implementations of the JMS API in different application servers: one for 1.1, and one for 1.0.2. In Spring 3.0, this 1.0.2 support in Spring is considered deprecated.

JMS 1.1 provides a domain-independent API, treating topic and queue as alternative message destinations. To address different JMS APIs, Spring provides two JMS template classes, JmsTemplate and JmsTemplate102, for these two versions of JMS. This chapter will focus on JMS 1.1, which is available for Java EE 1.4 and higher versions.

How It Works

Suppose that you are developing a post office system that includes two subsystems: the front desk subsystem and the back office subsystem. When the front desk receives mail from a citizen, it passes the mail to the back office for categorizing and delivering. At the same time, the front desk subsystem sends a JMS message to the back office subsystem, notifying it of new mail. The mail information is represented by the following class:

```
package com.apress.springenterpriserecipes.post;

public class Mail {

    private String mailId;
    private String country;
    private double weight;

    // Constructors, Getters and Setters
    ...
}
```

The methods for sending and receiving mail information are defined in the `FrontDesk` and `BackOffice` interfaces as follows:

```
package com.apress.springenterpriserecipes.post;

public interface FrontDesk {

    public void sendMail(Mail mail);
}
```

```
package com.apress.springenterpriserecipes.post;

public interface BackOffice {

    public Mail receiveMail();
}
```

Before you can send and receive JMS messages, you need to install a JMS message broker. For simplicity's sake, I have chosen Apache ActiveMQ (`http://activemq.apache.org/`) as my message broker, which is very easy to install and configure. ActiveMQ is an open source message broker that fully supports JMS 1.1.

■Note   You can download ActiveMQ (e.g., v5.2.0) from the ActiveMQ web site and extract it to a directory of your choice to complete the installation.

Sending and Receiving Messages Without Spring's Support

First, let's see how to send and receive JMS messages without Spring's support. The following `FrontDeskImpl` class sends JMS messages with the JMS API directly.

■Note   To send/receive JMS messages to/from a JMS message broker, you have to include the library of the message broker in your classpath. For ActiveMQ 5.0.0, it's `activemq-all-5.0.0.jar` (located in the root of the ActiveMQ installation). Alternatively, you can use the Maven project included for this book's source code, which includes the ActiveMQ and JMS jars.

```
package com.apress.springenterpriserecipes.post;

import javax.jms.Connection;
import javax.jms.ConnectionFactory;
import javax.jms.Destination;
import javax.jms.JMSException;
import javax.jms.MapMessage;
```

```
import javax.jms.MessageProducer;
import javax.jms.Session;

import org.apache.activemq.ActiveMQConnectionFactory;
import org.apache.activemq.command.ActiveMQQueue;

public class FrontDeskImpl implements FrontDesk {

    public void sendMail(Mail mail) {
        ConnectionFactory cf =
            new ActiveMQConnectionFactory("tcp://localhost:61616");
        Destination destination = new ActiveMQQueue("mail.queue");

        Connection conn = null;
        try {
            conn = cf.createConnection();
            Session session =
                conn.createSession(false, Session.AUTO_ACKNOWLEDGE);
            MessageProducer producer = session.createProducer(destination);

            MapMessage message = session.createMapMessage();
            message.setString("mailId", mail.getMailId());
            message.setString("country", mail.getCountry());
            message.setDouble("weight", mail.getWeight());
            producer.send(message);

            session.close();
        } catch (JMSException e) {
            throw new RuntimeException(e);
        } finally {
            if (conn != null) {
                try {
                    conn.close();
                } catch (JMSException e) {
                }
            }
        }
    }
}
```

In the preceding sendMail() method, you first create JMS-specific ConnectionFactory and Destination objects with the classes provided by ActiveMQ. The message broker URL is the default for ActiveMQ if you run it on localhost. In JMS, there are two types of destinations: queue and topic. As explained before, a *queue* is for the point-to-point communication model, while *topic* is for the publish-subscribe communication model. Because you are sending JMS messages point to point from front desk to back office, you should use a message queue. You can easily create a topic as a destination using the ActiveMQTopic class.

Next, you have to create a connection, session, and message producer before you can send your message. There are several types of messages defined in the JMS API, including TextMessage, MapMessage, BytesMessage, ObjectMessage, and StreamMessage. MapMessage contains message content in key/value pairs like a map. All of them are interfaces, whose super class is simply Message. In the meantime, you have to handle JMSException, which may be thrown by the JMS API. Finally, you must remember to close the session and connection to release system resources. Every time a JMS connection is closed, all its opened sessions will be closed automatically. So you only have to ensure that the JMS connection is closed properly in the finally block.

On the other hand, the following BackOfficeImpl class receives JMS messages with the JMS API directly:

```java
package com.apress.springenterpriserecipes.post;

import javax.jms.Connection;
import javax.jms.ConnectionFactory;
import javax.jms.Destination;
import javax.jms.JMSException;
import javax.jms.MapMessage;
import javax.jms.MessageConsumer;
import javax.jms.Session;

import org.apache.activemq.ActiveMQConnectionFactory;
import org.apache.activemq.command.ActiveMQQueue;

public class BackOfficeImpl implements BackOffice {

    public Mail receiveMail() {
        ConnectionFactory cf =
            new ActiveMQConnectionFactory("tcp://localhost:61616");
        Destination destination = new ActiveMQQueue("mail.queue");

        Connection conn = null;
        try {
            conn = cf.createConnection();
            Session session =
                conn.createSession(false, Session.AUTO_ACKNOWLEDGE);
            MessageConsumer consumer = session.createConsumer(destination);

            conn.start();
            MapMessage message = (MapMessage) consumer.receive();
            Mail mail = new Mail();
            mail.setMailId(message.getString("mailId"));
            mail.setCountry(message.getString("country"));
            mail.setWeight(message.getDouble("weight"));

            session.close();
            return mail;
```

```
        } catch (JMSException e) {
            throw new RuntimeException(e);
        } finally {
            if (conn != null) {
                try {
                    conn.close();
                } catch (JMSException e) {
                }
            }
        }
    }
}
```

Most of the code in this method is similar to that for sending JMS messages, except that you create a message consumer and receive a JMS message from it. Note that here we used the conn's start() method here, although we didn't in the FrontDeskImpl example before. When using a Connection to receive messages, you can add listeners to the connection that are invoked on receipt of a message, or you can block synchronously, waiting for a message to arrive. The container has no way of knowing which approach you will take and so it doesn't start polling for messages until you've explicitly called start(). If you add listeners or do any kind of configuration, you do so before you invoke start().

Finally, you create two bean configuration files—one for the front desk subsystem (e.g., beans-front.xml), and one for the back office subsystem (e.g., beans-back.xml)—in the root of the classpath.

```
<beans xmlns="http://www.springframework.org/schema/beans"
    xmlns:xsi="http://www.w3.org/2001/XMLSchema-instance"
    xsi:schemaLocation="http://www.springframework.org/schema/beans
        http://www.springframework.org/schema/beans/spring-beans-3.0.xsd">

    <bean id="frontDesk"
        class="com.apress.springenterpriserecipes.post.FrontDeskImpl" />
</beans>
```

```
<beans xmlns="http://www.springframework.org/schema/beans"
    xmlns:xsi="http://www.w3.org/2001/XMLSchema-instance"
    xsi:schemaLocation="http://www.springframework.org/schema/beans
        http://www.springframework.org/schema/beans/spring-beans-3.0.xsd">

    <bean id="backOffice"
        class="com.apress.springenterpriserecipes.post.BackOfficeImpl" />
</beans>
```

Now your front desk and back office subsystems are ready to send and receive JMS messages. You must start up your message broker before sending and receiving messages with the following main classes. To run them, first run FrontDeskMain; then run BackOfficeMain in another window or console.

■**Note**   To start ActiveMQ, you just execute one of the ActiveMQ startup scripts (the script itself is called
`activemq.sh`, or `activemq.bat` for Unix-variants and Windows, respectively, and is located in the `bin` directory)
for your operating system.

```java
package com.apress.springenterpriserecipes.post;

import org.springframework.context.ApplicationContext;
import org.springframework.context.support.ClassPathXmlApplicationContext;

public class FrontDeskMain {

    public static void main(String[] args) {
        ApplicationContext context =
            new ClassPathXmlApplicationContext("beans-front.xml");

        FrontDesk frontDesk = (FrontDesk) context.getBean("frontDesk");
        frontDesk.sendMail(new Mail("1234", "US", 1.5));
    }
}

package com.apress.springenterpriserecipes.post;

import org.springframework.context.ApplicationContext;
import org.springframework.context.support.ClassPathXmlApplicationContext;

public class BackOfficeMain {

    public static void main(String[] args) {
        ApplicationContext context =
            new ClassPathXmlApplicationContext("beans-back.xml");

        BackOffice backOffice = (BackOffice) context.getBean("backOffice");
        Mail mail = backOffice.receiveMail();
        System.out.println("Mail #" + mail.getMailId() + " received");
    }
}
```

■**Note**   You're encouraged to use your messaging middleware's reporting functionality. In these examples, we're
using ActiveMQ. With the default installation, you can open `http://localhost:8161/admin/queueGraph.jsp` to
see what's happening with `mail.queue`, the queue used in these examples.

Sending and Receiving Messages with Spring's JMS Template

Spring offers a JMS template that can significantly simplify your JMS code. To send a JMS message with this template, you simply call the send() method and provide a message destination, as well as a MessageCreator object, which creates the JMS message you are going to send. The MessageCreator object is usually implemented as an anonymous inner class.

```
package com.apress.springenterpriserecipes.post;

import javax.jms.Destination;
import javax.jms.JMSException;
import javax.jms.MapMessage;
import javax.jms.Message;
import javax.jms.Session;

import org.springframework.jms.core.JmsTemplate;
import org.springframework.jms.core.MessageCreator;

public class FrontDeskImpl implements FrontDesk {

    private JmsTemplate jmsTemplate;
    private Destination destination;

    public void setJmsTemplate(JmsTemplate jmsTemplate) {
        this.jmsTemplate = jmsTemplate;
    }

    public void setDestination(Destination destination) {
        this.destination = destination;
    }

    public void sendMail(final Mail mail) {
        jmsTemplate.send(destination, new MessageCreator() {
            public Message createMessage(Session session) throws JMSException {
                MapMessage message = session.createMapMessage();
                message.setString("mailId", mail.getMailId());
                message.setString("country", mail.getCountry());
                message.setDouble("weight", mail.getWeight());
                return message;
            }
        });
    }
}
```

Note that an inner class can access only arguments or variables of the enclosing method that are declared as final. The MessageCreator interface declares only a createMessage() method for you to implement. In this method, you create and return your JMS message with the JMS session provided.

A JMS template helps you to obtain and release the JMS connection and session, and sends the JMS message created by your MessageCreator object. Moreover, it converts the JMS API's JMSException hierarchy into Spring's JMS runtime exception hierarchy, whose base exception class is org.springframework.jms.JmsException. You can catch the JmsException thrown from send and the other send variants and then take action in the catch block if you want.

In the front desk subsystem's bean configuration file, you declare a JMS template that refers to the JMS connection factory for opening connections. Then you inject this template as well as the message destination into your front desk bean.

```
<beans ...>
    <bean id="connectionFactory"
        class="org.apache.activemq.ActiveMQConnectionFactory">
        <property name="brokerURL" value="tcp://localhost:61616" />
    </bean>

    <bean id="mailDestination"
        class="org.apache.activemq.command.ActiveMQQueue">
        <constructor-arg value="mail.queue" />
    </bean>

    <bean id="jmsTemplate"
        class="org.springframework.jms.core.JmsTemplate">
        <property name="connectionFactory" ref="connectionFactory" />
    </bean>

    <bean id="frontDesk"
        class="com.apress.springenterpriserecipes.post.FrontDeskImpl">
        <property name="destination" ref="mailDestination" />
        <property name="jmsTemplate" ref="jmsTemplate" />
    </bean>
</beans>
```

To receive a JMS message with a JMS template, you call the receive() method by providing a message destination. This method returns a JMS message whose type is the base JMS message type, an interface, javax.jms.Message, so you have to cast it into proper type before further processing.

```
package com.apress.springenterpriserecipes.post;

import javax.jms.Destination;
import javax.jms.JMSException;
import javax.jms.MapMessage;

import org.springframework.jms.core.JmsTemplate;
import org.springframework.jms.support.JmsUtils;

public class BackOfficeImpl implements BackOffice {

    private JmsTemplate jmsTemplate;
    private Destination destination;

    public void setJmsTemplate(JmsTemplate jmsTemplate) {
        this.jmsTemplate = jmsTemplate;
    }
```

```
    public void setDestination(Destination destination) {
        this.destination = destination;
    }

    public Mail receiveMail() {
        MapMessage message = (MapMessage) jmsTemplate.receive(destination);
        try {
            if (message == null) {
                return null;
            }
            Mail mail = new Mail();
            mail.setMailId(message.getString("mailId"));
            mail.setCountry(message.getString("country"));
            mail.setWeight(message.getDouble("weight"));
            return mail;
        } catch (JMSException e) {
            throw JmsUtils.convertJmsAccessException(e);
        }
    }
}
```

However, when extracting information from the received MapMessage object, you still have to handle the JMS API's JMSException. This is in stark contrast to the default behavior of the framework, where it automatically maps exceptions for you when invoking methods on the JmsTemplate. To make the type of the exception thrown by this method consistent, you have to make a call to JmsUtils.convertJmsAccessException() to convert the JMS API's JMSException into Spring's JmsException.

In the back office subsystem's bean configuration file, you declare a JMS template and inject it together with the message destination into your back office bean.

```
<beans ...>
    <bean id="connectionFactory"
        class="org.apache.activemq.ActiveMQConnectionFactory">
        <property name="brokerURL" value="tcp://localhost:61616" />
    </bean>

    <bean id="mailDestination"
        class="org.apache.activemq.command.ActiveMQQueue">
        <constructor-arg value="mail.queue" />
    </bean>

    <bean id="jmsTemplate"
        class="org.springframework.jms.core.JmsTemplate">
        <property name="connectionFactory" ref="connectionFactory" />
        <property name="receiveTimeout" value="10000" />
    </bean>
```

```
    <bean id="backOffice"
        class="com.apress.springenterpriserecipes.post.BackOfficeImpl">
        <property name="destination" ref="mailDestination" />
        <property name="jmsTemplate" ref="jmsTemplate" />
    </bean>
</beans>
```

Pay special attention to the receiveTimout property of the JMS template. By default, this template will wait for a JMS message at the destination forever, and the calling thread is blocked in the meantime. To avoid waiting for a message so long, you should specify a receive timeout for this template. If there's no message available at the destination in the duration, the JMS template's receive() method will return a null message.

In your applications, the main use of receiving a message might be because you're expecting a response to something or want to check for messages at an interval, handling the messages and then spinning down until the next interval. If you intend to receive messages and respond to them as a service, you're likely going to want to use the message-driven POJO functionality described later in this chapter. There, we discuss a mechanism that will constantly sit and wait for messages, handling them by calling back into your application as the messages arrive.

Sending and Receiving Messages to and from a Default Destination

Instead of specifying a message destination for each JMS template's send() and receive() method call, you can specify a default destination for a JMS template. Then you will no longer need to inject it into your message sender and receiver beans again.

```
<beans ...>
    ...
    <bean id="jmsTemplate"
        class="org.springframework.jms.core.JmsTemplate">
        ...
        <property name="connectionFactory" ref="connectionFactory" />
        <property name="defaultDestination" ref="mailDestination" />
    </bean>

    <bean id="frontDesk"
        class="com.apress.springenterpriserecipes.post.FrontDeskImpl">
        <property name="jmsTemplate" ref="jmsTemplate" />
    </bean>
</beans>

<beans ...>
    ...
    <bean id="jmsTemplate"
        class="org.springframework.jms.core.JmsTemplate">
        ...
        <property name="connectionFactory" ref="connectionFactory" />
        <property name="defaultDestination" ref="mailDestination" />
    </bean>
```

```
    <bean id="backOffice"
        class="com.apress.springenterpriserecipes.post.BackOfficeImpl">
        <property name="jmsTemplate" ref="jmsTemplate" />
    </bean>
</beans>
```

With the default destination specified for a JMS template, you can delete the setter method for a message destination from your message sender and receiver classes. Now when you call the send() and receive() methods, you no longer need to specify a message destination.

```
package com.apress.springenterpriserecipes.post;
...
import org.springframework.jms.core.MessageCreator;

public class FrontDeskImpl implements FrontDesk {
    ...
    public void sendMail(final Mail mail) {
        jmsTemplate.send(new MessageCreator() {
            ...
        });
    }
}
```

```
package com.apress.springenterpriserecipes.post;
...
import javax.jms.MapMessage;
...

public class BackOfficeImpl implements BackOffice {
    ...
    public Mail receiveMail() {
        MapMessage message = (MapMessage) jmsTemplate.receive();
        ...
    }
}
```

Instead of specifying an instance of the Destination interface for a JMS template, you can specify the destination name to let the JMS template resolve it for you, so you can delete the Destination object's declaration from both bean configuration files.

```
<bean id="jmsTemplate"
    class="org.springframework.jms.core.JmsTemplate">
    ...
    <property name="defaultDestinationName" value="mail.queue" />
</bean>
```

Extending the JmsGatewaySupport Class

Just like your DAO class can extend `JdbcDaoSupport` to retrieve a JDBC template, your JMS sender and receiver classes can also extend `JmsGatewaySupport` to retrieve a JMS template. You have the following two options for classes that extend `JmsGatewaySupport` to create their JMS template:

- Inject a JMS connection factory for `JmsGatewaySupport` to create a JMS template on it automatically. However, if you do it this way, you won't be able to configure the details of the JMS template.

- Inject a JMS template for `JmsGatewaySupport` that is created and configured by you.

Of them, the second approach is more suitable if you have to configure the JMS template yourself. You can delete the private field `jmsTemplate` and its setter method from both your sender and receiver classes. When you need access to the JMS template, you just make a call to `getJmsTemplate()`.

```
package com.apress.springenterpriserecipes.post;

import org.springframework.jms.core.support.JmsGatewaySupport;
...

public class FrontDeskImpl extends JmsGatewaySupport implements FrontDesk {
    ...
    public void sendMail(final Mail mail) {
        getJmsTemplate().send(new MessageCreator() {
            ...
        });
    }
}
```

```
package com.apress.springenterpriserecipes.post;
...

import org.springframework.jms.core.support.JmsGatewaySupport;

public class BackOfficeImpl extends JmsGatewaySupport implements BackOffice {
    public Mail receiveMail() {
        MapMessage message = (MapMessage) getJmsTemplate().receive();
        ...
    }
}
```

7-2. Converting JMS Messages

Problem

Your application receives messages from your message queue, but wants to transform those messages from the JMS-specific type to a business specific class.

Solution

Spring provides an implementation of SimpleMessageConvertor to handle the translation of a JMS message received to a business object and the translation of a business object to a JMS message. You can leverage the default or provide your own.

Approach

So far, you have been handling the raw JMS messages by yourself. Spring's JMS template can help you convert JMS messages to and from Java objects using a message converter. By default, the JMS template uses SimpleMessageConverter for converting TextMessage to/from a string, BytesMessage to/from a byte array, MapMessage to/from a map, and ObjectMessage to/from a serializable object. For your front desk and back office classes, you can send and receive a map using the convertAndSend() and receiveAndConvert() methods, and the map will be converted to/from MapMessage.

```
package com.apress.springenterpriserecipes.post;
...
public class FrontDeskImpl extends JmsGatewaySupport implements FrontDesk {
    public void sendMail(Mail mail) {
        Map<String, Object> map = new HashMap<String, Object>();
        map.put("mailId", mail.getMailId());
        map.put("country", mail.getCountry());
        map.put("weight", mail.getWeight());
        getJmsTemplate().convertAndSend(map);
    }
}
```

```
package com.apress.springenterpriserecipes.post;
...
public class BackOfficeImpl extends JmsGatewaySupport implements BackOffice {
    ...
    public Mail receiveMail() {
        Map map = (Map) getJmsTemplate().receiveAndConvert();
        Mail mail = new Mail();
        mail.setMailId((String) map.get("mailId"));
        mail.setCountry((String) map.get("country"));
        mail.setWeight((Double) map.get("weight"));
        return mail;
    }
}
```

You can also create a custom message converter by implementing the MessageConverter interface for converting mail objects.

```java
package com.apress.springenterpriserecipes.post;

import javax.jms.JMSException;
import javax.jms.MapMessage;
import javax.jms.Message;
import javax.jms.Session;

import org.springframework.jms.support.converter.MessageConversionException;
import org.springframework.jms.support.converter.MessageConverter;

public class MailMessageConverter implements MessageConverter {

    public Object fromMessage(Message message) throws JMSException,
            MessageConversionException {
        MapMessage mapMessage = (MapMessage) message;
        Mail mail = new Mail();
        mail.setMailId(mapMessage.getString("mailId"));
        mail.setCountry(mapMessage.getString("country"));
        mail.setWeight(mapMessage.getDouble("weight"));
        return mail;
    }

    public Message toMessage(Object object, Session session) throws JMSException,
            MessageConversionException {
        Mail mail = (Mail) object;
        MapMessage message = session.createMapMessage();
        message.setString("mailId", mail.getMailId());
        message.setString("country", mail.getCountry());
        message.setDouble("weight", mail.getWeight());
        return message;
    }
}
```

To apply this message converter, you have to declare it in both bean configuration files and inject it into the JMS template.

```xml
<beans ...>
    ...
    <bean id="mailMessageConverter"
        class="com.apress.springenterpriserecipes.post.MailMessageConverter" />

    <bean id="jmsTemplate"
        class="org.springframework.jms.core.JmsTemplate">
        ...
        <property name="messageConverter" ref="mailMessageConverter" />
    </bean>
</beans>
```

When you set a message converter for a JMS template explicitly, it will override the default SimpleMessageConverter. Now you can call the JMS template's convertAndSend() and receiveAndConvert() methods to send and receive mail objects.

```
package com.apress.springenterpriserecipes.post;
...
public class FrontDeskImpl extends JmsGatewaySupport implements FrontDesk {
    public void sendMail(Mail mail) {
        getJmsTemplate().convertAndSend(mail);
    }
}

package com.apress.springenterpriserecipes.post;
...
public class BackOfficeImpl extends JmsGatewaySupport implements BackOffice {
    public Mail receiveMail() {
        return (Mail) getJmsTemplate().receiveAndConvert();
    }
}
```

7-3. Managing JMS Transactions

Problem
You want to participate in transactions with JMS so that the receipt and sending of messages are transactional.

Approach
You can use the same strategy as you will everywhere else in Spring: leveraging Spring's many TransactionManager implementations as needed and wiring the behavior into your beans.

Solution
When producing or consuming multiple JMS messages in a single method, if an error occurs in the middle, the JMS messages produced or consumed at the destination may be left in an inconsistent state. You have to surround the method with a transaction to avoid this problem.

In Spring, JMS transaction management is consistent with other data access strategies. For example, you can annotate the methods that require transaction management with the @Transactional annotation.

```
package com.apress.springenterpriserecipes.post;

import org.springframework.jms.core.support.JmsGatewaySupport;
import org.springframework.transaction.annotation.Transactional;
...
```

```
public class FrontDeskImpl extends JmsGatewaySupport implements FrontDesk {

    @Transactional
    public void sendMail(Mail mail) {
        ...
    }
}

package com.apress.springenterpriserecipes.post;

import org.springframework.jms.core.support.JmsGatewaySupport;
import org.springframework.transaction.annotation.Transactional;
...
public class BackOfficeImpl extends JmsGatewaySupport implements BackOffice {

    @Transactional
    public Mail receiveMail() {
        ...
    }
}
```

Then, in both bean configuration files, you add the <tx:annotation-driven /> element and declare a transaction manager. The corresponding transaction manager for local JMS transactions is JmsTransactionManager, which requires a reference to the JMS connection factory.

```
<beans xmlns="http://www.springframework.org/schema/beans"
    xmlns:xsi="http://www.w3.org/2001/XMLSchema-instance"
    xmlns:tx="http://www.springframework.org/schema/tx"
    xsi:schemaLocation="http://www.springframework.org/schema/beans
        http://www.springframework.org/schema/beans/spring-beans-3.0.xsd
        http://www.springframework.org/schema/tx
        http://www.springframework.org/schema/tx/spring-tx-3.0.xsd">
    ...
    <tx:annotation-driven />

    <bean id="transactionManager"
        class="org.springframework.jms.connection.JmsTransactionManager">
        <property name="connectionFactory">
            <ref bean="connectionFactory" />
        </property>
    </bean>
</beans>
```

If you require transaction management across multiple resources, such as a data source and an ORM resource factory, or if you need distributed transaction management, you have to configure JTA transaction in your application server and use JtaTransactionManager. Of course, your JMS connection factory must be XA compliant (i.e., supporting distributed transactions).

7-4. Creating Message-Driven POJOs in Spring

Problem

When you call the receive() method on a JMS message consumer to receive a message, the calling thread is blocked until a message is available. During the duration, the thread can do nothing but wait. This type of message reception is called *synchronous reception* because your application must wait for the message to arrive before it can finish its work.

Starting with EJB 2.0, a new kind of EJB component called a *message-driven bean (MDB)* was introduced for *asynchronous reception* of JMS messages. An EJB container can listen for JMS messages at a message destination and trigger MDBs to react to these messages so that your application no longer has to wait for messages. In EJB 2.x, besides being a nonabstract, nonfinal public class with a public constructor and no finalize method, an MDB must implement both the javax.ejb.MessageDrivenBean and javax.jms.MessageListener interfaces and override all EJB life cycle methods (ejbCreate and ejbRemove). In EJB 3.0, an MDB can be a POJO that implements the MessageListener interface and is annotated with the @MessageDriven annotation.

Although MDBs can listen for JMS messages, they must be deployed in an EJB container to run. You may prefer to add the same capability to POJOs so that they can listen for JMS messages without an EJB container.

Solution

Spring allows beans declared in its IoC container to listen for JMS messages in the same way as MDBs. Because Spring adds message-listening capabilities to POJOs, they are called *message-driven POJOs (MDPs)*.

How It Works

Suppose that you want to add an electronic board to the post office's back office to display mail information in real time as it arrives from the front desk. As the front desk sends a JMS message along with mail, the back office subsystem can listen for these messages and display them on the electronic board. For better system performance, you should apply the asynchronous JMS reception approach to avoid blocking the thread that receives these JMS messages.

Listening for JMS Messages with Message Listeners

First, you create a message listener to listen for JMS messages. This negates the need for the approach taken in BackOfficeImpl in previous recipes. For example, the following MailListener listens for JMS messages that contain mail information:

```
package com.apress.springenterpriserecipes.post;

import javax.jms.JMSException;
import javax.jms.MapMessage;
import javax.jms.Message;
import javax.jms.MessageListener;

import org.springframework.jms.support.JmsUtils;
```

```java
public class MailListener implements MessageListener {

    public void onMessage(Message message) {
        MapMessage mapMessage = (MapMessage) message;
        try {
            Mail mail = new Mail();
            mail.setMailId(mapMessage.getString("mailId"));
            mail.setCountry(mapMessage.getString("country"));
            mail.setWeight(mapMessage.getDouble("weight"));
            displayMail(mail);
        } catch (JMSException e) {
            throw JmsUtils.convertJmsAccessException(e);
        }
    }

    private void displayMail(Mail mail) {
        System.out.println("Mail #" + mail.getMailId() + " received");
    }
}
```

A message listener must implement the javax.jms.MessageListener interface. When a JMS message arrives, the onMessage() method will be called with the message as the method argument. In this sample, you simply display the mail information to the console. Note that when extracting message information from a MapMessage object, you need to handle the JMS API's JMSException. You can make a call to JmsUtils.convertJmsAccessException() to convert it into Spring's runtime exception JmsException.

Next, you have to configure this listener in the back office's bean configuration file. Declaring this listener alone is not enough to listen for JMS messages. You need a message listener container to monitor JMS messages at a message destination and trigger your message listener on message arrival.

```xml
<beans xmlns="http://www.springframework.org/schema/beans"
    xmlns:xsi="http://www.w3.org/2001/XMLSchema-instance"
    xsi:schemaLocation="http://www.springframework.org/schema/beans
        http://www.springframework.org/schema/beans/spring-beans-3.0.xsd">

    <bean id="connectionFactory"
        class="org.apache.activemq.ActiveMQConnectionFactory">
        <property name="brokerURL" value="tcp://localhost:61616" />
    </bean>

    <bean id="mailListener"
        class="com.apress.springenterpriserecipes.post.MailListener" />

    <bean
        class="org.springframework.jms.listener.SimpleMessageListenerContainer">
        <property name="connectionFactory" ref="connectionFactory" />
        <property name="destinationName" value="mail.queue" />
        <property name="messageListener" ref="mailListener" />
    </bean>
</beans>
```

Spring provides several types of message listener containers for you to choose from in the `org.springframework.jms.listener` package, of which `SimpleMessageListenerContainer` and `DefaultMessageListenerContainer` are the most commonly used. `SimpleMessageListenerContainer` is the simplest one that doesn't support transaction. If you have a transaction requirement in receiving messages, you have to use `DefaultMessageListenerContainer`.

Now you can start your message listener with the following main class, which starts the Spring IoC container only:

```
package com.apress.springenterpriserecipes.post;

import org.springframework.context.support.ClassPathXmlApplicationContext;

public class BackOfficeMain {

    public static void main(String[] args) {
        new ClassPathXmlApplicationContext("beans-back.xml");
    }
}
```

Listening for JMS Messages with POJOs

While a listener that implements the `MessageListener` interface can listen for messages, so can an arbitrary bean declared in the Spring IoC container. Doing so means that beans are decoupled from the Spring framework interfaces as well as the JMS `MessageListener` interface. For a method of this bean to be triggered on message arrival, it must accept one of the following types as its sole method argument:

Raw JMS message type: For `TextMessage`, `MapMessage`, `BytesMessage`, and `ObjectMessage`

String: For `TextMessage` only

Map: For `MapMessage` only

byte[]: For `BytesMessage` only

Serializable: For `ObjectMessage` only

For example, to listen for `MapMessage`, you declare a method that accepts a map as its argument. This listener no longer needs to implement the `MessageListener` interface.

```
package com.apress.springenterpriserecipes.post;
...
public class MailListener {

    public void displayMail(Map map) {
        Mail mail = new Mail();
        mail.setMailId((String) map.get("mailId"));
        mail.setCountry((String) map.get("country"));
        mail.setWeight((Double) map.get("weight"));
        System.out.println("Mail #" + mail.getMailId() + " received");
    }
}
```

A POJO is registered to a listener container through a `MessageListenerAdapter` instance. This adapter implements the `MessageListener` interface and will delegate message handling to the target bean's method via reflection.

```
<beans ...>
    ...
    <bean id="mailListener"
        class="com.apress.springenterpriserecipes.post.MailListener" />

    <bean id="mailListenerAdapter"
        class="org.springframework.jms.listener.adapter.MessageListenerAdapter">
        <property name="delegate" ref="mailListener" />
        <property name="defaultListenerMethod" value="displayMail" />
    </bean>

    <bean
        class="org.springframework.jms.listener.SimpleMessageListenerContainer">
        <property name="connectionFactory" ref="connectionFactory" />
        <property name="destinationName" value="mail.queue" />
        <property name="messageListener" ref="mailListenerAdapter" />
    </bean>
</beans>
```

You have to set the `delegate` property of `MessageListenerAdapter` to your target bean. By default, this adapter will call the method whose name is `handleMessage` on that bean. If you want to call another method, you can specify it in the `defaultListenerMethod` property. Finally, notice that you have to register the listener adapter, not the target bean, with the listener container.

Converting JMS Messages

You can also create a message converter for converting mail objects from JMS messages that contain mail information. Because message listeners receive messages only, the method `toMessage()` will not be called, so you can simply return `null` for it. However, if you use this message converter for sending messages too, you have to implement this method. The following example reprints the `MailMessageConvertor` class written earlier:

```
package com.apress.springenterpriserecipes.post;

import javax.jms.JMSException;
import javax.jms.MapMessage;
import javax.jms.Message;
import javax.jms.Session;

import org.springframework.jms.support.converter.MessageConversionException;
import org.springframework.jms.support.converter.MessageConverter;

public class MailMessageConverter implements MessageConverter {
```

```java
    public Object fromMessage(Message message) throws JMSException,
            MessageConversionException {
        MapMessage mapMessage = (MapMessage) message;
        Mail mail = new Mail();
        mail.setMailId(mapMessage.getString("mailId"));
        mail.setCountry(mapMessage.getString("country"));
        mail.setWeight(mapMessage.getDouble("weight"));
        return mail;
    }

    public Message toMessage(Object object, Session session) throws JMSException,
            MessageConversionException {
        ...
    }
}
```

A message converter should be applied to a listener adapter for it to convert messages into objects before calling your POJO's methods.

```xml
<beans ...>
    ...
    <bean id="mailMessageConverter"
        class="com.apress.springenterpriserecipes.post.MailMessageConverter" />

    <bean id="mailListenerAdapter"
        class="org.springframework.jms.listener.adapter.MessageListenerAdapter">
        <property name="delegate" ref="mailListener" />
        <property name="defaultListenerMethod" value="displayMail" />
        <property name="messageConverter" ref="mailMessageConverter" />
    </bean>
</beans>
```

With this message converter, the listener method of your POJO can accept a mail object as the method argument.

```java
package com.apress.springenterpriserecipes.post;

public class MailListener {

    public void displayMail(Mail mail) {
        System.out.println("Mail #" + mail.getMailId() + " received");
    }
}
```

Managing JMS Transactions

As mentioned before, `SimpleMessageListenerContainer` doesn't support transactions. So, if you need transaction management for your message listener method, you have to use `DefaultMessageListenerContainer` instead. For local JMS transactions, you can simply enable its `sessionTransacted` property, and your listener method will run within a local JMS transaction (as opposed to XA transactions).

```
<bean
    class="org.springframework.jms.listener.DefaultMessageListenerContainer">
    <property name="connectionFactory" ref="connectionFactory" />
    <property name="destinationName" value="mail.queue" />
    <property name="messageListener" ref="mailListenerAdapter" />
    <property name="sessionTransacted" value="true" />
</bean>
```

However, if you want your listener to participate in a JTA transaction, you need to declare a `JtaTransactionManager` instance and inject it into your listener container.

Using Spring's JMS Schema

Spring, from 2.5 and onward, offers a new JMS schema to simplify your JMS listener and listener container configuration. You must add the jms schema definition to the <beans> root element beforehand.

```
<beans xmlns="http://www.springframework.org/schema/beans"
    xmlns:xsi="http://www.w3.org/2001/XMLSchema-instance"
    xmlns:jms="http://www.springframework.org/schema/jms"
    xsi:schemaLocation="http://www.springframework.org/schema/beans
        http://www.springframework.org/schema/beans/spring-beans-3.0.xsd
        http://www.springframework.org/schema/jms
        http://www.springframework.org/schema/jms/spring-jms-3.0.xsd">

    <bean id="connectionFactory"
        class="org.apache.activemq.ActiveMQConnectionFactory">
        <property name="brokerURL" value="tcp://localhost:61616" />
    </bean>

    <bean id="transactionManager"
        class="org.springframework.jms.connection.JmsTransactionManager">
        <property name="connectionFactory">
            <ref bean="connectionFactory" />
        </property>
    </bean>

    <bean id="mailMessageConverter"
        class="com.apress.springenterpriserecipes.post.MailMessageConverter" />
```

```
<bean id="mailListener"
    class="com.apress.springenterpriserecipes.post.MailListener" />

<jms:listener-container
    connection-factory="connectionFactory"
    transaction-manager="transactionManager"
    message-converter="mailMessageConverter">
    <jms:listener
        destination="mail.queue"
        ref="mailListener" method="displayMail" />
</jms:listener-container>
</beans>
```

Actually, you don't need to specify the `connection-factory` attribute for a listener container explicitly if your JMS connection factory's name is `connectionFactory`, which can be located by default.

Summary

This chapter explored Spring's support for JMS: how JMS fits in an architecture and how to use Spring to build message-oriented architectures. You learned how to both produce and consume messages using a message queue. You worked with Active MQ, a reliable open source message queue. Finally, you learned how to build message-driven POJOs.

The next chapter will explore Spring integration, which is an ESB-like framework for building application integration solutions, similar to Mule ESB and ServiceMix. You will be able to leverage the knowledge gained in this chapter to take your message-oriented applications to new heights with Spring integration.

CHAPTER 8

■ ■ ■

Spring Integration

In this chapter, you will learn the principles behind enterprise application integration, used by many modern applications to decouple dependencies between components. The Spring framework provides a powerful and extensible framework called Spring Integration, which provides the same level of decoupling to enterprise applications and data that the core Spring framework provides to components within an application.

This chapter aims to give you all the required knowledge to understand the patterns involved in *enterprise application integration (EAI)*, what an *enterprise service bus (ESB)* is, and how to build solutions using Spring Integration.

Upon finishing this chapter, you will be able to write fairly sophisticated Spring Integration processes to decouple applications from one another and to enable them to share services and data. You will learn Spring Integration's many options for configuration, including by XML and by annotation. You will also see why Spring Integration provides a very attractive alternative for people coming from a classic enterprise application integration background. If you've used another ESB before, such as Mule or ServiceMix, or a classical EAI server such as Axway's Integrator or TIBCO, the idioms explained here should be familiar, and the configuration refreshingly straightforward.

8-1. Getting Started with Spring Integration

Problem

You want to get started with Spring Integration, but the JARs aren't in the standard Spring distribution.

Solution

You can use Maven or Ivy, or you can download the JARs manually as a separate project. If you choose the Maven/Ivy route or want to use OSGi, there are different approaches you might take (discussed following).

How It Works

The simplest way to get started with Spring Integration is to simply download the Spring Integration binaries from http://www.SpringFramework.org/spring-integration and add the JARs provided to your classpath. The package is very modular, so if you don't need support for consumption of XML messages, for example, you can simply omit the JAR that provides it. There's no harm in loading them all, though! If you're just getting started with Spring Integration, you'll find there's a lot of value in downloading the whole distribution and reading through the numerous examples. The examples are in a separate folder, usually called Samples, in the root of the distribution.

If you decide to use the Open Services Gateway initiative (OSGi), you can use the SpringSource enterprise repository, which provides OSGi-friendly JAR files, both from SpringSource and from third-party projects. Be careful if you decide to use those JARs with Maven, however, because they import all the other SpringSource enterprise JARs for the core Spring framework and other OSGi-friendly, third-party libraries. If you already have Spring and all the other packages imported, relying on the SpringSource enterprise JARs will yield two of every JAR in the Spring framework! Yikes!

Instead, if you're not using OSGi, but still using Maven or Ivy, use the public JARs available on the main Maven repositories (e.g., http://www.ibiblio.org/maven/). A sample Maven Project Object Model (POM) is included in the source code for this book. The salient parts are extracted here:

```
<dependency>
    <groupId>org.springframework.integration</groupId>
    <artifactId>spring-integration-core</artifactId>
    <version>1.0.3.RELEASE</version>
</dependency>
<dependency>
    <groupId>org.springframework.integration</groupId>
    <artifactId>spring-integration-httpinvoker</artifactId>
    <version>1.0.3.RELEASE</version>
</dependency>
<dependency>
    <groupId>org.springframework.integration</groupId>
    <artifactId>spring-integration-file</artifactId>
    <version>1.0.3.RELEASE</version>
</dependency>
<dependency>
    <groupId>org.springframework.integration</groupId>
    <artifactId>spring-integration-jms</artifactId>
    <version>1.0.3.RELEASE</version>
</dependency>
<dependency>
    <groupId>org.springframework.integration</groupId>
    <artifactId>spring-integration-adapter</artifactId>
    <version>1.0.3.RELEASE</version>
</dependency>
```

8-2. Integrating One System with Another Using EAI

Problem

You have two applications that need to talk to each other through external interfaces. You need to establish a connection between the applications' services and/or their data.

Solution

You need to employ *enterprise application integration (EAI)*, which is the discipline of integrating applications and data using a set of well-known patterns. These patterns are usefully summarized and embodied in a landmark book called *Enterprise Integration Patterns*, by Gregor Hohpe, Bobby Woolf, et al. Today the patterns are canonical and are the lingua franca of the modern-day ESB.

How It Works

Picking an Integration Style

There are multiple integration styles, each best suited for certain types of applications and requirements. The basic premise is simple: your application can't speak directly to the other system using the native mechanism in one system. So you can devise a bridging connection, something to build on top of, abstract, or work around some characteristic about the other system in a way that's advantageous to the invoking system. What you abstract is different per application. Sometimes it's the location, sometimes it's the synchronous or asynchronous nature of the call, and sometimes it's the messaging protocol. There are many criteria for choosing an integration style, related to how tightly coupled you want your application to be, to server affinity, to the demands of the messaging formats, and so on. In a way, TCP/IP is the most famous of all integration techniques because it decouples one application from another's server.

You have probably built applications that use some or all of the following integration styles (using Spring, no less!). Shared Database, for example, is easily achieved using Spring's JDBC support; Remote Procedure Invocation is easily achieved using Spring's exporter functionality.

The four integration styles are as follows:

- **File Transfer**: Have each application produce files of shared data for others to consume and consume files that others have produced.

- **Shared Database**: Have the applications store the data they want to share in a common database. This usually takes the form of a database to which different applications have access. This is not usually a favored approach because it means exposing your data to different clients who might not respect the constraints you have in place (but not codified). Using views and stored procedures can often make this option possible, but it's not ideal. There's no particular support for talking to a database, per se, but you can build an endpoint that deals with new results in a SQL database as message payloads. Integration with databases doesn't tend to be granular or message-oriented, but batch-oriented instead. After all, a million new rows in a database isn't an event so much as a batch! It's no surprise then that Spring Batch (discussed in Chapter 9) included terrific support for JDBC-oriented input and output.

- **Remote Procedure Invocation**: Have each application expose some of its procedures so that they can be invoked remotely, and have applications invoke them to initiate behavior and exchange data. There is specific support for optimizing RPC (remote procedure calls such as SOAP, RMI, and HTTP Invoker) exchanges using Spring Integration.

- **Messaging**: Have each application connect to a common messaging system and exchange data and invoke behavior using messages. This style, most enabled by JMS in the JEE world, also describes other asynchronous or multicast publish/subscribe architectures. In a way, an ESB or an EAI container such as Spring Integration lets you handle most of the other styles as though you were dealing with a messaging queue: a request comes in on a queue and is managed, responded to, or forwarded onward on another queue.

Building on an ESB Solution

Now that you know how you want to approach the integration, it's all about actually implementing it. You have many choices in today's world. If the requirement is common enough, most middleware or frameworks will accommodate it in some way. JEE, .NET, and others handle common cases very well: SOAP, XMLRPC, a binary layer such as EJB or binary remoting, JMS, or a MQ abstraction. If, however, the requirement is somewhat exotic, or you have a lot of configuration to do, then perhaps an ESB is required. An ESB is middleware that provides a high level approach to modeling integrations, in the spirit of the patterns described by EAI. The ESB provides and manageable configuration format for orchestrating the different pieces of an integration in a simple high-level format.

Spring Integration, an API in the SpringSource Portfolio, provides a robust mechanism for modeling a lot of these integration scenarios that work well with Spring. Spring Integration has many advantages over a lot of other ESBs, especially the lightweight nature of the framework. The nascent ESB market is filled with choices. Some are former EAI servers, reworked to address the ESB-centric architectures. Some are genuine ESBs, built with that in mind. Some are little more than message queues with adapters.

Indeed, if you're looking for an extraordinarily powerful EAI server (with almost integration with the JEE platform and a very hefty price tag), you might consider Axway Integrator. There's very little it can't do. Vendors such as TIBCO and WebMethods made their marks (and were subsequently acquired) because they provided excellent tools for dealing with integration in the enterprise. These options, although powerful, are usually very expensive and middleware-centric: your integrations are deployed to the middleware.

Standardization attempts, such as JBI, have proven successful to an extent, and there are good compliant ESBs based on these standards (OpenESB, and ServiceMix, for example). One of the thought leaders in the ESB market is the Mule ESB, which has a good reputation; and is free/open source friendly, community-friendly, and lightweight. These characteristics also make Spring Integration attractive. Often, you simply need to talk to another open system, and you don't want to requisition a purchase approval for middleware that's more expensive than some houses!

Each Spring Integration application is completely embedded and needs no server infrastructure. In fact, you could deploy an integration inside another application, perhaps in your web application endpoint. Spring Integration flips the deployment paradigms of most ESBs on their head: you deploy Spring Integration into your application; you don't deploy your application into Spring Integration. There are no start and stop scripts, and no ports to guard.

The simplest possible working Spring Integration application is a simple Java `public static void main()` method to bootstrap a Spring context:

```
package com.apress.springenterpriserecipes.springintegration;

import org.springframework.context.support.ClassPathXmlApplicationContext;

public class Main {
    public static void main(String [] args){
        String nameOfSpringIntegrationXmlConfigurationFile = args[0];
        ClassPathXmlApplicationContext applicationContext = new
ClassPathXmlApplicationContext(
                nameOfSpringIntegrationXmlConfigurationFile) ;
        applicationContext.start();
    }
}
```

You created a standard Spring application context and started it. The contents of the Spring application context will be discussed in subsequent recipes, but it's helpful to see how simple it is. You might decide to hoist the context up in a web application, an EJB container, or anything else you want.

Indeed, you can use Spring Integration to power the e-mail polling functionality in a Swing/JavaFX application! It's as lightweight as you want it to be.

In subsequent examples, the configuration shown should be put in an XML file and that XML file referenced as the first parameter when running this class. When the main method runs to completion, your context will start up the Spring Integration bus and start responding to requests on the components configured in the application context's XML.

8-3. Integrating Two Systems Using JMS

Problem

You want to build an integration to connect one application to another using JMS, which provides location and temporal decoupling on modern middleware for Java applications. You're interested in applying more sophisticated routing and want to isolate your code from the specifics of the origin of the message (in this case, the JMS queue or topic).

Solution

While you can do this by using regular JMS code or EJB's support for message-driven beans (MDBs), or using core Spring's message-driven POJO (MDP) support, all are necessarily coded for handling messages coming specifically from JMS. Your code is tied to JMS. Using an ESB lets you hide the origin of the message from the code that's handling it. You'll use this solution as an easy way to see how a Spring Integration solution can be built. Spring Integration provides an easy way to work with JMS, just as you might using MDPs in the core Spring container. Here, however, you could conceivably replace the JMS middleware with an e-mail, and the code that reacts to the message could stay the same.

How it Works

Building an MDP Using Spring Integration

As you recall from Chapter 7, Spring can replace EJB's message driven bean (MDB) functionality by using message-driven POJOs (MDPs). This is a powerful solution for anyone wanting to build something that handles messages on a message queue. You'll build an MDP, but you will configure it using Spring Integration's more concise configuration and provide an example of a very rudimentary integration. All this integration will do is take an inbound JMS message (whose payload is of type Map<String,Object>).

As with a standard MDP, configuration for the JMSConnectionFactory exists. There's also a lot of other schema required for using the configuration elements available in Spring Integration. Shown following is a configuration file. You can store in on the classpath, and pass it in as a parameter to the Spring ApplicationContext on creation (as you did in the previous recipe, in the Main class.)

```xml
<?xml version="1.0" encoding="UTF-8"?>

<beans:beans xmlns:beans="http://www.springframework.org/schema/beans"
             xmlns:xsi="http://www.w3.org/2001/XMLSchema-instance"
             xmlns="http://www.springframework.org/schema/integration"
             xmlns:context="http://www.springframework.org/schema/context"
             xmlns:jms="http://www.springframework.org/schema/integration/jms"
             xsi:schemaLocation="http://www.springframework.org/schema/beans
```

```
http://www.springframework.org/schema/beans/spring-beans-3.0.xsd
http://www.springframework.org/schema/context
http://www.springframework.org/schema/context/spring-context-3.0.xsd
http://www.springframework.org/schema/integration
http://www.springframework.org/schema/integration/spring-integration-1.0.xsd
http://www.springframework.org/schema/integration/jms
http://www.springframework.org/schema/integration/jms/spring-integration-➥
jms-1.0.xsd">

    <context:annotation-config/>

    <beans:bean id="connectionFactory"  class="org.springframework. ➥
jms.connection.CachingConnectionFactory">
        <beans:property name="targetConnectionFactory">
            <beans:bean class="org.apache.activemq.ActiveMQConnectionFactory">
                <beans:property name="brokerURL" value="tcp://localhost:8753"/>
            </beans:bean>
        </beans:property>
        <beans:property name="sessionCacheSize" value="10"/>
        <beans:property name="cacheProducers" value="false"/>
    </beans:bean>

    <beans:bean id="inboundHelloWorldJMSPingServiceActivator"
class="com.apress.springenterpriserecipes.springintegration. ➥
InboundHelloWorldJMSMessageProcessor"/>

    <channel id="inboundHelloJMSMessageChannel"/>

    <jms:message-driven-channel-adapter
        channel="inboundHelloJMSMessageChannel"
        extract-payload="true"
        connection-factory="connectionFactory"
        destination-name="solution011"/>

    <service-activator input-channel="inboundHelloJMSMessageChannel"
ref="inboundHelloWorldJMSPingServiceActivator"/>
</beans:beans>
```

As you can see, the most intimidating part is the schema import! The rest of the code is standard boilerplate. You define a connectionFactory exactly as if you were configuring a standard MDP.

Then you define the salient beans specific to this solution: first, a bean that responds to messages coming in to the bus from the message queue, inboundHelloWorldJMSPingServiceActivator. A service-activator is a generic endpoint in Spring Integration that's used to invoke functionality_whether it be an operation in a service, or some routine in a regular POJO, or anything you want instead_in response to a message. Although this will be covered in some detail, it's interesting here only because you are using it to respond to messages. These beans taken together are the collaborators in the solution, and this example is fairly representative of how most integrations look: you define your collaborating components; then you define the configuration using Spring Integration schema that configures the solution itself.

The configuration starts with the inboundHelloJMSMessageChannel channel, which tells Spring Integration what to name the point-to-point connection from the message queue to the service-activator. You typically define a new channel for every point-to-point connection.

Next is a jms:message-driven-channel-adapter configuration element that instructs Spring Integration to send messages coming from the message queue destination solution011 to Spring Integration inboundHelloJMSMessageChannel. An *adapter* is a component that knows how to speak to a specific type of subsystem and translate messages on that subsystem into something that can be used in the Spring Integration bus. Adapters also do the same in reverse, taking messages on the Spring Integration bus and translating them into something a specific subsystem will understand. This is different from a service-activator (covered next) in that it's meant to be a general connection between the bus and the foreign endpoint. A service-activator, however, only helps you invoke your application's business logic on receipt of a message. What you do in the business logic, connecting to another system or not, is up to you.

The next component, a service-activator, listens for messages coming into that channel and invokes the bean referenced by the ref attribute, which in this case is the bean defined previously: inboundHelloWorldJMSPingServiceActivator.

As you can see, there's quite a bit of configuration, but the only custom Java code needed was the inboundHelloWorldJMSPingServiceActivator, which is the part of the solution that Spring can't infer by itself.

```
package com.apress.springenterpriserecipes.springintegration;

import org.apache.log4j.Logger;
import org.springframework.integration.annotation.ServiceActivator;
import org.springframework.integration.core.Message;
import java.util.Map;

public class InboundHelloWorldJMSMessageProcessor {
    private static final Logger logger =
Logger.getLogger(➥
InboundHelloWorldJMSMessageProcessor.class);

    @ServiceActivator
    public void handleIncomingJmsMessage(
        Message<Map<String, Object>> inboundJmsMessage
        ) throws Throwable {
        Map<String, Object> msg = inboundJmsMessage.getPayload();
        logger.debug(String.format(
        "firstName: %s, lastName: %s, id:%s",
        msg.get("firstName"), msg.get("lastName"), ➥
        msg.get("id")));

// you can imagine what we could do here: put
// the record into the database, call a websrvice,
// write it to a file, etc, etc

    }
}
```

Notice that there is an annotation, @ServiceActivator, that tells Spring to configure this component, and this method as the recipient of the message payload from the channel, which is passed to the method as Message<Map<String, Object>> inboundJmsMessage. In the previous configuration, extract-payload="true", which tells Spring Integration to take the payload of the message from the JMS queue (in this case, a Map<String,Object>) and extract it and pass *that* as the payload of the message that's being moved through Spring Integration's channels as a org.springframework.integration.core.Message. The Spring Integration Message is not to be confused with the JMS Message interface, although they have some similarities. Had you not specified the extract-payload option, the type of payload on the Spring Integration Message interface would have been javax.jms.Message. The onus of extracting the payload would have been on you, the developer, but sometimes getting access to that information is useful. Rewritten to handle unwrapping the javax.jms.Message, the example would look a little different:

```
package com.apress.springenterpriserecipes.springintegration;

import org.apache.log4j.Logger;
import org.springframework.integration.annotation.ServiceActivator;
import org.springframework.integration.core.Message;
import java.util.Map;

public class InboundHelloWorldJMSMessageProcessor {
    private static final Logger logger =
Logger.getLogger(InboundHelloWorldJMSMessageProcessor.class);

  @ServiceActivator
    public void handleIncomingJmsMessageWithPayloadNotExtracted(
            Message<javax.jms.Message> msgWithJmsMessageAsPayload
    ) throws Throwable {
        javax.jms.MapMessage jmsMessage = (MapMessage) ➡
msgWithJmsMessageAsPayload.getPayload();
        logger.debug(String.format("firstName: %s, lastName: %s, id:%s",➡
jmsMessage.getString("firstName"),
                jmsMessage.getString("lastName"), jmsMessage.getLong("id")));
    }
}
```

You could have specified the payload type as the type of the parameter passed into the method. If the payload of the message coming from JMS was of type Cat, for example, the method prototype could just as well have been public void handleIncomingJmsMessage(Cat inboundJmsMessage) throws Throwable. Spring Integration will figure out the right thing to do. In this case, I prefer access to the Spring Integration Message, which has header values and so on that can be useful to interrogate.

Also note that you don't need to specify throws Throwable. Error handling can be as generic or as specific as you want in Spring Integration.

In the example, you use the @ServiceActivator to invoke the functionality where the integration ends. However, you can forward the response from the activation on to the next channel by returning a value from the method. The type of the return value, be it a typed Message or a simple POJO, will be sent directly or wrapped in a Message and then sent out on the output channel configured on the service-activator. You can change the payload of the input Message for the Message on the outbound channel. Thus, a service-activator is a very flexible component in which to put hooks to your system and to help mold the integration.

This solution is pretty straightforward, and in terms of configuration for one JMS queue, it's not really a win over straight MDPs because there's an extra level of indirection to overcome. The Spring Integration facilities make building complex integrations easier than Spring Core or EJB3 could because the configuration is centralized. You have a birds-eye view of the entire integration, with routing and processing centralized, so you can better reposition the components in your integration. However, as you'll see, Spring Integration wasn't meant to compete with EJB and Spring Core; it shines at solutions that couldn't naturally be built using EJB3 or Spring Core.

8-4. Interrogate Spring Integration Messages for Context Information

Problem

You want more information about the message coming into the Spring Integration processing pipeline than the type of the message implicitly can give you.

Solution

Interrogate the Spring Integration Message for header information specific to the message. These values are enumerated as header values in a map (of type Map<String,Object>).

How it Works

Using MessageHeaders for Fun and Profit

The Spring Integration Message interface is a generic wrapper that contains a pointer to the actual payload of the message as well as to headers that provide contextual message metadata. You can manipulate or augment this metadata to enable/enhance the functionality of components that are downstream, too; for example, when sending a message through e-mail it's useful to specify the TO/FROM headers.

Any time you expose a class to the framework to handle some requirement (such as the logic you provide for the service-activator component or a transformer component), there will be some chance to interact with the Message and with the message headers. Remember that Spring Integration pushes a Message through a processing pipeline. Each component that interfaces with the Message has to act on it or do something with it. One way of providing information to those components, and of getting information about what's happened in the components up until that point, is to interrogate the MessageHeaders.

There are several values that you should be aware of when working with Spring Integration (see Table 8-1). These constants are exposed on the org.springframework.integration.core.MessageHeaders interface.

Table 8-1. Common Headers Found in Spring Integration Messages

Constant	Description
ID	This is a unique value assigned to the message by the Spring Integration engine.
TIMESTAMP	Timestamp assigned to the message.
CORRELATION_ID	This is optional. It is used by some components (such as aggregators) to group messages together in some sort of processing pipeline.
REPLY_CHANNEL	The String name of the channel to which the output of the current component should be sent. This can be overridden.

Continued

Constant	Description
ERROR_CHANNEL	The String name of the channel to which the output of the current component should be sent if an exception bubbles up into the runtime. This can be overridden.
EXPIRATION_DATE	Used by some components as a threshold for processing after which a component can wait no longer in processing.
SEQUENCE_NUMBER	The order in which the message is to be sequenced; typically used with a sequencer.
SEQUENCE_SIZE	The size of the sequence so that an aggregator can know when to stop waiting for more messages and move forward. This is useful in implementing "join" functionality.

Some header values are specific to the type of the source message's payload; for example, payloads sourced from a file on the file system are different from those coming in from a JMS queue, which are different from messages coming from an e-mail system. These different components are typically packaged in their own JARs, and there's usually some class that provides constants for accessing these headers. An example of component-specific headers are the constants defined for files on `org.springframework.integration.file.FileHeaders`: `FILENAME` and `PREFIX`. Naturally, when in doubt you can just enumerate the values manually because the headers are just a `java.util.Map` instance.

```
// …
public void interrogateMessage(Message<?> message) {
        MessageHeaders headers = message.getHeaders();
        for (String key : headers.keySet()) {
            logger.debug(String.format("%s : %s", key, headers.get(key)));
        }
    }
```

These headers let you interrogate the specific features of these messages without surfacing them as a concrete interface dependency if you don't want them. They can also be used to help processing and allow you to specify custom metadata to downstream components. The act of providing extra data for the benefit of a downstream component is called *message enrichment*. Message enrichment is when you take the headers of a given `Message` and add to them, usually to the benefit of components in the processing pipeline downstream. You might imagine processing a message to add a customer to a customer relationship management (CRM) that makes a call to a third-party web site to establish credit ratings. This credit is added to the headers so the component downstream is tasked with either adding the customer or rejecting it can make its decisions.

Another way to get access to header metadata is to simply have it passed as parameters to your component's method. You simply annotate the parameter with the @Header annotation, and Spring Integration will take care of the rest.

```
package com.apress.springenterpriserecipes.springintegration;
```

```
import org.springframework.integration.annotation.Header;
import org.springframework.integration.annotation.ServiceActivator;
import org.springframework.integration.core.MessageHeaders;
import org.springframework.integration.file.FileHeaders;
// …
import java.io.File;

public class InboundFileMessageServiceActivator {
    private static final  Logger logger = Logger.getLogger(
InboundFileMessageServiceActivator.class);

    @ServiceActivator
    public void interrogateMessage(
     @Header(MessageHeaders.ID)  String uuid,
     @Header(FileHeaders.FILENAME) String fileName,
     File file
) {
        logger.debug(String.format(
        "the id of the message is %s, and name of the file payload is %s",
            uuid, fileName));
    }
}
```

You can also have Spring Integration simply pass the Map<String,Object>:

```
package com.apress.springenterpriserecipes.springintegration;

import org.springframework.integration.annotation.Headers;
import org.springframework.integration.annotation.ServiceActivator;
import org.springframework.integration.core.MessageHeaders;
import org.springframework.integration.file.FileHeaders;

…

import java.io.File;
import java.util.Map;

public class InboundFileMessageServiceActivatorWithHeadersMap {
    private static final Logger logger = Logger.getLogger(
            InboundFileMessageServiceActivatorWithHeadersMap.class);

    @ServiceActivator
    public void interrogateMessage(@Headers Map<String, Object>➥
headers, File file) {
        logger.debug(String.format(
            "the id of the message is %s, and name of the file payload is %s",
                headers.get(MessageHeaders.ID),
                headers.get(FileHeaders.FILENAME)));
    }
}
```

8-5. Integrating Two Systems Using a File System

Problem

You want to build a solution that takes files on a well-known, shared file system and uses them as the conduit for integration with another system. An example might be that your application produces a comma-separated value (CSV) dump of all the customers added to a system every hour. The company's third-party financial system is updated with these sales by a process that checks a shared folder, mounted over a network file system, and processes the CSV records. What's required is a way to treat the presence of a new file as an event on the bus.

Solution

You have an idea of how this could be built by using standard techniques, but you want something more elegant. Let Spring Integration isolate you from the event-driven nature of the file system and from the file input/output requirements and instead let's use it to focus on writing the code that deals with the File payload itself. With this approach, you can write unit-testable code that accepts an input and responds by adding the customers to the financial system. When the functionality is finished, you configure it in the Spring Integration pipeline and let Spring Integration invoke your functionality whenever a new file is recognized on the file system. This is an example of an event-driven architecture (EDA). EDAs let you ignore how an event was generated and focus instead on reacting to them, in much the same way that event-driven GUIs let you change the focus of your code from controlling how a user triggers an action to actually reacting to the invocation itself. Spring Integration makes it a natural approach for loosely coupled solutions. In fact, this code should look very similar to the solution you built for the JMS queue because it's just another class that takes a parameter (a Message, a parameter of the same type as the payload of the message, and so on).

How It Works

Concerns in Dealing with a File System

Building a solution to talk to JMS is old hat. Instead, let's consider what building a solution using a shared file system might look like. Imagine how to build it without an ESB solution. You need some mechanism by which to poll the file system periodically and detect new files. Perhaps Quartz and some sort of cache? You need something to read these files in quickly and then pass the payload to your processing logic efficiently. Finally, your system needs to work with that payload.

Spring Integration frees you from all that infrastructure code; all you need to do is configure it. There are some issues with dealing with file system–based processing, however, that are up to you to resolve. Behind the scenes, Spring Integration is still dealing with polling the file system and detecting new files. It can't possibly have a semantically correct idea for your application of when a file is "completely" written, and thus providing a way around that is up to you.

Several approaches exist. You might write out a file and then write another 0-byte file and let Spring Integration detect that file. The presence of that file would mean it's safe to assume that the real payload is present. Configure Spring Integration to look for that file. If it finds it, it knows that there's another file (perhaps with the same name and a different file extension?) and that it can start reading it/working with it. Another solution along the same line is to have the client ("producer") write the file to the directory using a name that the glob pattern Spring Integration is using to poll the directory won't detect. Then, when it's finished writing, issue an mv command if you trust your file system to do the right thing there.

Let's revisit the first solution, but this time with a file-based adapter. The configuration looks conceptually the same as before, except the configuration for the adapter has changed, and with that has gone a lot of the configuration for the JMS adapter, like the connection factory. Instead, you tell Spring Integration about a different source from whence messages will come: the file system.

```xml
<?xml version="1.0" encoding="UTF-8"?>

<beans:beans xmlns:beans="http://www.springframework.org/schema/beans"
             xmlns:xsi="http://www.w3.org/2001/XMLSchema-instance"
             xmlns="http://www.springframework.org/schema/integration"
              xmlns:context="http://www.springframework.org/schema/context"
             xmlns:file="http://www.springframework.org/schema/integration/file"
             xsi:schemaLocation="http://www.springframework.org/schema/beans
http://www.springframework.org/schema/beans/➥
spring-beans-3.0.xsd http://www.springframework.org/schema/context
http://www.springframework.org/schema/context/➥
spring-context-3.0.xsd http://www.springframework.org/schema/integration
http://www.springframework.org/schema/integration/➥
spring-integration-1.0.xsd
http://www.springframework.org/schema/integration/jms
http://www.springframework.org/schema/integration/jms/➥
spring-integration-jms-1.0.xsd http://www.springframework.org/➥
schema/integration/file
http://www.springframework.org/schema/integration/file/➥
spring-integration-file-1.0.xsd">

  <context:annotation-config/>

    <poller id="poller" default="true">
        <interval-trigger time-unit="SECONDS" interval="10"/>
    </poller>

    <beans:bean id="inboundHelloWorldFileMessageProcessor"
                class="com.apress.springenterpriserecipes.springintegration. ➥
InboundHelloWorldFileMessageProcessor"/>

    <channel id="inboundFileChannel"/>

    <file:inbound-channel-adapter directory="${user.home}/inboundFiles/new/"
                                  channel="inboundFileChannel"
                                  filename-pattern="^new.*csv"
                                  />
    <service-activator input-channel="inboundFileChannel"➥
ref="inboundHelloWorldFileMessageProcessor"/>

</beans:beans>
```

Nothing you haven't already seen, really. The code for file:inbound-channel-adapter is the only new element, and it comes with its own schema, which is in the prologue for the XML itself.

The code for the service-activator has changed to reflect the fact that you're expecting a message containing a message of type Message<java.io.File>.

```
package com.apress.springenterpriserecipes.springintegration.solution014;

import org.apache.log4j.Logger;
import org.springframework.integration.annotation.ServiceActivator;
import org.springframework.integration.core.Message;

import java.io.File;

public class InboundHelloWorldFileMessageProcessor {
    private static final Logger logger = ➥
 Logger.getLogger(InboundHelloWorldFileMessageProcessor.class);

    @ServiceActivator
    public void handleIncomingFileMessage(
        Message<File> inboundJmsMessage) throws Throwable {
        File filePayload = inboundJmsMessage.getPayload();
        logger.debug(String.format("absolute path: %s, size: %s",
            filePayload.getAbsolutePath(), filePayload.length()));
    }
}
```

8-6. Transforming a Message from One Type to Another

Problem

You want to send a message into the bus and transform it before working with it further. Usually, this is done to adapt the message to the requirements of a component downstream. You might also want to transform a message by enriching it—adding extra headers or augmenting the payload so that components downstream in the processing pipeline can benefit from it.

Solution

Use a transformer component to take a Message of a payload and send the Message out with a payload of a different type. You can also use the transformer to add extra headers or update the values of headers for the benefit of components downstream in the processing pipeline.

How it Works

Spring Integration provides a transformer message endpoint to permit the augmentation of the message headers or the transformation of the message itself. In Spring Integration, components are chained together, and output from one component is returned by way of the method invoked for that component. The return value of the method is passed out on the "reply channel" for the component to the next component, which receives it as an input parameter.

A transformer component lets you change the type of the object being returned or add extra headers and that updated object is what is passed to the next component in the chain.

Modifying a Message's Payload

The configuration of a transformer component is very much in keeping with everything you've seen so far:

```java
package com.apress.springenterpriserecipes.springintegration;
import org.springframework.integration.annotation.Transformer;
import org.springframework.integration.core.Message;
import java.util.Map;

public class InboundJMSMessageToCustomerTransformer {
    @Transformer
    public Customer transformJMSMapToCustomer(
        Message<Map<String, Object>> inboundSpringIntegrationMessage) {
        Map<String, Object> jmsMessagePayload =
inboundSpringIntegrationMessage.getPayload();
        Customer customer = new Customer();
        customer.setFirstName((String) jmsMessagePayload.get("firstName"));
        customer.setLastName((String) jmsMessagePayload.get("lastName"));
        customer.setId((Long) jmsMessagePayload.get("id"));
        return customer;
    }
}
```

Nothing terribly complex happening here: a `Message` of type `Map<String,Object>` is passed in. The values are manually extracted and used to build an object of type `Customer`. The `Customer` object is returned, which has the effect of passing it out on the reply channel for this component. The next component in the configuration will receive this object as its input `Message`.

The solution is mostly the same as you've seen, but there is a new `transformer` element:

```xml
<?xml version="1.0" encoding="UTF-8"?>

<beans:beans xmlns:beans="http://www.springframework.org/schema/beans"
…
>

    <context:annotation-config/>

    <beans:bean id="connectionFactory"
 class="org.springframework.jms.connection.CachingConnectionFactory">
        <beans:property name="targetConnectionFactory">
            <beans:bean class="org.apache.activemq.ActiveMQConnectionFactory">
                <beans:property name="brokerURL" value="tcp://localhost:8753"/>
            </beans:bean>
        </beans:property>
        <beans:property name="sessionCacheSize" value="10"/>
        <beans:property name="cacheProducers" value="false"/>
    </beans:bean>
    <beans:bean id="jmsTemplate" class="org.springframework.jms.core.JmsTemplate">
        <beans:property name="connectionFactory" ref="connectionFactory"/>
    </beans:bean>
```

```
    <beans:bean id="inboundJMSMessageToCustomerTransformer"
            class="com.apress.springenterpriserecipes.springintegration. ➥
InboundJMSMessageToCustomerTransformer"/>

    <beans:bean id="inboundCustomerServiceActivator"➥
class="com.apress.springenterpriserecipes.springintegration. ➥
InboundCustomerServiceActivator"/>
    <channel id="inboundHelloJMSMessageChannel"/>
    <channel id="inboundCustomerChannel"/>
    <jms:message-driven-channel-adapter channel="inbound➥
HelloJMSMessageChannel" extract-payload="true"  connection-factory➥
="connectionFactory" destination-name="solution015"/>
    <transformer input-channel="inboundHelloJMSMessageChannel"➥
ref="inboundJMSMessageToCustomerTransformer" output-➥
channel="inboundCustomerChannel"/>
    <service-activator input-channel="inboundCustomerChannel"➥
 ref="inboundCustomerServiceActivator" />

</beans:beans>
```

Here, you're also specifying an output-channel attribute on the component, which tells a component on what channel to send the component's response output; in this case, the Customer.

The code in the next component can now declare a dependency on the Customer interface with impunity. You can, with transformers, receive messages from any number of sources and transform into a Customer so that you can reuse the InboundCustomerServiceActivator:

```
package com.apress.springenterpriserecipes.springintegration;

import org.apache.log4j.Logger;
import org.springframework.integration.annotation.ServiceActivator;
import org.springframework.integration.core.Message;


public class InboundCustomerServiceActivator {
    private static final Logger logger =
      Logger.getLogger(InboundCustomerServiceActivator.class);

    @ServiceActivator
            public void doSomethingWithCustomer(
                    Message<Customer> customerMessage) {
        Customer customer = customerMessage.getPayload();
        logger.debug(String.format("id=%s, firstName:%s, lastName:%s",
                                    customer.getId(),
                                    customer.getFirstName(),
                                    customer.getLastName()));


    }
}
```

Modifying a Message's Headers

Sometimes changing a message's payload isn't enough. Sometimes you want to update the payload as well as the headers. Doing this is slightly more interesting because it involves using the `MessageBuilder` class, which allows you to create new `Message` objects with any specified payload and any specified header data. The XML configuration is identical in this case.

```java
package com.apress.springenterpriserecipes.springintegration;

import org.springframework.integration.annotation.Transformer;
import org.springframework.integration.core.Message;
import org.springframework.integration.message.MessageBuilder;

import java.util.Map;

public class InboundJMSMessageToCustomerWithExtraMetadataTransformer {
    @Transformer
    public Message<Customer> transformJMSMapToCustomer(
        Message<Map<String, Object>> inboundSpringIntegrationMessage) {
        Map<String, Object> jmsMessagePayload =
                inboundSpringIntegrationMessage.getPayload();
        Customer customer = new Customer();
        customer.setFirstName((String) jmsMessagePayload.get("firstName"));
        customer.setLastName((String) jmsMessagePayload.get("lastName"));
        customer.setId((Long) jmsMessagePayload.get("id"));
        return MessageBuilder.withPayload(customer)
                .copyHeadersIfAbsent( inboundSpringIntegrationMessage.getHeaders())
                .setHeaderIfAbsent("randomlySelectedForSurvey", Math.random() > .5)
                .build();
    }
}
```

As before, this code is simply a method with an input and an output. The output is constructed dynamically using `MessageBuilder` to create a message that has the same payload as the input message as well as copy the existing headers, and adds an extra header: randomlySelectedForSurvey.

8-7. Error Handling Using Spring Integration

Problem

Spring Integration brings together systems distributed across different nodes, computers, and services/protocol/language stacks. Indeed, a Spring Integration solution might not even finish in remotely the same time period as when it started. Exception handling, then, can never be as simple as a language-level try/catch block in a single thread for any component with asynchronous behavior. This implies that many of the kinds of solutions you're likely to build, with channels and queues of any kind, need a way of signaling an error that is distributed and natural to the component that created the error. Thus, an error might get sent over a JMS queue on a different continent, or in process, on a queue in a different thread.

Solution

Use Spring Integration's support for an error channel, both implicit and explicitly via code. This solution works only for solutions that employ channels whose messages are received out of the client's thread.

How It Works

Spring Integration provides the ability to catch exceptions and send them to an error channel of your choosing. By default, it's a global channel called errorChannel. You can have components subscribe to messages from this channel to override the exception handling behavior. You can create a class that will be invoked whenever a message comes in on the errorChannel channel:

```xml
<?xml version="1.0" encoding="UTF-8"?>

<beans:beans xmlns:beans="http://www.springframework.org/schema/beans"
 …
>
    <context:annotation-config/>

    <beans:bean id="defaultErrorHandlingServiceActivator"➥
 class="com.apress.springenterpriserecipes.springintegration.DefaultError➥
HandlingServiceActivator"/>

    <service-activator input-channel="errorChannel" ref="defaultErrorHandling➥
ServiceActivator"/>

</beans:beans>
```

The Java code is exactly as you'd expect it to be. Of course, the service-activator doesn't need to be a service-activator. I just use it for convenience here. You could as easily send the error out on a channel to anywhere you want. The code for the following service-activator depicts some of the machinations you might go through to build a handler for the errorChannel:

```java
package com.apress.springenterpriserecipes.springintegration;

import org.apache.commons.lang.exception.ExceptionUtils;
import org.apache.log4j.Logger;
import org.springframework.integration.annotation.ServiceActivator;
import org.springframework.integration.core.Message;
import org.springframework.integration.core.MessagingException;

public class DefaultErrorHandlingServiceActivator {
    private static final Logger logger =
      Logger.getLogger( DefaultErrorHandlingServiceActivator.class );

    @ServiceActivator
    public void handleThrowable(Message<Throwable> errorMessage) throws Throwable {
        Throwable throwable = errorMessage.getPayload();
        logger.debug(String.format("message: %s, stack trace :%s",
            throwable.getMessage(),
            ExceptionUtils.getFullStackTrace(throwable)));
        if (throwable instanceof MessagingException) {
            Message<?> failedMessage =
```

```
            ((MessagingException) throwable).getFailedMessage();
        if (failedMessage != null) {
            // do something with the original message
        }
    } else {
        // it's something that was thrown in the
        // execution of code in some component you created
    }
}
}
```

All errors thrown from Spring Integration components will be a subclass of `MessagingException`. `MessagingException` carries a pointer to the original `Message` that caused an error, which you can dissect for more context information. In the example, you're doing a nasty `instanceof`. Clearly, being able to delegate to custom exception handlers based on the type of exception would be useful.

Routing to Custom Handlers Based on the Type of Exception

Sometimes more specific error handling is required. One way to discriminate by `Exception` type is to use the `org.springframework.integration.router.ErrorMessageExceptionTypeRouter`. This router is configured as a router component, which in turn listens to `errorChannel`. It then splinters off, using the type of the exception as the predicate in determining which channel should get the results.

```xml
<?xml version="1.0" encoding="UTF-8"?>

<beans:beans xmlns:beans="http://www.springframework.org/schema/beans"
...
>
    <context:annotation-config/>
    <channel id="customErrorChannelForMyCustomException"/>
    <beans:bean id="myCustomErrorRouter"➥
 class="org.springframework.integration.router.➥
ErrorMessageExceptionTypeRouter">
        <beans:property name="exceptionTypeChannelMap">
            <beans:map key-type="java.lang.Class">
                <beans:entry
    key="com.apress.springenterpriserecipes.➥
                springintegration.MyCustomException"
    value-ref="customErrorChannelForMyCustomException" />
            </beans:map>
        </beans:property>
    </beans:bean>
    <router input-channel="errorChannel" ref="myCustomErrorRouter"/>
</beans:beans>
```

Building a Solution with Multiple Error channels

The preceding might work fine for simple cases, but often different integrations require different error-handling approaches, which implies that sending all the errors to the same channel can eventually lead to a large "switch"-laden class that's too complex to maintain. Instead, it's better to selectively route error messages to the error channel most appropriate to each integration. This avoids centralizing all error handling. One way to do that is to explicitly specify on what channel errors for a given integration should go. The following example shows a component (service-activator) that upon receiving a message, adds a header indicating the name of the error channel. Spring Integration will use that header and forward errors encountered in the processing of this message to that channel.

```
package com.apress.springenterpriserecipes.springintegration;

import org.apache.log4j.Logger;
import org.springframework.integration.annotation.ServiceActivator;
import org.springframework.integration.core.Message;
import org.springframework.integration.core.MessageHeaders;
import org.springframework.integration.message.MessageBuilder;

public class ServiceActivatorThatSpecifiesErrorChannel {
    private static final Logger logger = Logger.getLogger(
        ServiceActivatorThatSpecifiesErrorChannel.class);

    @ServiceActivator
    public Message<?> startIntegrationFlow(Message<?> firstMessage)
        throws Throwable {
        return MessageBuilder.fromMessage(firstMessage).
            setHeaderIfAbsent( MessageHeaders.ERROR_CHANNEL,
                "errorChannelForMySolution").build();
    }
}
```

Thus, all errors that come from the integration in which this component is used will be directed to customErrorChannel, to which you can subscribe any component you like.

8-8. Forking Integration Control: Splitters and Aggregators

Problem
You want to fork the process flow from one component to many, either all at once or to a single one based on a predicate condition.

Solution
You can use a splitter component (and maybe its cohort, the aggregator component) to fork and join control, respectively.

How it Works
One of the fundamental cornerstones of an ESB is routing. You've seen how components can be chained together to create sequences in which progression is mostly linear. Some solutions require the capability to split a message into many constituent parts.

Splitter
It's often more useful to divide large payloads into separate messages with separate processing flows. In Spring Integration, this is accomplished by using a splitter component. A splitter takes an input message and asks you, the user of the component, on what basis it should split the Message: you're responsible for providing the split functionality. Once you've told Spring Integration how to split a

Message, it forwards each result out on the output-channel of the splitter component. In a few cases, Spring Integration ships with useful splitters that require no customization. One example is the splitter provided to partition an XML payload along an XPath query, XPathMessageSplitter.

One example of a useful application of a splitter might be a text file with rows of data, each of which must be processed. Your goal is to be able to submit each row to a service that will handle the processing. What's required is a way to extract each row and forward each row as a new Message.

The configuration for such a solution looks like this:

```xml
<?xml version="1.0" encoding="UTF-8"?>

<beans:beans xmlns:beans="http://www.springframework.org/schema/beans"
             xmlns:xsi="http://www.w3.org/2001/XMLSchema-instance"
             xmlns="http://www.springframework.org/schema/integration"
             xmlns:context="http://www.springframework.org/schema/context"
             xmlns:jms="http://www.springframework.org/schema/integration/jms"
             xmlns:file="http://www.springframework.org/schema/integration/file"
             xsi:schemaLocation="http://www.springframework.org/schema/beans
http://www.springframework.org/schema/beans/➥
spring-beans-3.0.xsd
http://www.springframework.org/schema/context
http://www.springframework.org/schema/context/➥
spring-context-3.0.xsd http://www.springframework.org/schema/integration
http://www.springframework.org/schema/integration/➥
spring-integration-1.0.xsd
http://www.springframework.org/schema/integration/jms
http://www.springframework.org/schema/integration/jms/➥
spring-integration-jms-1.0.xsd
http://www.springframework.org/schema/integration/file
http://www.springframework.org/schema/integration/file/➥
spring-integration-file-1.0.xsd">

    <context:annotation-config/>

   <poller id="poller" default="true">
        <interval-trigger interval="1000"/>
   </poller>
   <beans:bean id="fileSplitter"
                class="com.apress.springenterpriserecipes. ➥
springintegration.CustomerBatchFileSplitter"/>
    <beans:bean id="customerDeletionServiceActivator"
          class="com.apress.springenterpriserecipes. ➥
springintegration.CustomerDeletionServiceActivator"/>
    <channel id="customerBatchChannel"/>
    <channel id="customerIdChannel"/>
    <file:inbound-channel-adapter
        directory="file:${user.home}/customerstoremove/new/"
        channel="customerBatchChannel"  filename-pattern="^new.*txt$"/>

    <splitter input-channel="customerBatchChannel"
            ref="fileSplitter" output-channel="customerIdChannel" />
```

```
<service-activator input-channel="customerIdChannel"
                   ref="customerDeletionServiceActivator"/>
```

```
</beans:beans>
```

The configuration for this is not terribly different from the previous solutions. The Java code is just about the same as well, except that the return type of the method annotated by the @Splitter annotation is of type java.util.Collection.

```java
package com.apress.springenterpriserecipes.springintegration;

import org.apache.commons.io.IOUtils;
import org.springframework.integration.annotation.Splitter;
import java.io.File;
import java.io.FileReader;
import java.io.Reader;
import java.util.Collection;

public class CustomerBatchFileSplitter {
    @Splitter
    public Collection<String> splitAFile(File file) throws Throwable {
        Reader reader = new FileReader(file);
        Collection<String> lines = IOUtils.readLines(reader);
        IOUtils.closeQuietly(reader);
        return lines;
    }
}
```

A message payload is passed in as a java.io.File and the contents are read. The result (a collection or array value; in this case, a Collection<String>) is returned. Spring Integration executes a kind of "foreach" on the results, sending each value in the collection out on the output-channel configured for the splitter. Often, you split messages so that the individual pieces can be forwarded to processing that's more focused. Because the message is more manageable, the processing requirements are dampened. This is true in many different architectures: in map/reduce solutions (see Chapter 10 for more on this) tasks are split and then processed in parallel, and the fork/join constructs in a BPM system (see Chapter 11) let control flow proceed in parallel so that the total work product can be achieved quicker.

Aggregators

Ineluctably, you'll need to do the reverse: combine many messages into one, and create a single result that can be returned on the output-channel. An @Aggregator collects a series of messages (based on some correlation that you help Spring Integration make between the messages) and publishes a single message to the components downstream. Suppose that you know that you're expecting 22 different messages from 22 actors in the system, but you don't know when. This is similar to a company that auctions off a contract and collects all the bids from different vendors before choosing the ultimate vendor. The company can't accept a bid until all bids have been received from all companies. Otherwise, there's the risk of prematurely signing a contract that would not be in the best interest of the company. An aggregator is perfect for building this type of logic.

There are many ways for Spring Integration to correlate incoming messages. To determine how many messages to read until it can stop, it uses SequenceSizeCompletionStrategy, which reads a well known header value (aggregators are often used after a splitter. Thus, the default header value is provided by the splitter, though there's nothing stopping you from creating the header parameters yourself) to calculate how many it should look for and to note the index of the message relative to the expected total count (i.e., 3/22).

For correlation when you might not have a size but know that you're expecting messages that share a common header value within a known time, Spring Integration provides the HeaderAttributeCorrelationStrategy. In this way, it knows that all messages with that value are from the same group, in the same way that your last name identifies you as being part of a larger group.

Let's revisit the last example. Suppose that the file was split and subsequently processed. You now want to reunite the customers and do some cleanup with everyone at the same time. In this example, you use the default completion-strategy and correlation-strategy. The only custom logic is a POJO with an @Aggregator annotation on a method expecting a collection of Message objects. It could, of course, be a collection of Customer objects because they are what you're expecting as output from the previous splitter. You return on the reply channel a Message that has the entire collection as its payload:

```
<beans:bean id="customAggregator" class="com.apress.springenterpriserecipes. ➡
springintegration.MessagePayloadAggregator"/>
...
<channel id="messagePayloadAggregatorChannel"/>
<channel id="summaryChannel"/>
...
<aggregator input-channel="messagePayloadAggregatorChannel"
    ref="customAggregator"
    output-channel="summaryChannel" />
```

The Java code is even simpler:

```
package com.apress.springenterpriserecipes.springintegration;

import org.springframework.integration.annotation.Aggregator;
import org.springframework.integration.core.Message;
import org.springframework.integration.message.MessageBuilder;


import java.util.List;

public class MessagePayloadAggregator {
    @Aggregator
    public Message<?> joinMessages(
    List<Message<Customer>> customers
    ) {
        if (customers.size() > 0) {
            return MessageBuilder.withPayload(customers).copyHeadersIfAbsent(
                    customers.get(0).getHeaders()).build();
        }
        return null;
    }
}
```

8-9. Conditional Routing with Routers

Problem

You want to conditionally move a message through different processes based on some criteria. This is the EAI equivalent to an if-else branch.

Solution

You can use a router component to alter the processing flow based on some predicate. You can also use a router to multicast a message to many subscribers (as you did with the splitter).

How It Works

With a router you can specify a known list of channels on which the incoming Message should be passed. This has some powerful implications. It means you can change the flow of a process conditionally, and it also means that you can forward a Message to as many (or as few) channels as you want. There are some convenient default routers available to fill common needs, such as payload type–based routing (PayloadTypeRouter) and routing to a group or list of channels (RecipientListRouter).

Imagine for example a processing pipeline that routes customers with high credit scores to one service and customers with lower credit scores to another process in which the information is queued up for a human audit and verification cycle. The configuration is, as usual, very straightforward. In the following example, you show the configuration. One router element, which in turn delegates the routing logic to a class, is CustomerCreditScoreRouter.

```
<beans:bean id="customerCreditScoreRouter".➥
  class="com.apress.springenterpriserecipesspringintegration. ➥
CustomerCreditScoreRouter"/>
...
<channel id="safeCustomerChannel"/>
<channel id="riskyCustomerChannel"/>
...
<router input-channel="customerIdChannel" ref="customerCreditScoreRouter"/>
```

The Java code is similarly approachable. It feels a lot like a workflow engine's conditional element, or even a JSF backing-bean method, in that it extricates the routing logic into the XML configuration, away from code, delaying the decision until runtime. In the example, the Strings returned are the names of the channels on which the Message should pass.

```
import org.springframework.integration.annotation.Router;

public class CustomerCreditScoreRouter {
    @Router
    public String routeByCustomerCreditScore(Customer customer) {
        if (customer.getCreditScore() > 770) {
            return "safeCustomerChannel";
        } else {
            return "riskyCustomerChannel";
        }
    }
}
```

If you decide that you'd rather not let the Message pass and want to arrest processing, you can return null instead of a String.

8-10. Adapting External Systems to the Bus

Problem

You want to receive messages from an external system and process them using Spring Integration. The external system doesn't expose any messaging functionality.

Solution

The answer is a channel adapter that comes straight from the EIP book. Spring Integration makes it trivially easy to build one.

How It Works

You use a channel adapter to access an application's API or data. Typically this is done by publishing data from the application on a channel or receiving messages and invoking functionality on the application's API. Channels can also be used to broadcast events from an application to interested, external systems.

Adapters are opaque in nature. Your external system interfaces with the adapter. What functionality or scope of access the application provides to the adapter varies based on the requirements.

Some systems are insurmountable "walled gardens," and sometimes the worst solution is the only solution. Imagine, for example, a legacy terminal application based on curses that surfaces application functionality and data only via the user interface. In this case, a *user interface adapter* is required. This situation also presents itself often with web sites, which become data silos. These applications require an adapter to parse the emitted HTML for data or "screen-scrape" them.

Sometimes functionality is made available from within the application via a cohesive, stable API, but in a component model or form that isn't directly accessible to the bus. This type of adapter is called a *business logic adapter*. An application built in C++ that provides CORBA endpoints but needs to support SOAP endpoints is a good candidate for this approach.

A third type of adapter, which sits on the database and adapts an external system by way of the schema, is also an option. This is essentially an implementation of the *shared database* integration pattern.

An Inbound Twitter Adapter

Spring Integration already provides many useful implementations of channel adapters, as you have seen in previous exercises. You will build an example to receive messages from an external system for which there is no existing support (yet): Twitter. In Spring Integration, you use a MessageSource implementation to model components that can produce messages for consumption on the bus.

Most of you are familiar with Twitter, so indulge me in a quick overview and introduction, just to be thorough. Twitter is a social networking site founded in 2006. It allows users to broadcast a message (a *status* or a *tweet*) to all people who have subscribed to these status updates. The updates are limited to 140 characters. Subscribing to a person's status updates is called *following* that person.

Support for inspecting other peoples' updates and updating your own status is provided by the web site itself. Additionally, support is offered by a telephone integration that takes messages sent via a mobile phone (SMS) and correlates the phone number of the inbound message to a user's account and updates that person's status on her behalf.

Many people, from the everyman to the super famous, use Twitter. Reports have it as the third biggest social networking site as of this writing. Some people (presidents, celebrities, and so on) have hundreds of thousands of followers, and at least one has in excess of a million followers. As you can imagine, the difficulties and logistics of managing a graph as complex and sprawling as the one Twitter manages can be frustrating and has been the source of many well publicized outages.

Twitter furnishes a REST API through which users can interact with the system. The API lets one do anything she might do from the web site: follow users, stop following users, update status, and so on. The API is concise and has many language bindings already available. In the example, you'll use one project's API, called Twitter4J, which nicely wraps the API in simple approachable API calls.

Twitter4J was created by Yusuke Yamamoto and is available under the BSD license. It's available in the Maven repositories, and it has a fairly active support mailing list. If you want to find more about Twitter4J, visit http://yusuke.homeip.net.

Twitter Messages

In the first example, you'll build support for receiving messages, not for sending them. The second example will feature support for outbound messages. In particular, you'll build support for receiving the status updates of the people to which a particular account is subscribed, or *following*.

There are other types of Twitter messages. Although you won't build adapters for every type, it won't be difficult to imagine how it's done once you've completed the examples. Twitter supports direct messaging, in which you can specify that one recipient only sees the contents of the message; this is *peer-to-peer messaging*, roughly analogous to using SMS messaging. Twitter also supports receiving messages in which your screen handle was mentioned. These messages can often be messages directed to you and others, messages discussing you, or messages reposting (*retweeting*) something you said already.

A Simple MessageSource

There are two ways to build an adapter, using principally the same technique. You can create a class that implements MessageSource, or you can configure a method that should be invoked, effectively letting Spring Integration coerce a class into behaving like an implementation of a MessageSource. In this example, you'll build a MessageSource, which is very succinct:

```
package org.springframework.integration.message;
import org.springframework.integration.core.Message;

public interface MessageSource<T> {
    Message<T> receive();
}
```

In the example, you're building a solution that can pull status updates and return them in a simple POJO object called Tweet.

```
package com.apress.springenterpriserecipes.springintegration.twitter;

import java.io.Serializable;
import java.util.Date;
// …
```

```
public class Tweet implements Serializable, Comparable<Tweet> {
    private long tweetId;
     private String message;
    private Date received;
    private String user;
    // constructors, accessor/mutators, compareTo,
            // toString/equals/hashCode methods all ommited for brevity.
            // …
}
```

Thus, the implementation for the MessageSource will return Messages containing an object of type Tweet as the payload. Examining the outline of the implementation is telling because the approach for satisfying the interface becomes evident now that you know what interface requirements you're trying to meet. With any luck, the beginnings of the final solution will crystallize. It is that simple!

```
package com.apress.springenterpriserecipes.springintegration.twitter;

public class TwitterMessageSource
     implements MessageSource<Tweet>,  InitializingBean {
    public Message<Tweet> receive() {
     return null;
    }
    // …
 }
```

As you can see, the MessageSource reads from the external system, one message at a time. There are no other interfaces to implement. You do, however, have some design constraints imposed on you not by Spring Integration, but by the Twitter API. The Twitter API limits how many requests you can make to it per hour. The operative word here is *requests* because the limitation doesn't apply to updates. As of this writing, the API limits you to 100 requests per hour. After that, you are stalled until the top of the next hour.

So, what you want is to be able to handle 100 messages on each pull if you get 100 messages, but to not exceed the API request limit, which means using the API every 36 seconds at most. To be safe, let's just assume that the poller will be scheduled to run every minute.

Before diving into the code, let's examine the configuration:

```xml
<?xml version="1.0" encoding="UTF-8"?>
<beans:beans
    xmlns="http://www.springframework.org/schema/integration"
    xmlns:beans="http://www.springframework.org/schema/beans"
    xmlns:xsi="http://www.w3.org/2001/XMLSchema-instance"
    xmlns:p="http://www.springframework.org/schema/p"
    xmlns:context="http://www.springframework.org/schema/context"
    xmlns:util="http://www.springframework.org/schema/util"
    xmlns:tool="http://www.springframework.org/schema/tool"
    xmlns:lang="http://www.springframework.org/schema/lang"
    xsi:schemaLocation="http://www.springframework.org/schema/beans
```

```
http://www.springframework.org/schema/beans/spring-beans.xsd
http://www.springframework.org/schema/integration
http://www.springframework.org/schema/integration/spring-integration-1.0.xsd
http://www.springframework.org/schema/context
http://www.springframework.org/schema/context/spring-context-3.0.xsd
http://www.springframework.org/schema/util
http://www.springframework.org/schema/util/spring-util-3.0.xsd
http://www.springframework.org/schema/tool
http://www.springframework.org/schema/tool/spring-tool-3.0.xsd
http://www.springframework.org/schema/lang
http://www.springframework.org/schema/lang/spring-lang-3.0.xsd">


<beans:bean class="org.springframework.beans.factory. ➥
config.PropertyPlaceholderConfigurer"
  p:location="solution031.properties"
  p:ignoreUnresolvablePlaceholders="true" />

<channel id="inboundTweets" />

<beans:bean
    id="twitterMessageSource"
    class="com.apress.springenterpriserecipes. ➥
springintegration.twitter.TwitterMessageSource"
    p:password="${twitter.password}"
    p:userId="${twitter.userId}"
 />

<inbound-channel-adapter ref="twitterMessageSource" channel="inboundTweets">
    <poller max-messages-per-poll="100">
        <interval-trigger interval="10" time-unit="SECONDS" />
    </poller>
</inbound-channel-adapter>

<service-activator
    input-channel="inboundTweets" ref="twitterMessageOutput" method="announce" />

</beans:beans>
```

The bold parts are the only salient bits. As in previous examples, you start by declaring a channel ("inboundTweets"). Next, you configure an instance of the custom MessageSource implementation TwitterMessageSource. Finally, you use Spring Integration's inbound-channel-adapter element to wire the TwitterMessageSource and a poller element. The poller element is configured to run every 10 seconds, and to consume as many as 100 messages each time it runs. That is, if it runs 10 seconds from now, it will call read() without pause on the MessageSource implementation until it's given a null value, at which point it will idle until the scheduler starts the cycle again at the next 10-second interval. Thus, if you have 100 messages, this will consume all of them as quick as possible. Ideally, all the messages will be processed before the next scheduled pull occurs.

All this is provided by Spring Integration. All you have to do is avoid wastefully calling the service by caching the results and feeding the results back until the ache is exhausted. Then, you just wait for the next scheduled run. Simple, right? Let's look at the final result:

```
package com.apress.springenterpriserecipes.springintegration.twitter;

import java.util.Date;
import java.util.List;
import java.util.Queue;
import java.util.concurrent.ConcurrentLinkedQueue;

import org.apache.commons.lang.StringUtils;
import org.apache.commons.lang.exception.ExceptionUtils;
import org.apache.log4j.Logger;
import org.springframework.beans.factory.InitializingBean;
import org.springframework.context.support.ClassPathXmlApplicationContext;
import org.springframework.integration.channel.DirectChannel;
import org.springframework.integration.core.Message;
import org.springframework.integration.message.MessageBuilder;
import org.springframework.integration.message.MessageHandler;
import org.springframework.integration.message.MessageSource;
import org.springframework.util.Assert;

import twitter4j.Paging;
import twitter4j.Status;
import twitter4j.Twitter;
import twitter4j.TwitterException;

public class TwitterMessageSource implements MessageSource<Tweet>,
        InitializingBean {

    static private Logger logger = Logger.getLogger(TwitterMessageSource.class);

    private volatile Queue<Tweet> cachedStatuses;
    private volatile String userId;
    private volatile String password;
    private volatile Twitter twitter;
    private volatile long lastStatusIdRetreived = -1;

    private Tweet buildTweetFromStatus(Status firstPost) {
        Tweet tweet = new Tweet(firstPost.getId(), firstPost.getUser()
                .getName(), firstPost.getCreatedAt(), firstPost.getText());
        return tweet;
    }

    public Message<Tweet> receive() {
        Assert.state(cachedStatuses != null);

        if (cachedStatuses.peek() == null) {
            Paging paging = new Paging();
```

```
            if (-1 != lastStatusIdRetreived) {
                paging.sinceId(lastStatusIdRetreived);

            }
            try {
                List<Status> statuses = twitter.getFriendsTimeline(paging);
                Assert.state(cachedStatuses.peek() == null);// size() isn't
                // constant time
                for (Status status : statuses)
                    this.cachedStatuses.add(buildTweetFromStatus(status));

            } catch (TwitterException e) {
                logger.info(ExceptionUtils.getFullStackTrace(e));
                throw new RuntimeException(e);
            }
        }

        if (cachedStatuses.peek() != null) {
            // size() == 0 would be more obvious
            // a test, but size() isn't constant time
            Tweet cachedStatus = cachedStatuses.poll();
            lastStatusIdRetreived = cachedStatus.getTweetId();
            return MessageBuilder.withPayload(cachedStatus).build();
        }
        return null;
    }

    public void afterPropertiesSet() throws Exception {

        if (twitter == null) {
            Assert.state(!StringUtils.isEmpty(userId));
            Assert.state(!StringUtils.isEmpty(password));

            twitter = new Twitter();
            twitter.setUserId(userId);
            twitter.setPassword(password);

        } else { // it isnt null, in which case it becomes canonical memory
            setPassword(twitter.getPassword());
            setUserId(twitter.getUserId());
        }

        cachedStatuses = new ConcurrentLinkedQueue<Tweet>();
        lastStatusIdRetreived = -1;

    }

    public String getUserId() {
        return userId;
    }
```

```
public void setUserId(String userId) {
    this.userId = userId;
}

public String getPassword() {
    return password;
}

public void setPassword(String password) {
    this.password = password;
}

public Twitter getTwitter() {
    return twitter;
}

public void setTwitter(Twitter twitter) {
    this.twitter = twitter;
}

}
```

The bulk of the class is in the accessors and mutators for configuration. The class takes a userId and password, or can be configured with an instance of Twitter4J's Twitter class (which itself has userId and password properties). The read() method is the crux of the implementation. It attempts to take items off of the Queue, which it then returns. If it finds there's nothing to return_which it will when it either is first run or has exhausted all the cache items_it will attempt a query on the API. The API surfaces a Paging object, which works something like Criteria in Hibernate. You can configure how many results to return using the count property. The most interesting option is called the *sinceId*, which lets you search for all records occurring after the Status having the ID equal to the value given as the *sinceId*. It's a built-in duplication-prevention mechanism.

This means that while you are caching Status updates in the MessageSource, you can bound the growth because you don't have to forever store every previous message and test each new one for equality. This implementation does note the last ID that was processed and returned from the read() method. This value is then used in any subsequent queries to preclude it, and any Statuses before it, from appearing in the search results.

Note that there is no support in this implementation for durably storing the ID of the last read status between runtimes. That is, if you kill the Java process running Spring Integration, this MessageSource will simply start again with the last 100 messages from the instant it makes the query, regardless of whether they've been read or not in a previous or concurrent process. Care should be taken to either guard that state in something durable and transactional like a database, or at the very least to implement duplicate detection further on down the line.

A quick test of the component might look like the following:

```
public static void main(String[] args) throws Throwable {
    ClassPathXmlApplicationContext classPathXmlApplicationContext =
                new ClassPathXmlApplicationContext( "solution031.xml");
    classPathXmlApplicationContext.start();
    DirectChannel channel = (DirectChannel) classPathXmlApplicationContext
        .getBean("inboundTweets");
```

```
        channel.subscribe(new MessageHandler() {
            public void handleMessage(Message<?> message) {
                Tweet tweet = (Tweet) message.getPayload();
                logger.debug(String.format("Received %s at %s ", tweet
                        .toString(), new Date().toString())));
            }
        });
    }
```

Here, you've done very little except manually subscribe (which is what components do behind the scenes when you configure it in XML, although it's quite succinct) to messages that come onto the channel (from the MessageSource) and print them out.

An Outbound Twitter Example

You've seen how to consume Twitter status updates on the bus. Now, let's figure out how to send messages from the bus to Twitter. You will build an outbound Twitter adapter. This component will accept status updates (messages of type Tweet) coming in a channel and update the configured account with the new status.

In the last example, you built a class that implemented MessageSource, and explained that you could optionally configure a regular POJO and simply instruct Spring Integration to use a particular method in lieu of relying on the interface-enforced receive method of the MessageSource interface. The same is true in the opposite direction. You can implement MessageHandler<T>, whose API is similarly simple.

```
public interface MessageHandler {
        void handleMessage(Message<?> message)
                throws   MessageRejectedException,
                         MessageHandlingException,
                         MessageDeliveryException;
}
```

This time, you won't implement the interface, but it's useful to know it's there. The code for the outbound adapter is much simpler than the code for the inbound adapter because you have no quirks to contend with, and the mapping from Spring Integration to Twitter is sane: one message to one status update.

```
package com.apress.springenterpriserecipes.springintegration.twitter;

import org.apache.commons.lang.StringUtils;
import org.apache.commons.lang.exception.ExceptionUtils;
import org.apache.log4j.Logger;
import org.springframework.beans.factory.InitializingBean;
import org.springframework.context.support.ClassPathXmlApplicationContext;
import org.springframework.integration.channel.DirectChannel;
import org.springframework.integration.core.Message;
import org.springframework.integration.message.MessageBuilder;
import org.springframework.util.Assert;

import twitter4j.Twitter;
import twitter4j.TwitterException;

public class TwitterMessageProducer implements InitializingBean {
```

```java
static private Logger logger = Logger.getLogger(TwitterMessageProducer.class);

private volatile String userId;
private volatile String password;
private volatile Twitter twitter;

public void tweet(String tweet) {
    try {
        twitter.updateStatus(tweet);
    } catch (TwitterException e) {
        logger.debug(ExceptionUtils.getFullStackTrace(e));
    }
}

public String getUserId() {
    return userId;
}

public void setUserId(String userId) {
    this.userId = userId;
}

public String getPassword() {
    return password;
}

public void setPassword(String password) {
    this.password = password;
}

public Twitter getTwitter() {
    return twitter;
}

public void setTwitter(Twitter twitter) {
    this.twitter = twitter;
}

public void afterPropertiesSet() throws Exception {
    if (twitter == null) {
        Assert.state(!StringUtils.isEmpty(userId));
        Assert.state(!StringUtils.isEmpty(password));

        twitter = new Twitter();
        twitter.setUserId(userId);
        twitter.setPassword(password);

    } else { // it isnt null, in which case it becomes canonical memory
        setPassword(twitter.getPassword());
        setUserId(twitter.getUserId());
    }
}
}
```

Most of the code is boilerplate_exposed for configuration. Of note is one method, called tweet(Tweet). As you've seen in other places, you're relying on Spring Integration to unbundle the payload from the Message<T> coming in on a channel and to pass the payload as a parameter to this method.

The configuration inside the XML application context is strikingly similar to the configuration for the outbound adapter:

```
<?xml version="1.0" encoding="UTF-8"?>
<beans:beans
    xmlns="http://www.springframework.org/schema/integration"
    xmlns:beans="http://www.springframework.org/schema/beans"
    xmlns:xsi="http://www.w3.org/2001/XMLSchema-instance"
    xmlns:p="http://www.springframework.org/schema/p"
    xmlns:context="http://www.springframework.org/schema/context"
    xmlns:util="http://www.springframework.org/schema/util"
    xmlns:tool="http://www.springframework.org/schema/tool"
    xmlns:lang="http://www.springframework.org/schema/lang"
    xsi:schemaLocation="http://www.springframework.org/schema/beans
http://www.springframework.org/schema/beans/➥
spring-beans.xsd
http://www.springframework.org/schema/integration
 http://www.springframework.org/schema/integration/➥
spring-integration-1.0.xsd
http://www.springframework.org/schema/context
 http://www.springframework.org/schema/context/spring-context-3.0.xsd
 http://www.springframework.org/schema/util
http://www.springframework.org/schema/util/spring-util-3.0.xsd
http://www.springframework.org/schema/tool
http://www.springframework.org/schema/tool/spring-tool-3.0.xsd
http://www.springframework.org/schema/lang
http://www.springframework.org/schema/lang/spring-lang-3.0.xsd">

    <beans:bean class="org.springframework.beans.factory. ➥
config.PropertyPlaceholderConfigurer"
        p:location="solution031.properties"
        p:ignoreUnresolvablePlaceholders="true" />

    <beans:bean id="twitterMessageProducer"
  class="com.apress.springenterpriserecipes.springintegration. ➥
        twitter.TwitterMessageProducer"
        p:password="${twitter.password}"
        p:userId="${twitter.userId}"
    />

    <channel id="outboundTweets" />

    <outbound-channel-adapter ref="twitterMessageProducer"
            method="tweet"
            channel="outboundTweets" />

</beans:beans>
```

You renamed the `channel` and employed an `outbound-channel-adapter` instead of an `inbound-channel-adapter`. Indeed, the only thing novel is that you're employing the method attribute on the outbound-channel-adapter element to give the component an extra level of insulation from the Spring Integration APIs.

Using the component is easy, and a quick test might look like this:

```
public static void main(String[] args) throws Throwable {
    ClassPathXmlApplicationContext classPathXmlApplicationContext = new
                    ClassPathXmlApplicationContext( "solution032.xml");
    classPathXmlApplicationContext.start();
    DirectChannel channel = (DirectChannel)
                    classPathXmlApplicationContext.getBean("outboundTweets");
    Message<String> helloWorldMessage =
                    MessageBuilder.withPayload( "Hello, world!").build();
    channel.send(helloWorldMessage);
}
```

The example's even simpler than the test code for the inbound adapter! The code goes through the motions of setting up a `Message` and then simply sends it. Confirm by checking your status on twitter.com.

8-11. Staging Events Using Spring Batch

Problem

You have a file with a million records in it.

Solution

Spring Batch works very well with these types of solutions. It allows you to take an input file or a payload and reliably, and systematically, decompose it into events that an ESB can work with.

How It Works

Spring Integration does support reading files into the bus, and Spring Batch does support providing custom, unique endpoints for data. However, just like mom always says, "just because you can, it doesn't mean you *should*."

Although it seems as if there's a lot of overlap here, it turns out that there is a distinction (albeit a fine one). While both systems will work with files and message queues, or anything else you could conceivably write code to talk to, Spring Integration doesn't do well with large payloads because it's hard to deal with something as large as a file with a million rows that might require hours of work as an *event*. That's simply too big a burden for an ESB. At that point, the term *event* has no meaning. A million records in a CSV file isn't an event on a bus, it's a file with a million records, each of which might in turn *be* events.

It's a subtle distinction.

A file with a million rows needs to be decomposed into smaller events. Spring Batch can help here: it allows you to systematically read through, apply validations, and optionally skip and retry invalid records. The processing can begin on an ESB such as Spring Integration. Spring Batch and Spring Integration can be used together to build truly scalable decoupled systems.

Staged event-driven architecture (SEDA) is an architecture style that deals with this sort of processing situation. In SEDA, you dampen the load on components of the architecture by staging it in queues, and let advance only what the components downstream can handle. Put another way, imagine video processing. If you ran a site with a million users uploading video that in turn needed to be transcoded and you only had 10 servers, your system would fail if your system attempted to process each video as soon as it received the uploaded video. Transcoding can take hours and pegs a CPU (or multiple CPUs!) while it works. The most sensible thing to do would be to store the file and then, as capacity permits, process each one. In this way, the load on the nodes that handle transcoding is managed. There's always only enough work to keep the machine humming, but not overrun.

Similarly, no processing system (such as an ESB) can deal with a million records at once efficiently. Strive to decompose bigger events and messages into smaller ones. Let's imagine a hypothetical solution designed to accommodate a drop of batch files representing hourly sales destined for fulfillment. The batch files are dropped onto a mount that Spring Integration is monitoring. Spring Integration kicks off processing as soon as it sees a new file. Spring Integration tells Spring Batch about the file and launches a Spring Batch job asynchronously.

Spring Batch reads the file, transforms the records into objects, and writes the output to a JMS topic with a key correlating the original batch to the JMS message. Naturally, this takes half a day to get done, but it does get done. Spring Integration, completely unaware that the job it started half a day ago is now finished, begins popping messages off the topic, one by one. Processing to fulfill the records would begin. Simple processing involving multiple components might begin on the ESB.

If fulfillment is a long-lived process with a long-lived, conversational state involving many actors, perhaps the fulfillment for each record could be farmed to a BPM engine. The BPM engine would thread together the different actors and work lists, allow work to continue over the course of days instead of the small millisecond timeframes Spring Integration is more geared to. In this example, you used Spring Batch as a springboard to dampen the load for components downstream. In this case, the component downstream was again a Spring Integration process that took the work and set it up to be funneled into a BPM engine where final processing could begin.

To learn more about invoking a Spring Batch job, please see Chapter 9.

8-12. Gateways

Problem

You want to expose an interface to clients of your service, without betraying the fact that your service is implemented in terms of messaging middleware.

Solution

Use a gateway—a pattern from the classic book *Enterprise Integration Patterns* by Gregor Hohpe and Bobby Woolf (Addison-Wesley, 2004) that enjoys rich support in Spring Integration.

How It Works

A *gateway* is a distinct animal, similar to a lot of other patterns but ultimately different enough to warrant its own consideration. You used adapters in previous examples to enable two systems to speak in terms of foreign, loosely coupled, middleware components. This foreign component can be anything: the file system, JMS queues/topics, Twitter, and so on.

You all also know what a *façade* is, serving to abstract away the functionality of other components in an abbreviated interface to provide courser functionality. You might use a façade to build an interface oriented around vacation planning that in turn abstracts away the minutiae of using a car rental, hotel reservation, and airline reservation system.

You build a gateway, on the other hand, to provide an interface for your system that insulates clients from the middleware or messaging in your system, so that they're not dependent on JMS or Spring Integration APIs, for example. A gateway allows you to express compile time constraints on the inputs and outputs of your system.

There are several reasons why you might want to do this. First, it's cleaner. If you have the latitude to insist that clients comply with an interface, this is a good way to provide that interface. Your use of middleware can be an implementation detail. Perhaps your architectures messaging middleware can be to exploit the performance increases had by leveraging asynchronous messaging, but you didn't intend for those performance gains to come at the cost of a precise, explicit external facing interface.

This feature—the capability to hide messaging behind a POJO interface—is very interesting and has been the focus of several other projects. Lingo, a project from Codehaus.org that is no longer under active development, had such a feature that was specific to JMS and JCA. Since then, the developers have moved on to work on Apache Camel.

In this recipe, you'll explore Spring Integration's core support for messaging gateways, and explore its support for message exchange patterns. Then you'll see how to completely remove implementation details from the client-facing interface.

SimpleMessagingGateway

The most fundamental support for gateways comes from the Spring Integration class SimpleMessagingGateway. The class provides the ability to specify a channel on which requests should be sent and a channel on which responses are expected. Finally, the channel on which replies are sent can be specified. This gives you the ability to express in-out, and in-only patterns on top of your existing messaging systems. This class supports working in terms of payloads, isolating you from the gory details of the messages being sent and received. This is already one level of abstraction. You could, conceivably, use the SimpleMessagingGateway and Spring Integration's concept of channels to interface with file systems, JMS, e-mail, or any other system and deal simply with payloads and channels. There are implementations already provided for you to support some of these common endpoints such as web services and JMS.

Let's look at using a generic messaging gateway. In this example, you'll send messages to a service-activator and then receive the response. You manually interface with the SimpleMessageGateway so that you can see how convenient it is.

```
package com.apress.springenterpriserecipes.springintegration;

import org.springframework.context.support.ClassPathXmlApplicationContext;
import org.springframework.integration.core.MessageChannel;
import org.springframework.integration.gateway.SimpleMessagingGateway;

public class SimpleMessagingGatewayExample {
    public static void main(String[] args) {
        ClassPathXmlApplicationContext ctx =
                    new ClassPathXmlApplicationContext("solution042.xml");
        MessageChannel request = (MessageChannel) ctx.getBean("request");
        MessageChannel response = (MessageChannel) ctx.getBean("response");
        SimpleMessagingGateway msgGateway = new SimpleMessagingGateway();
```

```
    msgGateway.setRequestChannel(request);
    msgGateway.setReplyChannel(response);
    Number result = (Number) msgGateway.sendAndReceive(new Operands(22, 4));
        System.out.println("Result: " + result.floatValue());

    }
}
```

The interface is very straightforward. The SimpleMessagingGateway needs a request and a response channel, and it coordinates the rest. In this case, you're doing nothing but forwarding the request to a service-activator, which in turn adds the operands and sends them out on the reply channel. The configuration XML is sparse because most of the work is done in those five lines of Java code.

```
<?xml version="1.0" encoding="UTF-8"?>
<beans:beans … >
    <beans:bean id="additionService " class="com.apress.springenterpriserecipes. ➥
springintegration.AdditionService" />
    <channel id="request" />
    <channel id="response" />
    <service-activator  ref="additionService"
        method="add"
        input-channel="request"
        output-channel="response" />
</beans:beans>
```

Breaking the Interface Dependency

The previous example demonstrates what's happening behind the scenes. You're dealing only with Spring Integration interfaces and are isolated from the nuances of the endpoints. However, there are still plenty of inferred constraints that a client might easily fail to comply with. The simplest solution is to hide the messaging behind an interface. Let's look at building a fictional hotel reservation search engine. Searching for a hotel might take a long time, and ideally processing should be offloaded to a separate server. An ideal solution is JMS because you could implement the aggressive consumer pattern and scale simply by adding more consumers. The client would still block waiting for the result, in this example, but the server(s) would not be overloaded or in a blocking state.

You'll build two Spring Integration solutions. One for the client (which will in turn contain the gateway) and one for the service itself, which, presumably, is on a separate host connected to the client only by way of well-known message queues.

Let's look at the client configuration first. The first thing that the client configuration does is import a shared application context (to save typing if nothing else) that declares a JMS connection factory that you reference in the client and service application contexts. (I won't repeat all of that here because it's not relevant or noteworthy.)

Then you declare two channels, imaginatively named requests and responses. Messages sent on the requests channel are forwarded to the jms:outbound-gateway that you've declared. The jms:outbound gateway is the component that does most of the work. It takes the message you created and sends it to the request JMS destination, setting up the reply headers and so on. Finally you declare a generic gateway element, which does most of the magic. The gateway element simply exists to identify the component and the interface, to which the proxy is cast and made available to clients.

```
<?xml version="1.0" encoding="UTF-8"?>
<beans:beans
    xmlns:beans="http://www.springframework.org/schema/beans"
    xmlns:xsi="http://www.w3.org/2001/XMLSchema-instance"
```

```
        xmlns="http://www.springframework.org/schema/integration"
        xmlns:context="http://www.springframework.org/schema/context"
        xmlns:jms="http://www.springframework.org/schema/integration/jms"
        xsi:schemaLocation="http://www.springframework.org/schema/beans
http://www.springframework.org/schema/beans/ ➥
spring-beans-3.0.xsd
http://www.springframework.org/schema/context
http://www.springframework.org/schema/context/spring-context-3.0.xsd
http://www.springframework.org/schema/integration
http://www.springframework.org/schema/integration/ ➥
spring-integration-1.0.xsd
http://www.springframework.org/schema/integration/jms
http://www.springframework.org/schema/integration/jms/ ➥
spring-integration-jms-1.0.xsd
                ">

    <beans:import resource="solution041.xml" />
        <context:annotation-config />

    <channel id="requests" />
    <channel id="responses" />

    <jms:outbound-gateway
        request-destination-name="inboundHotelReservationSearchDestination"
        request-channel="requests"
        reply-destination-name="outboundHotelReservationSearchResultsDestination"
        reply-channel="responses"
        connection-factory="connectionFactory" />

<gateway id="vacationService"
                    service-interface="com.apress.springenterpriserecipes. ➥
springintegration.myholiday.VacationService" />

</beans:beans>
```

One thing that's conspicuously absent is any mention of an output or input channel from and to the gateway element. While it is possible to declare default request/reply message queues, realistically, most methods on an interface will require their own request/response queues. So, you configure the channels on the interface itself.

```
package com.apress.springenterpriserecipes.springintegration.myholiday;

import java.util.List;
import org.springframework.integration.annotation.Gateway;

public interface VacationService {

    @Gateway(requestChannel = "requests", replyChannel = "responses")
    List<HotelReservation> findHotels(HotelReservationSearch hotelReservationSearch);

}
```

This is the client facing interface. There is no coupling between the client facing interface exposed via the gateway component and the interface of the service that ultimately handles the messages. I use the interface for the service and the client to simplify the names needed to understand everything that's going on. This is not like traditional, synchronous remoting in which the service interface and the client interface match.

In this example, you're using two very simple objects for demonstration: HotelReservationSearch and HotelReservation. There is nothing interesting about these objects in the slightest; they are simple POJOs that implement Serializable and contain a few accessor/mutators to flesh out the example domain.

The client Java code demonstrates how all of this comes together:

```java
package com.apress.springenterpriserecipes.springintegration.myholiday;

import java.util.Calendar;
import java.util.Date;
import java.util.List;

import org.apache.commons.lang.time.DateUtils;
import org.springframework.context.support.ClassPathXmlApplicationContext;

public class Main {
    public static void main(String[] args) throws Throwable {
        ClassPathXmlApplicationContext classPathXmlApplicationContext = new
                ClassPathXmlApplicationContext("solution041_service.xml");
        classPathXmlApplicationContext.start();

        // setup the input parameter
        Date now = new Date();
        HotelReservationSearch hotelReservationSearch =  new HotelReservationSearch(
            200f, 2,
            DateUtils.add(now, Calendar.DATE, 1),
            DateUtils.add(now, Calendar.DATE, 8));

        ClassPathXmlApplicationContext classPathXmlApplicationContext1 =
                new ClassPathXmlApplicationContext("solution041_client.xml");
        classPathXmlApplicationContext1.start();

        // get a hold of our gateway proxy (you might
            // imagine injecting this into another service just like
            // you would a Hibernate DAO, for example)
        VacationService vacationService = (VacationService)
                classPathXmlApplicationContext1.getBean("vacationService");
        List<HotelReservation> results = vacationService.findHotels(
                            hotelReservationSearch);
        System.out.printf("Found %s results.", results.size());
        System.out.println();
        for (HotelReservation reservation : results) {
            System.out.printf("\t%s", reservation.toString());
            System.out.println();
        }
    }
}
```

It just doesn't get any cleaner than that! No Spring Integration interfaces whatsoever. You make a request, searching is done, and you get the result back when the processing is done.

The service implementation for this setup is interesting, not because of what you've added, but because of what's not there:

```xml
<?xml version="1.0" encoding="UTF-8"?>
<beans:beans
    xmlns:beans="http://www.springframework.org/schema/beans"
    xmlns:xsi="http://www.w3.org/2001/XMLSchema-instance"
    xmlns="http://www.springframework.org/schema/integration"
    xmlns:context="http://www.springframework.org/schema/context"
    xmlns:jms="http://www.springframework.org/schema/integration/jms"
    xsi:schemaLocation="http://www.springframework.org/schema/beans
http://www.springframework.org/schema/beans/spring-beans-3.0.xsd
http://www.springframework.org/schema/context
http://www.springframework.org/schema/context/ ➥
spring-context-3.0.xsd
http://www.springframework.org/schema/integration
http://www.springframework.org/schema/integration/spring-integration-1.0.xsd
http://www.springframework.org/schema/integration/jms
http://www.springframework.org/schema/integration/jms/ ➥
spring-integration-jms-1.0.xsd">
    <beans:import resource="solution041.xml" />
    <context:annotation-config />

    <channel id="inboundHotelReservationSearchChannel" />
    <channel id="outboundHotelReservationSearchResultsChannel" />

    <beans:bean id="vacationServiceImpl" . ➥
    class="com.apress.springenterpriserecipes.springintegration. ➥
myholiday.VacationServiceImpl" />

    <jms:inbound-gateway
        request-channel="inboundHotelReservationSearchChannel"
        request-destination-name="inboundHotelReservationSearchDestination"
        connection-factory="connectionFactory" />

    <service-activator
        input-channel="inboundHotelReservationSearchChannel"
        ref="vacationServiceImpl"
        method="findHotels" />

</beans:beans>
```

Here you've defined an inbound JMS gateway element. The messages from the inbound JMS gateway are put on a channel, inboundHotelReservationSearchChannel, whose messages are forwarded to a service-activator, as you would expect. The service-activator is what handles actual processing. What's interesting here is that there's no mention of a response channel, for either the service-activator, or for the inbound JMS gateway. The service-activator looks, and fails to find, an reply channel and so uses the reply channel created by the inbound JMS gateway, which in turn has created the reply channel based on the header metadata in the inbound JMS message. Thus, everything just works.

The implementation is a simple useless implementation of the interface:

```
package com.apress.springenterpriserecipes.springintegration.myholiday;
import java.util.Arrays;
import java.util.List;
import org.springframework.beans.factory.InitializingBean;

public class VacationServiceImpl implements VacationService, InitializingBean {
    private List<HotelReservation> hotelReservations;
    public void afterPropertiesSet() throws Exception {
        hotelReservations = Arrays.asList(
    new HotelReservation("Bilton", 243.200F),
    new HotelReservation("West Western", 75.0F),
    new HotelReservation("Theirfield Inn", 70F),
    new HotelReservation("Park Inn", 200.00F));
    }
    public List<HotelReservation> findHotels(HotelReservationSearch searchMsg) {
        try {
            Thread.sleep(1000);
        } catch (Throwable th) {
          // eat the exception
        }
        return hotelReservations;
    }

}
```

Summary

This chapter discussed building an integration solution using Spring Integration, an ESB-like framework built on top of the Spring framework. You were introduced to the core concepts of enterprise application integration (EAI). You learned how to handle a few integration scenarios, including JMS, and file polling. You saw how to build a custom endpoint to talk to Twitter and how to hide the integration functionality behind a POJO service interface using a gateway so that clients can interface synchronously while the server still enjoys the benefits of a decoupled, asynchronous, message-oriented architecture.

In the next chapter, you will work with Spring Batch, a batch-processing framework built on top of the Spring platform to handle long-running jobs.

CHAPTER 9

■ ■ ■

Spring Batch

Previous chapters discussed JMS and Spring Integration, which provide essential framework infrastructure for very common types of problems in an event-driven architecture (EDA). Another common kind of processing requirement is batch processing, which is both a complement and sometimes necessary extension to event-driven processing.

Batch processing has been around for decades. The earliest widespread applications of technology for managing information (information technology) were applications of batch processing. These environments didn't have interactive sessions and usually didn't have the capability to load multiple applications in memory. Computers were expensive and bore no resemblance to today's servers. Typically, machines were multiuser and in use during the day (time-shared). During the evening, however, the machines would sit idle, which was a tremendous waste. Businesses invested in ways to utilize the offline time to do work aggregated through the course of the day. Out of this practice emerged batch processing.

Batch processing solutions typically run offline, indifferent to "events" in the system. In the past, batch processes ran offline out of necessity. Today, however, most batch processes are run offline because having work done at a predictable time and having "chunks" of work done is a requirement for a lot of architectures. A batch processing solution doesn't usually respond to requests, although there's no reason it couldn't be started as a consequence of a message or request. Batch processing solutions tend to be used on large datasets where the duration of the processing may be unknown. A process might run for minutes, hours, or days!

Batch processing has had a long history that informs even modern batch processing solutions.

Mainframe applications used batch processing, and one of the largest modern day environments for batch processing, CICS on z/OS, is still fundamentally a mainframe operating system. Customer Information Control System (CICS) is very well suited to a particular type of task: take input, process it, and write it to output. CICS is a transaction server used most in financial institutions and government that runs programs in a number of languages (COBOL, C, PLI, and so on). It can easily support thousands of transactions per second. CICS was one of the first "containers," a concept familiar to Spring and Java EE users, even though CICS itself debuted in 1969! A CICS installation is very expensive, and although IBM still sells and installs CICS, many other solutions have come along since then. These solutions are usually specific to a particular environment: COBOL/CICS on mainframes, C on Unix, and, today, Java on any number of environments. The problem is that there's very little standardized infrastructure for dealing with these types of batch processing solutions. Very few people are even aware of what they're missing because there's very little "native" support on the Java platform for batch processing. Businesses that need a solution typically end up writing it in-house, resulting in fragile, domain-specific code.

The pieces are there, however: transaction support, fast I/O, schedulers such as Quartz and solid threading support, and a very powerful concept of an application container in Java EE and Spring. It was only natural that Dave Syer and his team would come along and build Spring Batch, a batch processing solution for the Spring platform.

It's important to think about the kinds of problems this framework solves before diving into the details. A technology is defined by its solution space. A typical Spring Batch application typically reads in a lot of data and then writes it back out in a modified form. Decisions about transactional barriers, input size, concurrency, and order of steps in processing are all dimensions of a typical integration.

A common requirement is loading data from a comma-separated value (CSV) file, perhaps as a business-to-business (B2B) transaction; perhaps as an integration technique with an older legacy application. Another common application is nontrivial processing on records in a database. Perhaps the output is an update of the database record itself. An example might be resizing of images on the file system whose metadata is stored in a database, or needing to trigger another process based on some condition.

■Note *Fixed-width data* is a format of rows and cells, quite like a CSV file. CSV file cells are separated by commas or tabs, however, and fixed-width data works by presuming certain lengths for each value. The first value might be the first nine characters, the second value the next four characters after that, and so on.

Fixed-width data, which is often used with legacy or embedded systems, is a fine candidate for batch processing. Processing that deals with a resource that's fundamentally nontransactional (for example, a web service or a file) begs for batch processing because batch processing provides retry/skip/fail functionality that most web services will not.

It's also important to understand what Spring Batch *doesn't* do. Spring Batch is a flexible but not all-encompassing solution. Just as Spring doesn't reinvent the wheel when it can be avoided, Spring Batch leaves a few important pieces to the discretion of the implementor. Case in point: Spring Batch provides a generic mechanism by which to launch a job, be it by the command line, a Unix cron, an operating system service, Quartz (discussed in Chapter 6), or in response to an event on an enterprise service bus (for example, the Mule ESB or Spring's own ESB-like solution, Spring Integration, which is discussed in Chapter 8). Another example is the way Spring Batch manages the state of batch processes. Spring Batch requires a durable store. The only useful implementation of a JobRepository (an interface provided by Spring Batch for storing runtime data) requires a database because a database is transactional and there's no need to reinvent it. To which database you should deploy, however, is largely unspecified, although there are useful defaults provided for you, of course.

Runtime Meta Model

Spring Batch works with a JobRepository, which is the keeper of all the knowledge/metadata for each job (including component parts such as JobExecution and StepExecution). Each job is composed of one or more steps, one after another. With Spring Batch 2.0, a step can conditionally follow another step, allowing for primitive workflows. These steps can also be concurrent: two steps can run at the same time.

When a job is run, it's often coupled with JobParameters to parameterize the behavior of the job itself. For example, a job might take a date parameter to determine which records to process. This coupling is called a JobInstance. A JobInstance is unique because of the JobParameters associated with it. Each time the same JobInstance (i.e., the same job and JobParameters) is run, it's called a

JobExecution. This is a runtime context for a version of the job. Ideally, for every JobInstance there'd be only one JobExecution: the JobExecution that was created the first time the JobInstance ran. However, if there were any errors, the JobInstance should be restarted; the subsequent run would create another JobExecution. For every step in the original job, there is a StepExecution in the JobExecution.

Thus, you can see that Spring Batch has a mirrored object graph, one reflecting the design/build time view of a job, and another reflecting the runtime view of a job. This split between the prototype and the instance is very similar to the way many workflow engines work, including jBPM.

For example, suppose that a daily report is generated at 2 AM. The parameter to the job would be the date (most likely the previous day's date). The job, in this case, would model a loading step, a summary step, and an output step. Each day the job is run, a new JobInstance and JobExecution would be created. If there are any retries of the same JobInstance, conceivably many JobExecutions would be created.

9-1. Getting Started with the Spring Batch Distribution

Problem

You want to get started with Spring Batch, but the JARs aren't in the standard Spring framework distribution.

Solution

You can use Maven or Ivy, or you can download them manually as a separate project. If you choose the Maven/Ivy route or want to use OSGi, there are some things to consider.

How It Works

The simplest thing to do is to simply download the JARS from http://static.springsource.org/spring-batch/, as usual, and add the JARs provided to your classpath. If you decide you want to use OSGi, you can use the SpringSource enterprise repository, which provides OSGi JARs. Be careful if you decide to use those JARs with Maven, however, because they import all other SpringSource enterprise JARs for the core Spring framework and other OSGi-friendly, third-party libraries. If you already have Spring and all other packages imported, relying on the SpringSource enterprise JARs will yield two of every JAR in the Spring framework! Yikes!

Instead, for Maven/Ivy, use the public ones available on the main Maven repositories. I included a sample POM in the source code for this book. I extract the salient dependency here. As of this writing, Spring Batch 2.0 had just been released.

```
<dependency>
    <groupId>org.springframework.batch</groupId>
    <version>2.0.1.RELEASE</version>
    <artifactId>spring-batch-core</artifactId>
</dependency>
```

Although all the Spring projects are pretty exhaustively documented, the Spring Batch project has a notably large sampling of demonstration projects. For this reason alone it might be worth downloading individually.

9-2. Setting Up Spring Batch's Infrastructure

Problem

Spring Batch provides a lot of flexibility and guarantees to your application, but it cannot work in a vacuum. To do its work, the JobRepository requires a database. Additionally, there are several collaborators required for Spring Batch to do its work. This configuration is mostly boilerplate.

Solution

In this recipe, you'll set up the Spring Batch database and also create a Spring XML application context that can be imported by subsequent solutions. This configuration is repetitive and largely uninteresting. It will also tell Spring Batch what database to use for the metadata it stores.

How It Works

The JobRepository is the first thing that you'll have to deal with when setting up a Spring Batch process. You usually don't deal with it in code, but in Spring configuration it is key to getting everything else working. There's only one really useful implementation of the JobRepository interface, which stores information about the state of the batch processes in a database. Creation is done through a JobRepositoryFactoryBean. Another standard factory, MapJobRepositoryFactoryBean is useful mainly for testing because its state is not durable. Both factories create an instance of SimpleJobRepository.

Because this JobRepository instance works on your database, you need to set up the schema for Spring Batch to work with. The simplest way for me to get that schema was to simply download the org.springframework.batch-2.0.0.RELEASE-with-dependencies.tar.gz and look in the sources folder at sources/org.springframework.batch.core/src/main/resources. You'll find a slew of .sql files, each containing the data definition language (DDL, the subset of SQL used for defining and examining the structure of a database) for the required schema for the database of your choice. Make sure you configure it and tell Spring Batch about it as in the following configuration:

```
<?xml version="1.0" encoding="UTF-8"?>
<beans:beans
    xmlns="http://www.springframework.org/schema/batch"
    xmlns:util="http://www.springframework.org/schema/util"
    xmlns:beans="http://www.springframework.org/schema/beans"
    xmlns:aop="http://www.springframework.org/schema/aop"
    xmlns:tx="http://www.springframework.org/schema/tx"
    xmlns:p="http://www.springframework.org/schema/p"
    xmlns:xsi="http://www.w3.org/2001/XMLSchema-instance"
    xsi:schemaLocation="http://www.springframework.org/schema/util
http://www.springframework.org/schema/util/spring-util-3.0.xsd
http://www.springframework.org/schema/beans http://www.springframework.org➡
/schema/beans/spring-beans-3.0.xsd http://www.springframework.org/schema/batch
http://www.springframework.org/schema/batch/spring-batch-3.0.xsd
http://www.springframework.org/schema/aop http://www.springframework.org/➡
schema/aop/spring-aop-2.0.xsd http://www.springframework.org/schema/tx
http://www.springframework.org/schema/tx/spring-tx-3.0.xsd"
>
```

```
    <beans:bean
        class="org.springframework.beans.factory.config.Property➥
PlaceholderConfigurer"
        p:location="batch.properties"
        p:ignoreUnresolvablePlaceholders="true" />

    <beans:bean
        id="dataSource"
        class="org.apache.commons.dbcp.BasicDataSource"
        destroy-method="close"
        p:driverClassName="${dataSource.driverClassName}"
        p:username="${dataSource.username}"
        p:password="${dataSource.password}"
        p:url="${dataSource.url}" />

    <beans:bean
        id="transactionManager"
        class="org.springframework.jdbc.datasource.DataSourceTransactionManager"
        p:dataSource-ref="dataSource" />

    <beans:bean
        id="jobLauncher"
        class="org.springframework.batch.core.launch.support.SimpleJobLauncher"
        p:jobRepository-ref="jobRepository" />

    <beans:bean
        class="org.springframework.batch.core.configuration.support.➥
JobRegistryBeanPostProcessor"
        p:jobRegistry-ref="jobRegistry" />

    <beans:bean
        id="jobRepository"
        class="org.springframework.batch.core.repository.support. ➥
JobRepositoryFactoryBean"
        p:dataSource-ref="dataSource"
        p:transactionManager-ref="transactionManager" />

    <beans:bean
        id="jobRegistry"
        class="org.springframework.batch.core.configuration.support. ➥
MapJobRegistry" />

</beans:beans>
```

Because the implementation uses a database to persist the metadata, take care to configure a
DataSource as well as a TransactionManager. In this example, you're using a PropertyPlaceholderConfigurer
to load the contents of a properties file (batch.properties) whose values you use to configure the data
source. You need to place values for your particular database in this file. This example uses Spring's
property schema ("p") to abbreviate the tedious configuration. In subsequent examples, this file will be
referenced as batch.xml.

9-3. Running Jobs

Problem

What deployment scenarios does Spring Batch support? How does Spring Batch "launch"? How does Spring Batch work with a system scheduler such as cron or autosys, or from a web application?

Solution

Spring Batch provides facilities to address execution inside of a web environment. It also provides a convenience class that can be readily used with cron or autosys to support launching jobs.

How It Works

Before you get into creating a solution, it's important to know what options are available for deploying and running these solutions. All solutions require, at minimum, a job and a JobLauncher. You already configured these components in the previous recipe. The job is configured in your Spring XML application context, as you'll see later. The simplest example of launching a Spring Batch solution from Java code is about five lines of Java code, three if you've already got a handle to the ApplicationContext!

```
package com.apress.springenterpriserecipes.springbatch.solution1;

import org.springframework.batch.core.Job;
import org.springframework.batch.core.JobParameters;
import org.springframework.batch.core.launch.JobLauncher;
import org.springframework.context.support.ClassPathXmlApplicationContext;

public class Main {
    public static void main(String[] args) throws Throwable {
        // build a standard ApplicationContext
        ClassPathXmlApplicationContext classPathXmlApplicationContext =
                            new ClassPathXmlApplicationContext➡
("customSolution.xml");
        classPathXmlApplicationContext.start();
         // launch the job
        JobLauncher jobLauncher = (JobLauncher)
            classPathXmlApplicationContext.getBean("jobLauncher");
        Job job = (Job)  classPathXmlApplicationContext.getBean(
                "nameOfCustomJobHere");
        jobLauncher.run(job, new JobParameters());
    }
}
```

This mechanism is the most flexible, and indeed it's sometimes required. If you plan to use the popular Quartz scheduling framework, you need to write a job that launches a batch job that looks something like what you see.

Launching From a Web Application

Launching a job from a web application requires a slightly different tact because the client thread (presumably an HTTP request) can't usually wait for a batch job to finish. The ideal solution is to have the job execute asynchronously when launched from a controller or action in the web tier, unattended by the client thread. Spring Batch supports this scenario through the use of a Spring TaskExecutor. This requires a simple change to the configuration for the JobLauncher, although the Java code can stay the same.

```
<beans:bean id="jobLauncher" class=" org.springframework. ➥
batch.execution.launch.SimpleJobLauncher"
        p:jobRepository-ref="jobRepository" >
  <beans:property name="taskExecutor">
    <beans:bean class="org.springframework.core.task.SimpleAsyncTaskExecutor" />
  </beans:property>
</beans:bean>
```

Running from the Command Line

Another common use case is deployment of a batch process from a system scheduler such as cron or autosys, or even Window's event scheduler. Spring Batch provides a convenience class that takes as its parameters the name of the XML application context (that contains *everything* required to run a job) as well as the name of the job bean itself. Additional parameters may be provided and used to parameterize the job. These parameters must be in the form name=value. An example invocation of this class on the command line (on a Linux/Unix system), assuming that you set up the classpath, might look like this:

```
java CommandLineJobRunner jobs.xml hourlyReport date➥
=`date +%m/%d/%Y` time=`date +%H`
```

The CommandLineJobRunner will even return system error codes (0 for success, 1 for failure, and 2 for an issue with loading the batch job) so that a shell (such as used by most system schedulers) can react or do something about the failure. More complicated return codes can be returned by creating and declaring a top-level bean that implements the interface ExitCodeMapper, in which you can specify a more useful translation of exit status messages to integer-based error codes that the shell will see on process exit.

9-4. Reading and Writing (but No Arithmetic)

Problem

You want to insert data from a file into a database. This solution will be one of the simplest solutions and will give you a chance to explore the moving pieces of a typical solution.

Solution

You'll build a solution that does a minimal amount of work, while being a viable application of the technology. The solution will read in a file of arbitrary length and write out the data into a database. The end result will be almost 100 percent code free. You will rely on an existing model class and write one class (a class containing the public static void main(String [] args() method) to round out the example. There's no reason why the model class couldn't be a Hibernate class or something from your DAO layer, though in this case it's a brainless POJO.

How It Works

This example demonstrates the simplest possible use of a Spring Batch: to provide scalability. This program will do nothing but read data from a CSV file, with fields delimited by commas and rows delimited by newlines) file and then insert the records into a table. You are exploiting the intelligent infrastructure that Spring Batch provides to avoid worrying about scaling. This application could easily be done manually. You will not exploit any of the smart transactional functionality made available to you, nor will you worry about retries.

This solution is as simple as Spring Batch solutions get. Spring Batch models solutions using XML schema. This schema is new to Spring Batch 2.0. The abstractions and terms are in the spirit of classical batch processing solutions, so will be portable from previous technologies and perhaps in subsequent technologies. Spring Batch provides useful default classes that you can override or selectively adjust. In the following example, you'll use a lot of the utility implementations provided by Spring Batch. Fundamentally, most solutions look about the same and feature a combination of the same set of interfaces. It's usually just a matter of picking and choosing the right ones.

When I ran this program, it worked on files with 20,000 rows, and it worked on files with 1 million rows. I experienced no increase in memory, which indicates there were no memory leaks. Naturally, it took a lot longer! (The application ran for several hours with the 1 million row insert.)

■**Tip**   Of course, it would be catastrophic if you worked with a million rows and it failed on the penultimate record because you'd lose all your work when the transaction rolled back! Read on for examples on "chunking." Additionally, you might want to read through Chapter 4 to brush up on transactions.

The following example inserts records into a table. I'm using PostgreSQL, which is a good mature open source database; you can use any database you want. (More information and downloads are available at http://www.postgresql.) The schema for the table is simple:

```
create table USER_REGISTRATION
(
  ID bigserial  not null  ,
  FIRST_NAME character varying(255) not null,
  LAST_NAME character varying(255) not null,
  COMPANY character varying(255) not null,
  ADDRESS character varying(255) not null,
  CITY character varying(255) not null,
  STATE character varying(255) not null,
  ZIP character varying(255) not null,
  COUNTY character varying(255) not null,
  URL character varying(255) not null,
  PHONE_NUMBER character varying(255) not null,
  FAX character varying(255) not null,
  constraint USER_REGISTRATION_PKEY primary key (id)
) ;
```

Data Loads and Data Warehouses

In this example, I didn't tune the table at all. For example, there are no indexes on any of the columns besides the primary key. This is to avoid complicating the example. Great care should be taken with a table like this one in a nontrivial, production-bound application,.

Spring Batch applications are workhorse applications and have the potential to reveal bottlenecks in your application you didn't know you had. Imagine suddenly being able to achieve 1 million new database insertions every 10 minutes. Would your database grind to a halt? Insert speed can be a critical factor in the speed of your application. Software developers will (hopefully) think about schema in terms of how well it enforces the constraints of the business logic and how well it serves the overall business model. However, it's important to wear another hat, that of a DBA, when writing applications such as this one. A common solution is to create a denormalized table whose contents can be coerced into valid data once inside the database, perhaps by a trigger on inserts. This is a common technique in data warehousing. Later, you'll explore using Spring Batch to do processing on a record before insertion. This lets the developer verify or override the input into the database. This processing, in tandem with a conservative application of constraints that are best expressed in the database, can make for applications that are very robust *and* quick.

The Job Configuration
The configuration for the job is as follows:

```
<job
    job-repository="jobRepository"
    id="insertIntoDbFromCsvJob">
    <step id="step1">
        <tasklet transaction-manager="transactionManager">
        <chunk
                reader="csvFileReader"
                writer="jdbcItemWriter"
                commit-interval="5"
            />
        </tasklet>
        </step>
        </job>
```

As described earlier, a job consists of steps, which are the real workhorse of a given job. The steps can be as complex or as simple as you like. Indeed, a step could be considered the smallest unit of work for a job. Input (what's read) is passed to the Step and potentially processed; then output (what's written) is created from the step. This processing is spelled out using a Tasklet. You can provide your own Tasklet implementation or simply use some of the preconfigured configurations for different processing scenarios. These implementations are made available in terms of subelements of the Tasklet element. One of the most important aspects of batch processing is chunk-oriented processing, which is employed here using the chunk element.

In chunk-oriented processing, input is read from a reader, optionally processed, and then aggregated. Finally, at a configurable interval_an interval specified by the `commit-interval` attribute to configure how many items will be processed before the transaction is committed_all the input is sent to the `writer`. If there is a transaction manager in play, the transaction is also committed. Right before a commit, the metadata in the database is updated to mark the progress of the job.

Input

The first responsibility is reading a file from the file system. You use a provided implementation for the example. Reading CSV files is a very common scenario, and Spring Batch's support does not disappoint. The `org.springframework.batch.item.file.FlatFileItemReader` class delegates the task of delimiting fields and records within a file to a `LineMapper`, which in turn delegates the task of identifying the end of a record, and the fields within that record, to `LineTokenizer` and `FieldSetMapper`, respectively.

In this example, you use an `org.springframework.batch.item.file.transform.DelimitedLineTokenizer`, and tell it to identify fields delimited by a comma (,). You name the fields so that you can reference them later in the configuration. These names don't have to be the values of some header row in the input file; they just have to correspond to the order in which the fields are found in the input file. These names are also used by the `FieldSetMapper` to match properties on a POJO. As each record is read, the values are applied to an instance of a POJO, and that POJO is returned.

```xml
<beans:bean
  id="csvFileReader"
  class="org.springframework.batch.item.file.FlatFileItemReader"
  p:resource="file:${user.home}/batches/registrations.csv">
  <beans:property
   name="lineMapper">
   <beans:bean
    class="org.springframework.batch.item.file.mapping.DefaultLineMapper">
    <beans:property
     name="lineTokenizer">
     <beans:bean
class="org.springframework.batch.item.file.transform.DelimitedLineTokenizer"
     p:delimiter=","
p:names="firstName,lastName,company,address,city,state,zip,county,url,phoneNumber,fax" />
    </beans:property>
    <beans:property
     name="fieldSetMapper">
     <beans:bean
class="org.springframework.batch.item.file.mapping.BeanWrapperFieldSetMapper"
p:targetType="com.apress.springenterpriserecipes.springbatch.solution1.UserRegistration" />
    </beans:property>
   </beans:bean>
  </beans:property>
</beans:bean>
```

The class returned from the reader, `UserRegistration`, is a rather plain JavaBean. The `BeanWrapperFieldSetMapper` class creates the POJO whose type is configured by the `targetType` property and sets the JavaBean properties corresponding to the names given to the `names` property of the `DelimitedLineTokenizer`.

Output

The next component to do work is the writer, which is responsible for taking the aggregated collection of items read from the reader. In this case, you might imagine a java.util.List<UserRegistration> containing up to as many elements as was configured for the commit-interval attribute on the chunk element. Because you're trying to write to a database, you use Spring Batch's org.springframework.batch.item.database.JdbcBatchItemWriter. This class contains support for taking input and writing it to a database. It is up to the developer to provide the input and to specify what SQL should be run for the input. It will run the SQL specified by the sql property, in essence reading from the database, as many times as specified by the chunk element's commit-interval, and then commit the whole transaction. Here, you're doing a simple insert. The names and values for the named parameters are being created by the bean configured for the itemSqlParameterSourceProvider property, an instance of org.springframework.batch.item.database.BeanPropertyItemSqlParameterSourceProvider, whose sole job it is to take JavaBean properties and make them available as named parameters corresponding to the property name on the JavaBean.

```
<beans:bean
        id="jdbcItemWriter"
        class="org.springframework.batch.item.database.JdbcBatchItemWriter"
        p:assertUpdates="true"
        p:dataSource-ref="dataSource">
        <beans:property name="sql">
          <beans:value>
            <![CDATA[
      insert into USER_REGISTRATION(
FIRST_NAME, LAST_NAME, COMPANY, ADDRESS,
CITY, STATE, ZIP, COUNTY,
URL, PHONE_NUMBER, FAX )
values (  :firstName, :lastName, :company, :address,  :city , :state, : ➥
zip, :county,  :url, :phoneNumber, :fax  )
]]> </beans:value>
</beans:property>
<beans:property name="itemSqlParameterSourceProvider">
<beans:bean
     class="org.springframework.batch.item.database.BeanPropertyItemSql➥
ParameterSourceProvider" />
</beans:property>
</beans:bean>
```

And that's it! A working solution. With little configuration and no custom code, you've built a solution for taking large CSV files and reading them into a database. This solution is bare bones and leaves a lot of edge cases uncared for. You might want to do processing on the item as it's read (before it's inserted), for example.

This exemplifies a simple job. It's important to remember that there are similar classes for doing the exact opposite transformation: reading from a database and writing to a CSV file.

9-5. Writing a Custom ItemWriter and ItemReader

Problem

You want to talk to a resource (you might imagine an RSS feed, or any other custom data format) that Spring Batch doesn't know how to connect to.

Solution

You can easily write your own `ItemWriter` or `ItemReader`. The interfaces are drop dead simple and there's not a lot of responsibility placed on the implementations.

How It Works

As easy and trivial as this process is to do, it's still not better than just reusing any of the numerous provided options. If you look, you'll likely find something. There's support for writing JMS (`JmsItemWriter`), JPA (`JpaItemWriter`), JDBC (`JdbcBatchItemWriter`), Files (`FlatFileItemWriter`), iBatis (`IbatisBatchItemWriter`), and more. There's even support for "writing" by invoking a method on a bean (`PropertyExtractingDelegatingItemWriter`) and passing to it as arguments the properties on the `Item` to be written! There's a slightly smaller but impressive set of implementations for `ItemReader` implementations.

Writing a Custom ItemReader

The `ItemReader` example is trivial. Here an `ItemReader` is created that knows how to retrieve `UserRegistration` objects from an (remote procedure call (RPC) endpoint:

```
package com.apress.springenterpriserecipes.springbatch.solution2;

import java.util.Collection;
import java.util.Date;

import org.springframework.batch.item.ItemReader;
import org.springframework.batch.item.ParseException;
import org.springframework.batch.item.UnexpectedInputException;
import org.springframework.beans.factory.annotation.Autowired;

import com.apress.springenterpriserecipes.springbatch.➥
UserRegistrationService;
import com.apress.springenterpriserecipes.springbatch.solution1.➥
UserRegistration;

public class UserRegistrationItemReader implements ItemReader<UserRegistration> {

    @Autowired
    private UserRegistrationService userRegistrationService;
```

```
public UserRegistration read() throws Exception,UnexpectedInputException,
ParseException {
    Date today = new Date();
    Collection<UserRegistration> registrations =

        userRegistrationService.getOutstandingUserRegistrationBatchForDate(
                1, today);
    if (registrations!=null && registrations.size() >= 1)
        return registrations.iterator().next();
    return null;
    }
}
```

As you can see, the interface is trivial. In this case, you defer most work to a remote service to provide you with the input. The interface requires that you return one record. The interface is parameterized to the type of object (the "item") to be returned. All the read items will be aggregated and then passed to the ItemWriter.

Writing a Custom ItemWriter

The ItemWriter example is also trivial. Imagine wanting to "write" by invoking a remote service using any of the vast support for remoting that Spring provides. The ItemWriter interface is parameterized by the type of item you're expecting to write. Here, you expect a UserRegistration object from the ItemReader. The interface consists of one method, which expects a List of the class's parameterized type. These are the objects read from ItemReader and aggregated. If your commit-interval were ten, then you might expect ten or fewer items in the List.

```
import java.util.List;

import org.apache.commons.lang.builder.ToStringBuilder;
import org.apache.log4j.Logger;
import org.springframework.batch.item.ItemWriter;
import org.springframework.beans.factory.annotation.Autowired;

import com.apress.springenterpriserecipes.springbatch.User;
import com.apress.springenterpriserecipes.springbatch.UserRegistrationService;
import com.apress.springenterpriserecipes.springbatch.solution1.UserRegistration;

/**
 *
 *
 * This class writes the user registration by calling an RPC service (whose
 * client interface is wired in using Spring
 */
public class UserRegistrationServiceItemWriter implements
        ItemWriter<UserRegistration> {

    private static final Logger logger = Logger
            .getLogger(UserRegistrationServiceItemWriter.class);
```

```
// this is the client interface to an HTTP Invoker service.
@Autowired
private UserRegistrationService userRegistrationService;

/**
 * takes aggregated input from the reader and 'writes' them using a custom
 * implementation.
 */
public void write(List<? extends UserRegistration> items)
throws Exception {
    for (final UserRegistration userRegistration : items) {
        User registeredUser = userRegistrationService
                .registerUser(userRegistration);
        logger.debug("Registered:"
                + ToStringBuilder.reflectionToString(registeredUser));
    }
  }
}
```

Here, you've wired in the service's client interface. You simply loop through the items and invoke the service. If you remove the gratuitous spacing, curly brackets and logging output, it becomes two lines of code to satisfy the requirement.

9-6. Processing Input Before Writing

Problem

While transferring data directly from a spreadsheet or CSV dump might be useful, one can imagine having to do some sort of processing on the data before it's written. Data in a CSV file, and more generally from any source, is not usually exactly the way you expect it to be or immediately suitable for writing. Just because Spring Batch can coerce it into a POJO on your behalf, that doesn't mean the state of the data is correct. There may be additional data that you need to infer or fill in from other services before the data is suitable for writing.

Solution

Spring Batch will let you do processing on reader output. This processing can do virtually anything to the output before it gets passed to the writer, including changing the type of the data.

How It Works

Spring Batch gives the implementor a chance to perform any custom logic on the data read from reader. The processor attribute on the chunk element expects a reference to a bean of type org.springframework.batch.item.ItemProcessor<I,O>. Thus, the revised definition for the job from the previous recipe looks like this:

```
        <job
    job-repository="jobRepository"
    id="insertIntoDbFromCsvJob">
```

```
<step id="step1">
    <tasklet transaction-manager="transactionManager">
                <chunk
            reader="csvFileReader"
            processor = "userRegistrationValidationProcessor"
            writer="jdbcItemWriter"
            commit-interval="5"
        />
    </tasklet>
</step>
</job>
```

The goal is to do certain validations on the data before you authorize it to be written to the database. If you determine the record is invalid, you can stop further processing by returning null from the ItemProcessor. This is crucial and provides a necessary safeguard. One thing that you want to do is ensure that the data is the right format (for example, the schema may require a valid two-letter state name instead of the longer full state name). Telephone numbers are expected to follow a certain format, and you can use this processor to strip the telephone number of any extraneous characters, leaving only a valid (in the United States) ten-digit phone number. The same applies for U. S. zip codes, which consist of five characters and optionally a hyphen followed by a four-digit code. Finally, while a constraint guarding against duplicates is best implemented in the database, there may very well be some other "eligibility" criteria for a record that can be met only by querying the system before insertion.

Here's the configuration for the ItemProcessor:

```
<beans:bean id="userRegistrationValidationProcessor"
class="com.apress.springenterpriserecipes.springbatch.solution1.➥
UserRegistrationValidationItemProcessor" />
```

In the interest of keeping this class short, I won't reprint it in its entirety, but the salient bits should be obvious:

```
package com.apress.springenterpriserecipes.springbatch.solution2;
import java.util.Arrays;
import java.util.Collection;

import org.apache.commons.lang.StringUtils;
import org.springframework.batch.core.StepExecution;
import org.springframework.batch.core.annotation.BeforeStep;
import org.springframework.batch.item.ItemProcessor;
import com.apress.springenterpriserecipes.springbatch.solution1.UserRegistration;

public class UserRegistrationValidationItemProcessor
    implements ItemProcessor<UserRegistration, UserRegistration> {

    private String stripNonNumbers(String input) { /* … */ }

    private boolean isTelephoneValid(String telephone) { /* … */ }

    private boolean isZipCodeValid(String zip) { /* … */ }

    private boolean isValidState(String state) { /* … */ }
```

```
    public UserRegistration process(UserRegistration input) throws Exception {
        String zipCode = stripNonNumbers(input.getZip());
        String telephone = stripNonNumbers(input.getPhoneNumber());
        String state = StringUtils.defaultString(input.getState());
        if (isTelephoneValid(telephone) && isZipCodeValid(zipCode) ➥
&& isValidState(state)) {
            input.setZip(zipCode);
            input.setPhoneNumber(telephone );
            return input;
        }
        return null;
    }
}
```

The class is a parameterized type. The type information is the type of the input, as well as the type of the output. The input is what's given to the method for processing, and the output is the returned data from the method. Because you're not transforming anything, in this example the two parameterized types are the same.

Once this process has completed, there's a lot of useful information to be had in the Spring Batch metadata tables. Issue the following query on your database:

```
select * from BATCH_STEP_EXECUTION;
```

Among other things, you'll get back the exit status of the job, how many commits occurred, how many items were read, and how many items were filtered. So if the preceding job was run on a batch with a 100 rows, each item was read and passed through the processor, and it found 10 items invalid (it returned null 10 times), the value for the filter_count column would be 10. You could see that a 100 items were read from the read_count. The write_count column would reflect that 10 items didn't make it, and would show 90.

Chaining Processors Together

Sometimes you might want to add extra processing that isn't congruous with the goals of the processor you've already set up. Spring Batch provides a convenience class, CompositeItemProcessor, which forwards the output of the filter to the input of the successive filter. In this way, you can write many, singly focused ItemProcessors and then reuse them and chain them as necessary.

```
    <bean id="compositeBankCustomerProcessor"➥
class="org.springframework.batch.item.support.CompositeItemProcessor">
        <property name="itemProcessors">
            <list>
                <bean ref = "creditScoreValidationProcessor" />
                <bean ref="salaryValidationProcessor" />
                <bean ref="customerEligibilityProcessor" />
            </list>
        </property>
    </bean>
```

The example created a very simple workflow. The first ItemProcessor will take an input of whatever's coming from the ItemReader configured for this job, presumably a Customer object. It will check the credit score of the Customer and, if approved, forward the Customer to the salary and income validation processor. If everything checks out there, the Customer will be forwarded to the eligibility processor, where the system is checked for duplicates or any other invalid data. It will finally be forwarded to the writer to be added to the output. If at any point in the three processors the Customer fails a check, the executing ItemProcessor can simply return null and arrest processing.

9-7. Better Living through Transactions

Problem
You want your reads and writes to be robust. Ideally, they'll use transactions where appropriate and also correctly react to exceptions.

Solution
Transaction capabilities are built on top of the first class support already provided by the core Spring framework. Where relevant, Spring Batch surfaces the configuration so that you can control it. Within the context of chunk-oriented processing, it also exposes a lot of control over the frequency of commits, rollback semantics, and so on.

How It Works

Transactions
Spring's core framework provides first class support for transactions. You simply wire up a TransactionManager and give Spring Batch a reference, just as you would in any regular JdbcTemplate or HibernateTemplate solution. As you build your Spring Batch solutions, you'll be given opportunities to control how steps behave in a transaction. You've already seen some of the support for transactions baked right in.

The batch.xml file, used in all these examples, established a DataSource and a DataSourceTransactionManager bean. The TransactionManager and DataSource were then wired to the JobRepository, which was in turn wired to the JobLauncher, which you used to launch all jobs thus far. This enabled all the metadata your jobs create to be written to the database in a transactional way.

You might wonder why there is no explicit mention of the TransactionManager when you configured the JdbcItemWriter with a reference to the DataSource. The TransactionManager can be specified, but in your solutions it wasn't required because Spring Batch will, by default, try to pluck the TransactionManager named transactionManager from the context and use it. If you want to explicitly configure this, you can specify the transactionManager property on the tasklet element. A simple TransactionManager for JDBC work might look like this:

```
<bean id="myCustomTransactionManager"
class="org.springframework.jdbc.datasource.DataSourceTransactionManager"
p:dataSource-ref="dataSource" />
    <job job-repository="jobRepository" id="insertIntoDbFromCsvJob">
        <step id="step1">
            <tasklet transaction-manager="myCustomTransactionManager" >
                <!-- ... -->
            </tasklet>
        </step>
    </job>
...
```

Items read from an `ItemReader` are normally aggregated. If a commit on the `ItemWriter` fails, the aggregated items are kept and then resubmitted. This process is efficient and works most of the time. One place where it breaks semantics is when reading from a transactional message queue. Reads from a message queue can and should be rolled back if the transaction they participate in (in this case, the transaction for the `writer`) fails:

```
<tasklet transaction-manager="customTransactionManager" >
    <chunk
        reader="jmsItemReader" is-reader-transactional-queue="true"
        processor="userRegistrationValidationProcessor"
        writer="jdbcItemWriter"
        commit-interval="5" />
</tasklet>
```

Rollbacks

Handling the simple case ("read X items and then, every Y items commit a database transaction every Y items") is easy. Spring Batch excels in the robustness it surfaces as simple configuration options for the edge and failure cases.

If a write fails on an `ItemWriter`, or some other exception occurs in processing, Spring Batch will roll back the transaction. This is valid handling for a majority of the cases. There may be some scenarios when you want to control which exceptional cases cause the transaction to roll back.

You can use the `no-rollback-exception-classes` element to configure this for the `step`. The value is a list of `Exception` classes that should not cause the transaction to roll back:

```
<step id = "step2">
    <tasklet>
        <chunk reader="reader" writer="writer" commit-interval="10" />
        <no-rollback-exception-classes>
com.yourdomain.services.exceptions.ZipCodeNotZipPlusFiveCompliantException,
com.yourdomain.services.exceptions.CustomerNotFoundException
        </no-rollback-exception-classes>
    </tasklet>
</step>
```

9-8. Retry

Problem

You are dealing with a requirement for functionality that may fail but is not transactional. Perhaps it is transactional but unreliable. You want to work with a resource that may fail when you try to read from or write to it. It may fail because of networking connectivity because an endpoint is down or for any other number of reasons. You know that it will likely be back up soon, though, and that it should be retried.

Solution

Use Spring Batch's retry capabilities to systematically retry the read or write.

How It Works

As you saw in the last recipe, it's easy to handle transactional resources with Spring Batch. When it comes to transient or unreliable resources, a different tack is required. Such resources tend to be distributed or manifest problems that eventually resolve themselves. Some (such as web services) cannot inherently participate in a transaction because of their distributed nature. There are products that can start a transaction on one server and propagate the transactional context to a distributed server and complete it there, although this tends to be very rare and inefficient. Alternatively, there's good support for distributed ("global" or XA) transactions if you can use it Sometimes, however, you may be dealing with a resource that isn't either of those. A common example might be a call made to a remote service, such as an RMI service or a REST endpoint. Some invocations will fail but may be retried with some likelihood of success in a transactional scenario. For example, an update to the database resulting in `DeadLockLoserException` might be usefully retried.

Configuring a Step

The simplest example is in the configuration of a `step`. Here, you can specify exception classes on which to retry the operation. As with the rollback exceptions, you can delimit this list of exceptions with newlines or commas:

```
<step id = "step23">
        <tasklet>
        <chunk reader="reader" writer="writer"
                            commit-interval="10"
                            retry-limit="3"
                            cache-capacity="10">
        <retryable-exception-classes>
                org.springframework.dao. ➥
DeadlockLoserDataAccessException
        </retryable-exception-classes>

        </chunk>
    </tasklet>
</step>
```

Retry Template

Alternatively, you can leverage Spring Batch's support for retries and recovery in your own code. For example, you can have a custom `ItemWriter` in which retry functionality is desired or even an entire service interface for which retry support is desired.

Spring Batch supports these scenarios through the `RetryTemplate` that (much like its various other `Template` cousins) isolates your logic from the nuances of retries and instead enables you to write the code as though you were only going to attempt it once. Let Spring Batch handle everything else through declarative configuration.

The `RetryTemplate` supports many use cases, with convenient APIs to wrap otherwise tedious retry/fail/recover cycles in concise, single-method invocations.

Let's take a look at the modified version of a simple `ItemWriter` from Recipe 9.5 on how to write a custom `ItemWriter`. The solution was simple enough and would ideally work all the time. It fails to handle the error cases for the service, however. When dealing with RPC, always proceed as if there are two things that could go wrong. The service itself may surface a semantic or system violation: i.e., duplicate database key, invalid credit card number, and so on. This is true whether the service is distributed or in-VM, of course.

Next, the RPC layer below the system may also fault. Here's the rewritten code, this time allowing for retries:

```java
import java.util.List;

import org.apache.commons.lang.builder.ToStringBuilder;
import org.apache.log4j.Logger;
import org.springframework.batch.item.ItemWriter;
import org.springframework.batch.retry.RetryCallback;
import org.springframework.batch.retry.RetryContext;
import org.springframework.batch.retry.support.RetryTemplate;
import org.springframework.beans.factory.annotation.Autowired;

import com.apress.springenterpriserecipes.springbatch.User;
import com.apress.springenterpriserecipes.springbatch.UserRegistrationService;
import com.apress.springenterpriserecipes.springbatch.solution1.UserRegistration;

/**
 *
 *
 * This class writes the user registration by calling an RPC service (whose
 * client interface is wired in using Spring
 */
public class RetryableUserRegistrationServiceItemWriter implements
        ItemWriter<UserRegistration> {

    private static final Logger logger = Logger
            .getLogger(RetryableUserRegistrationServiceItemWriter.class);

    // this is the client interface to an HTTP Invoker service.
    @Autowired
    private UserRegistrationService userRegistrationService;

    @Autowired
    private RetryTemplate retryTemplate;

    /**
     * takes aggregated input from the reader and 'writes' them using a custom
     * implementation.
     */
    public void write(List<? extends UserRegistration> items)
      throws Exception {
        for (final UserRegistration userRegistration : items) {
            User registeredUser = retryTemplate.execute(
            new RetryCallback<User>() {
                public User doWithRetry(RetryContext context) throws Exception {
                    return userRegistrationService.registerUser(userRegistration);
                }
            });
            logger.debug("Registered:"
                    + ToStringBuilder.reflectionToString(registeredUser));
        }
    }
}
```

As you can see, the code hasn't changed much, and the result is much more robust. The RetryTemplate itself is configured in the Spring context, although it's trivial to create in code. I declare it in the Spring context only because there is some surface area for configuration when creating the object, and I try to let Spring handle the configuration.

One of the more useful settings for the RetryTemplate is the BackOffPolicy in use. The BackOffPolicy dictates how long the RetryTemplate should "back off" between retries. Indeed, there's even support for growing the delay between retries after each failed attempt to avoid lock stepping with other clients attempting the same invocation. This is great for situations in which there are potentially many concurrent attempts on the same resource and a race condition may ensue. There are other BackOffPolicies, including one that delays retries by a fixed amount.

```
<beans:bean id="retryTemplate" class="org.springframework.batch.retry.➡
support.RetryTemplate">
    <beans:property name="backOffPolicy" >
        <beans:bean  class="org.springframework.batch.retry.backoff.➡
ExponentialBackOffPolicy"
        p:initialInterval="1000" p:maxInterval="10000" p:multiplier="2" />
    </beans:property>
</beans:bean>
```

You have configured a RetryTemplate's backOffPolicy so that the backOffPolicy will wait 1 second (1000 milliseconds) before the initial retry. Subsequent attempts will double that value (the growth is influenced by the multiplier). It'll continue until the maxInterval is met, at which point all subsequent retry intervals will level off, retrying at a consistent interval.

AOP-based Retries

An alternative is an AOP advisor provided by Spring Batch that will wrap invocations of methods whose success is not guaranteed in retries, as you did with the RetryTemplate. In the previous example, you rewrote an ItemWriter to make use of the template. Another approach might be to merely advise the entire userRegistrationService proxy with this retry logic. In this case, the code could go back to the way it was in the original example, with no RetryTemplate!

```
<aop:config>
    <aop:pointcut id="remote"
        expression="execution(* com...*RetryableUserRegistrationServiceItemWriter.*(..))" />
    <aop:advisor pointcut-ref="remote"  advice-ref="retryAdvice" order="-1"/>
</aop:config>

<bean id="retryAdvice"
        class="org.springframework.batch.retry.interceptor.➡
RetryOperationsInterceptor"/>
```

9-9. Controlling Step Execution

Problem

You want to control how steps are executed, perhaps to eliminate a needless waste of time by introducing concurrency or by executing steps only if a condition is true.

Solution

There are different ways to change the runtime profile of your jobs, mainly by exerting control over the way steps are executed: concurrent steps, decisions, and sequential steps.

How It Works

Thus far, you have explored running one step in a job. Typical jobs of almost any complexity will have multiple steps, however. A step provides a boundary (transactional or not) to the beans/logic it encloses. A step can have its own reader, writer, and processor. Each step helps decide what the next step will be. A step is isolated and provides focused functionality that can be assembled using the updated schema and configuration options in Spring Batch 2.0 in very sophisticated workflows. In fact, some of the concepts and patterns you're about to see will be very familiar if you have an interest in business process management (BPM) systems and workflows. (To learn more about BPM, and jBPM in particular, see Chapter 11.) BPM provides many constructs for process or job control that are similar to what you're seeing here.

A step often corresponds to a bullet point when you outline the definition of a job on paper. For example, a batch job to load the daily sales and produce a report might be proposed as follows:

Daily Sales Report Job

1. Load customers from the CSV file into the database.

2. Calculate daily statistics and write to a report file.

3. Send messages to the message queue to notify an external system of the successful registration for each of the newly loaded customers.

Sequential Steps

In the previous example, there's an implied sequence between the first two steps: the audit file can't be written until all the registrations have completed. This sort of relationship is the default relationship between two steps. One occurs after the other. Each step executes with its own execution context and shares only a parent job execution context and an order.

```
<job     id="nightlyRegistrationsJob"
    job-repository="jobRepository">
    <step id="loadRegistrations" next="reportStatistics" >
    <tasklet ref = "tasklet1"/>
    </step>
    <step id="reportStatistics" next="…" >
    <tasklet ref ="tasklet2"/>
    </step>
    <!-- … other steps …  -->
</job>
```

Notice that you specify the next attribute on the step elements to tell processing which step to go to next.

Concurrency

The first version of Spring Batch was oriented toward batch processing inside the same thread and, with some alteration, perhaps inside the virtual machine. There were workarounds, of course, but the situation was less than ideal.

In the outline for this example job, the first step had to come before the second two because the second two are dependent on the first. The second two, however, do not share any such dependencies. There's no reason why the audit log couldn't be written at the same time as the JMS messages are being delivered. Spring Batch provides the capability to fork processing to enable just this sort of arrangement:

```
<job      job-repository="jobRepository"
       id="insertIntoDbFromCsvJob">
       <step id="loadRegistrations" next="finalizeRegistrations"➥
> <!-- ... --> </step>
       <split id="finalizeRegistrations" >
              <flow>
                     <step id="reportStatistics" ><!-- ... --></step>
              </flow>
              <flow>
                     <step id="sendJmsNotifications" > <!-- ... --></step>
              </flow>
       </split>
</job>
```

In this example, there's nothing to prevent you from having many steps within the flow elements, nor was there anything preventing you from having more steps after the split element. The split element, like the step elements, takes a next attribute as well.

Spring Batch provides a mechanism to offload processing to another process. This feature, called *remote chunking*, is new in Spring Batch 2.0. This distribution requires some sort of durable, reliable connection. This is a perfect use of JMS because it's rock-solid and transactional, fast, and reliable. Spring Batch support is modeled at a slightly higher level, on top of the Spring Integration abstractions for Spring Integration channels. This support is not in the main Spring Batch code, though. Remote chunking lets individual steps read and aggregate items_as usual_in the main thread. This step is called the Master. Items read are sent to the ItemProcessor/ItemWriter running in another process (this is called the Slave). If the Slave is an aggressive consumer, you have a simple, generic mechanism to scale: work is instantly farmed out over as many JMS clients as you can throw at it. The aggressive-consumer pattern refers to the arrangement of multiple JMS clients all consuming the same queue's messages. If one client consumes a message and is busy processing, other idle queues will get the message instead. As long as there's a client that's idle, the message will be processed instantly.

Additionally, Spring Batch supports implicitly scaling out using a feature called *partitioning*. This feature is interesting because it's built in and generally very flexible. You replace your instance of a step with a subclass, PartitionStep, which knows how to coordinate distributed executors and maintains the metadata for the execution of the step, thus eliminating the need for a durable medium of communication as in the "remote chunking" technology.

The functionality here is also very generic. It could, conceivably, be used with any sort of grid fabric technology such as GridGain or Hadoop. (For more on GridGain, see Chapter 10.) Spring Batch ships with only a TaskExecutorPartitionHandler, which executes steps in multiple threads using a TaskExecutor strategy. This simple improvement might be enough of a justification for this feature! If you're really hurting, however, you can extend it.

Conditional Steps with Statuses

Using the ExitStatus of a given step to determine the next step is the simplest example of a conditional flow. Spring Batch facilitates this through the use of the stop, next, fail and end elements. By default, assuming no intervention, a step will have an ExitStatus that matches its BatchStatus, which is a property whose values are defined in an enum and may be any of the following: COMPLETED, COMPLETED WITH SKIPS, STARTING, STARTED, STOPPING, STOPPED, FAILED, ABANDONED or UNKNOWN.

Let's look at an example that executes one of two steps based on the success of a preceding step:

```
<step id="step1" >
    <next on="COMPLETED" to="step2" > <!-- ... --></step>
        <next on="FAILED" to="failureStep" > <!-- ... --></step>
</step>
```

It's also possible to provide a wildcard. This is useful if you want to ensure a certain behavior for any number of BatchStatus, perhaps in tandem with a more specific next element that matches only one BatchStatus.

```
<step id="step1" >
    <next on="COMPLETED" to="step2" > <!-- ... --></step>
        <next on="*" to="failureStep" > <!-- ... --></step>
</step>
```

In this example, you are instructing it to perform some step based on any unaccounted-for ExitStatus. Another option is to just stop processing altogether with a BatchStatus of FAILED. You can do this using the fail element. A less aggressive rewrite of the preceding example might be the following:

```
<step id="step1" >
    <next on="COMPLETED" to="step2" />
        <fail  on="FAILED"  />
        <!-- ... -->
</step>
```

In all these examples, you're reacting to the standard BatchStatuses that the Spring Batch framework provides. But it's also possible to raise your own ExitStatus. If, for example, you wanted the whole job to fail with a custom ExitStatus of "MAN DOWN", you might do something like this:

```
<step id="step1" next="step2"><!-- ... --></step>
<step id="step2" parent="s2">
  <fail on="FAILED" exit-code="MAN DOWN "/>
  <next on="*" to="step3"/>
</step>
<step id="step3"><!-- ... --></step>
```

Finally, if all you want to do is end processing with a BatchStatus of COMPLETED, you can use the end element. This is an explicit way of ending a flow as if it had run out of steps and incurred no errors.

```
<next on="COMPLETED" to="step2" />
<step id="step2" >
  <end on="COMPLETED"/>
  <next on="FAILED" to="errorStep"/>
  <!-- ... -->
</step>
```

Conditional Steps with Decisions

If you want to vary the execution flow based on some logic more complex than a job's ExitStatuses, you may give Spring Batch a helping hand by using a decision element and providing it with an implementation of a JobExecutionDecider.

```
package com.apress.springenterpriserecipes.springbatch.solution2;

import org.springframework.batch.core.JobExecution;
import org.springframework.batch.core.StepExecution;
import org.springframework.batch.core.job.flow.FlowExecutionStatus;
import org.springframework.batch.core.job.flow.JobExecutionDecider;

public class HoroscopeDecider implements JobExecutionDecider {

    private boolean isMercuryIsInRetrograde (){ return Math.random() > .9 ; }

    public FlowExecutionStatus decide(JobExecution jobExecution,
                                      StepExecution stepExecution) {
        if (isMercuryIsInRetrograde()) {
            return new FlowExecutionStatus("MERCURY_IN_RETROGRADE");
        }
        return FlowExecutionStatus.COMPLETED;
    }
}
```

All that remains is the XML configuration:

```
<beans:bean id="horoscopeDecider"class="com.apress.springenterpriserecipes. ➥
springbatch.solution2.HoroscopeDecider"/>

<job id="job">
    <step id="step1"  next="decision"  ><!-- ... --></step>
    <decision id="decision" decider="horoscopeDecider">
      <next on="MERCURY_IN_RETROGRADE" to="step2" />
      <next on="COMPLETED" to="step3" />
    </decision>
    <step id="step2" next="step3"> <!-- ... --> </step>
    <step id="step3" parent="s3">  <!-- ... --> </step>
</job>
```

9-10. Parameterizing a Job

Problem
The previous examples work well enough, but they leave something to be desired in terms of flexibility. To apply the batch code to some other file, you'd have to edit the configuration and hard-code the name in there.

Solution
Use JobParameters to parameterize a job, which is then available to your steps through Spring Batch's expression language or via API calls.

How It Works

Launching a Job with Parameters

A job is a prototype of a JobInstance. JobParameters are used to provide a way of identifying a unique run of a job (a JobInstance). These JobParameters allow you to give input to your batch process, just as you would with a method definition in Java. You've seen the JobParameters in previous examples, but not in detail. The JobParameters object is created as you launch the job using the JobLauncher. To launch a job called dailySalesFigures, with the date for the job to work with, you would write something like this:

```
ClassPathXmlApplicationContext classPathXmlApplicationContext = new
ClassPathXmlApplicationContext("solution2.xml");
classPathXmlApplicationContext.start();
JobLauncher jobLauncher = (JobLauncher) classPathXmlApplicationContext.➥
getBean("jobLauncher");
Job job = (Job) classPathXmlApplicationContext.getBean("dailySalesFigures");
jobLauncher.run(job, new JobParametersBuilder().addDate( "date",
    DateUtils.truncate(new Date(), Calendar.DATE)).toJobParameters());
```

Accessing JobParameters

Technically, you can get at JobParameters via any of the ExecutionContexts (step, job, and so on). Once you have it, you can access the parameters in a type-safe way by calling getLong(), getString(), and so on. A simple way to do this is to bind to the @BeforeStep event, save the StepExecution, and iterate over the parameters this way. From here, you can inspect the parameters and do anything you want with them. Let's look at that in terms of the ItemProcessor you wrote earlier:

```
// …
private StepExecution stepExecution;

@BeforeStep
public void saveStepExecution(StepExecution stepExecution) {
  this.stepExecution = stepExecution;
}

public UserRegistration process(UserRegistration input) throws Exception {

    Map<String, JobParameter> params =  stepExecution.getJobParameters().➥
getParameters();

  // iterate over all of the parameters
  for (String jobParameterKey : params.keySet()) {
     System.out.println(String.format("%s=%s", jobParameterKey,
  params.get(jobParameterKey).getValue().toString()));
     }

  // access specific parameters in a type safe way
  Date date = stepExecution.getJobParameters().getDate("date");
  // etc …
}
```

This turns out to be of limited value. The 80 percent case is that you'll need to bind parameters from the job's launch to the Spring beans in the application context. These parameters are available only at runtime, whereas the steps in the XML application context are configured at design time. This happens in many places. Previous examples demonstrated ItemWriters and ItemReaders with a hard-coded path. That works fine unless you want to parameterize the file name. This is hardly acceptable unless you plan on using a job just once!

The core Spring Framework 3.0 features an enhanced expression language that Spring Batch 2.0 (depending on Spring Framework 3.0) uses to defer binding of the parameter until the correct time. Or, in this case, until the bean is in the correct scope. Spring Batch 2.0 introduces the "step" scope for just this purpose. Let's take a look at how you'd rework the previous example to use a parameterized file name for the ItemReader's resource:

```
<beans:bean
        scope="step"
        id="csvFileReader"
        class="org.springframework.batch.item.file.FlatFileItemReader"
        p:resource="file:${user.home}/batches/#{jobParameters[input.fileName]}.csv">
    <!-- … this is the same as before…-->
</beans:bean>
```

All you did is scope the bean (the FlatFileItemReader) to the life cycle of a step (at which point those JobParameters will resolve correctly) and then used the EL syntax to parameterize the path to work off of.

Summary

This chapter introduced you to the concepts of batch processing, some of its history, and why it fits in a modern day architecture. You learned about Spring Batch, the batch processing from SpringSource, and how to do reading and writing with ItemReader and ItemWriter implementations in your batch jobs. You wrote your own ItemReader, and ItemWriter implementations, as needed, and saw how to control the execution of steps inside a job.

The next chapter will discuss Terracotta and GridGain. You'll learn how to use Terracotta to build a distributed cache and take your Spring applications onto the grid with GridGain.

CHAPTER 10

■ ■ ■

Distributed Spring

In this chapter, you will learn the principles behind various distributed computing concepts, and how to use Spring in conjunction with some very powerful, open-source–ish third-party products to build solutions leveraging those concepts. Grid computing is a very important concept in today's world, for many reasons. It solves many problems, some more ephemeral than others:

- *Scalability*: Distribution provides a mechanism by which to expand capability to scale an application to meet demand. This is simple, on the face of it: the more computers responding to the same request means more people can make requests. This is the quintessential reason behind clustering, and behind load balancing.

- *Redundancy*: Computers fail. It's built in. The only thing you can guarantee about a hard disk of any make? That it will, at some point or another, fail, and more than likely in your lifetime. Having the ability to have a computer take over when something else becomes ineffective, or to have a computer's load lessened by adjoining members in a cluster, is a valuable benefit of distribution.

- *Parallelization*: Distribution enables solutions designed to split problems into more manageable chunks, or to expedite processing by bringing more power to bear on the problem. Some problems are inherently, embarrassingly parallelizable. These often reflect real life. Take, for example, a process that's designed to check hotels, car rentals, and airline accommodations and show you the best possible options. All three checks can be done concurrently, as they share no state. It would be a crime not to parallelize this sort of thing. Other problem domains are not so clearly parallelizable. For example, a binary sort is an ideal candidate for parallelization.

The other reasons are more subtle, but very real. Over the course of computing, we've clung to the notion that computers will constantly expand in capacity with time. This has come to be known as Moore's Law, named for Gordon Moore of Intel. Looking at history, you might remark that we've, in fact, done quite well along that scale. Indeed, servers in the early 80s were an order of magnitude slower than computers in the early 90s, and computers at the turn of the millennia were roughly an order of magnitude faster than those in the early 90s. As I write this, in 2009, however, computers are not, strictly speaking, similarly faster than the computers in the late 90s. They've become more parallelized, and can better serve software designed to run in parallel. Thus, parallelization isn't just a good idea for big problems; it's a norm just to take full advantage of modern-day computing power.

On the Java landscape, this problem is even more pronounced because of Java's difficulty in addressing large amounts of RAM (anecdotally, 2GB to 4GB is about the max a single JVM can usefully address). There are garbage collectors in the works that seek to fix some of these issues, but the fact remains that a single computer can have far more RAM than a single JVM could ever usefully deal with. Parallelization is a must. Today, more and more enterprises are deploying entire virtualized operating system stacks on one server simply to isolate Java applications and fully exploit the hardware.

Thus, distribution isn't just a function of resilience or capability; it's a function of common-sense investing.

There are costs to parallelization, as well. There's always going to be some constraint, and very rarely is an entire system equally scalable. The cost of coordinating state between nodes, for example, might be too high because the network or hard disks impose latency. There are also other constraints. Notably, not all operations are parallelizable. It's important to design systems with this in mind. An example might be the overall processing of a person's uploaded photos (as happens in many web sites today). You might take the moment at which they upload the batch, to the moment a process has watermarked them and added them to an online photo album and measure the time during which the whole process is executed serially. Some of these steps are not parallelizable. The one part that is, the watermarking, will only lead to a fixed increase, and little can be done beyond that.

You can describe these gains. Amdahl's law, also known as Amdahl's argument, is a formula to find the maximum expected improvement to an overall system when only part of the system is improved. It is shown here:

$$\frac{1}{(1-P)+\left(\frac{P}{N}\right)}$$

It describes the relationship between a solutions execution time when serially executed and when executed in parallel with the same problem set. Thus, for 90 photos, if we know that it takes a minute for each photo, and that uploading takes 5 minutes, and that posting the resulting photos to the repository takes 5 minutes, the total time is 100 minutes when executed serially. Let's assume we add 9 workers to the watermarking process, for a total of 10 processes that watermark. In the equation, P is the portion of the process that can be parallelized, and N is the factor by which that portion might be parallelized (that is, the number of workers, in this case). For the process described, 90% of the process can be parallelized: each photo could be given to a different worker, which means it's parallelizable, which means that 90% of the serial execution is parallelizable. If you have 10 nodes working together, the equation is: 1/((1-.9) + (.9 / 10)), or 5.263. So, with 10 workers, the process could be 5x faster. With 100 workers, the equation yields 9.174, or 9x faster. It may not make sense to continue adding nodes as you'll achieve increasingly smaller gains.

Building an effective distributed solution, then, is an application of cost/benefit analysis. Spring has no direct support for distributed paradigms, *per se*, because plenty of other solutions do a great job already. Often, these solutions make Spring integration a first priority because it's a de-facto standard. In some cases, these projects forwent their own configuration format and use Spring itself as the configuration mechanism. If you decide to employ distribution, you'll be glad to know that there are many projects designed to meet the call, whatever it may be.

In this chapter, we discuss a few solutions that are Spring-friendly and ready. A lot of these solutions are possible because of Spring's support for "components," such as it's XML schema support and runtime class detection. These technologies often require you to change your frame of mind when building solutions, even if ever so slightly, as compared to solutions built using JEE, but being able to rely on your Spring skills is powerful. Other times, these solutions may not even be visible, except as configuration. Further still, a lot of these solutions expose themselves as standard interfaces familiar to JEE developers, or as infrastructure (such as, for example, backing for an HTTP session, or as a cluster-ready message queue) that goes unnoticed and isolated, except at the configuration level, thanks to Spring's dependency injection.

10-1. Cluster Object State Using Terracotta

Problem

You want to share object state across multiple virtual machines. For example, you'd like to be able to load all the cities in the United States into memory for faster lookup. Any other nodes in the cluster that need access to those objects should be able to get them from the cache, and not reload them.

Solution

You can use Terracotta to build such a solution. Terracotta works like many other clustered caches, except that it, in addition to being a good Hibernate clustered cache, also works as a mostly unnoticeable engine to enable API-free shared state across a cluster.

How It Works

Terracotta works as a JVM agent that monitors the object graph of a given JVM instance and ensures replication of object state across a cluster. It does this by deferring to a configuration file in which you specify which classes, methods, and fields should be clustered:

It does this for any object in the JVM, not just Hibernate entities or session entries, or objects otherwise updated by some caching API.

It's as simple as using a property on an object or updating a shared variable on an object. Instantly, across as many nodes as you want, that updated state is reflected in reads to that property on other instances.

To illustrate it, it's best to imagine a threaded application. Imagine a shared integer value in a threaded application. Three threads increment the value of an integer in lockstep, delayed every five seconds. Each thread acquires the lock, increments the integer, and then releases the lock. Other threads see the updated value and print it out. Eventually, as this goes on, the number rises and rises until some condition is met (you exit the program, for example.) to stop it. This is a very effective example of where Java's support for threading is useful, because it guarantees state through concurrent access. Now, imagine perhaps that you have that same integer, and each time a server hits a page, that integer is accessed and incremented. This page is deployed across several nodes, so that hitting the page on each of the nodes causes the integer, and thus the state, to change. Other servers see the new value on refresh, even though the change was last made on another server. The state is visible to all nodes in the cluster, and at the same times as the state would be visible to threads. This is what Terracotta does: it clusters object state. On the whole, your code will remain simple code (perhaps multithreaded in nature) that works across multiple VMs.

This is different than most clustered caches today because it has no visible API, and because it's far more efficient in conveying the changed state to nodes across the cluster. Most systems use some sort of Java serialization or broadcast mechanism, wherein each other node is given the entire object, or object graph, that's changed, regardless of whether they even they need to be aware of the new state. Terracotta does it differently: it deltas the memory of the object graphs itself and synchronizes other nodes in the cluster as they need a consistent view of the object state. Succinctly, it can do something tantamount to transmitting just one updated variable in an object, and not the entire object.

Deploying a Simple Example with Terracotta

You want to deploy Terracotta, and want to see what a simple application looks like, without Spring. We will walk through an example of how to do this, without using Spring. The example is a simple application that prompts for input and uses a service class that in turn keeps state. We cluster this state using Terracotta. A client manipulates a CustomerServiceImpl class, shown here, which is an implementation of CustomerService, which implements the following interface:

```
package
com.apress.springenterpriserecipes.distributedspring.terracotta.customerconsole.service;

import
com.apress.springenterpriserecipes.distributedspring.terracotta.customerconsole.entity.Custo
mer;

import java.util.Date;
import java.util.Collection;

public interface CustomerService {
    Customer getCustomerById( String id ) ;
    Customer createCustomer(
        String firstName, String lastName, Date birthdate ) ;
    Customer removeCustomer( String id ) ;
    Customer updateCustomer(
        String id, String firstName,
        String lastName, Date birthdate ) ;
    Collection<Customer > getAllCustomers() ;
}
```

As this is meant to be a gentle introduction to Terracotta, I'll forego building a complete Hibernate and Spring-based solution. The implementation will be an in-memory implementation.

```
package
com.apress.springenterpriserecipes.distributedspring.terracotta.customerconsole.service;

import com.apress.springenterpriserecipes.distributedspring.terracotta. ➥
customerconsole.entity.Customer;
import org.apache.commons.collections.CollectionUtils;
import org.apache.commons.collections.Predicate;

import java.util.*;

public class CustomerServiceImpl implements CustomerService {

    private final Set<Customer> customers;

    public CustomerServiceImpl() {
        customers = Collections.synchronizedSet(new HashSet<Customer>());
    }

    public Customer updateCustomer(
      String id, String firstName, String lastName, Date birthdate) {
        Customer customer;
        synchronized (customers) {
            customer = getCustomerById(id);
            customer.setBirthday(birthdate);
            customer.setFirstName(firstName);
            customer.setLastName(lastName);
```

```java
            removeCustomer(id);
            customers.add(customer);
        }
        return customer;
    }

    public Collection<Customer> getAllCustomers() {
        return (customers);
    }

    public Customer removeCustomer(String id) {
        Customer customerToRemove;
        synchronized (customers) {
            customerToRemove = getCustomerById(id);
            if (null != customerToRemove)
                customers.remove(customerToRemove);
        }
        return customerToRemove;
    }

    public Customer getCustomerById(final String id) {
        return (Customer) CollectionUtils.find(customers, new Predicate() {
            public boolean evaluate(Object o) {
                Customer customer = (Customer) o;
                return customer.getId().equals(id);
            }
        });
    }

    public Customer createCustomer(String firstName, String lastName, Date birthdate ){

        synchronized (customers) {
            final Customer newCustomer = new Customer(
                    firstName, lastName, birthdate);
            if (!customers.contains(newCustomer)) {
                customers.add(newCustomer);
                return newCustomer;
            } else {
                return (Customer) CollectionUtils.find(
                    customers, new Predicate() {
                    public boolean evaluate(Object o) {
                        Customer customer = (Customer) o;
                        return customer.equals(newCustomer);
                    }
                });
            }
        }
    }
}
```

The entity, Customer, is a simple POJO with accessors and mutators, and working equals, hashCode, toString methods.

```
// …
import java.io.Serializable;
import java.util.Date;
import java.util.UUID;

public class Customer implements Serializable {
    private String id;
    private String firstName, lastName;
    private Date birthday;
    // …
    // accessor/mutators, id, equals, and hashCode.
    // …
}
```

Note first that nothing we do in that class has any effect on Terracotta. We implement Serializable, ostensibly, because the class may very well be serialized in, for example, an HTTP session. The hashCode/equals implementations are just good practice.

The client that will allow us to interact with this service class is as follows:

```
package com.apress.springenterpriserecipes.distributedspring.terracotta. ➥
customerconsole.view;

import com.apress.springenterpriserecipes.distributedspring. ➥
terracotta.customerconsole.entity.Customer;
import com.apress.springenterpriserecipes.distributedspring. ➥
terracotta.customerconsole.service.CustomerService;
import org.apache.commons.lang.StringUtils;
import org.apache.commons.lang.SystemUtils;
import org.apache.commons.lang.exception.ExceptionUtils;

import javax.swing.*;
import java.text.DateFormat;
import java.text.ParseException;
import java.util.Date;

public class CustomerConsole {

        private void log(String msg) {
                System.out.println(msg);
        }

        private void list() {
                for (Customer customer : customerService.getAllCustomers())
                        log(customer.toString());
                log(SystemUtils.LINE_SEPARATOR);
        }
```

```java
private void create(String customerCreationString) {
        String cmd=
        StringUtils.defaultString(customerCreationString).trim();
        String[] parts = cmd.split(" ");
        String firstName = parts[1], lastName = parts[2];
        Date date = null;
        try {
           date =
        DateFormat.getDateInstance(DateFormat.SHORT).parse(parts[3]);
        } catch (ParseException e) {
           log(ExceptionUtils.getFullStackTrace(e));
        }
        customerService.createCustomer(firstName, lastName, date);
        list();
}

private void delete(String c) {
        log("delete:" + c);
        String id = StringUtils.defaultString(c).trim().split(" ")[1];
        customerService.removeCustomer(id);
        list();
}

private void update(String stringToUpdate) {
        String[] parts = StringUtils.defaultString(stringToUpdate).trim()
                         .split(" ");
        String idOfCustomerAsPrintedOnConsole = parts[1],
            firstName = parts[2],
            lastName = parts[3];
        Date date = null;
        try {
           date =
        DateFormat.getDateInstance(DateFormat.SHORT).parse(parts[4]);
        } catch (ParseException e) {
                log(ExceptionUtils.getFullStackTrace(e));
        }
        customerService.updateCustomer(idOfCustomerAsPrintedOnConsole,
                        firstName, lastName, date);
        list();
}

private CustomerService customerService;

public CustomerService getCustomerService() {
        return customerService;
}

public void setCustomerService(CustomerService customerService) {
        this.customerService = customerService;
}

enum Commands {
        LIST, UPDATE, DELETE, CREATE
}
```

381

```
public void handleNextCommand(String prompt) {
        System.out.println(prompt);

        String nextLine = JOptionPane.showInputDialog(null, prompt);
        if (StringUtils.isEmpty(nextLine)) {
                System.exit(1);
                return;
        }

        log(nextLine);
        if ((StringUtils.trim(nextLine).toUpperCase())
                        .startsWith(Commands.UPDATE.name())) {
                update(nextLine);
                return;
        }
        if ((StringUtils.trim(nextLine).toUpperCase())
                        .startsWith(Commands.DELETE.name())) {
                delete(nextLine);
                return;
        }
        if ((StringUtils.trim(nextLine).toUpperCase())
                        .startsWith(Commands.CREATE.name())) {
                create(nextLine);
                return;
        }

        if((StringUtils.trim(nextLine).toUpperCase()).startsWith(
         Commands.LIST.name())) {
                list();
                return;
        }
        System.exit(1);
}
```

Terracotta Architecture and Deployment

The client code is simple, as well. It's basically a dumb loop waiting for input. The client reacts to commands such as **create First Last 12/02/78**. You can test it out, without Terracotta, if you like. Simply run the class containing the `public static void main(String [] args)` method, as you would any other main class. If you're using Maven, you may simply execute:

mvn exec:java ➡

-Dexec.mainClass=com.apress.springenterpriserecipes.distributedspring

You can imagine how the client would work with Terracotta. The data managed by the CustomerService implementation is shared across a cluster. Changes to the data via an instance of the CustomerConsole on one machine should propagate to other machines instantly, and issuing a call to list() should reflect as much.

Let's dissect deployment. Terracotta is client/server architecture. The "server," in this case, is the one that contains the original working memory. It's what hands out deltas of changed memory to other nodes in the cluster. Other nodes "fault" in that memory as they need it. To deploy a Terracotta application, you first download the distribution. The distribution provides utility scripts, as well as jars. You may download Terracotta from http://www.terracotta.org.

For Terracotta to work, you need to provide it with a configuration file. This file is an XML file that we'll review shortly. You start Terracotta as follows:

```
$TERRACOTTA_HOME/bin/start-tc-server.sh -f $PATH_TO_TERRACOTTA_CONFIGURATION
```

For all virtual machine clients that you want to "see" and share that state, start it with a customized bootclasspath parameter when starting java. The arguments for this vary per operating system, so Terracotta provides a handy script for determining the correct arguments, dso-env.sh. When provided with the host and port of the Terracotta server, it can ensure that all configuration data for each client virtual machine is loaded dynamically from the server. As you might imagine, this greatly eases deployment over a grid of any substantive size! Here's how to use the script:

```
$TERRACOTTA_HOME/bin/dso-env.sh $HOST:$PORT
```

Replace $TERRACOTTA_HOME with the Terracotta's installation directory, and replace $HOST and $PORT with the host and port of the server instance. When run, it will print out the correct arguments, which you then need to feed into each client virtual machine's invocation scripts, for example in the $JAVA_OPTS section for Tomcat or any standard java invocation.

```
$ dso-env.sh localhost:9510
```

When executed, this will produce something like the following, which you need to ensure is used in your invocation of the java command:

```
...
-Xbootclasspath/p:c:\dev\terracotta-3.0.0\lib\dso-boot\dso-boot➥
hotspot_win32_160_14-ea.jar -Dtc.install-root=c:\dev\terracotta-3.0.0
```

How to Build a Terracotta XML Configuration File

The XML for the Terracotta configuration is verbose but self evident. Terracotta is a 99% code-incursion-free solution. Because Terracotta works at such a low level, you don't need to know about it when programming. The only thing of concern may be the introduction of threading issues, which you would not have to deal with in strictly serialized execution. There are no annotations, and no APIs, to direct Terracotta. Instead, Terracotta gets its information from the XML configuration file that you provide it. Our example XML file (tc-customerconsole-wo-spring.xml) is as follows:

```xml
<?xml version="1.0" encoding="UTF-8"?>
<tc:tc-config xmlns:tc="http://www.terracotta.org/config"
xmlns:xsi="http://www.w3.org/2001/XMLSchema-instance"
          xsi:schemaLocation="http://www.terracotta.org/schema/terracotta-4.xsd">
    <servers>
        <server host="%i" name="server1">
            <dso-port>9510</dso-port>
            <jmx-port>9520</jmx-port>
            <data>target/terracotta/server/data</data>
            <logs>target/terracotta/server/logs</logs>
            <statistics>target/terracotta/server/statistics</statistics>
        </server>
```

```xml
            <update-check>
                <enabled>true</enabled>
            </update-check>
        </servers>
        <system>
            <configuration-model>development</configuration-model>
        </system>
        <clients>
            <logs>target/terracotta/clients/logs/%(tc.nodeName)</logs>
            <statistics>target/terracotta/clients/statistics/%(tc.nodeName)</statistics>
        </clients>
        <application>
            <dso>
                <instrumented-classes>
                    <include>
                        <honor-transient>true</honor-transient>
                        <class-expression>
com.apress.springenterpriserecipes.distributedspring.terracotta. ➥
customerconsole.service.CustomerService*
                        </class-expression>
                    </include>
                    <include>
                        <honor-transient>true</honor-transient>
                        <class-expression>
com.apress.springenterpriserecipes.distributedspring. ➥
terracotta.customerconsole.entity.*
                        </class-expression>
                    </include>
                </instrumented-classes>
                <locks>
                    <autolock auto-synchronized="true">
                        <method-expression>*
com.apress.springenterpriserecipes.distributedspring. ➥
terracotta.customerconsole.entity.*.toString(..)
                        </method-expression>
                        <lock-level>read</lock-level>
                    </autolock>
                    <autolock auto-synchronized="true">
                        <method-expression>*
com.apress.springenterpriserecipes.distributedspring. ➥
terracotta.customerconsole.service.*.*(..)
                        </method-expression>
                        <lock-level>write</lock-level>
                    </autolock>
                </locks>
                <roots>
                    <root>
                        <field-name>
```

```
com.apress.springenterpriserecipes.distributedspring. ➥
terracotta.customerconsole.view.CustomerServiceImpl.customers</field-name>
            </root>
         </roots>
      </dso>
   </application>
</tc:tc-config>
```

The servers element tells Terracotta about how to the server behaves: on what port it listens, where logs are, and so forth. The application instance is what's of concern to us. Here, we first spell out which classes are to be clusterable in the instrumented-classes element.

The locks element lets us prescribe what behavior to ensure with regard to concurrent access of fields on classes. The last element, the field-name element, is the most interesting. This instruction tells Terrracotta to ensure that the changes to the customers field in the CustomerServiceImpl class are visible cluster-wide. An element inserted into the collection on one host is visible on other hosts, and this is the crux of our functionality.

10-2. Using Spring to Simplify Terracotta Configuration

Problem

You want to simplify configuration and have Terracotta cluster entire beans in Spring. Ideally, you'd like to let Terracotta resolve the information that we're already defining about classes in Spring.

Solution

Terracotta supports specialized configuration just for Spring. You can reference beans by bean name and it'll take care of resolving associated members of the object graph.

Approach

The configuration that we saw in the last recipe works fine for most cases, but it can quickly become tedious. Let's turn to Spring to simplify things, conceptually. In the previous example, we built an unnervingly simple application and then complicated it by introducing an XML configuration file. This situation would be further frustrating if we were using Spring, in which case we'd have to configure the same entity and service, two different ways.

Terracotta can benefit your Spring application directly and indirectly. In this example, we discuss using Terracotta to scale out Spring configured beans, directly. However, Terracotta also offers a powerful Ehcache integration and (in newer versions) there is Terracotta-based Hibernate provider as well. Thus, if you're using Ehcache with Hibernate, or as a separate install, this is a compelling option. Further, if you're using Hibernate and choose to use the Terracotta-based caching provider, there's value in Terracotta. Another area where Terracotta may significantly speed up your application is with its support for the HTTP Session. This can generally be useful to any web application, but in particular it can be very powerful for Spring Web Flow, which manages HTTP session memory.

Terracotta supports configuration using Spring-specific elements that let it infer a lot of the same data that we configured explicitly in the last example. First, let's take a look at the configuration of the classes as Spring beans. There's no need to put these collaborators together using Java; we merely need to acquire our reference from the context (customerconsole-context.xml).

```xml
<?xml version="1.0" encoding="UTF-8"?>

<beans xmlns="http://www.springframework.org/schema/beans"
       xmlns:xsi="http://www.w3.org/2001/XMLSchema-instance"
       xmlns:context="http://www.springframework.org/schema/context"
       xsi:schemaLocation="http://www.springframework.org/schema/beans
               http://www.springframework.org/schema/beans/spring-beans-3.0.xsd
http://www.springframework.org/schema/context
               http://www.springframework.org/schema/context/spring-context-3.0.xsd
http://www.springframework.org/schema/integration
                 ">

    <bean id="customerService"
class="com.apress.springenterpriserecipes.distributedspring.terracotta.customerconsole.servi
ce.CustomerServiceImpl"/>

    <bean id="customerConsole"
class="com.apress.springenterpriserecipes.distributedspring.terracotta.customerconsole.view.
CustomerConsole">
        <property name="customerService" ref="customerService"/>
    </bean>
</beans>
```

If we take a look at the revised (tc-customerconsole-w-spring.xml) example from the last recipe, the immediate benefit is apparent: it's much more concise! We've ripped out the application element entirely. Instead, we tell Terracotta about our Spring application context in the path element. It knows to consult that for information. Then, in the bean element, we specify which bean in the context to cluster:

```xml
<application>
        <spring>
            <jee-application name="*">
                <application-contexts>
                    <application-context>
                        <paths>
                            <path>customerconsole-context.xml</path>
                        </paths>
                        <beans>
                            <bean name="customerService"/>
                        </beans>
                    </application-context>
                </application-contexts>
                <locks>
                    <autolock>
                        <method-expression>*
com.apress.springenterpriserecipes.distributedspring.terracotta.customerconsole. ➥
service.CustomerServiceImpl.*(..)
                        </method-expression>
```

```
                    <lock-level>write</lock-level>
                </autolock>
            </locks>
        </jee-application>
    </spring>
</application>
```

You can still exercise all the same controls over the fields and so on as you could in the previous example, but in this case it might be easier to simply configure what shouldn't be clustered, such as injected connection pools, and so forth.

```
<beans>
<bean name="customerService">
    <non-distributed-field> connectionPool </non-distributed-field>
  </bean>
</beans>
```

Running this example is no different than in the last example; simply specify a different configuration XML file.

10-3. You Want to Farm Out Execution to a Grid

Problem
You want to distribute processing over many nodes, perhaps to increase result speed through the use of concurrences, perhaps merely to provide load balance and fault tolerance.

Solution
You can use something like GridGain, which was designed to transparently offload processing to a grid. This can be done many ways: one is to use the grid as a load alleviation mechanism, something to absorb the extra work. Another, if possible, is to split the job up in such a way that many nodes can work on it concurrently.

Approach
GridGain is an implementation of a processing grid. GridGain is different from Terracotta or Coherence because they are data grids. Data grids and processing grids are often used together, and in point of fact GridGain encourages the use of any number of data grids with its processing functionality. There are many data grids, such as Hadoop's HFS, which are designed to be fault-tolerant memory-based disks. These sorts of grids are natural compliments to a processing grid such as GridGain in that they can field massive amounts of data fast enough for a processing grid to keep busy. GridGain allows code to be farmed out to a grid for execution and then the results returned to the client, transparently. You can do this in many ways. The easiest route is to merely annotate the methods you want to be farmed out, and then configure some mechanism to detect and act on those annotations, and then you're done!

The other approach is slightly more involved, but it is where solutions such as GridGain and Hadoop really shine: use the Map/Reduce pattern to partition a job into smaller pieces and then run those pieces on the grid, concurrently. Map/Reduce is a pattern that was popularized by Google. Map/Reduce comes from functional programming languages, which often have map() and reduce() functions. The idea is that you somehow partition a job and send those pieces to be processed. Finally, you take the results and join them, and those results are then sent back. Often, you won't have results, per se; instead, you'll have sought only to distribute the processing asynchronously.

GridGain packs a lot of power in the few interfaces you're required to ever deal with. Its internal configuration system is Spring, and when you wish to avail yourself of anything besides the absolute minimum configuration options — for example, configuring a certain node with characteristics upon which job routing might be predicated — you do so using Spring. GridGain provides a Spring AOP Aspect for use on beans with the @Gridify annotation for the very simple cases.

Deployment

To get started, download GridGain from the web site, http://www.gridgain.com. Unzip the distribution and then descend into the bin directory and run gridgain.(bat|sh). If you're running a Unix/Linux instance, you may need to make the scripts executable:

```
chmod a+x *sh
```

You need to set up an environment variable, GRIDGAIN_HOME, pointing to the directory in which you installed the distribution for it to function correctly. If you're running Unix, you need to set the variable in your shell environment. Usually, this happens in something like ~.bashrc:

```
export GRIDGAIN_HOME=<YOUR DIRECTORY>
```

If you are running Windows, then you will need to go to System Properties -> Advanced -> Environment Variables and add a new system variable, GRIDGAIN_HOME, pointing to the directory of your installation. Regardless of what operating system you're using, you need to ensure that there are no trailing "/" or "\"s on the variable's path.

Finally, run the script.

```
./gridgain.sh
```

If you have more than a few hundred megabytes of RAM, you might run the script several times. Each invocation creates a new node, so that, in essence, you'll have started a grid on your local machine. GridGain uses multicast, so you could put GridGain on several boxes and run numerous instances on each machine, and they'd all join the same grid. If you want to expand your grid to 10 boxes, simply repeat the installation of the GridGain software and set up the environment variable on each. You can partition the grid and characteristics of the nodes using Spring, if you want, but for now we'll concern ourselves with the defaults.

Astonishingly, this is all that's required for deployment. Shortly, you'll create executable code (with numerous .jars, no doubt) and make changes on your local development machine, and then run the changed job and the rest of the nodes in the grid will just "notice" the updated job and participate in running it thanks to its first-rate class-loading magic. This mechanism, peer-to-peer class loading, means that you don't need to do anything to deploy a job besides run the code with the job itself once.

10-4. Load Balancing a Method

Problem

You want to quickly grid-enable a method on a bean using GridGain. You can see doing this, for example, to expose service methods that in turn instantiate longer-running jobs on the grid. One example might be sending notification e-mails, or image processing, or any process you don't want bogging down a single machine or VM instance, or whose results you need sooner.

Solution

You can use GridGain's @Gridify annotation along with some Spring AOP configuration to let GridGain know that it can parallelize the execution of the method across the grid.

Approach

The first use case you're likely to have is to simply be able to farm out functionality in a bean to other nodes, as a load-balancing precaution, for example. GridGain provides load balancing as well as fault tolerance and routing out of the box, which you get for free by adding this annotation. Let's take a look at a simple service bean with a single method that we want to farm out to the grid. The interface contract looks like the following:

```
package com.apress.springenterpriserecipes.distributedspring.gridgain;

public interface SalutationService {
    String saluteSomeoneInForeignLanguage( String recipient);
}
```

The only salient requirement here is the saluteSomeoneInForeignLanguage method. Naturally, this is also the method we want to be run on the grid when possible. The implementation looks like this:

```
package com.apress.springenterpriserecipes.distributedspring.gridgain;

import java.io.Serializable;
import java.util.HashMap;
import java.util.Locale;
import java.util.Map;
import java.util.Set;

import org.apache.commons.lang.StringUtils;
import org.gridgain.grid.gridify.Gridify;
import org.springframework.beans.BeansException;
import org.springframework.context.ApplicationContext;
import org.springframework.context.ApplicationContextAware;

/**
 * Admittedly trivial example of saying 'hello' in a few languages
 *
 */
public class SalutationServiceImpl implements SalutationService, Serializable,
ApplicationContextAware {

        private static final long serialVersionUID = 1L;

        private Map<String, String> salutations;

    public SalutationServiceImpl() {
        salutations = new HashMap<String, String>();
        salutations.put(Locale.FRENCH.getLanguage().toLowerCase(),
                    "bonjour %s!");
        salutations.put(Locale.ITALIAN.getLanguage().toLowerCase(),
                    "buongiorno %s!");
```

```java
        salutations.put(Locale.ENGLISH.getLanguage().toLowerCase(),
                        "hello %s!");
    }

    @Gridify
    public String saluteSomeoneInForeignLanguage(String recipient) {
        Locale[] locales = new Locale[]{
            Locale.FRENCH, Locale.ENGLISH, Locale.ITALIAN};
        Locale locale = locales[
            (int) Math.floor(Math.random() * locales.length)];
        String language = locale.getLanguage();
        Set<String> languages = salutations.keySet();
        if (!languages.contains(language))
            throw new java.lang.RuntimeException(
                String.format("this isn't supported! You need to choose " +
                        "from among the accepted languages: %s",
                        StringUtils.join(languages.iterator(), ",")));
        String salutation = String.format(
                salutations.get(language), recipient);
        System.out.println(String.format("returning: %s" ,salutation));
        return salutation;
    }

    @Gridify(taskClass = MultipleSalutationTask.class)
    public String[] saluteManyPeopleInRandomForeignLanguage(
        String[] recipients) {
        return recipients;
    }


    private ApplicationContext applicationContext;

    public void setApplicationContext(
        ApplicationContext applicationContext) throws BeansException {
        this.applicationContext = applicationContext;
    }
}
```

There are no tell-tale signs that this code is Grid-enabled except for the @Gridify annotation. Otherwise, the functionality is self-evident, and infinitely testable. We use Spring to ensure that this bean is given a chance to run. The configuration of the Spring file (gridservice.xml) side looks like this:

```xml
<?xml version="1.0" encoding="UTF-8"?>
<beans xmlns="http://www.springframework.org/schema/beans"
       xmlns:xsi="http://www.w3.org/2001/XMLSchema-instance"
       xmlns:util="http://www.springframework.org/schema/util"
       xmlns:aop="http://www.springframework.org/schema/aop"
       xsi:schemaLocation="
       http://www.springframework.org/schema/beans
http://www.springframework.org/schema/beans/spring-beans-3.0.xsd
        http://www.springframework.org/schema/aop
        http://www.springframework.org/schema/util/spring-aop-3.0.xsd
        http://www.springframework.org/schema/util
        http://www.springframework.org/schema/util/spring-util-3.0.xsd">
```

```
<bean id="myGrid" class="org.gridgain.grid.GridSpringBean"  scope="singleton">
    <property name="configuration">
            <bean id="grid.cfg" class="org.gridgain.grid.GridConfigurationAdapter"
scope="singleton">
                <property name="topologySpi">
                    <bean class="org.gridgain.grid.spi.topology.basic.GridBasicTopologySpi">
                        <property name="localNode" value="false"/>
                    </bean>
                </property>
            </bean>
    </property>
</bean>

<bean id="interceptor"
class="org.gridgain.grid.gridify.aop.spring.GridifySpringAspect"/>

<bean depends-on="myGrid" id="salutationService"
class="org.springframework.aop.framework.ProxyFactoryBean">
    <property name="autodetectInterfaces" value="false"/>
    <property name="target">
        <bean
class="com.apress.springenterpriserecipes.distributedspring.gridgain.SalutationServiceImpl"/
>
    </property>
    <property name="interceptorNames">
        <list>
            <value>interceptor</value>
        </list>
    </property>
</bean>
</beans>
```

Here, we use a plain, old-style AOP Proxy in conjunction with the GridGain aspect to proxy our humble service class. I override topologySpi to set localNode to false, which has the effect of stopping jobs from being run on the invoking node, which in this case is our service bean's node. The idea is that this node is, locally, the front for application services, and it's inappropriate to run jobs on that virtual machine, which may be handling highly transactional workloads. You might set the value to true if you don't mind a node bearing the load of both handling the services *and* acting as a grid node. Because you usually set up a Grid to offload work to some other node, this is usually not desirable. We know that invoking that service will cause it to be farmed out. Here's a simple client. The parameter is the only context we have and it's the only thing you can rely on being present on the node that's run. You can't, if you're running the nodes via the startup script mentioned previously, rely on the Spring beans being wired up. We'll explore this further. In the meantime, witness our client:

```
package com.apress.springenterpriserecipes.distributedspring.gridgain;

import org.springframework.context.ApplicationContext;
import org.springframework.context.support.ClassPathXmlApplicationContext;

import java.util.Locale;

public class Main {
```

```
    public static void main(String[] args) throws Throwable {

        ApplicationContext applicationContext = new
ClassPathXmlApplicationContext("gridservice.xml");

        SalutationService salutationServiceImpl = (SalutationService)
applicationContext.getBean("salutationService");

        String[] names =("Alan,Arin,Clark,Craig,Drew,Duncan,Gary,Gordon,Fumiko,"+
"Hicham,James,Jordon,Kathy,Ken,Makani,Manuel,Mario, "+
"Mark,Mia,Mike,Nick,Richard,Richelle, "+
"Rod,Ron,Scott,Shaun,Srinivas,Valerie,Venkatesh").split(",");

        Locale[] locales = new Locale[]{
          Locale.FRENCH, Locale.ENGLISH, Locale.ITALIAN};

        for (String name : names) {
            System.out.println("Result: " +
                salutationServiceImpl.saluteSomeoneInForeignLanguage(name));
        }
    }
}
```

When you run this, you'll witness — on as many command-line consoles as you've opened by clicking on the startup script — the jobs being handled in a round-robin fashion, each on its own node. If you had 100 names and 10 nodes, you'd notice that each node gets about 10 names listed on the command line, for example.

10-5. Parallelizing Processing

Problem
You want to build a parallelized solution for a problem that's intrinsically better-suited to parallelization or that, for want of resources, needs to be chunked.

Solution
Use Map/Reduce to approach the problem concurrently. As was mentioned earlier, decisions to parallelize shouldn't be taken lightly, but with an eye on the ultimate performance expectations and tradeoffs.

Approach
Underneath the hood, GridGain works with a GridTask, which tells GridGain how to handle the main unit of work, GridJob. Sometimes, GridTask splits up and reconciles large jobs. This process is simplified by abstract adapter classes. In this case, we'll use one called GridifyTaskSplitAdapter, which abstracts away most of the minutiae of building a map/reduce-oriented solution. It provides two template methods that we need to override.

In this example, we'll build a modified version of the previous solution that takes an array of String parameters. We intend for all entries in the array to be farmed out to the grid. Let's add the call from the client, which is the Main class we used earlier:

```
System.out.println("Results:" + StringUtils.join(
salutationServiceImpl.saluteManyPeopleInRandomForeignLanguage(names), ","));
```

We add one method to the original service interface and implementation.

```
@Gridify( taskClass = MultipleSalutationTask.class )
    public String[] saluteManyPeopleInRandomForeignLanguage(String[] recipients) {
        return recipients;
    }
```

As you can see, the method is simple. The only salient piece is the modified @Gridify annotation, which in this case has a taskClass parameter pointing to a MultipleSalutationTask class.

```
import java.io.Serializable;
import java.util.ArrayList;
import java.util.Collection;
import java.util.List;

import org.gridgain.grid.GridException;
import org.gridgain.grid.GridJob;
import org.gridgain.grid.GridJobAdapter;
import org.gridgain.grid.GridJobResult;
import org.gridgain.grid.gridify.GridifyArgument;
import org.gridgain.grid.gridify.GridifyTaskSplitAdapter;

public class MultipleSalutationTask extends GridifyTaskSplitAdapter<String[]> {

    private static final long serialVersionUID = 1L;

    protected Collection<? extends GridJob> split(int i,
            final GridifyArgument gridifyArgument) throws GridException {

        Collection<GridJob> jobs = new ArrayList<GridJob>();
        Object[] params = gridifyArgument.getMethodParameters();
        String[] names = (String[]) params[0];
        for (final String n : names)
            jobs.add(new GridJobAdapter<String>(n) {
                private static final long serialVersionUID = 1L;

                public Serializable execute() throws GridException {
                    SalutationService service =
                        (SalutationService) gridifyArgument.getTarget();
                    return service.saluteSomeoneInForeignLanguage(n);
                }
            });

        return jobs;

    }
```

393

```
public String[] reduce(List<GridJobResult> gridJobResults)
   throws GridException {
   Collection<String> res = new ArrayList<String>();
   for (GridJobResult result : gridJobResults) {
      String data = result.getData();
      res.add(data);
   }
   return res.toArray(new String[res.size()]);

   }
}
```

This code is pretty easy to follow, but there is some "magic" going on that you need to be aware of. When you call the method on the service with the @Gridify annotation pointing to this GridTask class, it stops execution of method and loads an instance of this class. The parameters, as passed to the method with the annotation, are passed to: split(int i, final GridifyArgument gridifyArgument), which is used to dole out GridJob instances, each one taking as their payload a name from the array. In this code, we create the GridJob instances inline using GridJobAdapter, which is a template class. The work of each GridJob instance is trivial; in this case, we actually just delegate to the first method on the service that we created: saluteSomeoneInForeignLanguage. Note that the invocation of the service in this case does *not* run the job on the grid again, as we're already on a node. The result is returned to the calling context, which in this case is another virtual machine altogether.

All the results are collected and then passed to the reduce method on the Task class. This method is responsible for doing something with the final results. In this case, the results are simply unwrapped and returned as an array of Strings. Those results are then again sent to the calling context, which in this case is our original method invocation on the service. The results returned from that invocation are the results of all the processing. Thus, if you invoke saluteManyPeopleInRandomForeignLanguage with new String[]{"Steve"}, you're likely to get "Bonjour Steve! " (or something like that), even though it appears you're merely returning the input parameter.

10-6. On GridGain Deployment

Problem

There are several issues to be aware of when deploying applications using GridGain. How do you configure nodes with specific properties that can be used for determining its eligibility for a certain job? How do you inject Spring beans into a node? What is a .GAR?

Solution

The issues you're likely to confront when using GridGaim stem mostly from the fact that what you develop on one node can't always automatically work on another node with no additional configuration. It becomes helpful to think about these deployment issues ahead of time, before you run into a wall in production.

Approach

In the previous examples, we deployed simple processing solutions that are deployable using GridGain's peer-to-peer class-loading mechanism. We haven't done anything too complex, however, and as they say, the devil's in the details.

Creating a Grid Node

Let's look at the infrastructural components of GridGain in detail. First, let's consider how a node is started up. As we saw before, GridGain lets you start up nodes using the startup script in the bin directory of the distribution. This script invokes a class of type GridLoader, of which there are many. The GridLoader's job is to hoist a grid node into existence. It responds to the lifecycle events and knows how to work in specific environments. The one that gets started when you use the script that comes with the distribution is the GridCommandLineLoader. There are others, though, including several for loading a grid instance from within a servlet container or application server instance. A GridLoader instance is responsible for many things, not the least of which is correctly calling GridFactory.start and GridFactory.stop.

GridFactory.start can take as its first parameter a GridConfiguration object or a Spring application context or a path to a Spring application context. This GridConfiguration object is what tells GridGain what is unique about a given node and the grid's topology. By default, it uses $GRIDGAIN_HOME/config/default-spring.xml, which in turn does things such as load a Grid object and configure user parameters about a specific node. These parameters may be queried to determine the candidacy of a node to handle a specific job. GridGain, because it is so deeply rooted in Spring, is very flexible and configurable. Different subsystems may be swapped out and replaced. GridGain provides several options via its SPIs. In the directory where default-spring.xml is located, there are several other Spring configurations for grids demonstrating integrations with many other technologies. Perhaps you'd like to use JMS as your message exchange platform? There are examples there for three different vendors. Perhaps you'd like to use Mule, or JBoss Cache?

Provisioning a Grid Node

In the previous examples, we deployed instances that were self-contained and had no dependency on any other components. When we do start introducing dependency — and you will, naturally — you'll want to be able to leverage Spring for dependency injection. At this point, we lose some of the elegance of GridGain's peer-to-peer class loading.

You can deploy a .GAR archive, for which there is an ant task, to package your .jars and resources and then deploy that to every node's $GRIDGAIN_HOME/work/deployment/file folder. This is far easier than it sounds if you can get away with an NFS mount or something like that to simplify deployment. Additionally, you can tell GridGain to load a resource from a, HTTP, or another remote, URL.

This mechanism has a lot of advantages for production: your extra .jars are visible to the node (which means you won't have to transfer megabytes of libraries over the wire each time you hot redeploy a node instance), and, most importantly, the custom beans inside the Spring application context we've been working with will be visible should you need them. When using this method, you can disable peer-to-peer class loading; this, while not significant, represents a gain in startup time.

A .GAR archive looks like a standard .JAR or .WAR. It provides several things that are mainly of concern for production. The first is that the libraries are already present, which we discussed. Secondly, the gridgain.xml file, which is optional, enables you to tell GridGain about which GridTask classes are deployed.

```
*class
lib/*jar
META-INF/{gridgain.xml,*}
```

The gridgain.xml is a simple Spring application context. An example configuration is as follows:

```
<?xml version="1.0" encoding="UTF-8"?>

<beans xmlns="http://www.springframework.org/schema/beans"
       xmlns:xsi="http://www.w3.org/2001/XMLSchema-instance"
       xmlns:util="http://www.springframework.org/schema/util"
       xsi:schemaLocation="
        http://www.springframework.org/schema/beans
http://www.springframework.org/schema/beans/spring-beans-3.0.xsd
        http://www.springframework.org/schema/util
http://www.springframework.org/schema/util/spring-util-3.0.xsd">
    <description>Gridgain configuration file in gar-file.</description>

    <util:list id="tasks">
        <value>org.gridgain.examples.gar.GridGarHelloWorldTask</value>
    </util:list>
</beans>
```

In this file, we provide a list with id "tasks." This file is consulted to help load any tasks contained in the GAR file. If you don't specify anything, GridGain will simply search for tasks itself.

Getting Access To The Spring Container From a Task

Instances of the ApplicationContext can be injected into the various GridGain class instances (GridTask, GridJob,and so forth) using GridGain's @GridSpringApplicationContextResource annotation. This example shows the Spring application context being injected using the @GridSpringApplicationContextResource annotation. This works like @Autowired or @Resource:

```
@GridSpringApplicationContextResource
private ApplicationContext applicationContext ;
```

Additionally, you can get components injected directly, using the @GridSpringResource:

```
@GridSpringResource(resourceName = "customerServiceBean")
private transient CustomerService customerService ;
```

Note the use of transient. These resources aren't copied across the wire, but rather, re-injected on each node's initialization. This is a crucial tool in your tool belt, especially with volatile resources that aren't amenable to being sent over the wire, such as DataSources.

Node-Specific GridGain Configuration

When you start GridGain via the gridgain.sh script, it provides very good defaults. However, sometimes you will want to exercise more control over the process.

When gridgain.sh is run, it consults (of all things!) a Spring application context for its configuration information. This file, located at **$GRIDGAIN_HOME/config/default-spring.xml**, contains all the information for GridGain to do what it does — communicate with other nodes, clusters, and so forth. Usually, this works well enough. However, there are *many* things you may want to configure, and because GridGain is Spring-friendly from the core, this is very easy. If instead you'd like to override the settings in that file, pass in your own application context:

```
./gridgain.sh my-application-context.xml
```

If you want even further control over the process, down to the last shell script, you can bootstrap the GridGain grid nodes yourself. The crux of the process is a call to

```
org.gridgain.grid.GridFactory.start( "my-application-context.xml") ;
```

There are many versions of the start method, but most of them take a Spring application context (either an instance of ApplicationContext, or a String or URL to an XML application context). The application context is where you configure the grid node.

There are many pre-built implementations for starting a Grid instance, however, and you'll rarely need to write your own. The implementations, called Grid Loaders, provide the necessary integration to start the Grid in many different environments. Summarized in Table 10-1 are some of the common ones.

Table 10-1 Common GridLoader implementations that you can use in different environments.

Table 10-1. Description of the various GridLoader implementations.

Class	Description
org.gridgain.grid.loaders.cmdline.GridCommandLineLoader	This is the default implementation. This is what is used when you run gridgain.sh or gridgain.bat.
org.gridgain.grid.loaders.servlet.GridServletLoader	This is likely the second most useful implementation. This provides a servlet that bootstraps the GridGain instance inside any web container as a servlet.
org.gridgain.grid.loaders.jboss.GridJbossLoader	Provides a hook for running a Grid inside of JBoss as JMX MBean
org.gridgain.grid.loaders.weblogic.GridWeblogicStartup, org.gridgain.grid.loaders.weblogic.GridWeblogicShutdown	Provides integration with Weblogic's infrastructure for JMX (monitoring), logging, and the WorkManager implementation.
org.gridgain.grid.loaders.websphere.GridWebsphereLoader	This GridGain loader is implemented as a JMX MBean. This, like the WebLogic integration, provides integration with logging, and the WorkManager implementation.
org.gridgain.grid.loaders.glassfish.GridGlassfishLoader	Provides integration with Glassfish as a lifecycle listener that works on both Glassfish 1 and 2.

In most of the loaders in Table 10-1 will be some sort of parameter that lets you provide the URL to a Spring XML application context file.

Because GridGain itself is built on top of Spring, most of its "plumbing" is configurable. You might, for example, want to use a JMS queue for the communications layer between nodes. You might want to override the discovery mechanism. You might want to make use of any of numerous caching solutions on the market. There are too many permutations to list, but the distribution itself will contain a config/ directory in which you can find numerous example configurations.

One common requirement is sharing one LAN with multiple grids. You could conceivably have 5 nodes doing one kind of processing, and another 10 doing another type for a different project, without requiring a separate subnet.

You partition the cluster by setting the gridName property. gridName enables you to start several grids on the same LAN without fear of one grid stealing another grid's jobs.

An example might be as follows:

```xml
<?xml version="1.0" encoding="UTF-8"?>

<beans xmlns="http://www.springframework.org/schema/beans"
       xmlns:xsi="http://www.w3.org/2001/XMLSchema-instance"
       xmlns:util="http://www.springframework.org/schema/util"
       xsi:schemaLocation="
        http://www.springframework.org/schema/beans
http://www.springframework.org/schema/beans/spring-beans-3.0.xsd
        http://www.springframework.org/schema/util
http://www.springframework.org/schema/util/spring-util-3.0.xsd">

    <bean id="grid.cfg" class="org.gridgain.grid.GridConfigurationAdapter"
scope="singleton">
        <property name="gridName" value="mygrid-001"/>

        <!-- ... other configuration … -->

    </bean>
</beans>
```

The next level of parameterization is user attributes. These parameters are specific to the node on which they're configured. You might imagine using these to partition your grid jobs, or to provide box-specific metadata like a NFS mount, or which FireWire or USB device to consult for something. In the following example, we use it to describe to the node on which countries' data it should concern itself with:

```xml
<?xml version="1.0" encoding="UTF-8"?>

<beans xmlns="http://www.springframework.org/schema/beans"
       xmlns:xsi="http://www.w3.org/2001/XMLSchema-instance"
       xmlns:util="http://www.springframework.org/schema/util"
       xsi:schemaLocation="
        http://www.springframework.org/schema/beans
http://www.springframework.org/schema/beans/spring-beans-3.0.xsd
        http://www.springframework.org/schema/util
http://www.springframework.org/schema/util/spring-util-3.0.xsd">
```

```
    <bean id="grid.cfg" class="org.gridgain.grid.GridConfigurationAdapter"
scope="singleton">
        <property name="userAttributes">
            <map>
                <entry key="countries">
                <util:list>
                        <value>FR</value>
                        <value>MX</value>
                        <value>CA</value>
                        <value>BG</value>
                        <value>JP</value>
                        <value>PH</value>
                </util:list>
                </entry>
            </map>
        </property>
    </bean>
</beans>
```

You may access parameters configured in this way using the GridNode interface:

```
GridNode gridNode = GridFactory.getGrid().getLocalNode();
Serializable attribute = gridNode.getAttribute("countries");
```

Summary

In this chapter, you explored the foundations of distributed computing and the use of grids for both processing and storage. You learned how to use Terracotta to synchronize your application's memory over a cluster so that it is highly available and in memory. You learned how to use GridGain to build a processing grid to distribute the load of a large job over smaller, more plentiful nodes. You learned about the basics of the map/reduce pattern, which enables you to build a parallelized solution for better performance, and you learned how to use GridGain's annotation-based approach to easily leverage a bean's methods on a cluster. Lastly, you learned how clustered GridGain jobs can access beans from a Spring application context.

In the next chapter, you'll learn about business process management and jBPM. You'll learn what BPM is, as a discipline and as a technology. You'll also learn how to use jBPM to build a processing solution with Spring.

CHAPTER 11

■ ■ ■

jBPM and Spring

A business is only as good as its processes. Often, businesses will thread together the contributions of multiple resources (people, automated computer processes, and so forth) to achieve a greater result. These individual contributions by people and automatic services are most efficient when single-focused and, ideally, reused. The simplest example of this might be a conveyor belt in a car factory, where work enters the line at the beginning of the conveyer belt and is worked on by any number of individuals or machines until finally the output of the work reaches the end of the line, at which point the job is done. One machine paints the chassis; another machine lowers the engine into the car. A person screws in and attaches the chairs and another person installs the radio. These people and machines do their work without worrying about what's going to happen to the car next.

A more complicated, interesting process—to take the car example even further—can be seen at a car dealership. There are many workers whose job depends on playing their role in selling you a car. It starts when you enter the car dealership and salesmen descend on you like wolves. Somebody walks with you, showing off models and features and answering questions. Finally, your eye catches the glimmer of a silver Porsche sitting an aisle over. You're sold. The next part of the process begins.

You're whisked away into the office where somebody starts prompting you for information to purchase the vehicle. You either have cash on hand, or you require a loan, or you've already got a loan from another bank. If you have cash on hand, you give it to them and wait an hour for them to count it. Perhaps you've got a check from the bank, in which case you give them that. Or, you begin the process of applying for a loan with the dealership. Eventually, the pecuniary details are sorted, credit scores checked, driver's license and insurance verified, and you begin signing paper work. If you've already paid for the car then the paper work to ensure proper title and registration is drawn up. If you're establishing a loan with the dealership, you fill out that paperwork, then work on registration, and so on.

Eventually, you're given the keys, the car, and the relevant paperwork and you're done. Or so you think. You make a break for the door, just itching to see how fast you can get the car to 65, which is the maximum speed limit in your area freeway, conditions permitting. As you arrive at the door, you're all but assaulted with one last packet of brochures and business cards and a branded pen and the good wishes of the grinning salesmen.

Baffled, you shrug them off and break for the car, jumping into the sporty convertible's driver's seat. As you leave, you turn the music up and speed off into the horizon. You'll remember that you left your wife at the dealership eventually, but for now, the fruit of all that bureaucracy is too sweet to ignore.

The process to buy the car may seem like it takes forever, and indeed, it does take a long time. However, the process is efficient in that all things that can be done at the same time are done at the same time, by multiple workers. Further, because each actor knows his part, each individual step is as efficient as possible. Being able to orchestrate a process like this is crucial in the enterprise.

You can extrapolate here, too. These examples are relatively small, though perhaps the inefficiencies of the worst-case scenario for the process are tolerable. The inefficiencies are overwhelmingly untenable in even slightly larger business processes, though! For example, imagine the new-hire process at a large company. Beyond the initial process of interviewing and a background security check, there's the provisioning that's required to get the new employee installed. The IT department needs to repurpose a laptop, image it, and install an operating system. Somebody needs to create a user account for that employee and ensure that LDAP and email are accessible. Somebody needs to ready a security card so that the employee can use the elevator or enter the building. Somebody needs to make sure the employee's desk station or office is cleaned, that remnants from the previous occupant are gone. Somebody needs to get forms for the health insurance or benefits, and somebody needs to give the new employee a walk around the office, introducing the employee to staff.

Imagine having only one person to do all of that for each employee! In a bigger company (such as a bank, for example) this process would soon become overwhelming! Indeed, many of the tasks mentioned themselves have many steps that are required to achieve the goal. Thus, the main process—integrating a new employee in the company—has multiple sub-processes. If all the tasks are performed concurrently by many people, however, the process becomes manageable. Additionally, not all people are suited to doing all of those tasks. A little specialization makes for a lot of efficiency here.

We see that processes, and the understanding of those processes, are *crucial* to a business. It is from this revelation that the study of business management emerged, called Business Process Management (BPM). BPM originally described how to best orchestrate technology and people to the betterment of the business, but it was a businessman's preoccupation, not a technologist's. As it became apparent that businesses were already leveraging technology, the next hurdle was to codify the notion of a business process. How could software systems know—and react to—what the immovable enterprises and unbending market forces demanded? BPM provides the answer. It describes in higher-level diagrams the "flow" a given process takes from start to finish. These diagrams are useful both to the business analyst and to the programmer, because they describe two sides of the same coin. Once a process is codified, it can be reused and reapplied in the same way a programmer reuses a class in Java.

Software Processes

Thus, the unit of work—that which is required to achieve a quantifiable goal—for a business is rarely a single request/response. Even the simplest of processes in a business require at least a few steps. This is true not just in business, but in your users' use-cases. Short of simple read-only scenarios such as looking at a web page for the news, most meaningful processes require multiple steps. Think through the sign-up process of your typical web application. It begins with a user visiting a site and filling out a form. The user completes the form and submits the finalized data, after satisfying validation. If you think about it, however, this is just the beginning of the work for this very simple process. Typically, to avoid spam, a verification e-mail will be sent to the user. When the e-mail is read, the user clicks on a link to confirm the intentions of the registrant, and that the registrant is not a robot. This tells the server that the user is a valid user, and that a welcome e-mail should be sent. A welcome e-mail is then sent. Here alone we had four steps with two different "roles!" This involved process, when translated into an activity diagram, is shown in figure 11-1.

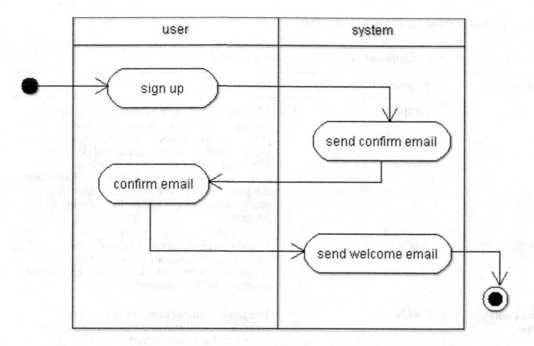

Figure 11-1. *The two roles(user, and system) are shown as swimlanes. Rounded shapes inside the swimlanes are states. Process flows from one state to another, following the path of the connecting lines.*

For such a simple process, it might be tempting to keep track of the state of the process in the domain model. After all, some of the state, such as the sign-up date, can certainly be regarded as business data, belonging to model entities. Such a date is valuable for revenue recognition. The date when the welcome e-mail was sent is probably not very important, though. The situation will escalate if you send out more e-mails. If you build other kinds of processes involving the user, then management of the user's state within those processes will become a burden on your system and will complicate the schema.

A workflow system extricates that process state from the domain and into a separate layer, called a business process. A workflow system also typically models which agents in the system do what work, providing work lists for different agents in the system.

A workflow engine lets you model the process in a higher-level form, roughly corresponding in code what a UML activity diagram can describe. Because a workflow is high-level, specifying how a business process is leveraged as an executable component of a system is a dizzyingly vast task. In industry, there are standards for the language used to model a business process as well as the model of the engine that's used to run the business process. Additionally, there are standards specifying interoperability, how endpoints are mapped to the agents being orchestrated by the process, and much more. Indeed, it can quickly become overwhelming.

Let's look at some of these standards in Table 11-1.

Table 11-1. some of the myriad, significant standards surrounding BPM

Standard Name	Standards Group	Description
WS-BPEL (BPEL)	OASIS	A language that, when deployed to a BPEL container, describes the execution of a process. It interfaces with the outside world via the invocation of external web services. This language describes the runtime behavior of a process. It has several flaws, not the least of which is the reliance on web service technology and the lack of work-list support.
WS-BPEL (BPEL 2.0)	OASIS	Largely an upgrade to its predecessor, clarifying the behavior at runtime of certain elements and adding more expressive elements to the language.
WS-BPEL for People (BPEL4People)	OASIS	The main feature common to traditional "workflow" systems is the ability to support work lists for actors in a process. BPEL had no such support as it didn't support human tasks (that is, wait states for people). This specification addresses that exact shortcoming.
Business Process Modeling Notation (BPMN)	Originally BPMI, then OMG, as the two organizations merged	Provides a set of diagramming notations that describe a business process. This notation is akin to UML's activity diagram, though the specification also describes how the notations relate to runtime languages such as BPEL. The notation is sometimes ambiguous, however, and one of the formidable challenges facing BPM vendors is creating a drawing tool that can round-trip to BPEL and back, providing seamless authoring.
XML Process Definition Language	Workflow Management Coalition (WfMC)	Describes the interchange of diagrams between modeling tools, especially how elements are displayed and the semantics of those elements to the target notation.

As you can see, there are some problems. Some of these standards are ill-suited to real business needs, even once the busywork is surmounted. Some of these standards lack adequate support for work lists—essentially making the processes useless for anything that models human interaction, a fairly typical requirement.

While a lot of this is slowly getting better, there's no reason to wait. There are viable de-facto standards that meet a lot of these problems and offer a compelling alternative. In this chapter, we will review jBPM, a popular open source environment. You might take a look at the alternative open source workflow engines (Enhydra Shark, or OpenWFE, for example) or, indeed, the proprietary engines from Tibco, IBM, Oracle, WebMethods, and so forth, before you decide on jBPM. In our opinion, it's powerful enough for easily 80% of the situations you're likely to encounter, and can at least facilitate solutions for another 10%.

Ultimately, jBPM integrates well with Spring, and it provides a very powerful complement to the features of the things we've discussed in this book and indeed to the core Spring framework itself. Just as a page-flow description language threads together multiple requests in a web application, workflows thread together many disparate actors (both people and automatic computer processes) into a process, keeping track of state. Workflow support becomes far more compelling in an architecture using even a few of the technologies we've covered in this book: messaging, distributed computing, ESB endpoints, web services, and long-lived processing infrastructure, for example! Workflow orchestrates these different, powerful tools and provides cohesion. Eventually, you'll even begin to reuse processes much like you might reuse a class or a Spring Integration endpoint.

11-1. Understanding Workflow Models

Problem

You understand the "why" behind business processes, and have identified types of problems that might be well-suited to this technology. Now you want to understand how—after all, it all sounds so nebulous and abstract. How do you describe and speak about a workflow, exactly?

Solution

It turns out, happily, that you probably already know most of what you need to describe a workflow engine. This is part of why a workflow engine is so powerful—it formalizes and facilitates solutions you're already struggling to build in other technologies. In fact, when you draw an activity diagram, the result is likely directly translatable into a workflow. As you'll see, a lot of the constructs used to build a business process are familiar. We've discussed many of them in our discussions of Spring Integration and Spring Batch and of the map/reduce pattern with GridGain.

Approach

One metric by which you might judge an engine is how well it lets you express workflow patterns. The workflow patterns describe different idioms that you might apply to a pattern. All patterns ultimately are built out of any mixture of a few key concepts, many of which we've discussed in other chapters of this book, as with Spring Batch and Spring Integration.

Table 11-2. A list of the kinds of constructs you will use when working with a BPM or workflow system and their description.

Concept	Description
State	A state can mean many things, but simply, it's a pause or window in the action. It's a way of letting your process rest in a known condition indefinitely. Perhaps during this time, an external event might take place, or the system might wait for an input. Perhaps the state is entered and then left as quickly as can be, serving only to provide record of the event. This is one of the simplest and most powerful functions of a workflow engine. Indeed, all discussions of long-lived state, of conversational state, and of continuations are centered on this concept. It allows your process to stop and wait for an event that tells it to proceed. This is powerful because it implies that no resources need to be wasted waiting for that event, and that the process can effectively sleep, or passivate, until such an event, at which point the workflow engine will "wake" the process up and start it moving.
Activity	An activity is a pause in the action that can only move forward when a known actor or agent in the system moves it forward. You might imagine the moderator or group admin who has to OK your subscription to a news group. In that case, only specified agents or roles may say the process may move forward.
Sequence	A sequence is simply an aggregation of states, activities, and other types of constructs that serializes them. You might have three states and an activity. You might imagine them as steps on a ladder, where the ladder is the sequence directing the process upwards to the ultimate goal.
Fork/Concurrence/ Split	The reason a sequence is important is because it implies there's another way of threading things along. A fork is a concurrent execution of multiple threads of execution at the same time, originating from a common thread. Some parts of a business process are inherently sequential, and some are readily concurrent. In the new employee example explored previously, you might imagine the security clearance, laptop provisioning, and other tasks could be done at the same time, thus increasing the speed of the process.
Sub Process	In the new employee example, we discuss several tasks that need to be performed by representatives of different departments. Each department may have its own task list to complete in order to achieve the goals of the overarching process. These sub-tasks (basically a separate process unto their own) may be modeled as a sub-process. Sub-processes afford your workflows the same flexibility through reuse that composition through functions or classes affords your programs.

11-2. Installing jBPM

Problem

You want to build a jBPM solution and need to know the simplest way to get the jars. There are many supported workflows for jBPM, so it isn't clear where to begin for what role. For a business analyst, the path is different than for a programmer, whose task it will be to employ jBPM, not deploy it. You will need a few libraries first.

Approach

You can use jBPM as an API, rather than as a server or service. This integration is the most natural to a developer, but not, for example, to a business user. We'll use Maven to get the dependencies.

While we'll focus on embedding jBPM in this chapter, it's useful to see the other ways you can integrate jBPM into your architecture.

- A developer may embed jBPM as services and Hibernate entities.

- A developer may deploy jBPM into a stand-alone server, and then use the administration console to deploy and test processes.

- jBPM 4.1 ships with a web application in which a user can diagram and test processes.

Solution

For this example, we're using a few libraries for AOP, transactions, the core Spring context, and, of course, jBPM itself.

If you're looking to find out more, read the documentation, and get the downloadable binaries for exploration, check out http://jboss.org/jbossjbpm/. There, you can find a lot of useful information.

Because we're looking to embed it, we'll simply get the libraries and use them in our own solution. If you're using Maven, the pom.xml file will contain the latest version of the following dependency entries. You may of course customize this as you see fit, but it's a good start. These are relatively current, and known-to-be-working, versions of the jars required to get started, as of the time of this writing.

```xml
<!-- JBPM -->
<dependency>
        <groupId>org.jbpm.jbpm4</groupId>
        <artifactId>jbpm-jpdl</artifactId>
        <version>4.0</version>
</dependency>

<!-- JSR 250 annotations -->
<dependency>
        <groupId>javax.annotation</groupId>
        <artifactId>jsr250-api</artifactId>
        <version>1.0</version>
</dependency>
```

```
<!--   GENERAL -->
<dependency>
        <groupId>commons-dbcp</groupId>
        <artifactId>commons-dbcp</artifactId>
        <version>1.2.1</version>
        <exclusions>
                <exclusion>
                        <groupId>xerces</groupId>
                        <artifactId>xercesImpl</artifactId>
                </exclusion>
        </exclusions>
</dependency>
<dependency>
        <groupId>xerces</groupId>
        <artifactId>xercesImpl</artifactId>
        <version>2.7.1</version>
</dependency>
<dependency>
        <groupId>commons-lang</groupId>
        <artifactId>commons-lang</artifactId>
        <version>2.2</version>
</dependency>
<dependency>
        <groupId>commons-io</groupId>
        <artifactId>commons-io</artifactId>
        <version>1.1</version>
</dependency>

<!--   ORM functionality  -->
<dependency>
        <groupId>org.hibernate</groupId>
        <artifactId>hibernate-entitymanager</artifactId>
        <version>3.4.0.GA</version>
</dependency>
<dependency>
        <groupId>javax.persistence</groupId>
        <artifactId>persistence-api</artifactId>
        <version>1.0</version>
</dependency>

<!--   Spring -->
<dependency>
        <groupId>org.springframework</groupId>
        <artifactId>spring-aspects</artifactId>
        <version>3.0.0 </version>
</dependency>
<dependency>
        <groupId>org.springframework</groupId>
        <artifactId>spring-tx</artifactId>
        <version>3.0.0 </version>
</dependency>
```

```
<dependency>
        <groupId>org.springframework</groupId>
        <artifactId>spring-beans</artifactId>
        <version>3.0.0 </version>
</dependency>
<dependency>
        <groupId>org.springframework</groupId>
        <artifactId>spring-context-support</artifactId>
        <version>3.0.0 </version>
</dependency>
<dependency>
        <groupId>org.springframework</groupId>
        <artifactId>spring-context</artifactId>
        <version>3.0.0 </version>
</dependency>
<dependency>
        <groupId>org.springframework</groupId>
        <artifactId>spring-core</artifactId>
        <version>3.0.0 </version>
</dependency>
<dependency>
        <groupId>org.springframework</groupId>
        <artifactId>spring-orm</artifactId>
        <version>3.0.0 </version>
</dependency>
<dependency>
        <groupId>org.springframework</groupId>
        <artifactId>spring-aop</artifactId>
        <version>3.0.0 </version>
</dependency>
<dependency>
        <groupId>org.springframework</groupId>
        <artifactId>spring-jdbc</artifactId>
        <version>3.0.0 </version>
</dependency>
```

Additionally, you may want to include the JBoss Maven repository. Include the following inside the repositories element of your Maven pom.xml:

```
<repository>
        <id>jboss</id>
        <url>http://repository.jboss.com/maven2/</url>
    </repository>
```

You might execute mvn dependency:tree to get a listing of all the dependencies those dependencies import, just to be sure it's compatible with your particular environment.

It's hard to find an exhaustive or conclusive list of supported databases for jBPM, but because it's built on Hibernate, you can expect it's going to work on the big-name databases: Oracle, SQL Server,

MySQL, PostgreSQL, and so forth. In this example, we're using Postgres 8.3, for which the driver's jar dependency is expressed in Maven as:

```
<dependency>
        <groupId>postgresql</groupId>
        <artifactId>postgresql</artifactId>
        <version>8.3-603.jdbc3</version>
</dependency>
```

11-3. Integrating jBPM 4 with Spring

Problem
You want to use jBPM 4 (the newer, and current, release) but you've got a Spring-based architecture and want to make use of jBPM from within a Spring application context.

Solution
jBPM ships with very good support for Spring, even providing a Spring-friendly configuration object (`org.jbpm.pvm.internal.cfg.SpringConfiguration`). This class makes it easy to set up the core pieces of the integration in a Spring-friendly manner. The balance of the configuration is fairly boilerplate transaction management and Hibernate integration, with some caveats. Andries Inzé started the project to integrate Spring and jBPM, and so much of the great work here is because of his efforts, on top of the great work behind jBPM itself, of course.

Approach
There are many ways to use jBPM. One approach is to use it as a stand-alone process server, perhaps deployed using JBoss. This solution exposes a console into which you can deploy business processes and even test the process out, and watch it move state forward. As it's written using Hibernate, it's not too difficult to get it working on JBoss' EJB environment. So, you might use it as a service. Indeed, JBoss itself supports deploying processes to a directory and loading those, with some configuration.

For our purposes, we want to flip that deployment on its head. We want to embed, rather than deploy to, jBPM, in the same way that we can use Spring to invert control for other things such as remote services, message driven POJOs, and the `HibernateTemplate`.

In this example, we'll host jBPM's services in the Spring context, just like we might any other Hibernate services. jBPM is, fundamentally, a runtime that stores its state and jobs in a database. It uses Hibernate as its persistence mechanism (though it may eventually move to a strict JPA–based model). When jBPM, with Hibernate, interacts with the database, it uses transactions and avails itself of many of the features that Hibernate provides to build a sophisticated object graph mapped to a database schema. Naturally, this isn't so bad, except that in order to use jBPM with other services inside of Spring, particularly ones that leverage transactions (other database resources, XA functionality including but not limited to JMS, other Hibernate models,and so forth), you need to exert control over jBPM's transactions. Otherwise, jBPM will commit and begin transactions independent of the Spring container's transaction lifecycle.

jBPM 4 is built cleanly, in such a way that delegating the lifecycle of the system to another container (such as JBoss's microcontainer or Spring) is feasible. The jBPM 4 and Spring integration builds on top of this, providing a recipe for accessing key services that jBPM provides at runtime. This is the key to the integration. With jBPM available to your beans as just another bean in the container, you can leverage it just like you might a Hibernate session or a JMS queue connection. Similarly, you can hide its use behind service methods that you expose to your applications clients.

Imagine exposing a service method for creating customer entities. It might use Hibernate to save the new record to the database, use JMS to trigger integration with an external financial system the company uses, and use jBPM to start a business process for fulfillment. This is a very robust, well-rounded service. You can use the services like you might any other transactional service—confident that the containing transaction will envelope the transactions of the jBPM process.

We will build a simple application context that contains the common elements you'll need to start using jBPM in your application, and then see where you may want to customize the solution to your environment.

In the example for jBPM 4, we will build a solution that models a simple customer registration workflow. In so doing, you will get a feeling for how you would set up the example, as well as get a chance to see a (very simple) jBPM solution. The namespaces of the work we'll do will sit below `com.apress.springenterpriserecipes.jbpm.jbpm4`.

The Application Context

The first thing to do is to set up basic database and Hibernate configuration. We will use the `tx`, `p`, `aop`, and `context` namespaces to build this solution. The skeletal frame for our Spring XML configuration is as follows:

```
<?xml version="1.0" encoding="UTF-8"?>
<beans xmlns="http://www.springframework.org/schema/beans"
        xmlns:tx="http://www.springframework.org/schema/tx"
xmlns:p="http://www.springframework.org/schema/p"
        xmlns:util="http://www.springframework.org/schema/util"
xmlns:xsi="http://www.w3.org/2001/XMLSchema-instance"
        xmlns:aop="http://www.springframework.org/schema/aop"
xmlns:context="http://www.springframework.org/schema/context"
        xsi:schemaLocation="http://www.springframework.org/schema/beans
http://www.springframework.org/schema/beans/spring-beans-3.0.xsd
                http://www.springframework.org/schema/util
http://www.springframework.org/schema/util/spring-util-3.0.xsd
                http://www.springframework.org/schema/context
http://www.springframework.org/schema/context/spring-context-3.0.xsd
                http://www.springframework.org/schema/util
http://www.springframework.org/schema/util/spring-util-3.0.xsd
                        http://www.springframework.org/schema/aop
http://www.springframework.org/schema/aop/spring-aop-3.0.xsd
                        http://www.springframework.org/schema/tx
http://www.springframework.org/schema/tx/spring-tx-3.0.xsd ">…
</beans>
```

In this example, we'll use two Spring application contexts. One application context will configure jBPM (`jbpm4-context.xml`), and the other will configure our sample application (simply, `context.xml`). The first application context is geared around configuring jBPM. You should be able to reuse this file later with no changes to the file itself. Mainly, you'd have to update the property file (naturally) and you'd have to tell the session factory about any annotated classes that you want it to know about from your own domain model. In this example, doing so is simple, as it involves overriding an existing `List` bean named `annotatedHibernateClasses` in a separate context. It's been done this way because it's not possible to have two sets of Hibernate classes that are registered with the Hibernate `SessionFactory`. To have an annotated class be registered as a Hibernate entity, it needs to be registered with the `AnnotationSessionFactoryBean`. The `annotatedClasses` property expects a list of Class names. Because our jBPM configuration uses Hibernate, we have to configure the AnnotatedSessionFactoryBean on behalf of jBPM, which means that you can't create a separate one if you're using the jbpm4-context.xml and want only one Hibernate session in your application. This is probably the case, because there's rarely a need for two Hibernate sessions as they can't share transactions and so on. So, we provide a "template" configuration, referencing a list that's created in the context. The list is empty, but you can in your Spring application context include (jbpm4-context.xml) and create your own list bean with the same bean name ("annotatedHibernateClasses"), effectively "overriding" the configuration. This delegation scheme works in much the same way an abstract method in a base class does.

Because we want this to be as automatic as possible, we'll exploit Spring's AOP schema support and transaction schema support. The first few lines of the application context are boilerplate: they instruct the context to enable annotation configuration and use a property file as values for placeholders in the application context's XML itself. The file jbpm4.properties is included and its values resolved. Those values are then available as expressions to other beans in the context file.

```
<context:annotation-config />

<bean

class="org.springframework.beans.factory.config.PropertyPlaceholderConfigurer"
        p:location="jbpm4.properties" p:ignoreUnresolvablePlaceholders="true" />
```

Next, the sessionFactory. It's key to get this right: we need to tell Spring about our database and give it the information on our schema. It does this by resolving the properties in the property file. When we configure the mappingLocations property, we are pointing it to classpath Hibernate mapping files so that it may resolve the various entities that ship with jBPM 4. These entities will exist in your database. They persist such information as process definitions, process variables, and so forth, that are important to the successful execution of the jBPM engine.

The final property we've configured here is the annotatedClasses property, which we basically punt. Providing an empty list object here allows us to "override" it in another context file, so we don't even need to modify the original one. If you don't want to provide any classes, than the original empty list declaration will still work, and you won't get any errors from Spring at runtime.

Note that we've specified p:schemaUpdate="true", which let's Hibernate generate the schema for us on load. Naturally, you probably want to disable this in production.

```
<bean id="sessionFactory"
class="org.springframework.orm.hibernate3.annotation.AnnotationSessionFactoryBean"
p:dataSource-ref="dataSource"
p:schemaUpdate="true">
        <property name="hibernateProperties">
                <props>
                        <prop key="hibernate.dialect">${dataSource.dialect}</prop>
                        <prop key="hibernate.show_sql">true</prop>
                        <prop key="hibernate.hbm2ddl.auto">create-drop</prop>
                        <prop key="hibernate.jdbc.batch_size">20</prop>
                        <prop key="hibernate.show_sql">true</prop>
                        <prop key="hibernate.use_sql_comments">true</prop>
                </props>
        </property>
```

```
        <property name="mappingLocations">
                <list>
                        <value>classpath:jbpm.execution.hbm.xml</value>
                        <value>classpath:jbpm.repository.hbm.xml</value>
                        <value>classpath:jbpm.task.hbm.xml</value>
                        <value>classpath:jbpm.history.hbm.xml</value>
                </list>
        </property>
        <property name="annotatedClasses" ref="annotatedHibernateClasses" />
</bean>

<util:list id="annotatedHibernateClasses" />
```

The next bean—the dataSource—is configured entirely at your discretion. The properties are set using properties in the properties file jbpm4.properties. The contents of jbpm4.properties:

```
hibernate.configFile=hibernate.cfg.xml
dataSource.password=sep
dataSource.username=sep
dataSource.databaseName=sep
dataSource.driverClassName=org.postgresql.Driver
dataSource.dialect=org.hibernate.dialect.PostgreSQLDialect
dataSource.serverName=sep
dataSource.url=jdbc:postgresql://${dataSource.serverName}/${dataSource.databaseName}
dataSource.properties=user=${dataSource.username};databaseName=${dataSource.databaseName};se
rverName=${dataSource.serverName};password=${dataSource.password}
```

Modify the values there to reflect your database of choice. As mentioned before, there are lots of supported databases. If you're using MySQL, I'd suggest something like the InnoDB table type to take advantage of transactions. In our experience, PostgreSQL, MySQL, Oracle, and so forth, all work fine. You'll also want to configure a transaction manager. You will use this later when setting up AOP–advised transaction management for our beans.

```
<bean id="dataSource" class="org.apache.commons.dbcp.BasicDataSource"
        destroy-method="close" p:driverClassName="${dataSource.driverClassName}"
        p:username="${dataSource.username}" p:password="${dataSource.password}"
        p:url="${dataSource.url}" />

<bean id="transactionManager"
        class="org.springframework.orm.hibernate3.HibernateTransactionManager"
        p:sessionFactory-ref="sessionFactory" />
```

Additionally, add a HibernateTemplate, as you'll need it to interact with both your and jBPM's entities.

```
<bean    id="hibernateTemplate"
        class="org.springframework.orm.hibernate3.HibernateTemplate"
        p:sessionFactory-ref="sessionFactory"   />
```

Finally, we begin configuring jBPM. This part is, in its most minimal incarnation, a very forgiving three lines of XML. The services we configure afterwards—processEngine, repositoryService, executionService, historyService, managmentService, and taskService—are configured for the express purpose of being able to inject them. You could as easily inject the jbpmConfiguration bean and manually access those services from the jbpmConfiguration. Succinctly, they're very much optional, and you're as good as done with just the jbpmConfiguration instance.

```
<bean id="jbpmConfiguration" class="org.jbpm.pvm.internal.cfg.SpringConfiguration"
      p:sessionFactory-ref="sessionFactory">
    <constructor-arg value="jbpm.cfg.xml" />
</bean>

<bean id="processEngine" factory-bean="jbpmConfiguration"
      factory-method="buildProcessEngine" />

<bean id="taskService" factory-bean=" jbpmConfiguration "
      factory-method="getTaskService" />

<bean id="repositoryService" factory-bean="jbpmConfiguration"
      factory-method="getRepositoryService" />

<bean id="executionService" factory-bean="jbpmConfiguration"
      factory-method="getExecutionService" />

<bean id="historyService" factory-bean="jbpmConfiguration"
      factory-method="getHistoryService" />

<bean id="managementService" factory-bean="jbpmConfiguration"
      factory-method="getManagementService" />
```

When you try to use these beans in your service or some client, be aware that several of these beans have the JbpmConfiguration super class (JbpmConfiguration is in turn the super class of SpringConfiguration.) Thus, you can't use @Autowired by itself on a single instance variable because, to Spring, the choice of which bean to inject is ambiguous. If you do use the @Autowired annotation, use an array or collection type so that the multiple matched instances can be injected because there's ambiguity.

To precisely specify the bean you're looking for, you can use Spring 3's @Value annotation and a Spring Expression Language expression, or JSR 250's @Resource annotation and a bean's name, or you could simply handle the configuration in Spring's XML format, referencing the bean by name.

At this point, all that remains is to specify the jBPM configuration itself (jbpm.cfg.xml), which is fairly boilerplate and you can use, unchanged, for a vast many solutions.

```
<?xml version="1.0" encoding="UTF-8"?>
<jbpm-configuration>
        <import resource="jbpm.jpdl.cfg.xml" />
        <import resource="jbpm.identity.cfg.xml" />
        <import resource="jbpm.jobexecutor.cfg.xml" />
```

```
<process-engine-context>
        <repository-service />
        <repository-cache />
        <execution-service />
        <history-service />
        <management-service />
        <identity-service />
        <task-service />
        <command-service>
                <retry-interceptor />
                <environment-interceptor />
                <spring-transaction-interceptor />
        </command-service>
        <script-manager default-expression-language="juel"
                default-script-language="juel"
                read-contexts="execution, environment, process-engine, spring"
                write-context="">
                <script-language name="juel"

factory="org.jbpm.pvm.internal.script.JuelScriptEngineFactory" />
        </script-manager>
        <authentication />
        <id-generator />
        <types resource="jbpm.variable.types.xml" />
        <address-resolver />
        <business-calendar>
                <monday hours="9:00-12:00 and 12:30-17:00" />
                <tuesday hours="9:00-12:00 and 12:30-17:00" />
                <wednesday hours="9:00-12:00 and 12:30-17:00" />
                <thursday hours="9:00-12:00 and 12:30-17:00" />
                <friday hours="9:00-12:00 and 12:30-17:00" />
                <holiday period="01/07/2008 - 31/08/2008" />
        </business-calendar>
</process-engine-context>
<transaction-context>
        <repository-session />
        <db-session />
        <message-session />
        <timer-session />
        <history-session />
        <hibernate-session current="true" />
</transaction-context>
</jbpm-configuration>
```

By and large, this is a pretty standard configuration for jBPM. It specifies many things that are safe defaults, and largely out of the scope of this book. Mainly, the configuration tells jBPM which services to bring up and defines some configuration for those services. Because we're integrating with Spring, we modify the transaction-context element and the command-service element, as those are the touch points with Spring. The hibernate-session element tells jBPM to reuse an existing Hibernate session (the one we created with our Hibernate Session factory) instead of creating its own. The spring-transaction-interceptor element is a special element to enable jBPM to defer to the TransactionManager defined in our application context. Here again, jBPM integrates by delegating to the Spring services, making for a very eloquent solution.

11-4. Building a Service With Spring

Problem

In the previous recipe, we configured Spring and jBPM, such that Spring's is successfully "hosting" jBPM. You set about writing a business process and want to work with jBPM inside of your service code, and to be able to delegate actions to Spring beans from within a business process.

Solution

Use Spring normally, injecting the services as you need them. For access within your business process, you can simply reference the services as you would any other process or environment variable in a business process. jBPM will expose beans using the jBPM expression language, and you can then just reference them by name.

Approach

In this recipe, we'll work through a simple example so you can see the pieces of a typical integration with Spring and jBPM. We've already laid the ground work in the previous example. Here, we'll actually build a simple Java service that works with Spring to move the process state forward.

The use case is a user registration, like the one described in Figure 11-1.

There are four steps:

1. A prospective customer (modeled here as a Hibernate entity, Customer) signs up via a form. (We'll leave the web page interactions to your imagination for this example; suffice it to say that the form, when submitted, invokes a service method, which we'll define.)

2. A verification e-mail is sent.

3. The user (ideally) will confirm the receipt of the e-mail by clicking on a link, which authorizes the user. This could happen in a minute, or in a decade, so the system can't afford to waste resources waiting.

4. Upon confirmation, the user will receive a "Welcome!" e-mail.

This is a simple use of a business process. It abstracts away the process of incorporating and processing a new Customer. Conceivably, the Customer object could have come from any number of channels: somebody sitting taking phone calls inputs them manually, the user self-subscribes to the system, in a batch process, and so on. All of these different channels can create and reuse this business process, though. When the processing for a new customer is standardized, the challenge becomes about surfacing the functionality for as many end users as possible.

Because the user could conceivably wait a few days (or weeks; it's arbitrary) before checking the e-mail and clicking the confirm link, state needs to be maintained but not burden the system. jBPM, and indeed most workflow engines, passivate state for you – allowing a process to "wait" on external events ("signals"). Indeed, because you've decomposed your process into a series of isolated steps, each of which contribute to the larger goal while remaining independently useful, you get the best of both worlds: stateful processes and stateless scalability. The state of the global business process is maintained, and throughout the state of customer's sign-up is persistent, but you get the benefits of not keeping things in memory when there's no progress in the business process, thus freeing it up to handle other requests.

To build our solution, we need to build a simple CustomerService class and configure it appropriately. We'll integrate jBPM and tailor transaction management for the CustomerService class. We'll also make our bean responsible for deploying the process definitions for us as the bean starts up, so that if they weren't already deployed, they will be.

The XML for the application context is stark, and simple.

```xml
<?xml version="1.0" encoding="UTF-8"?>
<beans xmlns="http://www.springframework.org/schema/beans"
       xmlns:tx="http://www.springframework.org/schema/tx"
xmlns:p="http://www.springframework.org/schema/p"
       xmlns:util="http://www.springframework.org/schema/util"
xmlns:xsi="http://www.w3.org/2001/XMLSchema-instance"
       xmlns:aop="http://www.springframework.org/schema/aop"
xmlns:context="http://www.springframework.org/schema/context"
       xsi:schemaLocation="http://www.springframework.org/schema/beans
http://www.springframework.org/schema/beans/spring-beans-3.0.xsd
                      http://www.springframework.org/schema/util
http://www.springframework.org/schema/util/spring-util-3.0.xsd
                      http://www.springframework.org/schema/context
http://www.springframework.org/schema/context/spring-context-3.0.xsd
                      http://www.springframework.org/schema/util
http://www.springframework.org/schema/util/spring-util-3.0.xsd
                                   http://www.springframework.org/schema/aop
http://www.springframework.org/schema/aop/spring-aop-3.0.xsd
                                   http://www.springframework.org/schema/tx
http://www.springframework.org/schema/tx/spring-tx-3.0.xsd
                                   ">
        <import resource="jbpm4-context.xml" />

        <context:annotation-config />

        <tx:advice id="txAdvice" transaction-manager="transactionManager">
                <tx:attributes>
                        <tx:method propagation="REQUIRED" name="*" />
                </tx:attributes>
        </tx:advice>

        <aop:config>
                <aop:advisor advice-ref="txAdvice"
                pointcut="execution(* com.apress.springenterpriserecipes..jbpm4.*.*(..))" />
        </aop:config>

<util:list id="annotatedHibernateClasses">
        <value>com.apress.springenterpriserecipes.jbpm.jbpm4.customers.Customer
</value>
</util:list>
```

417

```
<bean id="customerService"
class="com.apress.springenterpriserecipes.jbpm.jbpm4.customers.CustomerServiceImpl">
            <property name="processDefinitions">
            <list>
        <value>/process-efinitions/RegisterCustomer.jpdl.xml</value>
            </list>
            </property>
        </bean>
</beans>
```

The first few elements are familiar: we set up the AOP–based transaction management and apply it to the services deployed under the jbpm4 package in our solution. Next, we override the List bean (with id annotatedHibernateClasses) that we created for the last recipe (jbpm4-context.xml) to provide the session factory with a collection of annotated entities; here, the Customer entity. Finally, we have a bean to handle the customerService bean. This bean leverages Hibernate (through the HibernateTemplate instance) to handle persistence and it leverages jBPM (through the SpringConfiguration instance) to handle BPM. We provide the customerService bean with a list of business processes we want to ensure are deployed, which the bean handles as part of its duties in its post-initialization phase (the method annotated with @PostConstruct will be run after the bean's been configured to let the user inject custom initialization logic). In this case, we're deploying only one business process. Note that the business process file's name needs to end in jpdl.xml; otherwise jBPM won't deploy it. The customerService bean is an implementation of the interface CustomerService, whose definition is as follows:

```
package com.apress.springenterpriserecipes.jbpm.jbpm4.customers;

public interface CustomerService {

        void sendWelcomeEmail(Long customerId);

        void deauthorizeCustomer(Long customerId);

        void authorizeCustomer(Long customerId);

        Customer getCustomerById(Long customerId);

        Customer createCustomer(String email, String password, String firstName, String
lastName);

        void sendCustomerVerificationEmail(Long customerId);
}
```

The interface is trivial, and only provides creation and mutation services for a Customer record. The implementation is where we see all the pieces come together.

```
package com.apress.springenterpriserecipes.jbpm.jbpm4.customers;
```

CustomerServiceImpl is a simple class. At the top, we see that we've injected three dependencies: springConfiguration (which doesn't get used—though its configuration is worth noting because you may use it to access other services), repositoryService, and executionService. The class provides a few salient methods (some of which are required by its interface, CustomerService):

- void setupProcessDefinitions()

- Customer createCustomer(String email, String passphrase, String firstName, String lastName)

- void sendCustomerVerificationEmail(Long customerId)

- void authorizeCustomer(Long customerId)

In the bean, setupProcessDefinitions is run when the bean is created. It iterates through the processDefinitions collection and "deploys" the resource whose path it is given. If you monitor the logs, you'll witness SQL being issued against the database, creating the runtime structure of your process definition inside the database.

11-5. Building a Business Process

Problem

You've built a service that uses jBPM to create a working service. We've seen how jBPM is configured, and we've even built a service for a business requirement (the sign-up of customers). The last element that remains is the process definition itself. What does a business process definition look like? How does a process definition reference Spring beans?

Solution

We'll build a process definition that codifies the steps diagrammed in Figure 11-1 at the beginning of the chapter. This process definition will reference Spring beans using the JBoss expression language. Finally, we'll walk through how the business process uses our customerService bean and how the customerService bean uses the business process to handle the customer's sign-up.

Approach

Let's examine the business process itself (RegisterCustomer.jpdl.xml). In jBPM, a business process is built using jPDL. You can use the Eclipse plug-in to model jBPM processes, but the jPDL schema is so simple that you don't really need it. This is not like BPEL where it can become all but intolerably complicated to write the code by hand. What follows is the XML for the business process:

```
<?xml version="1.0" encoding="UTF-8"?>
<process name="RegisterCustomer" xmlns="http://jbpm.org/4.0/jpdl">

    <start>
        <transition to="send-verification-email" />
    </start>
```

```
    <java name="send-verification-email" expr="#{customerService}"
        method="sendCustomerVerificationEmail">
        <arg> <object expr="#{customerId}" /> </arg>
        <transition to="confirm-receipt-of-verification-email" />
    </java>

    <state name="confirm-receipt-of-verification-email">
        <transition to="send-welcome-email" />
    </state>

    <java name="send-welcome-email"
                expr="#{customerService}" method="sendWelcomeEmail">
        <arg> <object expr="#{customerId}" /> </arg>
    </java>
```

```
</process>
```

In the customerService bean, a client will use createCustomer to create a customer record. In a real-world example, you might imagine exposing these services as a SOAP endpoint to be consumed by various clients such as a web application or other business applications. You can imagine it being called as a result of a successful form on a web site. When it executes, it creates a new Customer object and uses Hibernate to persist it. Inside the createCustomer method, we use jBPM to start the business process to track the Customer. This is done with the startProcessInstanceByKey method. In the invocation, we give jBPM variables through a Map<String,Object> instance (acting as something of a context for the process variables). Those variables are accessible inside the business process as Expression Language expressions and allow you to parameterize the business process in much the same way you might parameterize a macro or a Java method. We give the process instance a custom business key, instead of letting it generate its own.

```
    executionService.startProcessInstanceByKey(
        REGISTER_CUSTOMER_PROCESS_KEY, vars, Long.toString(customer.getId()));
```

The last parameter is the key. Here we're using the String id of the customer as the key. This makes it easy to find the process instance later, though you could also query for the process instance, predicating on process variables that, taken together, should make the process instance unique. You might also query by roles or users assigned to certain tasks, or simply note the id of the business process itself in your domain model and reference that later when looking up the process instance. Here, we know that there's only ever going to be one sign-up process for a customer, so we key it with a valid ID that will only work once: the Customer's id value.

When the process starts, it will start executing the steps in your process definition. First, it will go to the <start> element. It will evaluate the one transition it has and proceed through that transition to the next step, send-verification-email.

Once in the java element named send-verification-email, jBPM will invoke sendCustomerVerificationEmail on the customerService bean in Spring. It uses an Expression Language construct to reference the Spring bean by name:

```
<java name="send-verification-email"
        expr="#{customerService}"
        method="sendCustomerVerificationEmail">
        …
</java>
```

The sendCustomerVerificationEmail method takes the customer's id and should send a notification. We leave the functionality of actually sending the e-mail to the reader, but you can imagine a unique, hashed link being generated and embedded in the body of the e-mail that lets the server trace the request back to a customer.

Once the process has left the send-verification-email java element, it'll proceed to confirm-receipt-of-verification-email state, where it'll wait indefinitely before proceeding. This is called a wait state. An external event is needed to "tell" it to proceed. In our scenario, this event will come when the user clicks on the link in the e-mail, which triggers the invocation of the authorizeCustomer method on our customerService bean. This method expects a customer ID as a parameter.

Inside authorizeCustomer, the service queries the server for the any processes waiting at the confirm-receipt-of-verification-email state and having this customer's ID. We know that there's only one instance of this process, but the query returns a collection of Execution instances. We then iterate through the collection, signaling (with the Execution instance's signalExecutionById method) the transition from a wait state to the next state. When a node in jBPM moves from one to another, it takes a transition. As we've seen before, it does so implicitly. Here, however, in the wait state, we have to explicitly tell it to take a transition to signal that it can proceed to the next node.

```
for (Execution execution : executions) {
        Execution subExecution = execution.findActiveExecutionIn(
                "confirm-receipt-of-verification-email");
        executionService.signalExecutionById(subExecution.getId());
}
```

The authorizeCustomer method also updates the Customer entity, marking it as authorized.

From there, execution proceeds to the send-welcome-email java element. As before, the java element will be used to invoke a method on the customerService bean. This time, it will invoke sendWelcomeEmail to send the newly registered Customer a welcome e-mail.

The name of the process (what we use when we call startProcessInstanceByKey) is in the process element. Here, that name is "RegisterCustomer."

Many of the expressions are in the JBoss expression language, which works very similarly to the unified EL found in Java Server Faces, or the Spring EL. You can use the EL here to reference parameters to the process.

You'll recall that when we invoked the service method for createCustomer, it in turn kicked off a business process whose progression the rest of the code followed. We use a Map<String,Object> to parameterize the business process. In this case, our Map<String,Object> was called vars.

```
Map<String, Object> vars = new HashMap<String, Object>();
vars.put("customerId", customer.getId());
executionService.startProcessInstanceByKey(
  REGISTER_CUSTOMER_PROCESS_KEY,
  vars,
  Long.toString(customer.getId()));
```

From within the running process, you can access the parameters from Java, or as an EL expression. To access the parameter using the EL, use something like: #{customerId}. To access the parameter from Java code at runtime, use:

```
Number customerId = (Number) executionService.getVariable(pi.getId(), "customerId") ;
```

At this point, you've got a working business process that lives inside of a Spring context, and you've got a working grasp of the constructs required to build a process.

Summary

In this chapter, you were given an introduction to business process management as a technology. You should have a big-picture view of the technology. There's much more to learn as BPM can become a key piece of architecture, providing a spine to otherwise isolated functionality. No single introduction to one particular brand of BPM will ever be adequate. There are lots of resources out there, though it helps to keep an eye on the bookshelf at your local bookstore, because often these technologies become irrelevant as quickly as the sands of the markets shift.

BPM is a discipline that's rooted in many decades of growth and concepts. The earliest tenants of workflow engines have their basis in a branch of mathematics called petri nets. The discipline's become more mainstream over the years, and the focus evolved from using BPM as a record-keeping mechanism to an enabling orchestration mechanism.

There are several very good discussions of the topic, if you're curious. To further explore the technology, there are several good sites on the Internet and many more good books readily had by searching for "BPM" in a search engine. For a deeper treatment of the discipline (though not necessarily the technology), we recommend the following:

- Frank Leymann and Dieter Roller. *Production Workflow: Concepts and Techniques.* Prentice Hall, 2000

- Michael Havey. *Essential Business Process Modeling.* O'Reilly, 2005.

- http://www.workflowpatterns.com/ - a comprehensive introduction to the patterns of workflow.

In the next chapter, you will learn about OSGi, and how to build OSGi solutions using Spring Dynamic Modules and SpringSource dm Server.

CHAPTER 12

■ ■ ■

OSGi and Spring

OSGi and Spring are, in many ways, a very natural technology combination. They approach different problems from different directions, but they do so in a similar spirit. It's only natural, then, that SpringSource, the company that stewards the Spring framework, should turn its eye to OSGi.

OSGi—which was formerly known as the Open Services Gateway initiative, though the name's obsolete now—has its roots in the embedded space, where dynamic service provisioning is far more important than it is in the gridiron world of enterprise applications. It provides a services registry as well as an application life-cycle management framework. Beyond this, OSGi provides such features as granular component visibility via a highly specialized class-loading environment, service versioning and reconciliation, and security. OSGi provides a layer on top of the JVM's default class loader. The deployment unit for OSGi is a bundle, which is essentially a jar with an augmented MANIFEST.MF. This manifest contains declarations that specify, among other things, on what other services the bundle depends, and what service the bundle exports.

OSGi has gained some notoriety because of Eclipse, which uses it for the plug-in model. This is a natural choice, because Eclipse needs to allow plug-ins to load and unload, and to guarantee that certain resources are made available to plug-ins. Indeed, the hope of an enhanced "module" system for Java has loomed large for many years, manifesting in at least a few JSRs: JSR-277, "Java Module System," and JSR-291, "Dynamic Component Support for Java SE." OSGi is a natural fit because it's been around for many years, matured, and has been improved on by many more vendors still. It is already the basis of the architecture of a few application servers.

OSGi is important today, more than ever, in the enterprise space because it represents a solution that can be gracefully layered on top of the Java Virtual Machine (JVM) (if not existing application servers) that can solve problems frequently encountered in today's environments. ".jar hell," the collision of two different versions of the same jar in the same class loader, is something most developers have encountered. Application footprint reduction provides another compelling use of OSGi. Applications today, be they .war or .ear, are typically bundled with numerous .jars that exist solely to service that application's requirements. It may be that other applications on the same application server are using the same jars and services. This implies that there are duplicated instances of the same libraries loaded into memory. This situation's even worse when you consider how large typical deployed .wars are today. Most .wars are 90% third-party jars, with a little application-specific code rounding out the mix. Imagine three .wars of 50 MBs, or 100 MBs, where only 5 MBs are application-specific code and libraries. This implies that the application server needs to field 300 MBs just to meet the requirements of a 15-30 unique MBs. OSGi provides a way of sharing components, loading them once, and reducing the footprint of the application.

Just as you may be paying an undue price for redundant libraries, so too are you likely paying for unused application server services, such as EJB1.x and 2.x support, or JCA. Here again, OSGi can help by providing a "server à la carte" model, where your application is provisioned by the container only with the services it needs.

OSGi is, on the large, a deployment concern. However, using it effectively requires changes to your code, as well. It affects how you acquire dependencies for your application. Naturally, this is where Spring is strongest, and where dependency-injection in general can be a very powerful tool. SpringSource has made several forays into the OSGi market, first with Spring Dynamic Modules, which is an enhanced OSGi framework that provides support for Spring and much more. Then, on top of Spring Dynamic Modules, SpringSource built SpringSource dm Server, which is a server wired from top to bottom with OSGi and Spring. SpringSource dm Server supports dynamic deployment, enhanced tooling, HTTP, and native .WAR deployment. It also sports superb administrative features.

OSGi is a specification, not a framework. There are many implementations of the specification, much like Java EE is a specification, not an implementation. Additionally, OSGi is not a user component model, like Spring or EJB 3. Instead, it sits below your components, providing life-cycle management for Java classes. It is, conceptually, possible to deploy to an OSGi runtime in the same way that you deploy to a Java EE runtime, completely unaware of how Java consumes your .jar files and MANIFESTS and so on. As you'll see in this chapter, however, there's a lot of power to be had in specifically targeting OSGi and exploiting it in your application. In this chapter, we will discuss Spring Dynamic Modules, and to a lesser extent, Spring dm Server.

12-1. Getting Started With OSGi

Problem
You understand OSGi conceptually, but you want to see what a basic, working example with raw OSGi looks like. It's hard to appreciate the sun, after all, if you've never seen the rain.

Solution
In this solution, we'll build a simple service and then use it in a client. Remember, in OSGi, anything used by something else is a service. "Service" doesn't imply any concrete inheritance, it doesn't imply transactional qualities, and it doesn't imply RPC. It's merely a class on whose concrete, black-box functionality and interface your class relies.

Approach
In this example, we'll use Eclipse's OSGi distribution, Eclipse Equinox. There are many distributions to choose from. Popular ones include Apache's Felix and Eclipse's Equinox. You may use any distribution you want, but for this example, the instructions will be for Felix. The concepts should be the same across implementations, but the specifics may vary wildly in both commands and mechanism.

Osgi and "JavaBeans™"
This is sort of like what a "JavaBean" was originally intended to be. These days, OSGi is starting to take on the very vivid marketing life that JavaBeans did before it. You'll occasionally note products promoting chief among their upgrades their new, internal use of OSGi, as products did years ago with JavaBeans and object-oriented programming ("Now object-oriented!"). Be mindful of the hype.

The "Service"

Let's first examine the Java code for the service's interface. It describes a service whose sole function is to take as inputs a target language and a name and to return as output a greeting.

```
package com.apress.springenterpriserecipes.osgi.helloworld.service;

public interface GreeterService {
    String greet(String language, String name);
}
```

The implementation's similarly plain. It hard-codes the greetings for three languages and satisfies the interface.

```
package com.apress.springenterpriserecipes.osgi.helloworld.service;

import java.util.HashMap;
import java.util.Locale;
import java.util.Map;

public class GreeterServiceImpl implements GreeterService {

    private Map<String, String> salutation;

    public GreeterServiceImpl() {
        salutation  = new HashMap<String, String>();
        salutation.put(Locale.ENGLISH.toString(), "Hello, %s");
        salutation.put(Locale.FRENCH.toString(), "Bonjour, %s");
        salutation.put(Locale.ITALIAN.toString(), "Buongiorno, %s");
    }

    /**
     * @param language Can be any language you want, so long as that language is one of
     *                 <code>Locale.ENGLISH.toString()</code>,
     *                 <code>Locale.ITALIAN.toString()</code>, or
     *                 <code>Locale.FRENCH.toString()</code>.
     *                 :-)
     * @param name     the name of the person you'd like to address
     * @return the greeting, in the language you want, tailored to the name you specified
     */
    public String greet(String language, String name) {
        if (salutation.containsKey(language))
            return String.format(salutation.get(language), name);
        throw new RuntimeException(String.format("The language you specified "+
                                                                             "(%s)
doesn't exist", language));
    }
}
```

As you can see, the code is simple, and in point of fact does nothing to betray the fact that we're going to deploy it on top of OSGi. The next class, called an Activator, is required for every bundle. The Activator registers services and receives a life-cycle hook to set the stage for the service. Similarly, it reacts to events and register listeners.

```
package com.apress.springenterpriserecipes.osgi.helloworld.service;

import org.osgi.framework.BundleActivator;
import org.osgi.framework.BundleContext;
import java.util.Properties;

public class Activator implements BundleActivator {

    public void start(BundleContext bundleContext) throws Exception {
        System.out.println("Start: ");
        bundleContext.registerService(
        GreeterService.class.getName(),
            new GreeterServiceImpl(),
            new Properties());
    }

    public void stop(BundleContext bundleContext) throws Exception {
        System.out.println("Stop: ");          // NOOP
    }
}
```

The Activator implements BundleActivator, which has a few life-cycle callback methods. We avail ourselves of the start method when the jar is installed to register the service that's contained. We could register many services. The first parameter, a String, is the service name, sort of like a JNDI name or a Spring beanName. The second parameter is the implementation of the service. The third parameter—the java.util.Properties object being passed to the registerService—are key/value pairs, called service attributes. The client can use them as a predicate to qualify what service should be returned when looking the service up in the registry. Here, we specify nothing.

This is all the Java code for this service, but we do need to expand on the MANIFEST itself a little bit, to specify extra metadata that OSGi uses in deploying the service. How you do this is entirely at your discretion, and it's simple enough that you could get away with doing it by hand. We use a Maven plug-in that handles the minutiae for us, though there are other approaches as well. Remember, OSGi bundles are simply standard .jar files with customized MANIFESTs that OSGi consumes at runtime.

What is Maven?

Maven's a build tool provided by the Apache foundation. To use it, download it from Apache.org: `http://maven.apache.org/`. Once downloaded, you can simply unzip it and add the bin directory your system's PATH variable. Maven projects rely on convention over configuration. If you examine the source for this chapter, you'll see the projects are all uniformly structured: `src/main/java` for Java class files, `src/main/resources` for anything that should be on the CLASSPATH at the root of the jar. At the root of these projects is a `pom.xml` file, which describes the projects information, including dependencies and plugins. The dependency information is used to download the required `.jars` as you compile the project. It creates a repository in your home directory (usually, `~/.m2/repository/`) where all jars are cached and used for subsequent builds. To compile a project, on the command line issue:

```
mvn install
```

Maven doesn't require you to explicitly tell it how to compile or jar source code. If there's java code in the `src/main/java` folder, it'll automatically compile it and deposit the resulting artifact (a `.jar`) in a target folder adjacent to the `pom.xml` file. All major IDE's (Eclipse, IntelliJ IDEA, and Netbeans) support opening projects and configuring the projects using Maven's `pom.xml` files. For Eclipse, you'll need the m2eclipse plug-in. The other two IDEs provide native support. The resulting project will already have all the correct jars on the classpath so you can begin editing and working with the code right away.

Maven builds follow a life cycle with phases. You can attach custom behavior to these phases (in much the same way you might listen with a PhaseListener in JSF's request/response processing stack). In the examples in this chapter, we use a Maven plug-in for building OSGi bundles.

The configuration of the Maven plug-in is simple. The plug-in wraps the bnd tool. The bnd tool dynamically interrogates classes for their imports and generates OSGi–compliant entries. We repeat it here mainly for illustrative purposes. For fully working code, see the source code for this book. Note that the plug-in produces OSGi–compliant bundles that work in any container. To read more on the plug-in itself, see: `http://felix.apache.org/site/apache-felix-maven-bundle-plugin-bnd.html`.

```
...
<plugin>
              <groupId>org.apache.felix</groupId>
              <artifactId>maven-bundle-plugin</artifactId>
              <extensions>true</extensions>
              <configuration>
                  <instructions>
<Export-Package>com.apress.springenterpriserecipes.osgi.➥
helloworld.service</Export-Package>
<Bundle-Activator>com.apress.springenterpriserecipes.osgi.➥
helloworld.service.Activator </Bundle-Activator>
                  </instructions>
              </configuration>
</plugin>
...
```

The relevant bits are in bold. It tells the plug-in to add to our MANIFEST certain properties: an Export-Package directive and a Bundle-Activator header. The Export-Package directive tells the OSGi environment that this jar, a "bundle," vends the classes in that package, and that those classes should be made visible to the client. The Bundle-Activator directive describes to the OSGi environment which class implements BundleActivator, and should be consulted when life-cycle events occur.

The preceding plug-in takes care of specifying upon which other bundles our bundle depends, using the Import-Package directive. The final, resulting MANIFEST.MF is telling.

```
Manifest-Version: 1.0
Export-Package: com.apress.springenterpriserecipes.osgi.➥
helloworld.service;uses:="org.osgi.framework"
Private-Package: com.apress.springenterpriserecipes.osgi.helloworld.service,
Built-By: Owner
Tool: Bnd-0.0.311
Bundle-Name: helloworld-service
Created-By: Apache Maven Bundle Plugin
Bundle-Version: 1.0.0.SNAPSHOT
Build-Jdk: 1.6.0_14-ea
Bnd-LastModified: 1243157994625
Bundle-ManifestVersion: 2
Bundle-Activator: com.apress.springenterpriserecipes.osgi.➥
helloworld.service.Activator
Import-Package: com.apress.springenterpriserecipes.osgi.helloworld.service,➥
org.osgi.framework;version="1.3"
Bundle-SymbolicName: com.apress.springenterpriserecipes.➥

helloworld-service
```

This describes the dependencies, exports, and layout of the bundle fully to the OSGi runtime, and makes it easy for clients to know what they're getting when they use this bundle. Take your compiled classes, the finalized META-INF/MANIFEST.MF, and jar them up.

This rounds out the code for the service. Let's install it into the OSGi environment and then start in using it as a client. The installation procedure is very specific to each tool.

Installing Equinox

Assuming that you've downloaded Equinox (http://www.eclipse.org/equinox/; this book was written against 3.4.2) and unzipped it, change to the installation directory and, on the command line, type:

```
java -jar eclipse/plugins/org.eclipse.osgi_YOUR_VERSION.jar -console
```

Naturally, substitute YOUR_VERSION for the one that applies to the version of the distribution that you downloaded. We're using 3.4, which is the latest stable release. This will start an interactive session. You can type help to see the list of available commands. You can issue the services command to list the bundles already installed. To install the bundle, assuming you've put the jar produced from previous steps for the service at the root of your file system (C:/, or /, perhaps?) issue:

```
install file://helloworld-service-1.0-SNAPSHOT.jar or install file:/C:/helloworld-service-
1.0-SNAPSHOT.jar
```

This installs the jar in the OSGi registry and produces an ID that can be used to refer to the bundle. Use it as the operand to the start command.

start 3

This will start the bundle and ready it for use by other bundles.

Using the Service in a Client Bundle

Using the service is almost exactly the same as creating the service, except that we need to specify our dependence on the service in the bundle. Let's first review the client-side Java code. In this case, we simply look up the service and demo it in the Activator for the client bundle. This is simple, and to the point, though not necessarily typical. In the source code for the book, this is a different Maven project, called helloworld-client.

```
package com.apress.springenterpriserecipes.osgi.helloworld.client;

import com.apress.springenterpriserecipes.osgi.helloworld.service.GreeterService;
import org.osgi.framework.BundleActivator;
import org.osgi.framework.BundleContext;
import org.osgi.framework.ServiceReference;
import java.util.Arrays;
import java.util.Locale;

public class Activator implements BundleActivator {

    public void start(BundleContext bundleContext) throws Exception {
        ServiceReference refs[] = bundleContext.getServiceReferences(
                GreeterService.class.getName(), null);
        if (null == refs || refs.length == 0) {
            System.out.println("there is no service by this description!");
            return;
        }
        GreeterService greeterService = (GreeterService)
                bundleContext.getService(refs[0]);

        String[] names = {"Gary", "Steve", "Josh", "Mario",➥
            "Srinivas", "Tom", "James", "Manuel"};

        for (String language : Arrays.asList(
                Locale.ENGLISH.toString(),
                Locale.FRENCH.toString(),
                Locale.ITALIAN.toString())) {
            for (String name : names) {
                System.out.println(greeterService.greet(language, name));
            }
        }
    }

    public void stop(BundleContext bundleContext) throws Exception {
        // NOOP
    }
}
```

The salient code is in bold. Here, we look up a ServiceReference in the OSGi registry. We use the same name as we provided when we registered the class in the registry. The second argument, null, is where we would specify any values to narrow the criteria for the search for a service. Because there's only one that could possibly match in this case, we won't specify anything. Note that there is no guarantee you'll get a reference to the service, or that you'll get only one. Indeed, you may be given any number of ServiceReferences, which is why the return type is scalar. This is a very different paradigm than more traditional component models such as EJB, which treat the inability to return a handle to a service as an error. This is also somewhat counter-intuitive from how traditional service registries (such as JNDI) work. When we're sure we have a handle to a service, we redeem it for an interface to the actual service itself, somewhat like an EJBHome, using the bundleContext.getService(ServiceReference) method. You can see, already, where Spring might be able to lend a hand—in this resource lookup and acquisition logic.

Let's examine the final MANIFEST for the client. It's not much different from what we've done before. It differs mainly in that it lists our service as a dependency. Apart from that, it's pretty boilerplate. The Activator is the only thing that's changed from the previous example. If you're following with Maven, don't forget to specify the changed Activator class in the plug-in. Additionally, we're using the interface from the service jar we produced in the last example. The Maven plug-in automatically adds this to your Import-Package MANIFEST header.

```
Manifest-Version: 1.0
Export-Package: com.apress.springenterpriserecipes.osgi.helloworld.client;➥
uses:="com.apress.springenterpriserecipes.osgi.helloworld.service,org.osgi.framework"
Private-Package: com.apress.springenterpriserecipes.osgi.helloworld.client,
Built-By: Owner
Tool: Bnd-0.0.311
Bundle-Name: helloworld-client
Created-By: Apache Maven Bundle Plugin
Bundle-Version: 1.0.0.SNAPSHOT
Build-Jdk: 1.6.0_14-ea
Bnd-LastModified: 1243159626828
Bundle-ManifestVersion: 2
Bundle-Activator: com.apress.springenterpriserecipes.osgi.➥
helloworld.client.Activator
Import-Package: com.apress.springenterpriserecipes.osgi.➥
helloworld.client,com.apress.springenterpriserecipes.osgi.➥
helloworld.service,org.osgi.framework;version="1.3"
Bundle-SymbolicName: com.apress.springenterpriserecipes.helloworld-client
```

Nothing too exceptional here, except the aforementioned Import-Package. Install the bundle as we did for the service. When the bundle begins to load, and start, it calls the start method of the Activator. You should see greetings being enumerated on the console. You've successfully completed your first OSGi deployment.

```
install helloworld-client-1.0-SNAPSHOT.jar.
start 2
```

You should see the output, as expected, greeting each name.

```
osgi> install helloworld-client-1.0-SNAPSHOT.jar.
Bundle id is 2

osgi> start 2
Hello, Gary
Hello, Steve
Hello, Josh
Hello, Mario
Hello, Srinivas
Hello, Tom
Hello, James
Hello, Manuel
Bonjour, Gary
Bonjour, Steve
Bonjour, Josh
Bonjour, Mario
Bonjour, Srinivas
Bonjour, Tom
Bonjour, James
Bonjour, Manuel
Buongiorno, Gary
Buongiorno, Steve
Buongiorno, Josh
Buongiorno, Mario
Buongiorno, Srinivas
Buongiorno, Tom
Buongiorno, James
Buongiorno, Manuel
osgi>
```

12-2. How do I get Started Using Spring Dynamic Modules?

Problem

You've got a feeling for how OSGi works, what it's capable of, and even how to go about creating a simple "hello, world!" example. Now, you want to start using Spring to smooth over some of the minutiae of resource acquisition and to help build more reliable systems in an OSGi environment.

Solution

Use Spring Dynamic Modules to provide the integration. Spring Dynamic Modules is a framework on top of OSGi that works with any OSGi environment. It provides tight integration for Spring dependency injection in the world of OSGi, which includes support for things like application context discovery, interface-based service injection, and versioning.

Approach

Spring Dynamic Modules is a very powerful API for integration with the OSGi environment. You need the Spring framework itself, and the Spring OSGi jars, as well. If you're following along using Maven, the jars can be added by using SpringSource's OSGi bundle repository. This repository exports the Spring framework jars, as well as those of countless other open source projects, in an OSGi–friendly format under a Maven/Ivy-friendly repository. For more information on the repositories, see http://www.springsource.com/repository/app/faq. To get access to them from Maven, add the repositories to your pom.xml configuration file, at the bottom, before the closing </project> element:

```
<repository>
         <id>com.springsource.repository.bundles.release</id>
         <name>SpringSource Enterprise Bundle Repository - SpringSource Bundle
Releases</name>
         <url>http://repository.springsource.com/maven/bundles/release</url>
     </repository>
     <repository>
         <id>com.springsource.repository.bundles.external</id>
         <name>SpringSource Enterprise Bundle Repository - External Bundle
Releases</name>
         <url>http://repository.springsource.com/maven/bundles/external</url>
</repository>
```

The SpringSource Enterprise Repository provides numerous OSGi–friendly jars files. To see if yours is already supported, search for it at http://www.springsource.com/repository.

We'll use this infrastructure to rebuild our previous helloworld example, this time relying on Spring to provide the injection of the service itself and to make writing the client more in line with what we've come to expect from Spring development. We've already deployed the service, so we don't need to rework any of that. Let's instead concentrate on a new client bundle.

Let's explore our revised client code. The entirety of the client is one Java class and two Spring XML application context files. One file has the OSGi–friendly Spring Dynamic Modules namespace imported; the other is a standard Spring application context.

When we deploy the final bundle to Equinox when we're finished, the XML context files loaded in the META-INF directory will be loaded. It is through the magic of OSGi extender models that this works. OSGi enables deployed bundles to scan other deployed bundles and react to qualities of those bundles. In particular, this is sort of like what Spring does when it scans a package for classes with annotations. Here, Spring Dynamic Modules scans our deployed bundles and loads an ApplicationContext (actually, the specific type of the Application Context is OsgiBundleXmlApplicationContext) into memory based on an event, or a "trigger." There are two ways to trigger this behavior. The first is to explicitly specify in the META-INF/MANIFEST.MF file the attribute Spring-Context, which allows you to override the default location it consults. Otherwise, by default, Spring Dynamic Modules will look for the XML file in the META-INF/spring directory of a bundle. Typically, you'll split your OSGi–specific Spring configuration and your plain-vanilla Spring configuration into two different files, of the form: *modulename*-context.xml and *modulename*-osgi-context.xml.

The Java code is like that of any other standard Spring bean. In fact, for all intents and purposes, this code has no knowledge of OSGi. It *does* have knowledge of Spring itself, though there's no reason it needs to. The @Autowired field-injection and InitializingBean interface are just for convenience and brevity's sake.

```
package com.apress.springenterpriserecipes.osgi.springdmhelloworld.impl;

import com.apress.springenterpriserecipes.osgi.helloworld.service.GreeterService;
import org.springframework.beans.factory.InitializingBean;
import org.springframework.beans.factory.annotation.Autowired;

import java.util.Arrays;
import java.util.Locale;

public class SpringDMGreeterClient implements InitializingBean {

    @Autowired
    private GreeterService greeterService;

    public void afterPropertiesSet() throws Exception {
        for (String name : Arrays.asList("Mario", "Fumiko", "Makani"))
            System.out.println(greeterService.greet(Locale.FRENCH.toString(), name));
    }
}
}
```

Let's explore the Spring XML files. The first one, src/main/resources/META-INF/spring/bundle-context.xml, a standard Spring XML application context, should not be very surprising. It contains just one bean definition.

```
<?xml version="1.0" encoding="UTF-8"?>
<beans xmlns="http://www.springframework.org/schema/beans"
  xmlns:xsi="http://www.w3.org/2001/XMLSchema-instance"
  xsi:schemaLocation="http://www.springframework.org/schema/beans
http://www.springframework.org/schema/beans/spring-beans.xsd">

  <bean name="springDMGreeterClient"
class="com.apress.springenterpriserecipes.osgi.➥
springdmhelloworld.impl.SpringDMGreeterClient" />

</beans>
```

Exploring the Spring Dynamic Modules application context (src/main/resources/META-INF/ spring/bundle-context-osgi.xml), we see little that's different or unusual, except an osgi namespace.

```
<?xml version="1.0" encoding="UTF-8"?>
<beans xmlns="http://www.springframework.org/schema/beans"
  xmlns:xsi="http://www.w3.org/2001/XMLSchema-instance"
  xmlns:osgi="http://www.springframework.org/schema/osgi"
  xsi:schemaLocation="http://www.springframework.org/schema/beans
http://www.springframework.org/schema/beans/spring-beans-2.5.xsd
                    http://www.springframework.org/schema/osgi
http://www.springframework.org/schema/osgi/spring-osgi.xsd">


    <osgi:reference id="greeterService"
interface="com.apress.springenterpriserecipes.osgi.➥
helloworld.service.GreeterService"/>


</beans>
```

Here, we've imported a new namespace, osgi, which enables us to use the osgi:reference element. The osgi:reference element proxies an OSGi service. The proxy manages awareness of whether the service has been removed or not. This might happen, for example, if you unload the service to replace it. If the service is removed and you make a call against the proxy, it will block, waiting for the service to be reinstalled. This is called *damping*. Furthermore, the proxy itself can be referenced for standard dependency injection into other beans. Remember: when we registered the service with OSGi in the Activator for the greeter service, we passed in an interface as well as the implementation to the bundleContext.registerService invocation. This interface is what we're using to look up the service here.

Already, we've reaped the benefits of OSGi and Spring Dynamic Modules. This application is infinitely more robust because, as a client to a service, it's immune to outages in the service itself and because any number of other clients can now also use the service in the same way, without loading duplicate versions of the jar.

In order for this example to run, we need to deploy all the dependencies of the client into Equinox so that they can be managed. In this case, that implies that we have to install all the bundles for Spring and all the dependencies that Spring itself has. In order to simplify this process, we'll have Equinox automatically load the jars at startup. The simplest way to do this is to modify Equinox's config.ini file. The file will be located under the configuration directory, under the eclipse/plugins folder. The folder won't be present if you haven't run the console as explained in previous exercises. The configuration folder is where Equinox keeps state between sessions. Create the file with a text editor. We're going to reference the jars that are required by this project. In order to obtain those jars using the Maven project, you can issue mvn dependency:copy-dependencies, which will place the jars in the target/lib folder of the current project, where you can grab them. I would put them in a folder under the OSGi Equinox directory so that you may reference them quickly, using relative paths. You can visit the source code for this book to see the exact Maven configuration I've used. Now that you've got the jars, modify the config.ini file and list the jars. My config.ini looks like this:

```
osgi.bundles=spring/com.springsource.org.aopalliance-1.0.0.jar@start,➥
spring/com.springsource.org.apache.commons.logging-1.1.1.jar@start, ➥

spring/helloworld-service-1.0-SNAPSHOT.jar@start, ➥

spring/org.osgi.core-1.0.0.jar@start, ➥
```

```
spring/org.osgi.core-4.0.jar@start, ➡

spring/org.springframework.aop-2.5.6.A.jar@start, ➡

spring/org.springframework.beans-2.5.6.A.jar@start, ➡

spring/org.springframework.context-2.5.6.A.jar@start, ➡

spring/org.springframework.core-2.5.6.A.jar@start, ➡

spring/org.springframework.osgi.core-1.1.3.RELEASE.jar@start, ➡

spring/org.springframework.osgi.extender-1.1.3.RELEASE.jar@start, ➡
spring/org.springframework.osgi.io-1.1.3.RELEASE.jar@start➡

eclipse.ignoreApp=true
```

These declarations tell Equinox to load and start the jars at launch time. I put the jars in a folder called spring, which itself is located under the eclipse/plugins folder.

We have one last thing to do to see it all working. We need to install and start the client. There is no change in this process from before. We repeat it here for clarity. Run the Equinox console:

```
java -jar eclipse/plugins/org.eclipse.osgi_YOUR_VERSION.jar -console
```

Then, install and start the client:

```
install file:/path/to/your/client/jar.jar
start 12
```

If everything goes to plan, you should see the application contexts recognized by Spring and you should, towards the end of the output, see the output from the invocation of the service.

```
…terService,org.springframework.context.annotation.internalAutowiredAnnotationPro…
equiredAnnotationProcessor,springDMGreeterClient]; root of factory hierarchy
Bonjour, Mario
Bonjour, Fumiko
Bonjour, Makani
May 25, 2009 11:26:04 PM org.springframework.osgi.context.support.AbstractOsgiBu…
INFO: Publishing application context as OSGi service with properties {org.spring…
iserecipes.springdmhelloworld, Bundle-SymbolicName=com.apress.springenterprisere…
```

12-3. How do I Export a Service Using Spring Dynamic Modules?

Problem

You want to create services and have those automatically installed in the registry, as we did in the first recipe, available for other services to depend on. This process is different because we will no longer register the services in Java code, and instead will let Spring export the service on our behalf.

Solution

You can use Spring Dynamic Modules configuration schema to export a service. The service will be made available to other beans as well as other OSGi components.

Approach

The approach is similar to that of the other configurations. We will create a bundle and deploy it. Create a Spring XML configuration (src/main/resources/META-INF/spring/bundle-context.xml) for our regular Spring beans, just as we did in the previous recipe.

```xml
<?xml version="1.0" encoding="UTF-8"?>
<beans xmlns="http://www.springframework.org/schema/beans"
       xmlns:xsi="http://www.w3.org/2001/XMLSchema-instance"
       xmlns:context="http://www.springframework.org/schema/context"
       xsi:schemaLocation="http://www.springframework.org/schema/beans
http://www.springframework.org/schema/beans/spring-beans.xsd
http://www.springframework.org/schema/context
http://www.springframework.org/schema/context/spring-context.xsd ">

    <context:annotation-config/>

    <bean id="greeterService"
class="com.apress.springenterpriserecipes.osgi.helloworld. ➥
service.GreeterServiceImpl"/>

</beans>
```

Here, we declare a bean named greeterService that we will reference.

In a separate file (src/main/resources/META-INF/spring/bundle-osgi-context.xml), we will export the service using the Spring Dynamic Modules configuration schema. Here, we'll use the osgi:service element to export the bean as an OSGi service, classified by the interface we specify. Note that we could, technically, have specified a concrete class for the value of interface, though it's not recommended. In our example, we want our service to advertise that it supports multiple interfaces, so we'll specify both of them.

```xml
<?xml version="1.0" encoding="UTF-8"?>
<beans xmlns="http://www.springframework.org/schema/beans"
       xmlns:xsi="http://www.w3.org/2001/XMLSchema-instance"
         xmlns:osgi="http://www.springframework.org/schema/osgi"
       xmlns:util="http://www.springframework.org/schema/util"
       xmlns:context="http://www.springframework.org/schema/context"
       xsi:schemaLocation="http://www.springframework.org/schema/beans
http://www.springframework.org/schema/beans/spring-beans.xsd
http://www.springframework.org/schema/util
http://www.springframework.org/schema/beans/spring-util.xsd
http://www.springframework.org/schema/context
http://www.springframework.org/schema/context/spring-context.xsd
http://www.springframework.org/schema/osgi
http://www.springframework.org/schema/osgi/spring-osgi.xsd">
```

```
<context:annotation-config/>

<osgi:service auto-export="all-classes" ref="greeterService">
    <osgi:interfaces>
<value>com.apress.springenterpriserecipes.osgi. ➥
helloworld.service.GreeterService</value>
            <value>com.apress.springenterpriserecipes.osgi. ➥
helloworld.service.GreetingRecorderService</value>
    </osgi:interfaces>
</osgi:service>

</beans>
```

You can abbreviate the syntax by using an anonymous bean. An anonymous bean specified inside of the osgi:service element allows you to avoid cluttering the namespace. The previoussalient pieces, slightly changed to use an anonymous bean, look like this:

```
<osgi:service   interface="com.apress.springenterpriserecipes. ➥

osgi.helloworld.service.GreeterService">
    <bean class="com.apress.springenterpriserecipes.osgi.helloworld. ➥
service.GreeterServiceImpl"/>
</osgi:service>
```

Remember, as these beans are proxies, some may load asynchronously, or take a longer time to register. This implies that you may have timing issues to resolve in configuring your service. For this, Spring Dynamic Modules provides the depends-on attribute, which lets your bean *wait* for another bean. Suppose our greeterService depended on a dictionaryService, which itself took a long time to load:

```
<osgi:service   depends-on="dictionaryService"
interface="com.apress.springenterpriserecipes.osgi.helloworld. ➥
service.GreeterService">
    <bean class="com.apress.springenterpriserecipes.osgi.helloworld. ➥
service.GreeterServiceImpl"/>
</osgi:service>
```

Interfacing With the OSGi Runtime

You can interact with the OSGi infrastructure in some interesting, more metaprogramming-oriented ways. Spring surfaces a lot of this functionality if you want to use it. The first, most direct connection to OSGi is the bean that's created on your behalf when you export a service. This bean, an instance of org.osgi.framework.ServiceRegistration, is in turn a delegate to the Spring bean you have defined. You can inject this instance if you want and manipulate it, just as with any other Spring bean. Define an id on the osgi:service element to be able to reference it.

By default, beans created in a Spring application context are global to the entire OSGi runtime, including all clients that use it. Sometimes you may want to limit the visibility of a service so that multiple clients each get their own instance of the bean. Spring Dynamic Modules provides a clever use of the scope attribute here, allowing you to limit beans exported as services to the client, or service importer.

```xml
<bean scope ="bundle"  id="greeterService"
class="com.apress.springenterpriserecipes.osgi.helloworld.service.GreeterServiceImpl"/>

<osgi:service   interface="com.apress.springenterpriserecipes.osgi. ➥
helloworld.service.GreeterService" ref="greeterService"        />
```

The OSGi runtime surfaces events based on the life cycle of services. You can register a listener to react to the life cycle of a service. There are two ways to do this, one using anonymous inner beans and one using a named reference.

```xml
<osgi:service  id="greeterServiceReference"
interface="com.apress.springenterpriserecipes.osgi.helloworld. ➥
service.GreeterService">
    <registration-listener registration-method="greeterServiceRegistered"
                                unregistration-method="greeterServiceUnRegistered">
 <bean class="com.apress.springenterpriserecipes.osgi.helloworld.service. ➥
GreeterServiceLifeCycleListener"/>
    </registration-listener>
</osgi:service>
```

Spring Dynamic Modules is relatively flexible with respect to the prototype of the method:

```java
public void serviceRegistered(  ServiceInstance serviceInstance, Map serviceProperties)
public void serviceUnregistered(ServiceInstance serviceInstance, Dictionary
serviceProperties)
```

Naturally, there's a similar feature for client-side proxies. The feature is a listener on the osgi:reference element. Here, we use an inner bean inside the osgi:listener element, though you can also use the ref attribute on the osgi:listener element and avoid the inner bean if you wish.

```xml
    <osgi:reference id="greeterService"

interface="com.apress.springenterpriserecipes.osgi. ➥
helloworld.service.GreeterService">
    <osgi:listener bind-method="greeterServiceOnBind"
            unbind-method="greeterServiceOnUnbind" >
        <bean class = "com.apress.springenterpriserecipes.osgi. ➥
helloworld.client.GreeterClientBindListener"/>
    </osgi:listener>
</osgi:reference>
```

Spring Dynamic Modules also supports injection and manipulation of bundles themselves. An injected bundle is of type org.osgi.framework.Bundle instances. The simplest use case is that you want to obtain an instance of the org.osgi.framework.Bundle class from an already loaded bundle in the system. You specify the symbolic name to help Spring look it up. The Symbolic-Name is a MANIFEST.MF attribute that every bundle should specify. Once acquired, the Bundle can be interrogated to introspect information about the bundle itself, including any entries, its current state (which can be any of: UNINSTALLED, INSTALLED, RESOLVED, STARTING, STOPPING, or ACTIVE), and any headers specified on the bundle. The Bundle class also exposes methods to dynamically control the life cycle of the bundle, in much the same way as you might from the Equinox shell. This includes things like stopping a bundle, starting it, uninstalling it, and updating it (that is, replacing it with a new version at runtime, for example.)

```
<osgi:bundle id ="greeterServiceBundle"

        symbolic-name="symbolic-name-from-greeter-service" />
```

You can inject into a variable of type org.osgi.framework.Bundle, just as you would any other bean. More powerful, however, is the prospect of dynamically loading and starting bundles using Spring. This sidesteps the shell we used earlier to install a service. Now, that configuration is built into your application and it will be enforced on your application context's startup. To do this, you need to specify the location of the .jar to be installed, and optionally an action to take, such as start, when the bundle is installed into the system.

```
<osgi:bundle
    id ="greeterServiceBundle"
        location= "file:/home/user/jars/greeter-service.jar"
        symbolic-name="symbolic-name-from-greeter-service"
        action="start"
 />
```

You can specify what action the bundle should take on the event that the OSGi runtime is shut down using the destroy-action attribute.

12-4. Finding a Specific Service in the OSGi Registry

Problem
OSGi will let you maintain multiple versions of a service in your registry at the same time. While it is possible to ask the registry to simply return all instances of the services that match (that is, by interface), it can be useful to qualify them when searching.

Solution
OSGi, and Spring Dynamic Modules on top of it, provides many tools for discriminating services both in publishing and consuming services.

Approach
Multiple services of the same interface may be registered inside of an OSGi environment, which necessitates a conflict-resolution process. To aid in that, Spring Dynamic Modules provides a few features to help.

Ranking
The first feature is ranking. Ranking, when specified on a service element, allows the ascription of a rank relative to other beans with the same interface. Ranking is specified on the service element itself. When encountered, the OSGi runtime will return the service with the highest-ranking integer value. If a version of a service is published with a higher integer, any references will rebind to that.

```
<osgi:service
ranking="1"
interface="com.apress.springenterpriserecipes.osgi. ➡
helloworld.service.GreeterService">
    <bean class="com.apress.springenterpriserecipes.osgi. ➡
helloworld.service.GreeterServiceImpl">
</osgi:service>
...
<osgi:service
ranking="2"
interface="com.apress.springenterpriserecipes.osgi. ➡
helloworld.service.GreeterService">
    <bean class="com.apress.springenterpriserecipes.osgi. ➡
helloworld.service.GreeterServiceImpl">
</osgi:service>
```

If you want to bind to a specific service of a particular ranking, you can use a filter on your osgi:reference element.

```
<osgi:reference id="greeterServiceReference"
    interface="com.apress.springenterpriserecipes.osgi. ➡
helloworld.service.GreeterService"
  filter="( service.ranking = 1 )"
  />
```

Service Attributes

A more robust solution to service discrimination is service attributes. A service attribute is an arbitrary key and value pair that the service exports, and on which lookups for a service with multiple matches can be predicated. The service properties are specified as a Map element. You may have as many keys as you want.

```
<osgi:service  ref="greeterService"  interface="com.apress.springenterpriserecipes. ➡
osgi.helloworld.service.GreeterService">
 <osgi:service-properties>
   <entry key="region" value = "europe"/>
</osgi:service-properties>
 </osgi:service>
```

If you wanted to look this service up, you would use a filter attribute for the client. Here's how you might specify the osgi:reference element to find this service as a client.

```
<osgi:reference id="greeterService" interface="com.apress.springenterpriserecipes. ➡
osgi.helloworld.service.GreeterService"
filter="(region=europe)"
  />
```

There are also many standard attributes that the runtime configures for all services. For a good list, consult http://www.osgi.org/javadoc/r2/org/osgi/framework/Constants.html. You may also use the bean name of the original service as a predicate for finding a service. This will be very familiar.

```
<osgi:reference id="greeterServiceReference"
interface="com.apress.springenterpriserecipes.➥
osgi.helloworld.service.GreeterService"
bean-name="greeterService"
  />
```

Cardinality

There are frequently situations where OSGi will return more than one instance of a service that satisfies the interface, especially if you aren't able to specify which one you're looking for using the methods discussed before. Take, for example, a deployment where you have multiple GreeterServices deployed for various regions. Spring Dynamic Modules provides the set and list interfaces to retrieve multiple references and populate a java.util.Set and java.util.List, respectively.

```
<list id="greeterServices"
    interface ="com.apress.springenterpriserecipes.osgi.helloworld.service.GreeterService"
    cardinality="1..N" />
```

Note the cardinality element, which stipulates how many instances are expected. 0..N stipulates that any number of references are expected. 1..N stipulates that at least one instance is expected. On a single reference element, only two values for cardinality are acceptable: 0..1, and 1..1. This has the effect of saying that fulfillment of the dependency for a reference is not mandatory (0..1) or that it's mandatory (1..1).

You may fine-tune the collections returned to you. For example, you might specify a comparator element or attribute to sort the collection returned. The bean you reference should implement java.util.Comparator. Unless this logic is extraordinarily involved, it might be an ideal place for using Spring's scripting support to inline the java.util.Comparator implementation in the Spring application-context XML file.

```
<list id="greeterServices"
    interface ="com.apress.springenterpriserecipes.osgi.helloworld.service.GreeterService"
    cardinality="1..N"  comparator-ref="comparatorReference" />
```

12-5. Publishing a Service Under Multiple Interfaces

Problem

Your bean implements many interfaces and you want those interfaces to be visible to clients of the service.

Solution

Spring Dynamic Modules supports registering beans under multiple interfaces. It also provides extra flexibility in auto-detecting the interfaces.

Approach

Spring Dynamic Modules creates a proxy for you based on the interface you specify. A side effect is that the other interfaces your bean implements won't be visible. To be able to access a bean by other interfaces, you may enumerate the other interfaces in the bean's registration, which will make it

441

available under all of those interfaces. Note that it's illegal to specify both the `interface` attribute *and* the `interfaces` attribute: use one or the other.

```xml
<?xml version="1.0" encoding="UTF-8"?>
<beans xmlns="http://www.springframework.org/schema/beans"
       xmlns:xsi="http://www.w3.org/2001/XMLSchema-instance"
       xmlns:osgi="http://www.springframework.org/schema/osgi"
       xmlns:context="http://www.springframework.org/schema/context"
       xsi:schemaLocation="http://www.springframework.org/schema/beans
http://www.springframework.org/schema/beans/spring-beans-2.5.xsd
http://www.springframework.org/schema/context
http://www.springframework.org/schema/context/spring-context-2.5.xsd
http://www.springframework.org/schema/osgi
http://www.springframework.org/schema/osgi/spring-osgi.xsd">

    <context:annotation-config/>

    <bean id="greeterService"
class="com.apress.springenterpriserecipes.osgi.helloworld.service.GreeterServiceImpl"/>

    <osgi:service ref="greeterService">
        <osgi:interfaces>
<value>com.apress.springenterpriserecipes.osgi. ➥
helloworld.service.GreeterService</value>
<value>com.apress.springenterpriserecipes.osgi. ➥
helloworld.service.GreetingRecorderService</value>
        </osgi:interfaces>
    </osgi:service>
</beans>
```

This is powerful in its own right, but Spring Dynamic Modules can help even more. The service element supports an auto-export attribute, which starts auto detection of interfaces on the bean and publishes them under the detected interfaces. There are four options: `disabled`, `interfaces`, `class-hierarchy`, and `all-classes`.

The first option, `disabled`, is the default behavior. It works with whatever interfaces you've explicitly configured on the bean using the `interfaces` element or the `interface` attribute. The second, `interfaces`, registers the service using the interfaces implemented by a bean, but not its super classes or the implementation class. If you want to include all super classes as well as the current implementation class, use `class-hierarchy`. If you want everything: super classes, implementation class, as well as all interfaces on the implementation class, choose `all-classes`.

Having said this, you should probably stick to explicitly specifying the interfaces of your bean. The auto detection may overexpose your bean, revealing crucial private implementation knowledge. More to the point, sometimes it may not expose enough. Perhaps you forgot that the functionality that you're trying to export is specified on an interface on a super class? Don't risk either, and instead prefer explicit configuration.

12-6. Customizing Spring Dynamic Modules

Problem

Spring Dynamic Modules is a powerful tool, and it provides reasonable defaults (and results) for very little investment. The main work of Spring Dynamic Modules is done through extenders, which sometimes require customization.

Solution

Spring Dynamic Modules provides strong support for fragments, part of the OSGi specification, to override key infrastructure beans Spring uses in service of the extenders.

Approach

Extenders provide a way to let a bundle control the loading process of another bundle. This magic is most clearly exemplified in Spring Dynamic Modules' ability to auto-load Spring XML application contexts detected in the META-INF/spring/ folder, or those configured by the Spring-Context MANIFEST.MF attribute. Spring provides two extenders: one for web-based bundles (spring-osgi-web-extender, whose trigger is being deployed in a bundle ending in .WAR) and one for normal bundles (spring-osgi-extender).

Customizing these extenders is key to customizing Spring Dynamic Modules' behavior at runtime. Fragments permit the injection of resources, classes, and functionality into a bundle on the same ClassLoader as the host bundle. Fragments do not, however, let you remove functionality or override MANIFEST.MF values that are already established. Additionally, a fragment cannot contain its own Activator. The OSGi runtime knows a bundle is a fragment if it encounters a Fragment-Host header in the MANIFEST.MF file. The Fragment-Host attribute in turn is the Symbolic Name of another bundle. In this case, because we are interested in configuring the two bundles with the extenders, we will reference one of org.springframework.bundle.osgi.extender or org.springframework.bundle.osgi.web.extender.

Spring will check bundles that are configured this way and look for Spring XML application contexts inside the META-INF/spring/extender folder. These Spring XML application contexts are loaded and any beans with the same names as well known beans used by Spring will be given priority and used instead. Let's go through some examples of where this might be useful.

You Want Spring To Process OSGi Annotations on Beans

Spring provides the ability to inject OSGi services using annotations. This functionality is available as an extension, and requires a little configuration to enable it. The annotation serves the same function as the reference element discussed earlier.

```
@ServiceReference
public void  setGreeterService(GreeterService greeterService) {
 // …
}
```

To see this work, you need to enable it using a fragment. Let's first take a look at the Spring XML configuration. Here, we declare a properties bean that in turn contains our property key, process.annotations.

```xml
<?xml version="1.0" encoding="UTF-8"?>
<beans xmlns="http://www.springframework.org/schema/beans"
       xmlns:xsi="http://www.w3.org/2001/XMLSchema-instance"
        xmlns:context="http://www.springframework.org/schema/context"
       xsi:schemaLocation="http://www.springframework.org/schema/beans
http://www.springframework.org/schema/beans/spring-beans.xsd
http://www.springframework.org/schema/context
http://www.springframework.org/schema/context/spring-context.xsd">

 <bean name="extenderProperties"
class="org.springframework.beans.factory.config.PropertiesFactoryBean">
        <property name="properties">
            <props>
                <prop key="process.annotations">true</prop>
            </props>
        </property>
    </bean>
 </beans>
```

Change the Default HTTP Server that Spring Uses When Deploying a .WAR

Spring Dynamic Modules provides the ability to install OSGi bundles as web applications. It uses an instance of org.springframework.osgi.web.deployer.WarDeployer to perform this feat. Currently, the default is org.springframework.osgi.web.deployer.tomcat.TomcatWarDeployer. You can change this to use Jetty, should you like.

```xml
<?xml version="1.0" encoding="UTF-8"?>
<beans xmlns="http://www.springframework.org/schema/beans"
       xmlns:xsi="http://www.w3.org/2001/XMLSchema-instance"
        xmlns:context="http://www.springframework.org/schema/context"
       xsi:schemaLocation="http://www.springframework.org/schema/beans
http://www.springframework.org/schema/beans/spring-beans.xsd
http://www.springframework.org/schema/context
http://www.springframework.org/schema/context/spring-context.xsd">

<bean name="warDeployer"
class="org.springframework.osgi.web.deployer.jetty.JettyWarDeployer"/>

 </beans>
```

12-7. Using SpringSource dm Server

Problem

You're convinced of the potential of OSGi, but you feel that perhaps, even with Spring Dynamic Modules, the investment might be hard to justify without some serious upgrades to the tooling and a general smoothing out of the road. Such upgrades would enhance monitoring, provide better, more thoroughly baked support for deployment of traditional `.war` artifacts, enable use of some of the standard Java EE libraries, provide useful defaults for many de-facto standard libraries, and provide fully integrated support for Spring Dynamic Modules.

Solution

Use Spring dm Server, SpringSource's venerable OSGi–oriented server built on many technologies including Equinox and the Spring framework itself.

Approach

OSGi is a framework, on top of which more sophisticated solutions are built. OSGi doesn't solve framework concerns, instead focusing on infrastructure requirements for Java applications. OSGi is a specification that is well-represented in implementations. Spring Dynamic Modules provides functionality that sits on top of those implementations, providing very powerful runtime sophistication for developers looking to produce and consume OSGi services in a Spring-friendly fashion.

Realizing that Spring Dynamic Modules was, while powerful for those already invested in an OSGi platform, not the most natural accommodations for those trying to migrate large code into the OSGi environment, SpringSource created SpringSource dm Server. SpringSource dm Server is a robust solution. There are several editions available. The community edition is licensed under the GPL 3.0. You may download the source code and build it yourself. SpringSource dm Server provides tooling via Eclipse to help design solutions designed for dm Server.

SpringSource dm Server's many advances focus on delivering a solution, and not just a framework, for delivering OSGi–based enterprise applications. The lack of support for core enterprise features stems from OSGi's suitability for any of a number of target environments, including embedded devices. While you are able to use OSGi–friendly HTTP servlet containers to deploy web applications, it's been up to you to build that solution. Imagine piecing together a proper Java EE server, component by component! Thus, SpringSource dm Server provides value above and beyond a regular OSGi solution because it's already well-integrated.

SpringSource dm Server provides a number of features geared towards minimizing the hassle of deploying large applications in an OSGi environment. It reduces the number of redundant jars on a server through the use of a shared library repository, where jars shared among many other artifacts may be stored. Significantly, this reduces the need to redeploy bundles because they are automatically loaded from this repository. Large enterprise packages tend to be composed of a tapestry of dependencies, each of which depends on any permutation of other dependencies. OSGi–enabling all of these interwoven dependencies via the granular use of the `Import-Package` header would be tedious. Spring dm Server provides the ability to wholesale import an entire library and all packages therein to expedite the process. Additionally, SpringSource dm Server can effect an even more flexible isolation of services in an OSGi environment, preventing collisions caused by deployment of the same service with the same name without a need to use a service attribute or other discriminator.

SpringSource dm Server also allows you to bend the rules where necessary. For example, consider the application of an aspect using Spring's AOP. This might require weaving of classes, which in the case of a point cut that matches classes deployed across multiple bundles, would prove cumbersome. SpringSource dm Server can intervene on Spring's behalf, propagating such changes across multiple bundles where necessary.

SpringSource dm Server works with four types of deployment formats. The first is a **bundle**, which we've discussed, and that works as you'd expect. The second is a **native Java EE `.war`** file. This is revolutionary because it provides support for out-of-the-box deployment of legacy `.WAR`–based applications. However, this format should be viewed as an intermediary step, as it loses out on many of the advantages of OSGi. Hybrid approaches are supported; a **shared-library `.WAR`** lets you deploy a `.WAR` whose dependencies are satisfied by the shared library. The server supports an enhanced format called a web module, which is an enhanced shared-library `.WAR`. The format removes the need for XML configuration to describe your web application to the container, relying entirely on the OSGi manifest. It, like a shared-library .WAR, can use Spring to inject OSGi services. The final format is called a **platform archive**. A platform archive is the ultimate form of an application. It provides the ability to group bundles together and provides application isolation. Application isolation is critical because it allows you to solve the issue of reconciliation of two services whose interfaces collide. You can use a .PAR to isolate services within the deployment unit.

SpringSource dm Server provides the robustness needed to commoditize enterprise application development in an OSGi environment, and definitely deserves a look. For a *really* good reference, specifically on SpringSource dm Server, I (Josh Long) would humbly recommend you investigate my co-author's in-depth treatment of the subject, *Pro SpringSource dm Server*, by Gary Mak and Daniel Rubio (Apress, 2009).

12-8. SpringSource's Tooling

Problem
You want to begin with SpringSource dm Server, but need a way to rapidly turnaround development.

Solution
Use the SpringSource dm Server tooling available as part of SpringSource Tool Suite (STS).

Approach
One of the best parts about dealing with OSGi, and in particular SpringSource's implementation, is that the tooling is prolific and refined. SpringSource has provided solid tooling for Eclipse, called dm Server Tools, which facilitate executing applications directly in a development environment. These tools—part of the broader SpringSource Tools Suite (STS)—are available as either a plug-in or as a stand-alone environment.

The path of least resistance, especially if you're just starting or if you plan on doing a lot of Spring development, is to download the standalone installation and use it, as it contains built-in support for Spring applications. I prefer the first approach, as interfacing with OSGi rarely requires more than a few minutes and rarely distracts from primary Java application development. We'll explore both approaches in this recipe.

SpringSource Tool Suite requires Eclipse Ganymede (3.4), as well as the corresponding Web Tools Platform (WTP) to work, though, as of this writing, milestone releases for the recently released Eclipse 3.5 (Galileo) are available.

We'll walk through installing the SpringSource Tool Suite plug-ins into an existing installation, and not the individual dm Server Tools or Spring IDE. Both of these products are folded into SpringSource Tool Suite, and SpringSource Tool Suite was just recently made available for free.

Assuming you have a compatible build of Eclipse (the Eclipse Java EE Developer's package is a solid start on top of which to install the tooling because it contains WTP and a lot of other useful tooling). The simplest installation mechanism is to point the update manager inside of Eclipse to the SpringSource Eclipse update site. To do this, choose "Software Updates" from Eclipse's "Help" menu and then open the "Available Software" tab. You can add the SpringSource update site(s) by clicking the "Add Site" button, and enter the following URLs (one at a time):

- `http://www.springsource.org/update/e3.4`

- `http://www.springsource.org/milestone/e3.4`

■ **Note** There are two recommended update sites due to the plug-in release schedule targeting dm Server version 2.0. At the time of this writing, the main update site—http://www.springsource.org/update/e3.4— only contains plug-ins for dm server version 1.0. Therefore, updates are also performed on the milestone update site, which contains plug-ins targeting dm server version 2.0

Once you enter both URLs, the Eclipse update screen will present you with two "SpringSource Update Site for Eclipse 3.4" options. By choosing the top-level box, all SpringSource-related Eclipse plug-ins will be selected for download, including the dm Server Tools plug-in. Next, click the "Install" button to begin the installation. The next screen will prompt you to confirm your selection. Ensure that the dm Server Tools for dm Server 2.x.x is selected. Then, proceed. Be aware that the installation may take quite a while, because it'll download a copy of SpringSource tc Server (the enhanced Tomcat Server) as well as dm Server and all the required Spring IDE tooling, as well.

Summary

In this chapter, you got an introduction to OSGi, the specification as well as the Equinox platform implementation, which guarantees that certain resources are made available to plug-ins. OSGi, a module system that can be layered on top of the JVM, is important for its simplicity and powerful problem-solving abilities. You learned how to write simple raw OSGi clients and services. Remember that anything used by something else is called a service in OSGi. You then deployed the same client and service using Spring Dynamic Modules, a framework that sits on top of OSGi and is a powerful API for integration with OSGi. Spring dm Server is the OSGi-based Java server that minimizes the hassles of deploying large applications in an OSGi environment. You learned about a number of its capabilities and the four types of deployment formats with which it works. Finally, you learned how to install powerful tooling from SpringSource to support your Spring dm Server and OSGi applications.

This is the last chapter of the book. Congratulations on having learned so much about the Spring framework and surrounding projects, and we hope you enjoy using it!

Index

C